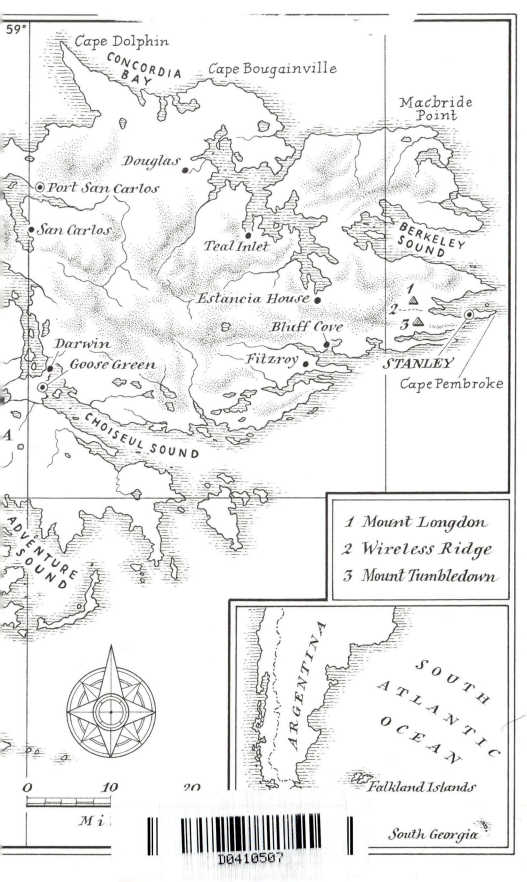

59°

Cape Dolphin

CONCORDIA BAY

Cape Bougainville

Macbride Point

Douglas

⊙ Port San Carlos

• San Carlos

Teal Inlet

BERKELEY SOUND

Estancia House

1

2

3

Bluff Cove

STANLEY

Darwin

Goose Green

Fitzroy

Cape Pembroke

4

CHOISEUL SOUND

ADVENTURE SOUND

1 Mount Longdon
2 Wireless Ridge
3 Mount Tumbledown

ARGENTINA

SOUTH ATLANTIC OCEAN

0   10   20

Mi

Falkland Islands

South Georgia

D041050

Our Boys

Our Boys

The story of a Paratrooper

HELEN PARR

ALLEN LANE
an imprint of
PENGUIN BOOKS

ALLEN LANE

UK | USA | Canada | Ireland | Australia
India | New Zealand | South Africa

Penguin Books is part of the Penguin Random House group of companies
whose addresses can be found at global.penguinrandomhouse.com.

First published in 2018

001

Set in 12/14.75 pt Bembo Book MT Std
Typeset by Jouve (UK), Milton Keynes
Printed and bound in Great Britain by Clays Ltd, Elcograf S.p.A.

A CIP catalogue record for this book is available from the British Library

ISBN: 978–0–241–28894–8

www.greenpenguin.co.uk

Penguin Random House is committed to a
sustainable future for our business, our readers
and our planet. This book is made from Forest
Stewardship Council® certified paper.

Contents

List of Photographs   vii

Introduction   ix

PART ONE

1. Britain and the Parachute Regiment:
   A Short History   3

2. Joining Up in the 1970s   27

3. Training: Making Men   58

PART TWO

4. Falkland Islands   85

5. Orders: The Battle of Darwin and
   Goose Green   97

6. Momentum: The Battle of Mount Longdon   118

7. Comrades   130

8. Fear   146

9. Killing   162

10. Death   185

PART THREE

11. Our Boys   195

12. Grief   229

13. Trauma   251

14. Memory   282

   Appendix   300
   Notes   303

   Bibliography   349

   Index   369

List of Photographs

Chapter 2: Joining Up in the 1970s

1. and 2. Dave Parr playing in the garden of the bungalow, aged five, c.1967. (© Helen Parr)
3. Chris Parr, Dave Parr and author (as a baby) in the back room of the bungalow, early 1975: Dave aged twelve, Chris aged sixteen. (© Helen Parr)
4. Dave Parr out on the marshes, 1980–81, aged eighteen. (© Helen Parr)
5. Dave Parr out on the marshes, with Blue Cole, autumn 1981, aged nineteen. (© Blue Cole)

Chapter 4: Falkland Islands

6. On the *Norland* with members of Dave Parr's section, 11 Platoon D Company 2 Para (Photograph courtesy of Walter McAuley)
7. D Company 2 Para on the *Norland*.

Chapter 7: Comrades

8. Dave Parr at Fitzroy, between the battles of Goose Green and Wireless Ridge, after coming back to the battalion from the field hospital. Photo taken by Private Terry Stears. (© Terry Stears)
9. Dave Parr (on the left), waiting to move by helicopter from Fitzroy, 10 June 1982. With Private Terry Stears and Lance Corporal Neil Turner. (Imperial War Museum, FKD2124)

Chapter 11: Our Boys

10. and 11. Gun carriage arriving at St Michael's Church, Oulton Broad, 2 December 1982. (© Eastern Counties Newspaper Limited/Archant Community Media Limited)
12. and 13. Mourners at Dave Parr's funeral, 2 December 1982. (© Eastern Counties Newspaper Limited/Archant Community Media Limited)

Chapter 14: Memory

14. Commemorative cairn to Dave Parr on the top of Wireless Ridge, built by the author, Harmer Parr and Patrick Watts, October 2012. (© Helen Parr)
15. Dedications to British paratroopers on summit of Mount Longdon, October 2012. (© Helen Parr)
16. Soldado Argentino, Argentine cemetery on the Falkland Islands, October 2012. (© Helen Parr)

Introduction

On East Falkland, the war was over. British soldiers rushed towards Port Stanley, disbelieving at first, and then relieved, exhilarated, joyously alive. Around 10,000 men, Argentine prisoners as well as British troops, massed into the small island capital. Rubble, clothing, ammunition, sewage, were strewn through its mud streets.[1] Two Argentine bodies lay discarded on the roadside. On Wireless Ridge, a Scout helicopter landed, and men descended to collect the Parachute Regiment's last dead, already frozen solid in the early winter snow.

Life carried on. Soldiers requisitioned Falklands' houses, rested, played with guns, drank whisky and beer, joked with their Argentine prisoners, listened to the World Cup on the radio. They felt tremendous – and they felt dreadful. They had won, and men had died. For some, the comfort of indoors was a relief, the opportunity to sleep, cook and eat with no possibility of deadly interruption. For others, the warmth of home felt alien, their thin and roughened bodies trapped in someone else's world.

In the Suffolk town of Oulton Broad, Joy Parr, my grandmother, heard news of the Argentine surrender on BBC radio. She wrote a letter to her son Dave, a nineteen-year-old Private in the 2nd Battalion, The Parachute Regiment. She told him how proud she was of him and the part he had played in what the British had done. She said how pleased she would be to see him again soon.

Three days later, on Thursday, 17 June, at 11.15 a.m., a military car drew up at the petrol station where Joy worked as a secretary. Inside the car was a man in uniform.[2] He cannot have relished the task he had to fulfil. He parked, crossed the forecourt and arrived at the door. Did she see him approach? He must have knocked, and although she cannot have wanted to, she must have let him in. The man told Joy that her son had been killed serving in the Falklands. He said he was very sorry.

The man instructed Joy's work colleague Caroline to ring her eldest son, my father, Harmer. Harmer was teaching French to the fifth form at Hadleigh High School when the school secretary opened the classroom door and told him to take a call in the office. He returned with her and picked up the handset. Caroline said, 'You're to come home to be with your mother.' Caroline had been advised not to tell him that his brother was dead, but he said, 'It's Dave, isn't it, he's been killed', and she had to confirm what he suspected. The head teacher appeared and said he must leave straight away. Harmer dialled our home number, standing there in the school office, concerned staff all around him.

I was seven years old in June 1982 and absent from school because I was ill. I was asleep in bed and I remember the sound of the phone ringing. It woke me. I heard my mother running up the stairs and when she came into my room she was crying. She said, 'Uncle Dave is dead.' My mother must then have closed all the curtains, as the next thing I remember is waiting in the darkened front room with our next-door neighbour. After a silence, and somewhat unexpectedly, our neighbour said, 'He is with Jesus now.' My father arrived home for a moment, but I did not see him, only his car pulling away from the end of the lane.

My father reached my grandmother's home about an hour later. She was sitting in the back garden of her bungalow with her husband Con. Con lived a few streets away. The two had been separated for several years and they rarely spoke to each other. My father scarcely recognized them as he approached, in this altered landscape in which they now lived. Old people together, but irrevocably apart.

Harmer had to phone his middle brother, Chris, who had left Oulton Broad in the summer of 1981 to trek across Asia. In the late British spring of 1982 Chris was working in a building yard and living in a commune in Australia. The call came at midnight. The phone rang for a long time. A man answered it, and he was initially annoyed to be disturbed. Chris said the man, the leader of the commune, had roused him from sleep and told him, 'It's England ringing, you'd better come.' My father said it was the hardest thing he ever had to do. Two brothers, talking on the phone.

★

Thirty years later, I stood in Aldershot military cemetery with my parents and a couple of hundred people who had congregated to mark the Falklands anniversary. I had begun research for this book and consequently, for the first time in many years, my father and I had been in contact with the Parachute Regiment and with some of the men who had served with my uncle.

I remembered the soldiers in my grandmother's bungalow after his funeral, crammed into her narrow conservatory, wearing uniform, talking the way men do, and of course they did not remember the presence of a child. They had had other things on their minds. Now – like me – they wore dark suits. They looked respectable, fit, younger, many of them, than their fifty or so years. They were friendly and humorous. I stood with them and someone took a photo. They did not know me and I did not know them, but we were caught there together, connected because in 1982 my uncle had been one of them and, had he lived, he would be among them now.

One man, Phil Francom, had recently been in touch with my father by email. He had been standing near to Dave when Dave was killed, and he had not even been scratched. He said that Dave had lost his gloves, and had had cold hands.[3] The night he was killed, it was freezing. When Phil went back to the Falkland Islands, he left gloves for Dave, and a letter. He wanted us to know how bad he felt, that Dave had died and he had lived. He was worried about seeing us, in case we were angry with him for not dying in Dave's place. He came up to my father and they embraced for a long time.

In that small cemetery, the eighteen Falklands paratrooper graves were in three neat lines.[4] The trees, deliberately chosen to bear leaves of different colours, were designed to show the coexistence of individual complexions within the collective form. In the memorials and the photographs, everything was neat and everything was ordered. Everything had its place and everything had its history. But that cemetery contained, even then, thirty years after the conflict, so much simmering emotion.

I began to realize that the history of the Parachute Regiment and the Falklands War was not quite as I had supposed. My grandmother painted a picture of Dave from an old photo and it hung above the door to the back room of her bungalow. She conjured him there as a child – her son, her boy – smiling, blue-eyed, his hair blond, shoulder-length and wavy. Standing there in that cemetery, it was evident to me that my grandmother's painting, the way I had seen my uncle all my life, was only a partial picture. His death became my grand-parents' history. After he died, it felt as if everything had been leading to that point and nothing else could ever matter as much. But now it was plain that he – and all of us – played such a tiny part in a history that was bigger than any one person's fate.

★

Who were the men who wore the maroon red berets of the Parachute Regiment? This is a question normally answered in one of two ways. Most writers about military subjects follow Field Marshal Montgomery's original appraisal of the men he ordered into Arnhem in 1944. The Paras, Montgomery said, were 'men apart – every man an Emperor'.[5] Their eagerness, courage, and discipline, their willingness to conduct their duty in the 'van of battle' made them exemplars to other soldiers and other men. On the other hand, critics of the military sometimes write about soldiers as if they were not people, but only symbols: 'avatars of a nation's sanctioned violence'.[6] Paratroopers, priding themselves on their ability to endure extreme conditions, were designated 'dangerous men', even 'uniformed psychopaths'.[7]

Neither of these starting points was particularly satisfactory. I realized in Aldershot military cemetery that I too had a relationship with the Parachute Regiment. My uncle had been a paratrooper, and so I was part of the regimental family. This struck me as odd. My parents and my grandmother had not been inclined to military ideals and I was not military minded. Born in 1974, I grew up at a time when neither I nor my classmates at school had to think about military service. But I could see – indeed, because of my own family, I had always known – that paratroopers were more than brave combatants, or sadistic lovers of violence, or emblems of nationalism. As I got closer to the subject of my study – the men in the red-maroon berets – gaining a sense of who they were became both more complicated and more interesting.

Indeed, paratroopers were intriguing even if my uncle had not been one of them. They were a young regiment, their incipient corps formed in 1940 to demonstrate modern fortitude as Britain prepared itself to resist the Nazi challenge. The regiment's reputation was for its extremes and it depended upon the prowess of the men in the ranks, the infantry soldiers. Famous for their part in the doomed battle of Arnhem Bridge in September 1944, post-war they were deployed in various wars resulting from the end of the British Empire. Then, in the 1970s, they had a difficult role in a conflict closer to home, and they made unwelcome headlines when soldiers from the 1st Battalion, The Parachute Regiment, shot and killed thirteen Irish civilians marching in Londonderry on 30 January 1972.

Ten years later, the Falklands War created the modern paratrooper. After the British government despatched a Task Force in response to the Argentine occupation of British territory overseas, the British press reported the naval spectacle of the fleet sailing from Portsmouth docks. Later, as the dispute turned to war, attention moved to the operations on land. There, the Parachute Regiment was central. The 2nd and 3rd Battalions sailed to the Falklands as part of a brigade comprised of the most elite elements of the British armed services. The Royal Marines fought at Mount Harriet and Two Sisters; the Scots Guards at Mount Tumbledown; and the 1st Battalion, 7th Duke of Edinburgh's Own Gurkha Rifles, were engaged as they advanced towards Mount William. The 3rd Battalion, The Parachute Regiment, fought at Mount, Longdon, and the 2nd Battalion, the only unit to go twice into battle, at Darwin Goose Green and then at Wireless Ridge.

The contest on Falklands soil made a lasting public impression because of the terrible weather, the poor terrain and the elemental sight of men carrying packs and weapons over long distances. The land battles were iconic because, for the first time in a generation, British soldiers engaged a static enemy on open fields and ridges. The battles were intense, fought at night, at close quarters, sometimes hand to hand with bayonets. Two hundred and fifty-five British servicemen died during the campaign; a figure that includes six men serving with the Merchant Navy, four from the Royal Fleet Auxiliary and eight sailors from Hong Kong.[8] One hundred and twenty-three of the dead were with the Army. Of the regiments, the Welsh Guards sustained heavy losses when the Argentine air force bombed their waiting ship in the bay at Fitzroy. The SAS took their greatest number of casualties in a single day since the Second World War, when eighteen of their soldiers were killed in a helicopter crash. The Parachute Regiment bore the highest toll in battle, and the largest overall number of deaths. Fifteen paratroopers were killed at Goose Green, twenty-one on Longdon and three at Wireless Ridge. The Parachute Regiment received both the war's Victoria Crosses. The first was for Lieutenant Colonel Jones, the Commanding Officer of 2 Para, killed at Darwin. The second was for Sergeant Ian McKay, killed as he charged towards a machine-gun post near the summit of Mount Longdon.

McKay's award illustrated how much the Falklands War transformed the reputation of the Parachute Regiment. In 1972, McKay had been a private soldier and he was named later as having been the Widgery and Saville Reports' Private T, who fired two shots from the car park of the Rossville Flats on Bloody Sunday.

★

To research this book, I talked to former paratroopers of all ranks, other soldiers who fought in the Falklands, as well as the mothers, fathers, siblings and, where possible, children of soldiers who were killed. Talking to them forced me to listen, and to try to understand what it was they wanted to say. Listening opened my eyes to histories that I did not previously know, and to ways of understanding the world that were new – and sometimes uncomfortable – for me.

I needed to see what it had been like for them. I did not want to glorify or to damn them. I had to appreciate their courage and their spirit; but I could not ignore parts of their histories that were distressing or disquieting. People's memories, of course, are not absolutely reliable, but the way that people remember, what they choose to say and how they say it, what they recall and what they omit or forget can be as revealing as the details they convey.[9] They did not have to spell it out in so many words for me to see how the Parachute Regiment had shaped the lives of the men who had been part of it.

I was aware that I do not have what former Gurkha officer and Falklands veteran Mike Seear calls 'existential authority'.[10] I was not there. I have never been in battle and I would not want to be. The divide between those who have been in combat and those who have not has always been important to military writing. It used to be conceived as a fault-line between men, an unofficial measure of masculinity, with the courage to face death at its pinnacle.[11] Now it is understood as a barrier between those who have been in the military and the majority who have not. I would not have used the word 'civilian' before I started this book. Rapidly, it became obvious to me that, from the point of view of paratroopers, and probably many former soldiers, this could be an incision in society difficult to bridge. Military personnel often saw their lives as different – even in opposition – to those of civilians. Post-war, out of the Army, ex-soldiers often struggled with the loss of their military status.

I was not there; but surely military writing should not be the exclusive preserve of those who share the assumptions of their subjects. I was not accustomed to a military mindset, and so I wanted, in some ways, to understand more about them than they did themselves. As well as the interviews I conducted, I read memoirs and listened to oral history collections deposited in the Imperial War Museum, the Airborne Forces Museum and the National Army Museum; and I read documents kept at the time by the Parachute Regiment, the Ministry of Defence and the government. I needed to examine the mentalities they had that were unfamiliar to me; and I wanted to see paratroopers, and their family members, in the contexts in which they had lived.

This book therefore became a social history of the Parachute Regiment. In Part One, I examine the history of the Parachute Regiment, the backgrounds of men joining up in the 1970s, and how they were trained. Part Two goes into depth about what the Paras saw and did in the Falkland Islands, and Part Three explores the personal and political aftermaths of the Falklands War. One theme of the book is the relationship between army and society. The Parachute Regiment had an elite and aggressive reputation, and it came under unwelcome scrutiny after the events in Londonderry. In 1980, members of the SAS abseiled into the Iranian Embassy in London to rescue hostages held by Iranian dissidents. The live screening of their actions on the BBC turned Special Forces into a household name, and the Falklands War had the same effect for the Paras. Margaret Thatcher called the men in the Task Force 'our boys'. Her familiar words revealed, conversely, the growing distance between the professional armed services and the British population. In that sense at least the Falklands War marked a moment when Britain moved out of the period of history defined in large part by the experiences and legacies of total war.

The second theme of this book is the human experiences of close-quarters combat. What was the Falklands War like for the paratroopers who had to fight it? This generation of soldiers was born for the most part in the early 1960s. They lived under a twin shadow of war. Their fathers and grandfathers had often served in the Second World War or had done peacetime National Service; but their schoolmates were increasingly influenced by 1960s counter-culture, itself formed, at least in part, in antipathy to the form and restrictions of wartime and military life. The principles of their military training were the same as they had been in the 1940s, if not earlier, and their training taught them the high standard of regimental history, as well as the constant rigour of fitness, discipline and drill. Combat on the Falklands did not last long, but it was brutal. The organization of the battles usually determined what soldiers had to do. How they thought about it often depended on how they had been trained to see themselves as paratroopers. This war was their test, and combat could enhance – or subvert – their expectations. Looking back later to what they had done, those experiences could appear in a different light – sometimes easier, but sometimes more painful.

A study of the Parachute Regiment is also a study of the lives of paratroopers, the third theme of this book. Examining the lives of paratroopers opens a window into parts of British society usually overlooked in general histories. Officers in the Parachute Regiment tended to come from military families and had usually attended public school. Greater numbers of men from grammar schools and universities were beginning to enlist, but army cultures were guided by past standards. Men who joined the ranks of the Parachute Regiment in the 1970s had often grown up knowing deprivation and violence. Their histories trace how the outlooks and fortunes of those boys changed, or did not change, as they grew older in the 1980s and beyond. The lives of their families – mothers born into poverty in the 1930s, fathers who had done National Service, and the young widows they left – suggest the pride derived from tradition, and the endurance of social inequalities, as people adjusted to life recast after a death in the Falklands.

As I wrote, I often asked myself whether I was for or against the Parachute Regiment; whether I was for or against war. In a way, it is a redundant question. An army regiment, particularly one like the Paras, is a tough place, disciplined as other institutions are not. War is terrible, even when it is necessary. When it happens, it is not a single experience. Soldiers see things differently from each other, and some experiences in combat are worse than others.

For me, the point was that, although the Parachute Regiment was in some ways separate from society, and although this war happened a long way from home, neither the Army nor war makes sense in isolation. The British Army, the Parachute Regiment and the Falklands War were part of the same society I lived in: the unmilitary niece of a man who was killed as a paratrooper in the Falklands.

PART ONE

1. Britain and the Parachute Regiment: A Short History

The Parachute Regiment was without a heritage, being spawned at the fulcrum of the twentieth century in Britain, in June 1940, as France surrendered to the Nazis and continental Europe reached an uneasy peace.

Winston Churchill, taking office after the parliamentary crisis that deposed Neville Chamberlain, asked on 5 June for a corps of 5,000 parachutists. After a faltering start, the numbers grew, and in 1942 the Parachute Regiment was born.

The parachute battalions created their own, independent ethos. That ethos became a tradition, a very powerful one. The two most important elements in the Parachute Regiment's reputation were first, that they were capable of going to extreme lengths, willing to accept tasks that other regiments would not; and secondly, that they were meritocratic, a unique band of brothers, whose spirit reached across the ranks.

Who were the paratroopers? In 1940, they stood for Britain's fighting will at the time of its deepest peril. After the Second World War, they were tasked with managing the difficult winding down of the British Empire. In the 1970s, they were deployed in Northern Ireland, and their operations in the province brought them into the public eye.

★

Great Britain was forged from the threat of invasion and experience of war, and Britain grew great on expansion, in part made good by war. In the twentieth century, Britain was twice a key participant in total world war. Despite the obvious importance of war to Britain's history, the British saw themselves as an unmilitary nation.[1] In 1941, George Orwell characterized their unmilitary nature. He said the British would not tolerate a military despot. The jackboot and the goose-step would not make them quail, but laugh.[2]

The roots of the British people's non-military perception of themselves were geographic, but also social. Britain was an island, its power was naval, and it had not been invaded. It kept a small standing army. Britain's state was liberal and did not compel its subjects into uniform except under threat to its survival. These features distinguished Britain from America and France, both republics created from revolution and war, and for whom military service was linked to a civic as well as patriotic pride, and obviously separated Britain from Germany, who had taken too zealous an interest in its military prowess.[3] Britain's armed services had political influence, but were formally separate from politics. They took instruction from government in Parliament, but their allegiance was to the monarch, a long-standing historical tradition which, it was thought, helped to avoid their becoming too politicized.[4]

The armed services were therefore vital, but at the same time not central, to Britain's national life. All three armed services were woven into the fabric of British society and traditionally connected to the principal institutions – public schools, the Church, landed county families – that nourished the careers of Britain's aristocracy and gentry. However, the armed services did not dominate the British upper middle classes. Military service, perhaps particularly army service, was always slightly looked down upon. Between 1870 and 1959, the majority of men in the rank of officer were not from the really great ruling families, but 'lesser landowners, senior administrators, soldiers and independent professionals – the "supporting class" '.[5] More often than not, a career in the army was viewed as the pastime of somewhat eccentric figures, or of families who liked the trappings of gentlemanly life – uniforms, medals and the imposed formalities of rank – but who lacked the means or the breeding to achieve it in ways that were less physically demanding.[6]

The Second World War, and the period of conscription that followed it, stood out as an unusual, and an extraordinarily influential, period in British history. As in 1916, conscription resulted from the enormous centralization of power and mobilization of resources necessary to defeat Germany. To win the war, Britain needed to compel ordinary men – shopkeepers, mechanics, teachers, factory workers – to join the services; sometimes to spend long months polishing buttons and shining boots in army barracks, sometimes to fight.

Perhaps because it often reflected reality, or because the British were predominantly fighting the Nazis, whose militarism did not need much elucidation, the image of the fighting man then was not a violent one. The soldier was in service to the nation. In joining the Army, he was fulfilling his duty and responsibility: he was shouldering the burden of his manhood with stoic acceptance of whatever might be his fate. Of course, an important part of this construction was social class. Service and stoicism – the stiff upper lip – were middle-class virtues. The prevalence of their appeal meant violence was never centre-stage in British understandings of their military traditions, and the British always retained a frisson of fear about the possibility that working-class men could return from war brutalized, their passions inflamed and unquenchable.

★

In a strange way, the creation of the Parachute Regiment was bound up with the inception of modern Britain. In May and June 1940, the country's future hung in the balance. Belgium, the Netherlands, France, Luxembourg, Denmark and Norway were all overrun, while Soviet Russia in 1939 and then Vichy France made their allegiances with Nazi Germany. Only the conquest of Britain stood between Hitler and domination of Western Europe. Isolation, at this time of peril, made Britain militarily distinct, its resolve unquestioned; and their separateness became an important part of how British people later thought about the war. But the country was not alone. In 1940, Britain had an Empire and could call on the economic resources of the sterling area, as well as the manpower of the colonies and Dominions, and could reach out to the United States of America, to help in this great struggle.

Winston Churchill requested a corps of parachutists, seeing them as a modern type of force. He wanted them because the Germans had them and had used them to powerful effect in Norway, Denmark and the Netherlands; they had also used an elite, mobile force in the conquest of France. Parachuting was inherently modern. Hardly any soldiers had been in a plane before, let alone dropped out of the sky. Early parachutists had attempted to exit the plane by crawling onto the tail, hanging from a bar, and then letting go, but swiftly decided it was preferable to plunge through a hole specially cut in the fuselage.

Parachutists represented Britain's determination to continue the effort against Nazi Germany, as part of 'a vigorous, enterprising and ceaseless offensive against the whole German occupied coastline'.[7] They stood for Britain's fighting will and ability to match German violence. They also girded the country's defences against invasion. In the spring and summer of 1940, British people feared a German onslaught from the air. Newspapers reported that enemy parachutists would float to earth, speaking perfect English and in civilian disguise. Britain would not be so much subjugated as infiltrated by this almost alien force. The public must prepare to fight against this terrifying invasion, and many men rushed to volunteer their services.[8]

Churchill intended that the parachutists – elite troops – would shake up the gentlemanly amateurism of the British Army, an amateurism that seemed to invoke, however inaccurately, the languid habits of the upper middle classes who had preferred appeasement, and whose performance in France had to many appeared disturbingly ineffective. It was difficult to train parachutists, but Churchill persevered. He recalled that the colonels of many of Britain's finest regiments were aggrieved by the idea of crack squads of brothers-in-arms. 'The idea that large bands of favoured "irregulars" with their unconventional attire and free-and-easy bearing should throw an implied slur on the efficiency and courage of the Regular battalions was odious to men who had given all their lives to the organised discipline of permanent units.'[9]

It was only the ongoing success of German airborne forces that convinced the Army of the need to invest in its parachutists. In 1941, the Nazis used gliders and parachutists to take Crete; thereafter the numbers of parachutists in Britain grew. Initially, they were called No. 2 Commando, then the 11th Special Air Service Battalion. On 1 August 1942, they became the Parachute Regiment with two battalions, up to 2,000 men, under Major General Browning, the Commander of the 1st Airborne Division.

Frederick Browning came from a military family, had a very distinguished military record and had been decorated in the First World War. He also lived with his own demons, and his personal life was unusual in that he had an influential and equally complicated wife: the feminist novelist Daphne du Maurier. He appreciated the importance of form, and the power of illusions to create it. He gave the Parachute Regiment identity, their own maroon red berets, and created the emblem of the airborne forces: Pegasus, the winged horse of Greek myth, born from the blood of the beheaded Medusa, and Pegasus' rider, Bellerophon.

★

The parachutists were initially to be used as a guerrilla force, dropping behind enemy lines to disrupt communications, damage infrastructure and upset morale. Their first objective was the Tragino Aqueduct in Italy in February 1941. A year later, the Bruneval raid on 27 February 1942 drew attention to their daring success. Major John Frost's company stole a piece of radar equipment that had been spotted by a Spitfire pilot on a cliff north of Le Havre. The paratroopers took the radar after a firefight and wheeled it on a trolley to the beach, where they waited under heavy fire for the Navy to extricate them. They lost two killed and six wounded.

In the winter of 1942, airborne forces were deployed into North Africa, and their role, as well as their numbers, expanded. At first, carrying little, they were dropped to capture airfields, but after heavy losses at Oudna, the 1st Parachute Brigade went into battle as conventional infantry in the freezing Tunisian hills.[10] They suffered nearly 80 per cent casualties, losing 1,700 men. In the 1st Battalion, only fourteen officers out of twenty-four survived, and 346 of the original 588 soldiers.[11] After this, German troops nicknamed the paratroopers the 'Red Devils'.

Right from the start, the parachutists prided themselves on their meritocracy. This marked them out from the grander regiments, where a military lineage and education at the right public school were thought to guarantee a commission or the appropriate promotion. The key determinant in advancement in the Paras was not social standing, many believed, but fighting spirit. Among the ranks, the early parachutists volunteered to transfer from their existing units because they wanted to have a go at 'Jerry'. They were not medically examined; they just needed to have 'guts'.[12] When the supremely phlegmatic John Frost – later a Parachute Regiment legend – was given the job of putting together the 2nd Battalion, a large number of men were recruited from a Scottish regiment. According to Frost, 'Fully 95 per cent of this company had decided to become parachutists as they thought it would be the quickest way of seeing some action. They weren't particular who they fought and if there was no one else available as an enemy, then the English would do very well.'[13]

Among officers, the idea of parachuting did tend to attract men who were in some ways unconventional. Frost, the son of a brigadier, was born in India and grew up in Iraq, where his father was serving. He followed in many ways a well-trodden path, attending public schools with military and Christian backgrounds, Wellington and Monkton Combe School, and then Sandhurst. But he wanted excitement, and asked to transfer to a parachute unit from his home regiment, the Cameronians. In his selection interview, he was asked if he thought strict military discipline should be enforced among a formation of volunteer parachutists. His response was that strict discipline tended to cramp initiative. He imagined this answer had gone down badly with the brigadier conducting the interview, but in fact he was chosen.[14]

The Paras' meritocratic ethos arose also from the collaboration and enterprise some of their operations demanded. In the summer of 1943 2 Para were sent into Sicily. Adjutant Captain Dover was dropped far from the intended destination on the slope of Mount Etna. He and Corporal Wilson spent twenty-three days trying to find the rest of their unit, evading German capture and subsisting almost entirely on apples. They cut telephone wires, killed a German sentry and a despatch rider and created a road-block. They obviously displayed extraordinary personal judgement and team work across ranks even to survive.[15]

Nevertheless, the Parachute Regiment's voluntarism and meritocracy had limits. For a start, the regiment was created during a period of conscription. Between 1939 and 1945, 5.8 million men and 640,000 women were called up. Of those, 3.8 million men went into the Army.[16] Most men stayed in Britain – until D-Day over half the Army was at home: 'For most soldiers, therefore, the experience of war was not one of daring deeds at the "sharp end", but rather of a sedentary existence in camps or depots across the country polishing their brasses and wondering why they were there'.[17] Their 'choice', therefore, was not a completely free one, and many transferred to the parachutists just because they were bored. In addition, while recruitment began with volunteers from other units, as the parachute brigades expanded, recruitment became more targeted. In 1942, whole battalions – the 7th Queen's Own Cameron Highlanders, the 10th Battalion Royal Welch Fusiliers, the 10th Somerset Light Infantry, the 13th Royal Warwickshires and the 10th Essex – were asked to transfer. If men did not pass selection, they were moved elsewhere.[18]

Anthony (Tony) Crosland, who later became a Labour Cabinet minister and was famous for his part in 1950s revisionist socialism, was a lieutenant, later a captain, in the Parachute Regiment. He joined in 1942, as part of the transfer of the Royal Welch Fusiliers. If he had to spend time in the Army, then he wanted to become a parachutist: 'vanity, bravado, browned-off-ness with the infantry, a feeling of the utter absurdity of spending three years of one's life in khaki without even getting an interesting psychological experience'.[19] Even inside the Paras, Crosland was dismayed by the atmosphere of conformity and xenophobia among the officers, and found himself almost demoted because of his tendency to question his superiors' judgement.[20] Mostly, men and officers did not mix at all. The ranks got drunk and fraternized with women; the officers were not seen by their men to do either. Crosland attempted to convert his men to socialism and in speaking with them developed a limited rapport.[21]

★

The other most important element of the Paras' reputation was their willingness to endure extreme conditions. Initially, this was simply because of the difficulty and danger of jumping out of planes. By 21 September 1940, twenty-one officers and 321 soldiers had passed the selection procedure to undergo parachute training. Of this number, thirty had not dared to jump, two had been killed when their parachutes failed to open, and twenty were either unsuitable or had sustained injuries that ruled them out.[22]

As operations intensified during the war, the problems of depositing men in the right places became more manifest, particularly at night or under heavy fire. In Sicily, a number of men simply disappeared, having been dropped, it was assumed, into the crater of Mount Etna, twenty-five miles away from the drop zone.[23] In June 1944, the 6th Airborne Division parachuted into Northern France ahead of the main allied D-Day landings. The Commanding Officer of 9 Para could only find 150 of his 635 men, but even with a weakened force they captured the well-defended Merville gun battery.

Landing correctly could also prove difficult and dangerous. Men often found themselves alone, separated from their troop; sometimes they landed in trees, and dangled helplessly while being shot at, or worse. In Normandy, one soldier got entangled upside down in a tree and, unable to free himself, had his throat slit and his genitals cut off and stuffed in his mouth. Other men landed in the water, as one recalled: 'The tide was out on the [River] Dives but it was very deep in mud and slime . . . it was a real struggle to get out. I managed to hang on to my rifle and about 50 rounds of ammunition. I lost everything else. It was pitch-black. I couldn't see any of the others.'[24] Many others drowned as their parachutes formed a seal over the surface of even shallow water and they floundered, unable to escape. Brigadier General James Gavin commented: 'We lost a surprising number that way.'[25]

Parachute troops also had to cope with high casualties. The 6th Airborne Division in Normandy spent eighty-two consecutive days in the field. Their losses were huge, with 542 killed, 1,623 wounded and 725 missing. Almost one man in five became a casualty.[26] They saw and did some terrible things. Colonel Hill, the commander of the

3rd Parachute Brigade, was dropped into the flooded valley of the River Dives with forty-two other men. They struggled out, and were then bombed by a squadron of British aircraft. Only Hill and one other man survived: 'The rest were either dying or dead. So what do you do? Do you look after the wounded or do you push on? It is obviously your job to push on. So we gave morphia to the chaps who were dying, took morphia off the dead and gave it to the living, and moved on. The memory I can't get out of my mind, and sometimes I wished I could, is that as the two of us pushed off all these other chaps, every one of whom died, gave us a cheer.'[27]

★

The most important battle in the Parachute Regiment's short history was the battle of Arnhem in September 1944. Field Marshal Montgomery's objective was to drop two American and one British division – the 1st Airborne – of around 10,000 men apiece, and a Polish parachute brigade, in an 'airborne carpet' through German-occupied Northern Holland. He wanted to secure the Rhine bridges to enable Allied armoured troops to cross, making Arnhem the bridgehead for the Allied push eastwards.[28]

The plan failed. Montgomery felt confident because the initial Allied advance had been so swift, but the troops were dropped in daylight and not all at once, as the air force could only release one load per day. They had to advance over land, losing the benefit of surprise, and thus they became separated and their lines of communication disrupted. They did not have adequate air or fire support.[29] The German resistance was stronger than expected, and this, added to bad weather, meant the paratroopers were not resupplied, reinforced or rescued.

Only one battalion, under Colonel John Frost, made it to the final bridge at Arnhem. The rest of the division was beaten back to Oosterbeek before they reached the river. Frost's men held out for three days and four nights under heavy attack. Frost was shot in the legs and sheltered with the other wounded in the cellar of the battalion headquarters a short distance from the bridge. Here the injured were piled on top of each other. When the building eventually caught fire, Frost had no choice but to organize a truce with the Germans to bring the casualties to safety. He spent the rest of the war in a prison camp. He felt bitter: 'No living enemy had beaten us. The battalion was unbeaten yet, but they could not have much chance with no ammunition, no rest and with no positions from which to fight. No body of men could have fought more courageously and tenaciously than the officers and men of the 1st Parachute Brigade at Arnhem bridge.'[30]

Frost's words defined the Paras' ethos. They had accepted what they could not avert, but, against terrible odds, their spirit was not broken. Only 2,183 men of the 1st Airborne Division succeeded in crossing the river: 1,400 had died and 6,000 were taken prisoner.[31] Such a desperate end brought its own glory. The extraordinary courage of men fighting on in the face of death defined the regiment. That unbreakable spirit was on display again in March 1945, when the 6th Airborne Division crossed the Rhine in the final push against German forces. Airborne troops descended, packed closely together in a relatively small area, assaulted by anti-aircraft guns, their sight of the ground obscured by smoke. Some wondered afterwards whether the cost of life was not too high to justify the airborne contribution. From the paratroopers' perspective, they had helped to open the routes across the Rhine and so led the way to the German surrender.

★

In 1945, with Germany and Japan defeated, the military necessity that had been imposed on people's everyday lives did not cease immediately. Conscription continued. During the period of post-war National Service, a further 2 million men were called up.[32] In its external relations, Britain faced three overlapping challenges: the threat from the communist Soviet Union; the dwindling of Britain's imperial reach; and the creation of atomic and then thermonuclear weaponry. In the atomic era, the prospect of atomic bombs dropped on British cities threatened Britain's survival; in the thermonuclear age, war could mean the end, not just of Britain, but of recognizable forms of human society.

The severity, reach and complexity of these challenges led the government to retain conscription. In the event of a crisis leading to nuclear escalation, there would be time to hold off a Soviet advance, but not enough time to train and develop a force of volunteers. Britain's army had to be prepared in order 'to hit back hard at the outset to defend our very existence'.[33] Britain was still a world power. The 1945 Labour government oversaw the independence of India and quit Britain's mandate in Palestine, but by 1948 Britain's post-war military commitments had expanded. National Servicemen would find themselves fighting in Korea, Malaya, Egypt, Cyprus and Kenya. Korea was a Cold War conflict; the rest, except Suez, were insurgencies arising from the end of Empire, usually complicated by Cold War factors.

The experience of the Second World War and post-war conscription had a mixed influence on British attitudes towards the army. People had served and, usually, if they complained about it they did so privately rather than politically. They accepted the reasons they had had to be there in the first place. In a general sense, many men had resented the intrusion of military service and disliked the tedium of army life.[34] That distaste, deepened perhaps by the absurdity of having to spend years in uniform rather than pursuing other, more interesting, pastimes, did sometimes create a muted anti-militarism. Even defence planners thought so. One of their challenges in the 1970s was to 'dispel the picture of the services which some former conscripts present to their children – of a dull routine of pointless and over-disciplined activity'.[35] On the other hand, conscription created 'military families' where they had not previously existed. The shadow of totalitarianism gave armed service respectability; and the fathers and grandfathers of men who chose to join up in the 1970s had usually enlisted in either the First or Second World War, or had done National Service afterwards.

The Second World War meant the armed services intruded into daily life, but it did not lead to a single national experience. All conscripted men had the course of their lives disrupted by the call-up, and people knew what the army was like. However, distinctions between regiments, divisions of class, the rigid hierarchy of rank and simple chance meant that, once in the army, men's experiences were then very different.[36] Class background usually determined men's progression within the Army. Leslie Ives remembered, 'my mates and I had about as much chance of becoming officers as becoming king'.[37] It was also often luck whether men ended up in the humid, treeless wastes of Korea, or mundanely ironing trousers in Aldershot.

Conscription also meant that the differences between regiments were widely understood. People knew that the Paras were tough. The film *Theirs is the Glory* (1946) brought the 1st Airborne Division to a national audience. It used 200 veterans of Arnhem to reconstruct the battles: perhaps exorcizing ghosts for some of those men, and allowing British viewers vicariously to experience the extremes – the insanity, even the futility – of this airborne assault.[38] It was uncontroversial that the ranks of the Paras were swelled by the boys who were keenest to fight. Even their own officers sometimes saw their men as 'aggressive criminals', 'very live wires', who required 'careful handling'.[39]

★

After the Second World War, the Parachute Regiment was cut by half, from two divisions to one (up to 15,000 men), and then, by 1948, to a single brigade. The idea of airborne infantry fell out of favour, partly because of the loss at Arnhem and the large numbers of casualties throughout the war, and partly because, it was argued, the further development of anti-aircraft weaponry and jet fighter planes made parachute assaults seem not just much more dangerous, but also unnecessary.[40]

The Paras also began to feel the contradictions of Britain's shrinking world role. For servicemen who grew up in Britain, Britain's Empire was often a background fact that rarely cost them a thought. After the Second World War, servicemen could be surprised to find that this was not the case for people living in other countries. In Palestine between 1944 and 1948, the Paras were compelled to conduct counter-insurgency operations against well-organized radical Jewish units. They were shocked to find that these units did not welcome them as liberators from the Nazis in Europe. Rather, the Jewish fighters, determined on their own sovereignty, saw the British as a colonizing power. Two British intelligence corps sergeants were hanged 'for membership of the criminal Nazi British Army of Occupation'.[41] In Cyprus, from 1955 to 1957, the Paras similarly found themselves on the receiving end of the hatred of Greek nationalists, EOKA, who were determined to free Cyprus from colonial control and unite it with Greece. An EOKA gunman shot and killed one sergeant in the back. He had been out shopping with his four-year-old son.[42] This morally difficult and defensive world was a long way from the global drama of 1939–45.

The Paras' only post-war battalion parachute assault was in the Suez Canal Zone in November 1956. Aircraft flying at low level delivered a battalion of 16 Independent Parachute Brigade onto the El Gamil airfield, with the intention of attacking coastal defences and advancing up the canal. Egyptian fighters shot at them as they descended, but British and French air support was superior. They bombed a cemetery in which local soldiers were hiding. The British fought through the graveyard: 'there were these disinterred corpses, enormous mausoleums with bits and pieces of them falling down and collapsing on themselves under fire . . . half a body here and half a body there. Coffins sticking up, quite a few dead Egyptian soldiers and quite a few live ones.'[43]

The attack at Suez was a military success. The British and French achieved victory swiftly. Politically, however, it was a disaster. The European allies had secretly colluded with the Israelis to invade Egypt, whose president, Colonel Nasser, had nationalized the Suez Canal and leaned towards the Soviets. The Americans, who had not been consulted, refused to support the action. The weakness in Britain's global political power was exposed and Britain and France had to withdraw. Four British men died; thirty-two were injured, and over 100 Egyptians were killed. At Suez, perhaps the widespread wartime tendency to accept Britain's military commitments, while feeling 'browned off' about having to be involved in them, began to weaken. One Para lieutenant said: 'I thought it was simply terrible. We'd gone off on this bloody expedition, which nobody could justify and these boys had been ruined and died for nothing. That doesn't seem right.'[44]

★

Suez was one factor contributing to the reduction in Britain's role overseas in 1957, the year that the Conservative government declared National Service would soon end. After it did, a 'veritable chasm' opened between army and society.[45] National Service had not democratized the Army. The officer corps continued to come chiefly from certain public schools and established military families. In the ranks, men in the Paras tended to hail from parts of the industrial working class and some of the sections of society that were outside classification or were right at the bottom of the pile. As the size of the army, and the numbers of men in it who did not intend to make a career in the military, diminished, so the Parachute Regiment both slipped from public view and became more associated with the difficult practices of counter-insurgency. They polarized opinion – if, as was becoming more doubtful, people thought about them at all.

One reason for that polarization was the growing association of the Paras with violence. The British prided themselves on the comparatively moderate conduct of their counter-insurgency, believing they were good at winning 'hearts and minds'. Britain's experience was contrasted favourably with that of France, whose end-of-Empire experiences in Algeria and Indo-China were protracted and brutal. Later, Britain's counter-insurgency doctrines also looked moderate compared to those of the Americans in Vietnam. The size of America's military machine always seemed excessive in relation to the peasant landscapes and people they were seen to strafe.[46]

The reality, however, was usually more complicated. The Paras were on the receiving end of violence that demonstrated just how much insurgents detested a former colonial power. In Borneo in 1962–5, the British protected newly formed Malaysia (an amalgamation of former British colonies the Malayan Federation, Singapore and Borneo/Sarawak) from communist-influenced Indonesian fighters. B Company 2 Para were attacked in their camp at night: 'it was hand to hand stuff, actually one to one combat. It was very frightening but it became a survival experience.'[47] In the Federation of South Arabia (formerly the Aden Protectorate) in 1964–7, the Paras struggled in the extreme heat against different tribal and nationalist groups. The Commander of A Squadron SAS, also deployed, said:

'We did not appreciate the intensity of the violence or the tribal re-action to our presence. I expected a few dissidents to poop a few rounds and then go home again . . . so often we underrate our enemy.'[48] Covering Britain's retreat from Aden in 1967, 1 Para Private Boot's memory was 'of being really scared in a dirty narrow Arab street and seeing people who have one ambition: to kill a British soldier'.[49]

The Paras had to adapt their methods and, while winning over hearts and minds could be part of it, they also used force to coerce and intimidate populations. In Cyprus, the Paras worked alongside the local police to find insurgents, while also searching houses in specific areas to discourage locals from siding with EOKA. In Radfan – north of Aden – Britain aimed to starve tribal groups out of the mountains by bombing their cattle, grain stores and irrigation systems.[50] They asserted themselves to show the locals they were in charge, and there-fore who ultimately controlled the area. After one fire-fight, General Sir Anthony Farrar-Hockley recalled, 'The British force now looked down into the Wadi Dhubsan. This area, hitherto a safe base for Rad-fani operations, was to be entered as a demonstration of power, and the grain stocks held there were to be destroyed.' Brigadier Blacker told Farrar-Hockley, who was a Lieutenant Colonel at the time: 'The aim is not to slaughter tribesmen, but to teach them that we will come wherever we need to if they misbehave.'[51]

★

The Parachute Regiment's engagements in the Persian Gulf and Aden/Yemen in the 1960s were often conducted beyond much public scrutiny. Everything changed, though, when in 1969 British troops were sent to Northern Ireland.

The proximate cause of the Troubles was the growing attempt to improve the rights of Catholics in Northern Ireland, and the heavy-handed reactions of the Royal Ulster Constabulary and the Ulster Special Constabulary, the B Specials. In August 1969 riots in Londonderry led the British government to send in reinforcements, initially to protect Catholics from violence against them. The first Parachute Regiment action in the province was to control loyalist riots sparked by

anger at the disbandment of the B Specials. There were armed gun-
men among the rioters and the Parachute Regiment held the line
between the Shankill and the Catholic Falls Road.[52] They claimed
early success. As they saw it, they had quelled a sectarian escalation.
The Paras' magazine *Pegasus* reported jauntily: 'When our patrols
walk down Shankill Road today, they are greeted with warm smiles
and cheery comments.' But *Pegasus* was not blind to the likelihood
of further bloodshed: 'the slightest tension could set off another
holocaust'.[53]

Violence led to violence. In December 1969, the Provisional Irish
Republican Army (PIRA) formed, and then Sinn Féin split into
Official and Provisional wings. In the summer of 1970, the Army
enforced a curfew on Falls Road, searching houses and looking for
weapons. This provoked riots, and the PIRA began operations
against the security forces. In March 1971, children found in a ditch
the bodies of three soldiers, all shot in the head. The three were from
Scotland, two of them brothers, aged seventeen and eighteen. They
had last been seen drinking in a bar with five civilians. They had been
lured out to the countryside on the promise of attending a party, and
they were probably killed as they relieved themselves by the side of
the road.[54]

In the streets, relations became more volatile. In August 1971 the
government in Westminster agreed to introduce internment without
trial, and in October authorized an intensification of military efforts
to find PIRA fighters. It was difficult work. One Para officer described
how his patrol was using an empty house as an observation post. From
the house, they shot a man aiming a rifle at them. A soldier went to
pick up the gun, but a second man also came out to grab it. It all happened in an open street. A crowd of 200 gathered. The Paras' patrol
vacated their house and 'the mob began attacking [it]. They took it
apart brick by brick, and within a day there was nothing of it left
standing, so that it couldn't be used again.'[55]

Opinions became more polarized. Internment was a blunt instrument, and it turned many Catholics against the British Army. In the
Paras, some thought that the PIRA deserved whatever they got. The
terrorist groups were hard and dirty fighters, who did not have to

operate within the same constraints as British soldiers.[56] Others thought that overbearing British tactics exacerbated the conflict. One officer in the Parachute Regiment remarked: 'for every one we have picked up, we have recruited ten for the IRA'.[57]

In early 1972, the British government advised British troops to adopt a policy of 'rather less provocative activity than recent weeks'. In Londonderry, troops should enter the 'no-go' areas of the Bogside and Creggan only 'on specific information and for a minimum of routine patrolling'.[58] Unsurprisingly, there were divisions on the ground as to how British forces should operate. General Sir Robert Ford, the Commander of land forces in Northern Ireland, believed that the Army were failing, and were losing control in Londonderry, where western parts of the city lay in ruins. One of the suggestions he made was that 'the minimum force necessary to achieve a restoration of law and order is to shoot selected ring leaders amongst the Derry Young Hooligans'.[59]

When a civil rights march was planned in Derry on 30 January 1972, in contravention of the ban on marches, Ford asked for 1 Para to patrol it. According to the detailed evidence given to the Saville Inquiry, which reported in 2010, Ford did not plan on confrontation; nor did he advocate shooting to kill. What he envisaged was a large-scale arrest operation, which could only be authorized by Brigadier Patrick MacLellan, the Commander of 8th Infantry Brigade.[60]

Nevertheless, calling for the Paras was provocative. The Paras had not operated in Londonderry before, and so had had no time to form their own relationships with the city and its residents. As a regiment, they were already somewhat isolated within the Army. According to one journalist, they were 'almost uniformly disliked by the other Army units in Northern Ireland as being the mailed fist of this increasingly aggressive military posture'.[61] They were also gaining notoriety among the Catholic population. In November 1971, after a mother of eleven was blinded by a rubber bullet, *The Guardian* reported: 'Undoubtedly the Regiment is one of the most hated by Catholics in troubled areas where among local people at any rate it has a reputation for unnecessary brutality.'[62]

The Paras themselves often enjoyed their notoriety, and regarded complaints against them with a degree of pride.[63] A member of 1 Para commented that 'a guy can't throw a stone if he's running away from you, and therefore we used to get stuck into them'.[64] Ex-Para Michael Asher said: 'The Paras had been chosen for the job [on Bloody Sunday] because of their toughness and aggression. It was this reputation that mattered to us. We were proud . . . Morale was high as a kite.'[65] Asher portrayed the Parachute Regiment of the 1970s as brutal and conformist. The job of the men in the ranks was never to question or to think, but to follow and obey. In the ranks, they were not taught about the subtleties of the conflict in Northern Ireland, and had no idea that their aggression might be a propaganda tool for the IRA.

The march started, and as marchers reached the junction of William Street and Rossville Street, they turned to Army Barrier 14. Rioting began, and the Royal Green Jackets, stationed at the barrier, fired rubber bullets and water cannon into the crowd. Colonel Derek Wilford, the Commanding Officer of 1 Para, requested permission from Brigadier MacLellan to send a company of Paras through Barrier 14 into William Street to make arrests. As he did so, two paratroopers from Machine Gun Platoon fired five shots from the derelict building in which they were based, across William Street, into the waste ground, at a boy they could see there. He had been throwing stones and, in their own apprehension, they may have feared he was about to throw a nail bomb.[66] He was fifteen-year-old Damien Donaghey, and was wounded in the thigh; beyond him, fifty-five-year-old John Johnston was hit by shrapnel. Almost immediately afterwards, an IRA gunman, who had been positioned to snipe at soldiers, also opened fire.

Wilford then received authorization to mount an arrest operation along William Street. MacLellan had delayed the authorization because he wanted to be sure that rioters and peaceful marchers were not mixed up together. Consequently, MacLellan ordered Wilford not to chase rioters down Rossville Street. Wilford either 'deliberately disobeyed' the order he had been given, or 'failed for no good reason to appreciate the clear limits on what he had been authorized to do'.[67] He sent troops through Barrier 14, but also sent Support Company in vehicles through Barrier 12. He did not tell Major

Loden, the officer commanding Support Company, about the Brigadier's orders not to chase people down Rossville Street. The soldiers of Mortar Platoon drove down Rossville Street and disembarked. British paratroopers were now in the febrile 'no-go' area of the Bogside, among many civilians. Some had been rioting, most had not.

Lieutenant N. got out of his armoured vehicle and walked to the entrance of an alleyway. The soldiers had never been in the Bogside before. The paratroopers were beginning to make arrests and people were throwing stones and missiles at them. N. fired two shots into the air. Those two shots, fired to frighten people, were the spark that set off the shootings, and almost certainly led some troops to believe they were being fired on.[68]

Private R., in the car park of the Rossville Flats, shot at a boy he could see, Jackie Duddy. R. may have been afraid, he may have panicked, but seventeen-year-old Duddy was shot in the back and killed. Two more platoons, the Anti-Tank Platoon and Composite Platoon, arrived in armoured vehicles.[69] One of the new arrivals, Lance Corporal F., shot and killed another teenager, seventeen-year-old Michael Kelly, who was behind a rubble barricade on Rossville Street. He did not fire in fear, but in the knowledge that no one at the barricade was posing a threat of death or serious injury – or not caring whether anyone was or not.[70]

Soldiers then shot and killed five more civilians at the rubble barricade, four of them teenagers, the other aged twenty. The father of William Nash was shot and injured as he went to tend to his son. The shots fired by Lance Corporal F., Lance Corporal J., Corporal P. and Corporal E. were not fired in fear or panic. Private U. shot Hugh Gilmour while he was running away; and either Private L. or Private M. shot Kevin McElhinney, probably on the order of Colour Sergeant 002 or Corporal 039, or both, as McElhinney tried to crawl away on his knees.[71] Four soldiers went into Glenfada Park. They killed two more men, William McKinney and Jim Wray, both shot in the back, and Wray was shot again while he lay on the ground.[72]

Private G. went on into Abbey Park. He shot Gerard McKinney, and the shot passed through McKinney and mortally wounded Gerald Donaghey. Donaghey was a member of the youth wing of the

PIRA and had nail bombs in his pocket, but when he was shot he was trying to escape from the soldiers.[73] Some of the soldiers went back towards Rossville Street. Lance Corporal F. then shot Patrick Doherty and Bernard McGuigan, who was waving a white piece of cloth, and wounded two more men.[74]

The incident lasted ten minutes, during which time British paratroopers fired 108 rounds. Thirteen civilians were killed outright, one received fatal injuries, and fourteen were wounded. More soldiers fired their guns than those who killed. Three fired more than ten rounds, on occasion indiscriminately. Private S. fired twelve, Lance Corporal F. fired thirteen and Private H. fired twenty-two.[75] The only one found to have fired in response to a threat of injury was Private T., who discharged two shots in the car park of the Rossville Flats after someone in the flats threw bottles of acid at British soldiers.[76]

The day's events had an immediate impact. In Northern Ireland, the testy, unsatisfactory balance of a 'hands-off' operation was over. Stormont was suspended, and in March the British government agreed to impose Direct Rule, as they could no longer avoid it. In July, Britain's military policy intensified and Operation Motorman sought to penetrate the PIRA's 'no go' areas.[77] In the province, Bloody Sunday cemented the reputation of the Parachute Regiment as a brutal instrument of the state's oppression. According to one ex-Para, graffiti in Belfast's Unity Flats read: 'KILL BRITS, PARAS = EVIL BASTARDS and FUCK THE QUEEN'.[78]

In mainland Britain, reactions to the shootings were much more muffled. In the House of Commons on 31 January 1972, parliamentarians called for an inquiry, and the MP for Mid Ulster, Bernadette Devlin, twice shouted out that the troops had committed murder. She crossed the House and hit the Home Secretary, Reginald Maudling, and aimed blows at the Prime Minister, Edward Heath.[79] Devlin's emotion illustrated just how lacklustre other responses were. The general attitude of the British public seemed to be indifference. If they expressed an opinion about Northern Ireland, it was usually that the troops should be brought home and the Protestants and Catholics left to fight it out among themselves.[80] For the most part, politicians waited to hear the results of the investigation conducted by the Lord Chief Justice, Lord Widgery. When he did report in April, he said that some soldiers' firing had 'bordered on the reckless', but troops had been fired on first, and some of the deceased had used weapons.[81] Nationalist opinion saw the report as a whitewash, but the rapid inquiry, and Direct Rule, took the sting from criticism of the Army.

The escalation of terrorist violence also drew attention away from what British soldiers had done. On 22 February 1972, an IRA car bomb exploded at Aldershot barracks, killing five women working in the kitchen and a Catholic priest. In July, the IRA set twenty-three car bombs in and around Belfast city centre, at least nineteen of which exploded without warning in an hour and twenty minutes, killing two soldiers and seven civilians; and three no-warning car bombs in Claudy, outisde Derry, killing nine more people, including one child. Subsequently, on 4 February 1974, the IRA detonated a bomb on a coach carrying off-duty soldiers and their families on the M62. Among the twelve dead were a family of four with two pre-school-age children. In June, a bomb went off in the Houses of Parliament, and in July a bomb at the Tower of London killed one person; in October and November bombs left in pubs in Guildford and Birmingham killed twenty-six and injured over 200 people.

In 1971, two paratroopers had been killed in Northern Ireland, and between 1972 and the end of 1976, seventeen more lost their lives.[82] On 27 August 1979, sixteen paratroopers and two soldiers from the Queen's Own Highlanders were killed in an ambush at Warrenpoint, in South Armagh, on the border between Northern Ireland and the Republic. The first bomb was in a hay trailer. The IRA had planned to explode it for any suitable target passing along the country road, but they got lucky. A small convoy of vehicles carrying men from 2 Para drove by. The IRA detonated the device. Private Paul Burns, travelling in the final truck, said: 'The noise must have been enormous, but I have no memory of it, or of any of the events that followed . . . Of the eight people in our truck, only two survived, myself and Tom'. Burns lost his leg, and 'Tom's leg was damaged and he sustained terrible burns, but he knew he was only alive because he'd swapped seats with Barney.'[83]

The hay-trailer bomb was a lure. The IRA calculated that the Army would set up a temporary base to investigate, and the nearest likely building was the gatehouse of a medieval castle. As soldiers arrived at the gatehouse, IRA fighters set off a huge second bomb, hidden in a milk pail. The bomb devastated its surroundings. General Sir Mike Jackson, then a major, said: 'There were some very gruesome sights. All that was left of the driver of the rear lorry [from the first bomb] was his pelvis, which had been welded to the seat by the intense heat.' A face lay in the estuary, that of Major Peter Fursman, the thin line of his moustache still visible.[84]

The level of violence in Northern Ireland was extraordinary. Between 1968 and 1998, 3 per cent of the population were killed or injured.[85] Given that, and the extent of the threat from the IRA, debate in England about what was happening in Northern Ireland was extremely constrained. The majority saw it as a sectarian conflict; the questions it potentially raised about Britain's Empire and the post-imperial British state remained unanswered.

Britain's world role was contracting. The Empire was almost completely dismantled and, to some extent at least, the Cold War confrontation was turning to detente. In 1968, under financial constraint, Britain decided to accelerate withdrawal from its bases 'East of Suez', and to focus its defence efforts primarily in NATO. Britain's membership of the European Economic Community looked set. In 1975, the Defence Review projected 12 per cent budgetary cuts and an 11 per cent reduction in manpower over the next ten years. Up to 15,000 people in the Army were likely to lose their jobs. By the end of the 1970s, some military thinkers believed that Britain's global defence role was over.[86]

Partly because of cuts, and partly because of the Parachute Regiment's unpopularity with the rest of the Army, in 1977 16 Parachute Brigade was disbanded and the Paras were reduced to one parachute battalion group, consisting of three battalions of around 2,700 men. They were ready to do anything they were asked, but the subtle requirements of counter-insurgency operations in Northern Ireland led some to wonder whether Britain needed a crack squad of tough-minded men at all.

★

Who were the paratroopers? In the 1970s, that question only made sense in the context of Britain's relative decline. In 1940 Britain had an Empire; by 1980, it did not. Only the outposts and anomalies remained. Britain's economy had not been as productive as that of her closest European neighbours in France and West Germany. For Andrew Shonfield and Michael Shanks, who authored the two most influential 'declinist' manifestos in 1958 and 1961, the problem ran deep. Decline showed just how much the persistence of outmoded class structures inhibited economic dynamism and prevented Britain from launching itself confidently into the modern age.[87] The Army was Old Britain: rigid in its hierarchy, defensive of the landed interests of its upper echelons, dependent upon the labour and loyalty of men from the working classes and beneath, and formed from the certainties of a divided class order.

The question of decline took on a new acuity in the 1970s. The violence in Northern Ireland gave the Army a sharpened edge at home, something it had previously avoided. It was also one ingredient in the growth of anxiety that Britain was becoming not just ungovernable, but also increasingly violent. Richard Clutterbuck, an Exeter-based academic who had been a major general in the army, wrote that the years 1971–7 were, by British standards, 'exceptionally violent years . . . in terms of internal political violence: in strikes, demonstrations and terrorism'.[88]

Clutterbuck was careful to confine his remarks to deliberate political violence, but other commentators saw the rise of industrial strikes as the tip of a wider social, even moral, decay. Britain's youth had become wayward, led astray by the counter-culture. Violence lurked in the sweaty dance halls where punk bands played; violence slept lightly in the inner-city streets, the stamping ground of groups of young black men; and violence rose on football terraces and in town centres, where young white men ran in hooligan gangs.[89] For some, the Army was an antidote to the erosion of disciplined standards among the lower orders. Former Commander-in-Chief of Allied Forces in Northern Europe, General Sir Walter Walker, talked about the 'communist Trojan horse' of industrial strife and in 1974 joined the anti-communist Unison in Action group. The group sought to raise funds in order to run the country in the event of a general strike.[90]

In contrast, left-wing commentators focused their criticism on what they saw as the 'conservative backlash' of a state whose credentials were tainted by colonialism and corroded by its propensity to violence.[91] In the 1970s, the Army appeared simply as an instrument of oppression, and the paratroopers, therefore, were its most violent manifestation. During the five states of emergency called between 1970 and 1974, soldiers had been on standby to keep ports open and to clear decaying rubbish off the streets; the prospect of their guarding power stations and maintaining public order while the lights went out seemed very real. The pop group The Clash wrote in a song of 1978: 'The British Army is waiting out there / An' it weighs fifteen hundred tons.'[92]

But General Sir Walter Walker and The Clash were both expressing views that could be considered extreme or just plain odd. For most people, the 1970s were a period of contentment. More people were richer and had access to more material comfort than ever before in the country's history. The imminent danger of thermonuclear war seemed to have passed. The Second World War, and the misery, brutality, terror, discomforts and restrictions it had brought, receded from the pressing memory of the recent past.[93] In 1977 Richard Attenborough's enormously successful film *A Bridge Too Far* cast the Parachute Regiment at Arnhem in an epic drama of extremes, lived and endured, but also long gone. In a British society emerging from the shadows of total war, and one whose rigid class divides were becoming more fluid, what kind of men were these who wanted to join a regiment like the Paras?

2. Joining Up in the 1970s

Dave Parr was born in September 1962 in Oulton Broad, a small town outside Lowestoft on the Suffolk coast. He entered Depot Para, the Parachute Regiment's recruit company in Aldershot, in June 1980, passed selection at the first attempt on 5 December 1980 and joined D Company 2 Para. His parents were working class, but had advanced from their own origins. Dave's father was a motor mechanic and dealt in second-hand cars; he was classed as a skilled manual worker. His mother was a housewife until she began secretarial work at a garage. They were Conservative voters; his father was impressed by money and the appearance of success. Both of Dave's parents had a country upbringing, descended on his mother's side from agricultural labourers, and on his father's side from a man who roasted hops in the brewery and a woman who, in her spare time, attended to the bodies of the dead.

Dave did not grow up accustomed to personal space. His childhood home was a bungalow that his father had bought. It comprised two equally sized rooms at the front, two rooms at the back, one reasonably large and one tiny, and a kitchen. At the rear of the house, there was a conservatory, not one of the kind that became fashionable in the later 1980s, but a stone outhouse with a corrugated plastic roof. In the conservatory, there was a room for the toilet, and in 1965 they added an indoor bathroom. Before that, the bath was behind a curtain at the end of the kitchen.

A striking feature of the period was the improvement in bathrooms. Tony Banks, who joined D Company the year after Dave, remembered that, growing up in 1970s Dundee, he still used to go with his father to the public baths to wash.[1] When he was a young child, Dave slept in a double bed in one of the front rooms with his two brothers. The brothers were quite far apart in age: his oldest brother, my father Harmer, was born in 1949, and Chris in 1958.

Harmer moved into the small backroom when he began his A levels, in order to have somewhere to study. When Harmer left home, Dave shared that backroom with his middle brother Chris.

★

On 2 June 1980, Dave arrived in Aldershot to begin Parachute Regiment selection. Like all recruits, on presenting himself at the Depot he had a preliminary interview with the lieutenant in charge of Recruit Platoon. The lieutenant's job was to record on an index card his impression of each of the youths in front of him. On the card, the lieutenant always recorded the location of the recruiting office through which the youngster had been sent, the boy's age, and aptitude levels attained in the Army's intelligence proficiency tests. He then briefly noted his assessment of the newcomer. In some cases, the lieutenant followed up with further comments, particularly if the boy did not pass training. The lieutenants were free to write whatever they liked – they did not have to trouble with political correctness – and while they tended to be sparing with their remarks, the Depot index cards open a window on a world that would otherwise remain opaque.

The Depot Para records show that men came from a wide geographical range of recruiting offices. Unlike, perhaps, the County Regiments or the Guards, the Paras were a national recruiter. In 1980, of 100 records, the majority were from England – normal given the size of the population – nine were from Scotland, two from Wales and three from Northern Ireland. The only significant group of men not from the UK were from the Republic of Ireland: in 1973, forty-nine of the Paras' 2,687 men were either 'Eirean' or 'British and Eirean'.[2] Mirroring the distribution of the population, most men came from big cities.[3]

All bar a tiny number were white: 'pale-faced', as the lieutenants often put it. Racist attitudes in the Army were probably common, given the very small number of black recruits, but did not necessarily lead to discrimination on grounds of race alone. Race was always visible and in so far as it is possible to tell, the lieutenants always commented on it. On one card, a lieutenant wrote: 'Maltese lad who like many Mediterranean types does not like hard work'; but on another: 'a very tall, well-built coloured lad with a Lancashire accent. Quiet but confident and I feel he will make a willing recruit.' The Paras probably had slightly more recruits recorded as 'coloured' than other regiments. Following a request to return figures to the Army, a Scots Guard respondent remarked: 'We have no coloured male adult soldiers serving in the Regiment.'[4]

Dave probably came from a slightly more comfortable background than many recruits. The lieutenants nearly always commented on the new soldier's bearing, regional background and accent. On Dave's card, the lieutenant wrote: 'Medium height, slim build, fresh face and fair hair. No noticeable accent. Youngish and a bit immature but would seem to have the ability if he gets stuck in.' The lieutenant evidently did not have an ear for the rural East Anglian accent Dave must have had. He was probably attuned to the northern city manners of speech he would have heard more frequently, and Dave might not have talked for long. The observation that he was 'youngish and a bit immature' was probably a comment on his living arrangements. Unlike many of the young men stepping into the Depot, Dave lived at home with his mother, and probably did not have the range of life experiences some men had gained at a younger age.

Dave's background also showed that boys sometimes grew up in households that were difficult to pigeonhole in terms of class. Dave joined the Paras, while my father did well at grammar school, won a scholarship, read modern languages at Cambridge and became a teacher. Tony Banks's oldest brother trained as a lawyer, and another of his brothers was a nurse. Banks's parents wanted Tony to become an accountant. Mark Eyles-Thomas was a private in 3 Para during the Falklands. His mother was a primary school head teacher, and Paul Burns, who had experienced the bombing at Warrenpoint, had a father who was a local manager for an area TV company. Often the decision to step into an army recruiting office was born not of unemployment, but out of dreams of adventure. Men came to the Paras usually because it was an aspiration.

★

Some men did come from deprived backgrounds, and joined to survive, or to escape. Tom Harley, who was a corporal during the
Falklands War, had no family, and lived in an orphanage. Aged fourteen, he was forced to leave. He joined the Merchant Navy and stayed
until he was eighteen. He had nowhere to go: 'I was on the streets for
about six months, living in the Salvation Army, and I saw an advert
saying, "Join the Army, get three meals a day". So I joined the Army.'
The Army offered him the infantry. He struggled with taking orders
at first – 'I've always been on my own, on the streets you become
pretty tough. And you won't . . . in orphanages you've been ordered
all your life to do things, and I found it very, very difficult to take
orders', but he got to like army life in the end.[5]

Some men who grew up in Northern Ireland joined because the
Troubles sharpened division and forced men to choose which side
they were on. The lieutenant at Depot Para in 1980 wrote on the card
of one young recruit from County Down seeking to leave training:
'This young lad probably would not have made the grade anyway,
just as well he goes now. Another waste of a slot that could have
been filled by a better boy. A stone thrower in the making.' Another
man wanted to join because his brother had been a Para killed in the
IRA ambush at Warrenpoint. The lieutenant wrote: 'seems unaffected
by his brother's death', but perhaps he wanted to preserve his
brother's memory, or to find a way to show his brother's death had
not been in vain.

At the time of the Troubles, the Army might have looked like the
least violent and dangerous of a young man's career options. One
man, who grew up in Shankill, a Protestant area of Belfast, said he
had been caught after helping a Catholic friend escape a Protestant
reprisal in a shipyard. His parents had had to flee, and he was picked
up, presumably by a paramilitary: 'So all I was given was a .45 pistol,
a feller picked me up on the back of a motorbike. I never shot a
weapon before, a hand full of big, bulky ammo, said you're coming
with us . . . and the IRA got me, I caught a bullet in the back of the
leg, so you know. When the troubles started, the UVF, UDA, my
dad just said, he knows me, if you don't join the army you're going to
end up dead or in jail.'[6]

Other men had violent home lives. Lee Smith joined the Army at the age of fifteen, in 1974. He did not come from a military family. His father had not served in the Second World War and had managed to miss National Service. Lee reflected that this probably made him feel 'less of a man'. Perhaps this was one reason why his father regularly beat him. Lee said he knew when he was going to be beaten because his father would send him upstairs to the toilet, as he did not want his children wetting themselves under his fists. His household was evidently a troubled one. His older brother used to ask him to masturbate him in return for a ride on his motorbike, and his sister also wanted him to feel her up. He was only a young teenager, but he knew it would be incest if he had sex with her. He thought that was normal life.[7]

Lee was a bright boy, top of his class in primary school. So he could not understand why he failed the 11-plus. He went to a secondary modern, but could never engage with school again; the escape route of educational attainment he had perhaps perceived now appeared to be closed to him. He discovered at the end of the 1980s that he had passed after all, but his father had kept the letter from him.

He went into the army recruiting office, he said, to give himself a future, a goal he could hold onto. He needed to get away, and he did not realize he could join at the age he was – fifteen – so long as his parents signed the papers. He did not dare to ask them, but the recruiting sergeant came to his house, an enormous man in uniform, intimidating and charming his parents by telling them that this boy wanted to join the Army and he had to join 'my corps'. By personalizing it, the sergeant – evidently a skilled evaluator of likely recruits and their domestic circumstances[8] – won his mother over and she signed his form. It was November. He left school in May and went straight to the boys' division of the Royal Engineers.

Lee said that the violence he encountered in the Army was more comprehensible than the violence at home. Army brutality had logic and meaning. It could be controlled if you behaved. Violence at home was arbitrary, disorienting and far more frightening. Lee knew nothing about the Army before he joined up; he had not fantasized about being a soldier. He joined to escape from something worse.[9]

Lee's domestic background was extreme, but not unusual. Colin Black was also beaten by his father as a child: 'Life before the military was horrendous. A very violent father, [he] used to beat the crap out of me for no apparent reason – there probably was, I was probably a horrible child, but all I remember was getting beaten up and thrown around and taken to hospital by my mum, until she finally left him.'[10] Robin Horsfall, who went from the Paras to the SAS, had a stepfather who regularly beat him: 'My fear of him grew into an intense dislike, which he obviously sensed, and that of course made matters even worse.'[11] Mark Eyles-Thomas's parents divorced, remarried and divorced again. His father was not violent, but when he did take an interest in his son it was to drive him hard to perfect his cricketing skills. His father's constant criticism, sometimes drunkenly delivered in the middle of the night, became difficult for Eyles-Thomas to take.[12]

Women joining the Army in this period were also sometimes pushed to do so because of poor family circumstances. Janet Findlay joined the Army in 1969 and subsequently married a paratrooper. Her father 'was an alcoholic and used to beat us up. Especially my mum.' She joined to get away from him: 'I just went into town one day and I saw this army recruitment office. I went in: you're talking someone a stone and a half underweight, chronic bronchitis, I couldn't even stand up straight. But I was brainy, so I got in just like that.' In the Army, 'it was the first time I'd ever had my own bed, because three of us [she and her sisters] used to share a bed in a three-quarter bed . . . I mean it was a luxury because not only did I have my own bed, but I could have a bath whenever I felt like it, and I could have a shower whenever I felt like it. [At home] we had to get in everyone else's bathwater.'[13]

These stories are not just anecdotes. Probably a sizeable minority of men entering the Paras came from backgrounds of deprivation and domestic violence. In 1980, in a sample of 182 Depot Para records chosen randomly, four men had grown up in children's homes. On one of those records, the lieutenant had commented: 'Parents divorced when he was young and [he] lived in a home for eleven years and is keen to join the Regt'; and on another, 'Brought up in a home since the age of three and should have no problems about settling in.'

Two more men were orphans, and one reported that his mother was dead. Three made suicide attempts during their training: one with an overdose and two by slashing their wrists. Eight others confessed to a 'difficult home life' or unspecified welfare problems. One man requested a discharge because his alcoholic father was beating up his mother and he thought he could stop it if he went back home.[14]

It was also reasonably common that boys joined to escape from detention. In the same sample of 182 cards, fifteen men had been in trouble with the law. Ostensibly, the Army was not keen on men of potentially poor character. Post-war experience showed that enlisting men who had shown a disregard for the law generally led to 'unreliable and unsatisfactory soldiers' who found it hard to avoid further trouble. Nevertheless, men with convictions were permitted to join if they could show themselves to be reformed, well motivated or intelligent; or if they had good recommendations and would not need additional supervision.[15] Men from approved schools, children's homes or borstals could have the waiting time of six months to two years from the date of the offence to enlistment waived if they had not committed a serious offence and had good recommendations from the heads of those institutions.[16]

Of the fifteen men in the sample, one had a motorbike offence, another had been involved in football hooliganism. One had a charge for being drunk and disorderly, two for breach of the peace and another for fighting. One had a formal charge of assault, one had a charge of Actual Bodily Harm and one man had multiple charges or cautions for criminal damage, ABH, burglary and breach of the peace (he qualified). One had been charged with shoplifting, another had spent time in junior detention, while another was on remand in jail at the time he went to the Depot. Two spent time in military prison, and two more admitted they had been in trouble with the police for 'discipline problems' in their younger days. Five others had outstanding debts, but nothing criminal. They owed money on hire purchase for motorbikes, a car, a stereo and weight-lifting equipment.

Sometimes, boys slipped into crime because of their social and family problems. Dominic Gray, who went into 3 Para, was brought up by a succession of family members after his parents divorced. He was happy with an aunt who lived in France, but his father insisted Dominic came back to England, which meant separating him from his brother. When his father remarried, Dominic did not get along with his stepmother and her children, and he was soon in trouble with the law. Jerry Phillips grew up in Singapore because his father was an RAF technician. His parents divorced and he came back to England with his mother, living in a one-bedroom flat with three siblings. They were poor, and Jerry took to burglary to make ends meet.[17]

What explains the noticeable incidence of men with convictions arriving at Depot Para? It could be that fighting on the streets and football terraces made a job in the Paras look attractive. Jon Cook said that he was involved in football violence at Luton. He joined Junior Para so he could channel his violence: 'I used to go and watch football at Luton so I was a bit of a boot-boy, and really I joined Junior Para and got away from that side of things – the fighting and this, that and the other. So really I was a skinhead . . . We were a little bit thuggish then as kids, and we were as a junior soldier, but you were proud.'[18]

It could also be that men facing detention were given the choice of the Army as an alternative to a prison sentence. Vincent Bramley grew up in a block of flats in Aldershot, in a loving home but in what he called a 'slum area'. He left school with no qualifications and said he could barely read and write. He became involved in football violence and, as civilian boys did in the home of the Parachute Regiment, sometimes got into fights with soldiers: 'I was heavily into football fights, having a ruck at a disco, driving around on my scooter – because I was a mod – and thinking I was the bee's knees and a hard man.'

Vince had an apprenticeship with an electrician, but he was restless, a little irrepressible, wanting more. But there was no more to be had. Like many other youngsters who found their way towards the Paras, he was soon in trouble: 'By the age of seventeen and a half I was in a detention centre, for two counts of ABH, and I served three months in what we'd call a young offender's place now, but a detention centre in 1975 was a hard regime, you wouldn't be able to do what they do now – we were beaten daily, and kicked around, marched around in a grey uniform, and it was a hard, hard . . . I served eight weeks there . . . for what I duly think I deserved, for beating up a couple of people with a gang, you think you're hard . . . The ironic thing about it was that I actually quite enjoyed the discipline.'

It took Vince a bit longer to reconcile himself to that discipline, as he was straight back out onto the streets, and it was two or three years later when he finally joined up. His girlfriend's father, a paratrooper himself, bet him a fiver that he could not qualify as a Para. He joined then to give himself an alternative to the wayward life he seemed to be drifting into and the risk that he might end up in prison. He said: 'The Army did know about my troubles, they said keep that quiet, get through, blah blah blah. But without a doubt, I would say it was the best thing I did.'[19]

Vince's girlfriend's family played an important part in pushing him into the Paras. Most men believed that being in uniform made them attractive to women. Tony Banks said, 'The girls loved it. It never failed!'[20] On the other hand, one element in explaining why men went to the Depot and made it through training was often that they didn't have girlfriends, or that their girlfriends didn't mind or perhaps didn't care that they were there. If men wanted to spend a lot of time with their spouses or partners, or if they wanted sometimes to be more involved in the lives of their children, then army life was unsuitable. Perhaps at that time, like Banks they preferred carefree liaisons, brief encounters and having the possibility of many women rather than one.

Seven men of the sample of 182 going into the Depot mentioned that they already had children. Some were in a relationship with the mother of those children, others were not but were making maintenance payments. Three were married, and of those only one completed training, while the rest asked to leave. To get through training, they needed an ability to separate themselves from the temptations of home, and to give primacy to military needs over domestic comforts. Over-dominating girlfriends were a repeated refrain on the Depot Para cards. One comment read: 'Excellent young soldier (aged 18) whose girl of 16 yrs 5 months is pregnant and he allows her to dominate him'; and, in another case, the lieutenant wrote: 'Rather wet and pathetic individual with no moral values, no mental stamina, no physical ability, using a "groin injury" as an excuse for not taking P Company [the toughest part of selection training]. Yet he managed to impregnate his girlfriend. Ugh! Not recommended for re-enlistment.'

Of course, it is difficult to say from the Depot records how many men with significant problems did become Paras and how many dropped out. Of those who had been in trouble with the law, about half failed. Often, men's personal difficulties presented themselves on the discharge notes, rather than at the initial interview. On one card, the lieutenant wrote on the recruit's arrival: 'Slightly above average height, medium build, darkish features, small moustache and Liverpool accent. Young but seems keen enough to get stuck in. I see no reason why he should not make a reasonable recruit.' A few weeks later, the same lieutenant noted: 'Wants to leave the army and as he is a potential problem he should be allowed to as soon as possible. Has attempted to slash his wrist and failed.'

At the same time, if men made it through training, their private histories might never have been recorded. We just do not know how often men came into the Depot and withheld information from the lieutenants about their home lives. Dave Parr was not reported as coming from a 'broken home' even though his parents had been living separately for several years. Recruits' success in training depended in part on being able to put family problems, girlfriends or emotional distress behind them. The process of training was part of the process of making boys into men, whether those boys had grown up in relatively stable circumstances or in a sort of modern-day hell.

*

Why did men choose to become officers in the Parachute Regiment? Often, they had military fathers who expected or wanted their sons to follow in their footsteps. David Chaundler, a lieutenant colonel in the Falklands who came to lead 2 Para after Commanding Officer Herbert 'H' Jones had been killed, had a father who had been an officer at Dunkirk. He said he joined up because his father told him to grow up and take responsibility for himself: 'I joined the army because I was something of a layabout and my father told me it was about time I went and earned a living. So, I thought I suppose I'd better go and join the Army.'[21] He did not consider doing anything else.

Other men at the rank of major during the Falklands – Dair Farrar-Hockley, who commanded A Company 2 Para, and Philip Neame, Officer Commanding D Company 2 Para – had fathers with very distinguished military records. Neame's father, who had children late in life, had won the Victoria Cross in the First World War; and Farrar-Hockley's father Anthony had been decorated for his service to the Parachute Regiment. Growing up with fathers who modelled such excellence could mean a son might want to fulfil family expectations, or to pursue a career that he grew up comprehending. Nothing else would quite match up. Becoming a soldier was about more than the Army. It was about reaching maturity, and therefore about becoming a man. Deciding to join signalled readiness to assume responsibilities, to continue a family tradition, perhaps to improve prospects for marriage and, if called upon, to assume duty to the country.

Some men may have carried an almost spiritual view of duty as an honour and a calling. It was a destiny, perhaps one granted or chosen by God, and one that emulated the responsibility, heredity and service by Britain's monarch. Boys were raised understanding that they were to suppress the instincts of their individual selves and fulfil the obligations to which they were born. The Commanding Officer of 3 Para, Hew Pike, came from a family for whom service was a privilege and a necessity. To fail to continue the family's heritage would colour the family's memories and diminish past sacrifice. The path was there, and a young man had to display the form and standards to continue along it. Pike's father had been a soldier and his grandparents 'lived with their memories and sadnesses from the First World War'. In his mother's family, 'everyone seems to have been either a soldier or a clergyman since time immemorial . . . lives well spent, many in the service of the country'.[22]

These traditional ideas of duty as honour probably mixed with a sense that joining the Army, particularly a regiment like the Paras, was the toughest test of a man's fitness and nerve. Perhaps men did not so much think in terms of Victorian, gentlemanly gamesmanship, but rather they wanted to demonstrate their strength, endurance and physical aptitude, and to thrive outdoors. Men tended to enjoy competitive sports. The Army offered nearly constant physical activity and war would be the greatest competition on earth. Philip Neame relished a challenge and had nearly made it to the top of Mount Everest before he went to the Falklands.[23] Chip Chapman – a lieutenant in 2 Para in the Falklands, retiring as Major General Chapman – chose the Paras because he was good at boxing and football.[24] Others were into freefall parachuting, rowing or rugby. They were sports that required not only brute force, but also courage, measured risk-taking, stamina and judgement.

The connection between becoming a man and becoming a soldier was about stepping up to the responsibility of service, but it was also about the ability to demonstrate manly attributes such as authority, aggression, strength, resolve and confidence. Ultimately, wanting to become a soldier was a desire to be tested as men, to see how they, as individuals, would measure up in circumstances endured by many thousands of men before them. Chaundler said: 'I rather liken it to the African tribe, where to prove you're a man you have to kill a lion. It's the sort of macho side.'

In the late 1970s and early 1980s the social background of officers was becoming more diverse, but there remained a strong link between public-school education and army service. The majority of middle-class men who joined the Army had been to public school, and in 1974 44 per cent had been to one of the more distinguished schools that made up the 'Headmasters' Conference'.[25] Seven per cent had been to Eton, Harrow or Winchester.[26] Even though the Parachute Regiment was more meritocratic than other, more traditional regiments, it probably opened up more during the 1980s, and senior officers who went to the Falklands generally were public-school educated.[27] The Commanding Officer of 2 Para, Lieutenant Colonel Jones, went to Eton, Hew Pike to Winchester. Major Chris Keeble, who temporarily took over from Jones after his death, went to the Roman Catholic Douai School, run by Benedictine monks; David Chaundler attended Eastbourne College. Farrar-Hockley went to Exeter School, and

John Crosland, the major in charge of B Company, 2 Para, to Wellington, a regular feeder school to the Army and, as he put it, 'Broadmoor Secondary Modern'.[28]

Attending public school probably helped to instil in men notions that manhood meant taking responsibility – of yourself and others – and accustomed men to maintaining a stoical hold over their emotions, and to living communally in often austere conditions.[29] School life also acclimatized men to discipline. Chaundler was too old when he joined to go to Sandhurst for a regular commission, and so went in as a private soldier in the ranks. He said that his public-school background had great advantages: 'I was used to mindless discipline, I was used to living in a barrack room, I was used to lousy food.' It also gave him the confidence to use the kind of currency that was understood in the barracks: 'More to the point, at school we all had to box, so when I was put in charge of jobs I was wise enough to put this Irish docker down for cleaning the latrines.'[30] The docker challenged him, and Chaundler was able to silence his challenge by flooring him with a straight left and a right hook.

Above all, perhaps public school gave men loyalty to institutions that looked after them, and a sense that they should exhibit independence from notions of home comfort and motherly affection. John Crosland's father was in the Indian Army during the Second World War. Aged eight, Crosland was sent to boarding school while his parents were in Singapore, and he did not see them for three years.[31] Mike Jackson – who ended his career as General Sir Mike Jackson – went to Sandhurst in 1962. He came from a military family but not a wealthy one. He boarded at Stamford School from the age of eight: 'In general I was quite happy at school . . . There was a fagging system in place which required small boys to "fag" for their seniors, running errands and generally acting as drudges: perhaps a little archaic, but it taught you to obey orders unquestioningly.'[32]

There were increasing numbers of men at Sandhurst who had not gone to public school and for whom these connections between service, discipline and communal living were not second nature. Sometimes, middle-class men joined the Army because they needed to get away from home. The Army paid them, and thus could give them independence from their families, as well as allowing them some status among their peers. If they were at university, they could earn money by joining the Officer Training Corps and could differentiate themselves from other students. Chip Chapman, who went to Lancaster University, recounted a farcical meeting of the student anarchist society, saying, 'student politics were absurd'.[33] David Benest, a captain at the time of the Falklands and later Commanding Officer of 2 Para, said he had a place to read Geography at Queen's University Belfast. But his father refused to sign the form to enable him to get a grant. He went to Sandhurst instead, much to his father's annoyance, and later did an in-service degree at Keele University, paid for by the Army.[34] Another man who was a captain during the Falklands, said, 'I needed to be independent.' He studied medicine with the Army because he could not, or did not want to, rely on his parents to give him financial support.[35]

For any boy or young man, joining up could be an expression of rebelliousness, unwillingness to conform to civilian mores, or it could be a badge of status, especially if they felt other avenues were closed to them. 'H' Jones (who was called 'H' because he did not like his first name, Herbert), who was Commanding Officer of 2 Para during the Falklands, did not come from a military family. His father was a wealthy, liberal American, given to philanthropy, whose family had made money from mining. Jones senior married a relatively impoverished Welsh nurse. He was an Anglophile, and he sent H to Eton to turn him into a 'proper English gentleman'.[36] At Eton, according to his biographer and friend John Wilsey, Jones did not excel academically and was an awkward fit.

Sixty per cent of Eton's schoolboys were the sons of old Etonians, in possession of an effortless self-confidence. Jones was shy and spent a lot of time alone, reading war books and developing strongly held notions of valour. He was dismissive of traditions that excluded him. In his senior year at Eton, the school selected boys to hold social positions. Jones was offered a lowly post. He rejected it. A schoolmate remembered: 'In the conditions of the time, this was an event on a par with a Spartacus revolt. It had a dramatic impact on those of us resigned to having been born into some teenage underclass for reasons not explained by our education or upbringing.'[37]

Fascinated by things military, Jones went to Sandhurst after Eton. He was what the Army call a 'late developer', but his wealth enabled him to take risks. From Cyprus, he flew to England twice in one weekend to see his girlfriend Sara; on another occasion, he climbed through a hotel window three storeys up to join her in their bedroom; and as a practical joke he let off the fire hydrants at Dartmouth's Naval Commissioning Ball, covering the guests with water coloured by rust. When told off, he had the temerity to suggest that if the Navy cleaned their hydrants more often the damage would have been less serious and he could afford to compensate the guests for their ruined outfits.[38] He was impetuous, romantic and immensely loyal to those who knew him well; but he could also be blunt and rude, and underneath his brashness and arrogance was uncertainty and vulnerability.

After Sandhurst in 1960, he went to his county regiment, the Devonshire and Dorset Regiment (the Devon and Dorsets). In 1965, he did an attachment with the Parachute Regiment and passed out of Staff College in 1973 as a major. He chose then to rejoin his parent regiment as adjutant. He was one of three candidates considered to command the Devon and Dorsets, but he did not get that job.

The reasons why he lost out in his county regiment seem to say something about the Army, and something too about Jones. One successful candidate was senior to the other two. The second was junior to Jones, and although that candidate had not been with the Devon and Dorsets for ten years, his father had served with them and that might have counted for something. As for Jones, he seemed to split opinion among army senior command. He had energy, determination and enthusiasm without bounds, and therefore undoubted ability. Nevertheless, he sometimes behaved irreverently to his superiors, and did not listen to others' concerns. One of his Staff College reports read: 'He has tended to dominate each syndicate he has been in. In full spate he interrupts other speakers and is deaf to all counter argument.'[39] Brigadier Randle, the Acting Commanding Officer of the Devon and Dorsets, wrote: 'There were question marks over H's judgement. Now, if you project that forward to a commanding officer in that position – being awkward and not accepting orders – it could do a battalion untold harm.'[40] Jones assumed command of the 2nd Battalion, The Parachute Regiment on 3 April 1981.

★

The Second World War, and the conscription that followed it, meant millions of British men had to devote part of their lives to military service. This legacy impacted the generation born after the war, and was the backdrop for all individuals' decisions to join up in this period. Conscription created military families. The records of Depot Para show that a family military background, or prior military experience, was the largest common factor (although still a relatively minor one – twenty candidates out of 182) among men trying to join in 1980.

For some, a military childhood opened worlds they believed they would not otherwise have accessed. Les Davis, a private in the Army Catering Corps attached to 3 Para during the battle of Mount Longdon, grew up on army bases around the world. His father had stayed in the Royal Army Service Corps as a butcher after National Service. As a young child, Les lived in Singapore. Later, he was sent to boarding school. He loved it, because of the opportunities it gave him for life outdoors, horse-riding for example, and he got to fly out to Hong Kong, where his parents now were, for holidays. He said it was a 'very privileged' upbringing. It was secure; he did not have to make hard choices for himself. Les was attracted to the 'job security, and the travel, it was still a big army then'. He did not consider a different career.[41]

For many men, therefore, joining up was normal. They were treading in the footsteps of their fathers, their schoolmates' fathers, and their neighbours. Joining the Army was not particularly about wanting to fight a war. In the 1970s, it did not seem as if war was likely, unless it was the war that presaged nuclear apocalypse. Even for men whose fathers had been Paras, service did not necessarily mean combat. Dean Edwards, a private in 2 Para in 1982, joined up because his father had been a Para who was proud of the regiment. Eighteen when he joined during the Second World War, Dean's father had had malaria and therefore did not go to Arnhem – 'hardly any of his mates came back'.[42] In 1948 in Palestine, his father managed to sleep through an attack, and later left the Paras to get married. 3 Para's Private Mark Dodsworth had a father, Bryan, who had been a paratrooper at Suez in 1956. Bryan left the regiment shortly afterwards to marry his young girlfriend Carole, Mark's mother.[43] Phil Francom's grandfather was a paratrooper in the Second World War. He had been injured in a parachute jump. As a child, Phil, who was in D Company with my uncle, had 'synovitis and as a result had one leg shorter than the other. I was in callipers for many years trying to correct this. When the callipers came off I was like a horse out of the stalls.' He wanted to follow his grandfather's path and make his grandparents proud.[44]

There might have also been a sense of romance about military life in families who did not have much military experience. In this era, boys' comics and books were filled with Second World War adventure and toys were modelled on the glamour of combat.[45] 2 Para's Private Paul Burns lived near an army training centre and watched the vehicles and soldiers coming and going.[46] Tony Coxall, also a private in 2 Para, said his father had been in the RAF, but that did not influence Tony's decision. Rather, he saw pictures of the battle of Arnhem in a local library when he was a child and knew that he wanted to become a paratrooper, like those men.[47]

Boys might also have been influenced by the fact that their fathers, in the military or not, were often away from home for long periods of time. Martin Margerison, a corporal during the Falklands War, said that his dad was in the Merchant Navy, but was a 'great guy – never swore, my dad'.[48] His father modelled ideals Martin wanted to emulate, but he was not a daily presence in the lives of his children, and it probably never occurred to most of the fathers – or sons – that they could be.

Jon Cook and Vince Bramley, both lance corporals with 3 Para, said their fathers were both long-distance lorry drivers – a profession that might have been encouraged by being able to obtain their

driving licences during National Service. As a result of his father
being away so much, Vince commented, 'I'd say I'm a mother's son.'[49]
Jon said that because his mother worked too, he was regularly left to
his own devices: 'My dad was a lorry driver, so I didn't see much of
him. My mum was a nurse, we were a bit like latchkey kids, she was
always doing home visits and my dad wasn't home.'[50]

In practice, most men were brought up by their mothers. Mothers'
attitudes towards military service could sometimes be more indul-
gent than those of fathers, perhaps because they wanted their sons to
pursue their ambitions, or at least they did not feel they should stand
in their sons' way – or else they did not have sufficient time and
energy to dissuade them. Ian McKay's father did not want Ian, who
was a sergeant with 3 Para in the Falklands, to join the Parachute
Regiment, because he had not particularly enjoyed his own National
Service. Freda, Ian's mother, encouraged him, pleased that he wanted
to do something with his life and that he sought independence from
the family home. She loved him and she felt she had to allow him to
do the things he wanted to do: 'It was hard, but I've always been told:
let them go, you keep them.'[51]

At other times, mothers' acceptance of military service could be
because they wanted their sons to fit in. Theresa Burt signed her son
Jason's papers to join the Parachute Regiment when he was sixteen.
She was a Catholic who grew up in Ireland; her husband was Jewish,
his grandmother having fled with her family to England from the
Soviet Union. They were market traders in London's East End. They
did not want Jason to join the Army. Jason was perhaps struggling at
school and in the streets because he was small and had a 'Mediterranean' complexion. Theresa said that when he went to the Depot, one
senior soldier asked him which of his parents was a 'wog'. Jason was
in rebellion. He threatened his parents that if they did not sign him
up, he would leave home as soon as he could and they would never
see him again.[52]

Mothers also probably respected and admired the kind of masculinity their sons exhibited in uniform. Rita Hedicker grew up in an
orphanage in the north of Scotland, abandoned, she subsequently discovered, by her unmarried teenage mother. She came to London to

go into domestic service and met her husband at a Reel Club. He had been in the Royal Army Service Corps and stayed on after National Service. She was a bit concerned when her son Peter joined the infantry, because her husband and her older son had both had clerical roles in the army, but she knew what he had trained for, and she felt more fear for him riding his motorbike than she did when he was out in Northern Ireland.[53]

★

As for Dave Parr, it is hard to know what made him decide to join the Paras, how his family's history and its relationship to military service might have influenced him. His father Con had been in the Royal Naval Patrol Service during the Second World War, driving a boat around local ports. Dave's cousin on his mother's side, Billy Allen, had been in the 10th Battalion, The Parachute Regiment. He had been killed, aged nineteen, at Arnhem. Perhaps that kindled Dave's imagination; but his mother Joy was not close to her oldest brother, Billy's father. They rarely saw each other, and it is unlikely that Billy Allen's death impinged on Dave at all. He probably did not even know about it.

Dave's family background perhaps influenced him in less obvious ways. His mother Joy was born in 1925, the youngest of four children. When her own mother was dying in 1958, Joy discovered that the man she knew as her father, also called Billy, was not her real father. Her biological father was the family lodger, Jack. It possibly explains the fact she did not always get on with her siblings, who could claim their father as legitimate. She was ashamed of her parentage, and hid it all her life.

Billy had been exempt from war service in the First World War because he was head horseman on the estate of the village landlord, Lord Somerleyton. Jack, on the other hand, had been in the 9th Battalion Norfolk Regiment and had been at the front on the Somme in 1916. After the war, Jack became an itinerant labourer, and that was how he ended up staying with Joy's parents. He lived there for thirty years while her mother was alive, and continued to live with Billy after her mother's death. Jack outlived Billy, and still resided in the family home when I was a young child.

Joy wanted to leave the village of her birth. She was the only child in Somerleyton, so the story goes, to pass the school entrance exam, but her parents did not want her to go to the grammar school. During the Second World War she joined the Auxiliary Training Service and went away to training camps in Newmarket and Guildford. She enjoyed it. The war offered her some chance of escape, but then it ended.

She needed a man to establish her independence. Joy conceived my father before she was married and she never told anyone this, although it must have been obvious when Harmer was born six months after her wedding.[54] Nobody will ever know if she contrived his conception to marry Con, if it was an accident or if it was something worse than that. Con was not violent but he was unreliable and restless, and she could never live up to the domestic standards he hankered after.

She probably believed she was on the wrong side of respectable. She regularly referred to herself as a 'slut', in the old-fashioned sense of the word, as a woman who could not properly keep house. She was untidy, and not particularly strict. She was not military minded, she just liked boyish misdemeanours. When her sons came home dirty from football and running or playing out on the marshes, she often referred to them as 'mudlarks': the name given to people from the lower orders, who eked a living picking junk from the mud of the Thames.

Like many boys, Dave played war games when he was a child and loved toy soldiers. Con had never been a soldier, but he always spoke very highly of the Army, and he was particularly keen on the SAS. He left home when Dave was about twelve, to live with another woman, and he probably did not talk much to Dave about what he was to do with his life. As a young teenager, Dave was into sports like cross-country running and skateboarding. Later, Dave hung around with his friend Blue Cole, whose father had been in the Parachute Regiment during National Service. Blue joined the Army as a junior, and did not want anything else but to be a Para.

1. and 2. Dave playing in the garden of the bungalow, aged five, *c*.1967.

Perhaps Dave joined up because he wanted to impress his father, and they seemed to share an appreciation of special forces. Maybe the steadiness of Blue's father, who often bailed Blue and Dave out of scrapes or fights, appealed to him; or it could be that Blue's choice of career helped him decide. We do not know. On his way to the

3. Chris, Dave and the author (as a baby) in the back room of the bungalow, early 1975; Dave aged twelve, Chris aged sixteen.

Falklands, Dave wrote more frequently to his mother than he did to his father, but in the one letter he did write to his dad, just before troops landed on the islands, he alluded to his father's fascination with elite troops: 'I can tell you that "your friends" are playing a very big roll at the moment.'[55] Dave's ambition was to join the SAS, and no doubt, like many men, he saw the Paras as his first step towards it.

He wanted, I suspect, to follow his ambitions, and it was a goal Joy would have fully supported. She wanted her children to do well for themselves and going into the Army was a mark of advancement. Joining up made Dave into a man, and she respected a man in uniform much as she had admired the soldiers she had met during the war. She probably supposed it would increase his prospects, make it more likely he would attract a nice girl, settle down and father children. She was so proud when Dave passed out and stood on a parade ground with members of the Royal Family. She was not noticeably patriotic, but she was thrilled he had made something of himself. He could look forward to an exciting and reliable career.

★

In a 1960s recruiting pamphlet, the Parachute Regiment stressed that the Army provided a steady job with the possibility of promotion, paid holidays and housing for married men.[56] By the 1970s, army advertising campaigns featured sunshine, water-skiing, weapons and attractive young women in bikinis.[57] The Army deliberately presented itself so as to tap into young men's sense of fun and excitement: 'adventurous and overseas training . . . although expensive, play an important part in fostering job satisfaction . . . Training of this kind is warmly welcomed on manning grounds since it helps to retain men in the Army and encourages young men of the right character and spirit to enlist.'[58]

Britain's military presence was contracting, but still global, and the Army could open up worlds – tropical beaches, extreme sports, enticing-looking women – that might have been more easily accessible to wealthier teenagers, but harder to find for men from the backstreets of Glasgow. Men could seek a life in the Army because they wanted adventures they would not have if they stayed at home. Those adventures were not about war and violence, but about glamorous and adrenaline-fuelled sports, hot weather and sex. In 1982 the BBC followed 480 Platoon through their recruit training. Among the reasons the new recruits gave for joining up were: 'the glamorous reasons . . . the combination of adventure and travel was by far the most popular'.[59] In this way, the great freedoms of the 1960s influenced the aspirations of young recruits, even if they were not expressly into the things – free love, greater equality for homosexuals, women and people of colour, world peace – that the counter-culture promoted.

Why did boys seek adventure in the military rather than through other career avenues? The ranks of the British infantry in the 1970s often hailed from what might be termed an educational underclass, and that may have circumscribed the choices open to them. The school-leaving age was raised to sixteen on 1 September 1972. It was difficult after that for men to leave school with no qualifications at all; but the majority joining the ranks of the Paras had done very poorly at school. Dave, who came from a family who supported, although did not encourage, educational success, left school in 1978 with two CSEs. In 1980, none of the Paras' intake had a degree or had done A levels. Only 2.7 per cent had O levels, or CSE level 1; 12.5 per cent had CSEs Grade 2–5; 79.1 per cent had no school-leaving certificate; and 5.7 per cent were at a lower level than that, although nobody was classed in band level 8 (illiterate).[60] The figures suggest poor schooling rather than lack of ability to figure things out. In their general aptitude tests, the Paras recorded 41.5 per cent of recruits in level 2 (the second highest level), compared with 13.7 per cent in the infantry overall.[61]

These statistics indicate that schools were not managing to convince some boys of the value of formal education. The numbers of comprehensive schools in Britain were growing, but mentalities formed in a period when education had been more clearly stratified along class lines had not died out.[62] The legacy of the selection exam, old-fashioned curricula and traditions of 'streaming' forced children to know where they stood at an early point in their lives, and to understand that academic success was no longer expected. Schools were often segregated by gender, and methods of discipline could be harsh. Mark Eyles-Thomas said that at one of the schools he went to, a Catholic school run by nuns, he was tied to a chair to prevent him from running around.[63] If men felt that their schools expected them to become failures, then success in the Army became an act of resistance or rebellion.

Underwhelming experiences at school were often compounded by attitudes fostered in boys' homes and local streets. Gary Williams, who was with the Royal Marines in the Falklands at the time of the Argentine occupation, said: 'In 1975 you didn't take any notice of what you did at school, so I had no exam grades.'[64] The legacy of full male employment meant many families saw school as irrelevant. Boys looked up not to their teachers but to men they knew in their neighbourhoods, and emulated the attributes they thought they would need to get ahead in the all-male world of work: quick wit, independence, strength and prowess with girls.[65]

Some men believed that school-based education enabled people who lacked initiative to succeed. Doing what you were told, unless you were earning money for it, was just sucking up to those in charge. For Tony Banks, his classmates at college when he studied accountancy had never known struggle, had never lived. They were mediocre, except that they could do their sums, and yet they assumed they deserved more: 'What really got to me about college was the air of superiority that the would-be accountants had. They truly believed they were better than everyone else. I never understood that.'[66] Further education could bring with it a charge of snobbery, the view that boys rejected the worlds they grew up in. In contrast, a boy who went to Depot Para came home as he was before, but more so. He came home a man.

Sometimes, men disliked the more liberal influences their classmates developed. Recruits-in-waiting did not want to listen to music, wear fashionable clothes or go to discos in mixed groups. Rejection of those influences was one factor ruling out higher education, even for academically more able boys. Ian McKay went to grammar school. One of his school friends recalled: 'The hippie era started and for a bunch of us our interests moved from sport to music and girls. Ian never showed any interest in either topic. About 90 per cent of our class grew long hair, listened to what was then called "progressive music" and spent most of our spare time going out with girls. Ian seemed to carry on in the same old way and preferred to retain what we'd have referred to at the time as old-fashioned values.'[67]

Perhaps some men joined the Army to feel more comfortable with those 'old-fashioned values'. The soon-to-be singer-songwriter Billy Bragg wrote of his time in the Royal Armoured Corps in 1980 that army culture was dominated by 'white Anglo-Saxon Protestants, anti-Catholic, anti-black, anti-Semitic out-and-out bigots'. Bragg decided to leave when Bob Marley died: 'The other guys in the Regiment just kept asking why we listened to that nigger music.'[68]

However, recruits were young, and their views were not fixed. Like many Paras, Mike Curtis grew up in a mining village. He lived in Rhondda, in the Welsh valleys. His father and grandfathers were miners and his parents urged him never to go down the pits. Mike went to grammar school and his parents wanted him to become a gym teacher. He was looking for independence and, to get that, he needed money. His girlfriend, whom he had known since she was thirteen and he fifteen, was unhappy at home and Mike wanted to get a mortgage for a house for the two of them, which he managed to do when they were old enough. At sixteen and a half, he began to train as a fitter's apprentice at the coal mine. Gradually, it dawned on him that this would be it for the rest of his life: 'There was just a sameness about the existence and a realization that it hadn't changed in generations.'

His parents were not keen on his becoming a Para, but it was not such a clean break with his past as it might superficially appear. Rhondda was staunchly socialist, even communist. But Rhondda miners had fought against fascism in the Spanish Civil War; his grandfathers had both fought in the First World War. He knew men in his village who had been in the Army. The harsh conditions of the mine, the physical strength and endurance men needed to go to the coalface day after day, the salvation of their camaraderie – attributes found in many traditional industrial workplaces – would all overlap with conditions in the Paras.

Curtis was working on the surface of the mine when there was a terrible accident underground, and he decided then he had to leave. He married his girlfriend, and he thought he could enlist for a few years and have an adventure: 'It was this very sense of permanence which finally gave me the confidence to leave the Rhondda: there was something comforting about the thought that if I did head off to see the world, the valley would still be waiting when I got back, just the same as always.'[69]

★

Curtis was thus influenced by the fact of full male employment, not lack of work. Unemployment did not become a major factor in recruitment until 1982–3, by which time the numbers of unemployed dramatically increased; from 1,464,000 in July 1979 to 3,225,000 in January 1983.[70] In a sample of recruits in 1980, men were most likely to come from the North, Manchester, Glasgow and Newcastle. By 1982, the Depot Para records suggest that the proportion of recruits from northern cities had increased. In a similar sample in that year, 17 per cent now came from Manchester, as opposed to 7 per cent in 1980, and 11 per cent from Glasgow and Leeds, as opposed to 7 per cent each in 1980. The 1982 recruits were also marginally older than those in 1980, indicating that they had spent longer looking for work before coming to the Depot. The mean age of the 1982 cohort was 20.09 years, and of the 1980 cohort 19.4. The median age in 1982 was 19.83 years, and in 1980 it was a year younger, 18.83. The authorities noticed the change too. In March 1983, when Her Majesty's Inspectorate inspected the Aldershot barracks of Junior Para, they commented on the increase in IQ levels of new recruits, because of 'the higher number of more able youngsters who are attracted to an Army career at a time of high unemployment'.[71]

For Paras who went to the Falklands, therefore, it was not usually a lack of potential jobs that encouraged men to join the Army, but that the kinds of jobs they could otherwise do were dull by comparison. They did not want 'shit work'.[72] Paul Burns said the guys he had been at school with only talked about going out with a new girl, or which pub to drink in. He was in Junior Para, and was out in the wilds camping, potholing and canoeing.[73] Michael Asher said he could not bear the 'drudgery' of repetitive work: 'I had only one life to live, and I had no intention, even then, of living it in an office or a factory.'[74]

It was the same, I think, for Dave Parr. After he left school, he lived with his mum and his dog, a black Labrador, and worked as an unskilled labourer at Morton's pea factory, 'pushing a pea with a broom'. Dave's brother, my uncle Chris, left home in 1981 to travel across Asia. Chris said: 'Leaving school and going to work is a very debilitating experience for most people. Life could be very dry and disappointing.'[75] It was at that point, entering the labour market after school, that the boyhood dreams of work and women, the assumed status of earning money, hit against reality: unqualified, you were no longer the joker of the classroom (and Dave had never been that anyway), but the lowest of the low. Surely Dave was aware that, stuck where he was, his horizons had narrowed in comparison to those of his brothers. He kicked against the fatalism that might have kept him there, and he wanted to travel, to see the world.

Dave might have looked for openings that reflected the type of things he was already familiar with, the pastimes he had already developed. Growing up in a semi-rural area, Dave spent a lot of time down on the marshes, wildfowling and fishing – pursuits that required a kind of masculine proficiency. He had a knowledge of the countryside and his surroundings, the patience to move with the natural world and an acceptance of its brutality, and the ability to endure the physical discomfort of rain, mud and wind. Those were skills he could use once he was in the Paras.

Most recruits grew up in big cities. On the city streets, men were often forced to reckon with an everyday masculine power rooted in survival of a different kind. It could be hard to avoid violence. Robin Horsfall, who never fitted in, was beaten by boys in and out of school. Tony Banks wrote of the filthy crush on the football terraces at Celtic, the drunkenness, the regular fights between rival, or just different, gangs of men. Chris Parr said that, in places, Lowestoft was a very violent little town.[76] Men came off the fishing fleet looking to release their aggression. If the inhabitants of the town wanted a fight, they

4. Dave, out on the marshes, 1980–81, aged eighteen.

5. Dave, out on the marshes with Blue Cole, autumn 1981, aged nineteen.

knew where to go to find it. Men grew accustomed to judging the
mood of a pub room or a street corner, to relying on their friends to
support them or cover for them, to using their physical strength
when it was required, and to bearing pain.

But in many ways, their leisure (if that is the word for it) was innocent. When he was an older teenager, Dave spent his free time with
his brother Chris, and his friend Blue. They hung around in Lowestoft, the nearest big town to Oulton Broad, drinking to excess, having
a laugh. Anything and everything could make them laugh: hiding
under the bridge in Everitt Park and roaring to scare passers-by;
stealing an empty police car, driving it up the road and running
away; falling into and avoiding fights; and getting drunk, always
getting drunk. They would stay in the pub until closing time and
then take bottles of wine to the beach, pushing the cork into the
bottle with their thumbs.

Blue remembered Dave on his hands and knees in a back alley, vomiting Pernod and black.[77] Chris said that he and Dave, full of drink, would sleep in the cemetery on the outskirts of Lowestoft town before making the three-mile walk home to Oulton Broad. If Dave was with Blue, they slept in whichever home they got to first, fully clothed, lying on the backroom floor. Theirs was an unmaterialistic, inward-looking and self-reliant culture. Their heroes even not war heroes, but John Wayne and Clint Eastwood: elemental men, silent, sharp and spare.

Out on the streets, they felt the power of their youth, their male physicality; at home they had the tolerance of their mothers, chiding but proud of their masculine high spirits. Beneath that endless, wanton larking about was a terror of boredom that could be utterly relentless, and a dim knowledge that in the world of labour they were nothing. If they did not want what their fathers were supposed to have, then life stretched ahead, long and dull and pointless.

★

Becoming a soldier became entwined with everyday views of youthful male behaviour; a boy who went into the Army came home a man: fit, emotionally independent, ready to assume his responsibilities. Military service was still 'normal', because of the experience of the Second World War and National Service. Joining the Army meant serving the nation, and for many families enlisting gave them respectability, a sense that men were making something of themselves.

Some men joined because they could not find other work, or because they had no other choices open to them. But on the whole men joined up because they did not want the jobs that were otherwise available to them. They sought adventure of a specific kind, lured by the promise of leisure and excitement; they dreamed of a better life, perhaps stimulated also by raised expectations that came with the 1970s.

At the same time, only small numbers of men wanted to join the Army. According to the army planners, the poor pay, difficult conditions and long periods away from home put most men off even trying. Those who did choose to join either did not mind, or in fact relished, those things.

Many men were already accustomed to violence; they had grown up without privacy or personal possessions. Many had uncomfortable relations with their families and had not enjoyed school. They did not trust others and were used to relying only on themselves. They sometimes saw joining up as being non-conformist. Men often opposed the authorities of school and civilian workplaces, and sometimes the cultures of their neighbourhoods, their families and the idea of domestic life. Their lives had been shaped by their physical abilities: their capacity for endurance, their quickness, their strength.

Once they were in, success at selection in the Paras gave men power and a sense of belonging. It enhanced their individual status when they went back home. Even in a traditional Labour mining community, a soldier attracted welcome attention. It made men proud. John Gartshore, whose father and brothers were miners, and who was a corporal during the Falklands War, said: 'As a young boy you didn't leave school with O levels and A levels. Some of us were probably a little bit . . . not thick, we knew how to work out life, but our education wasn't up to standard. But you'd get five weeks off during summer, you could go home, in uniform, show your mates. It was brilliant.'[78]

3.   Training: Making Men

The aim of Parachute Regiment training was to turn recruits into paratroopers. Selection training – time spent at Depot Para and then at RAF Brize Norton – took twenty-two weeks. At its centre was P Company (pre-parachute selection), a week of extremely demanding tests to determine whether men were ready for parachute training. Many paratroopers saw P Company as the toughest infantry selection test in the world. The goal of recruit training was explicit: a man had to show the moral fibre to endure the physical and mental strain of his conditions and to give himself freely to the regiment. P Company sought 'to test physical courage, military aptitude, fitness, endurance, and determination under conditions of stress, to determine whether the individual has the ability, self-discipline and motivation to become an airborne soldier'.[1]

Arriving at the Depot, recruits were immediately assessed, and then reassessed after the eighth week in the field in Brecon, a week's training known as 'Basic Wales'. Thereafter, the officers in charge of the recruit platoons made selection choices. The wastage rate in training was high. In the early 1960s, 49 per cent of the Para trainees dropped out. This was a higher figure than for the rest of the infantry, and by the 1970s it was reckoned that fewer than one in three trainees got through.[2] The week of P Company claimed the most drop-outs. When the BBC followed 480 Platoon through their basic training in the first months of 1982, of the forty-one initial recruits, only eight passed P Company at the first try.[3]

Training often changed young men's perceptions of themselves. Jon Cook, a lance corporal in 3 Para during the Falklands War, said: 'Basically . . . you're broken down from what you were and rebuilt to what they want you to be . . . you come in as a civvie and they take it all out of you and build you up, they train you to be a soldier, what they want you to be.'[4] New recruits were removed from their former lives, put through this rigorous selection, and then they returned to their families and childhood homes. Tony Banks said, 'I knew I couldn't go back to Dundee without a red beret. I would've been ashamed. So no matter how bad it got, I knew I would never give up.'[5]

The passing out parade at the end of training was the point at which they could wear the maroon red beret. It was a huge achievement. Becoming a paratrooper not only gave recruits technical proficiency and the skills to be a soldier, but it also often made them into men. As Michael Asher said, 'For me it was a symbol of passing from childhood to manhood . . . Money could not buy this: no friends, connections or privileges of birth could attain it.'[6] The feeling that becoming a man and becoming a soldier was one and the same thing was accepted in the places boys had grown up, just as it was in the Parachute Regiment. It meant that the process of training itself often transformed young men's lives.

★

When Mark Eyles-Thomas arrived at Aldershot railway station to go to Junior Para (the boys' division of the Parachute Regiment), he realized straight away he had to learn how to exist in this new world. Alighting from the train with the other boys, the sergeant on the platform asked him his name. 'Mark Robert Jason Eyles-Thomas,' he replied keenly. 'He burst out laughing and said in a sadistic tone, "With names like that you should have been an officer. Do you think you're better than everyone else?"'[7] Mark vowed never to repeat his full name again, and from that point on he retained only the name Thomas. Michael Asher, arriving at adult recruit training, remembered calling the sergeant 'mate'. 'I'm not your fucking mate,' came the reply.[8] Most men identified that the best way to get through was to keep their heads down and not to draw attention to themselves.

These anecdotes point to the first process of adjustment in becoming a paratrooper: separation from their former lives, control of their routine, and concentration, through physical activity, on their new environment. On arrival at the Depot, the lieutenant commanding the recruit platoon interviewed each one of them, issued them with their kit and ordered them to their rooms. They were allowed to keep their civilian clothes, but had to pack them away. Men shared: four to a room. They had a bunk and a locker that they had to keep in regulation order. Even in 1983, Her Majesty's Inspectors inspecting the junior barracks at Aldershot described the set-up as 'austere', and the senior barracks would be no different. They had no luxury, and virtually no material possessions. The list of one man's personal effects kept at Bruneval Barracks in Aldershot, and sent to his mother after his death, ran simply to: 'braces, shirt, jacket, trousers, badges, raincoat, khaki tie'. Dave Parr had little more. When his kit was returned after the Falklands, aside from his uniforms he had five T-shirts, four pairs of socks, some 'pyjama type drawers' and a towel.[9]

Soon after arrival, the men were sent for haircuts. They began to look the same, and they had to do the same things together. The first week was spent adjusting to their new routine. Right from the start, they had regular drill. Drill was essential as an expression of their discipline: 'drill teaches obedience, precision, alertness and self-respect'. The week began with an hour and forty-five minutes of drill, and each day started with forty-five minutes of drill practice.[10] Drill also helped to instil an endurance of tedium as well as habits of repetition that could become useful in moments of peril.

The early days were also about separating them from the ideas of their mothers and home comforts, and enforcing strict domestic rules. They learnt how to make their beds, shine their boots and fold their clothes. According to one member of Depot staff, 'For many of them, their mothers make their beds, and tea has always been on the table. They have never even picked up an iron.'[11] They were sent running and for preliminary fitness tests. They had to clean their rooms, polish the floors and clean the lavatory block. At the end of the first week they went to sleep out in the field, and the Depot staff remarked that even at that point some men had not made the adjustment from civilian life or domestic camping trips, and tried to bring their pyjamas and pillows with them.

Nobody thought to remark on the sometimes inelegant proximity of shared living. This was clear in Dave Parr's first letter home: 'I had a good journey down here with no problems. I've made some friends and it's not really too bad at all. I've done a bit of training and I think it's going to be tough. I haven't had much time to myself and I'm going to get even less, so don't expect too many letters. At the moment we are not allowed to use the phone, I don't why. Don't worry about me I'm OK, the food's not to bad.'[12] In the first week, they could leave without penalty, but the records would suggest such voluntary, swift departures were comparatively rare. It was hard, perhaps, to give up before they had undergone a full and proper test of training.

Gradually, their worlds narrowed. As the intensity of training heightened, so too did the effort not to give up, and so too did their sense of exhaustion. Fatigue meant they did not have time to think about the outside world, still less to regret that they could not be part of it. Getting through each day required their full attention, and each day was crammed with tremendous physical challenges, as well as with the acquisition of new skills in fieldcraft and weapons-handling.

As they learnt the barracks language and ways to behave, their reference points became their worth in relation to each other: who was the fastest, who got coldest the quickest, who had endurance, who could punch the hardest. They learnt to steal tiny moments of relief, to scrounge any extra food they could get away with, to subvert rules without being caught, but never to look as if they thought they were better – worth more – than their mates.[13] Small alliances, rivalries and informal hierarchies began to form.

Dave wrote to his mother: 'The training is getting tough now, we had to go over the Bridge again on Wednesday but it wasn't so bad this time. Most of our time is spent having lectures about map reading ect. Today we went on a NAVEX (map reading) walk which was pretty good although on the way back along the canal I fell in along with two others. We had just been paid so all my money got wet through. Luckily it wasn't to deep, only up to my neck!' He'd been paid £60. Later in the letter (the rest of it was about train times for his visit home, ending with 'I can't think of anything else to tell you') he said he had enclosed the money and asked his mother to bank it.[14]

Two weeks in, he was proud of his earnings and wanted to take responsibility for saving them, or perhaps they did not have the privacy in the barracks to keep money safe. Dave liked the technical skills he was gaining and, while he suggested that he had not found it easy, he could cope with the physical challenges. But why would he and his colleagues fall in the canal? He was coming back from an exercise, not from the pub. It was more likely he and his fellow trainees were full of their first pay – cocky – and were pushed in to teach them a lesson. If that was the case, then he gives us a glimpse of the kind of regime that forced new recruits to know their place, and encouraged them to internalize what was happening as a necessary, even amusing, part of their initiation.

★

Training issued from the principle that men should develop a love and loyalty to their regiment. That love was not abstract and loyalty was not just about wearing the right hat. For the British Army, the regiment was the means for a man to value his reputation more highly than his life. It was the essence of what made a soldier: courage, moral certainty, self-abnegation for the good of the collective and a willingness and ability to use aggression when it was called for.

Since the Second World War, army planners had grappled with the problem of how to ensure soldiers would fire their guns in combat. One study of American soldiers – however flawed it was later shown to be – revealed that only one in four men reliably did so, and this made some military analysts worry that some soldiers would prefer to die rather than to kill.[15] At the same time, the Army always had to reckon with the idea that men – facing the real prospect of death – might go to ground and hide, rather than risk their own lives. The Army needed men who would prove capable of displaying an aggressive instinct and would have the fortitude to die for their cause.

Psychologists studying the military argued that the primacy of the small group gave men the impetus to do both. The small group made good an individual's relationship with the regiment. If men could see their comrades around them, if they could steady each other's nerves with a hand on the shoulder, then they were more likely to fight. The physical proximity of other men could give them courage, and the deep-rooted fear of appearing frightened – of not being man enough for the job – would both encourage men to fire and open them to accept the possibility of death.[16]

In 1977, Lieutenant General Sir William Scotter, then Vice Chief of the General Staff at the Ministry of Defence, told the Infantry Commanders' Conference that 'the frightened infantryman, taking shelter in a shell-scrape and out of immediate contact with the rest of his section, can so easily persuade himself that he alone, by staying put, can have no effect on the course of the battle. What makes him get up and fight is that his mates are doing so, and trust him to support them and he trusts them. Thus, it is small group loyalty, and loyalty to leaders, that impart the motivation to the individual.'[17]

Training thus instilled a formidable loyalty between men, and, through that, an *esprit de corps*. They learnt to fight for and with each other because it was each other they could see; but their love was not so much for each other as individuals, it was love for other men equally trained: the knowledge that they were all working together, they would do the same things and make the same sacrifices, for the objective they had been given. They stood together because they all comprehended their own part as representatives of the regiment, past, present and future. The coming together of the component parts, moving in harmony, in absolute trust each cog would carry out its tasks to its full capability, created an almost sublime beauty. Men would become masters – emperors – overcoming their human limits of compassion and fear.

★

Regimental pride came first, but regimental pride could not be totally separated from national pride. History was important to paratrooper training. Britain had been an Empire, and in the Second World War had stood alone. It was a singular history, a superior history, that depended on Britain's military tradition, and therefore on the extreme endurance Britain's paratroopers had shown against the Nazi menace. Recruits were drilled in the character of those Second World War paratroopers. During D-Day, 'the Paras breached the defences and, in bitter hand to hand fighting, killed or wounded all but 20 of the enemy, who surrendered. Though it lost 70 men killed or wounded, the battalion succeeded in getting through to the guns.' At Arnhem, 'We did what we could – but it wasn't bloody well possible.'[18]

Recruits came to Depot Para from all over the British Isles, but the history they were taught and the regiment they were part of was English-centred and white. 480 Platoon's forty-one recruits comprised twenty-five Englishmen, ten Scotsmen, four men from Wales and two from the Republic of Ireland. The two Irishmen both left: one bought himself out; the other ran away. The Scottish men stuck together. Once the platoon was whittled down to twenty-five men, the ten were all still present. One unhappy recruit from Glasgow did not want to be the first to go. The only black recruit in 480 Platoon was regularly teased about jungle warfare: 'the darkest of dark horses, [he] wore camouflage cream anyway just to keep the others company'. At the same time, becoming a Para forced recruits to put regional, and even racial, differences aside. One man from England reflected that the Welshmen were now his comrades-in-arms: 'If he'd met him in a pub in civvy street, he'd have called him a stupid effing Welsh twit and probably gone and smacked him one. Whereas here he was one of his mates.'[19]

The recruits also understood that the history of the regiment gave them a blazing standard it was all but impossible to meet. Soldiers in the past had been tougher and more impressive than those of the present day. Today's young were untested; their characters innately softer than their forebears'. They were growing up, so they were told, in less hardened times, 'with the ever-increasing cushiness of British lifestyle, with all its mod-cons and lack of discipline in society'. They could aspire to the high bar set in the Second World War, but they were always so far from achieving it: the twenty-eight battle honours and two Victoria Crosses.[20] Fallen heroes hung in photo frames from bar-room walls. If called upon, the present-day recruits had to emulate the achievements of the dead, to show themselves worthy of their sacrifice.

They came to appreciate that they were required to be both capable of extreme action and endurance and, at the same time, to embody high moral standards. The licence to take another man's life in battle made the Army different from any other career. Paratroopers were always, in a sense, rebels, because they entered an exclusive club beyond the pale for most civilian men. Simultaneously, the world of the elite soldier – perhaps of any soldier – was about selflessness, because, if it came to it, they would have no choice but to give their lives for their regiment and their country. The facts of service gave a paratrooper moral courage. A paratrooper, or any soldier, had to sub-jugate his own life in order to open himself to the possibility of death. He had to believe that the honour of his regiment and the survival of the other soldiers around him mattered more than he did. The moral-ity of armed service gave regimental life coherence. Training was hard because it had to be. It took them towards that higher purpose.

If teaching regimental history was one way to turn men into proud Paras, then physical training made good their absorption into the col-lective body of the regiment. The challenges the men were set compelled them to understand just how much the small group mat-tered, and made them overcome their individual weaknesses for the good of the unit. P Company was singularly important, aiming to test more than men's fitness and willingness to push beyond the limits of their endurance, although those things were also vital. They com-pleted a ten-mile battle march, an assault course and steeplechase; they dug trenches and slept outdoors; and they had to master the 'trainasium', a giant scaffold with the illusion of no safety net.

The key element in men's ability to pass was to demonstrate how far they could go to do what they were told by their superiors and to stand with their comrades-in-arms. In the stretcher race, men had to carry a 180-lb stretcher in teams, with two men as relief. If more than two dropped out, the others had more weight to bear: 'I detested the individuals who had packed it in as it meant more work and more pain for those of us that were left.'[21] In the log race, teams of six had to carry a log the size of a telegraph pole, the symbol of a gun team. If one man fell, he had to get up immediately or the momentum of the others would trample him, and he would fail the test. 'It is designed to find out whether a recruit will "pull his weight" when the going gets tough, and whether he will push himself to his limits rather than let down his mates.'[22]

Many failed, and the toughness of the challenge was part of its appeal. Success gave them confidence. But it was not just confidence in their personal accomplishments. Rather, it was the sense that they too might be able to follow in the footsteps of those elite paratroopers. Confidence was about daring to see themselves as paratroopers-in-waiting, and so, through their physical mastery of the obstacles in their way, developing their sense of their *esprit de corps*. As Eyles-Thomas commented: 'The Parachute Regiment was an elite fighting force and only those who could maintain its reputation for fitness and courage would succeed. This was never regarded as brainwashing or an indoctrination process, but plain and simple fact.'[23]

The process of training encouraged recruits to accept their tiny part in the regiment's proud history. Right now, they were nothing, they had proved nothing. At the same time, each day they lived out the reality of how fit and strong, and potentially impressive, they were becoming. The glory of dying in service, and at the same time the crushing sense that their lives could be cut short, was ever-present, but their view of the indisputable superiority of the Parachute Regiment gave them strength: 'All through your Para training, you become very confident. It's in-bred into you, if you like. You're expected to be good at stuff. I think that's why you do the selection process, because if you're not up to that standard then you're out.'[24]

As a result, recruits gave their loyalty to the regiment. Their voluntary submission to the demands made on them gave recruits their individual power. It was not who they were but what they stood for that was important, and the fact that, as individuals, they had the determination and the willpower to represent what they believed was the best regiment in the world. They had to display those proud traditions always, even if they might not know whether they had succeeded in living up to them. Martin Margerison said: 'They put a flying horse in my head, and it's still flying round to this day.'[25] John Gartshore described the thought of parachuting into battle: 'I get a hard-on thinking about it.'[26] His potency came in the dream of being that man, that paratrooper, dropping gently from the sky to earth, a man that all men, somewhere in themselves, desired to become, and a man that, surely, all women wanted.

★

Training connected the process of becoming a paratrooper with that of becoming a man. Men who failed training lacked grit and were weak: 'a crying, pathetic individual who says he can't make it'.[27] On the surface, recruits were encouraged to adopt coarse masculine attributes in contrast to perceived ideas of femininity or softness. A female journalist following the Paras in 1990 asked one sergeant what happened to vegetarians in the army. 'They die, ma'am,' he replied.[28] One man was called a 'pansy' for using a handkerchief rather than blowing his nose onto the floor.[29] The officers responsible for making the final assessments of the 480 Platoon's recruits saw another man as an 'intelligent guy' with a 'sensitive and artistic' temperament. He loved playing his trumpet, was 'totally unfit' for the Paras and was therefore transferred to the band.[30] Femininity could also be synonymous with homosexuality, and there was often intolerance to the idea of homosexuality in infantry regiments, because many believed sexual jealousy between men could undermine the cohesion of the small group.[31] One of the corporals filmed by the BBC in 1982 expressed this tersely: 'If he's a poof then he's out.'[32] All this created a harsh, conformist, masculine environment.

However, the Army had accepted since the 1950s that officers and soldiers alike would want to marry, and it made provision for married men. In many ways, marriage connected army, society and nation. A soldier loved his regiment because it was through his regiment that he could protect his woman and defend his home. Marriage, heading a household and fathering children were badges of maturation, markers on the route to manhood. Many soldiers married at a young age. In 1980, although in the general population the age of first marriage was rising, 6.9 per cent of paratroopers were married by the age of nineteen, and 52 per cent by twenty-three. The proportion of sergeants married at twenty-three was higher (64.4 per cent) than that of corporals (59.6 per cent), lance corporals (56.7 per cent) and privates (43.1 per cent). The figures suggest that the longer a man had been in the Parachute Regiment, or the more ambitious he was to climb the ranks, the more likely he was to be married.[33]

Perhaps young soldiers chose to marry because after a few years in the ranks they wanted somewhere nicer to live than the barracks, or perhaps they were tired of casual relationships and wanted a woman to settle down with. Lee Smith said that in Northern Ireland some girls were so desperate to leave their home towns they would agree to virtually any sexual requests from visiting soldiers.[34] For a teenage boy from the sticks, the prospect of marriage could thus be an expectation of long-term sexual nirvana. On the other hand, if a soldier met a girl he liked, and wanted privacy, somewhere to spend the night, they often did not have much choice but to get married. Girls often lived with their parents, and cohabiting before marriage was uncommon. As Jon Cook said, 'I got married at nineteen, but at the time it didn't seem young, because I'd been away from home from since I was fifteen, by the time then I thought I knew it all. I obviously didn't.'[35]

A wife and home brought status, as it could make young soldiers seem steady and respectable. Marriage and the discipline of earning money, establishing a lineage and upholding the family name, went hand in hand. A man was expected to take charge of his household; and the behaviour of his wife could reflect on him. Divorce and adultery, particularly among officers and their wives, were taken seriously and could be career-limiting.[36] Home was therefore always subordinate to a man's responsibilities to the Army. When Mike Curtis arrived at recruit training in Aldershot from the Welsh valleys with his young wife, she said: 'Oh, look at those horrible flats over there. Who lives in them, poor things? "You and me, love," I said, and she burst into tears.'[37]

Recruits were also young, away from home and in all-male company. On nights out, they often drank to excess, sometimes extraordinarily so, and played foul pranks on each other. Sexual appetite was seen as natural, part of their youthful enthusiasm, their physical well-being and their reward for the unpleasantness of some parts of their job. They had not yet grown to full maturity and tamed their sexual hunger. In barracks talk, women were divided into two groups: respectable, the kind of girl a man would take home to his mother, and 'dogs'.[38] 'Dogs' could be readily found in Aldershot, and were available for the soldiers at leisure. Paratroopers, the infantry's elite, could be expected to take their pick of these women, even when they were still in training.

The nickname for paratroopers was not 'squaddies', which was insulting, but 'Toms', with its connotations of tomcats out on the prowl. Tomcats were sexually promiscuous and fought with each other for the right to be so. Sex and violence were, in that sense, connected, because the application of violence was about winning a competition with another man, and therefore showing who had authority, the right to take his pick of sexual partners.

★

Some authors have seen a connection between bayonet training and sexual identity, because imagining the insertion of a bayonet into flesh had psychological overlaps with the act of penetration during sex.[39] Historically, some army planners had regarded bayonet drill as instilling in men the confidence and aggression to attack and kill in battle, and some thought that the prospect of bayoneting would awaken their 'lust for blood'.[40] However, the link between bayoneting, sex and violence may have been over-emphasized. The Depot timetable suggests there was only one session on bayonet fighting – for two hours on a Saturday morning at the end of the third week. It was right before a Current Affairs lecture on 'Europe and the Common Market', scheduled perhaps to dissipate any frisson that may have arisen as men handled their most personal weapons for the first time.

More likely, bayonet practice was unremarkable – it is not mentioned in many memoirs – because it was just one very small part of their routine. Its purpose was chiefly to give a practical means of giving the recruits a link with the past – to armed traditions stretching back centuries, and to moments of peril in the more recent past.[41] Learning to use a gun was much more important, took more time and was something most men outside the army could not do. Technical proficiency with firearms gave recruits soldierly skills and a great deal more power.

Focusing on the bayonet also overlooks the most important part of paratrooper training: milling. This was boxing against a comrade, with gloves but no protective headgear. Milling was the first challenge of P Company. For one minute, two trainees had to fight, while all their comrades watched. The qualities the assessors sought were controlled aggression (they were not allowed to bite, kick or head-butt, for example) and the will to win. Recruits had to fight without regard to the rules of boxing or the safety of their opponent. When, in 480 Platoon, one recruit tried to use 'fancy footwork' to dodge blows, the staff yelled at him that this was not *Come Dancing*. The aim was to punch, repeatedly; to bear those punches and to hit back. If they staggered or fell over, their comrades returned them to the ring, yelling 'kill him, kill him, kill him!'[42]

The bout only lasted one minute, but it was perhaps the most important minute of their assessment. Trainees had to overcome their instincts (if they had them) not to hurt their mates. They were publicly exposed. Everyone could see who was the strongest, the most determined. They were on display to the recruit company commanders, who held the recruits' futures in their hands and wanted to see if they were up to it.

Recruits were theoretically matched with opponents their own size, but many remember being pitted against a larger, stronger adversary – a memory perhaps symbolic of their fear. As one man recalled, 'I turned my insanity switch on.' Suddenly, they found they could funnel whatever it was in their former lives that had made them feel bullied, degraded or scared, and let it out of themselves, and show that they could overcome whatever had stood in their way.[43] Kevin Connery, who had been badly bullied at school, depicted himself as spindly and afraid, accustomed to taking a beating. The platoon sergeant took him aside and said, 'Go in there and fight all the people who ever bullied you and all the people who ever put pressure on you. Go in there and just fight, just let it go, son.' Connery stepped into the ring and pounded his opponent. He had to be pulled away. Afterwards the sergeant said, 'You'll do.'[44]

In that one minute of milling, everything became connected. Milling really hurt. Training was about confidence and conquering their fear, but it was also about the acclimatization to – and the ability to bear and to push beyond physical and mental – pain. In milling, the hurt reminded some of them of the beatings they had taken and the humiliations they had felt. Robin Horsfall said: 'In fighting situations I had always been afraid of being hurt; now I did my utmost to completely destroy my aggressor first.'[45] To succeed at milling, men had to overcome any sense of inferiority and harness their aggressive power for a purpose bigger than themselves. In so doing, they showed they could stand among the best.

★

After P Company, the recruits went for four weeks of parachute training at RAF Brize Norton. Parachuting was the defining act of the airborne brotherhood. They had to do it. To refuse to jump meant an instant fail. Those four weeks were different in tone from the rest of the training programme. The staff at Brize Norton did not just order them around, but explained why they had to behave in a certain way.[46] The focus was on learning how to parachute. They spent a week practising how to land properly, and half a week preparing by jumping from a tower and an exit trainer. Those exercises made plain why drill was so exact and discipline so repetitive. Parachuting brought a real operation a little bit closer. Jumping out of a plane was dangerous, and landing wrongly could kill them. They did not have to be told too many times that if they did not come up to standard, they might die.

The first jump was from the cage under a barrage balloon; the subsequent ones from aircraft. From the balloon basket men had to step out into the air, just as if they were walking from the edge of the pavement. There was total silence. The recruit dropped like a stone for 200 feet before he felt the jerk of his parachute opening and he floated to earth. In the plane, there was a lot of noise. He jumped through the door into the slipstream, the turbulence caused by the engine, and dropped. Then the parachute deployed.

Each jump was, in a sense, a miniature death: a step into the unknown, an act of trust in the cosmic justice of the universe. Once he had stepped out, the recruit was totally on his own. It was perhaps the only time during training that, for the seconds it took, he was utterly free. 'Brilliant, unbelievable . . . just falling is great . . . the chute opens and you are just floating there.'[47] The sensation was awesome: 'My God, this is marvellous. The parachute is open and I'm just

hanging here in space.'[48] For those pure moments, suspended in mid-
air, it felt as if anything was possible – and then the ground rose up
and the moment was gone. It felt timeless, but also short: 'Very similar to my first sexual encounter, I thought.'[49]

They landed, and they were still alive. The recruit felt utter
elation, elation immediately squashed by the instructors rushing to
get him out of the way before the next drop.[50] And then, the next day
or a few days later, he had to do it again. The subsequent times could
be harder, because they all knew that bad accidents did happen. The
sight of canopies opening across the sky was the symbol of airborne forces. It showed the mastery by man of his environment, but
the throwing of the individual into the lap of the gods. The feeling of
possibility, the joy of survival, was fleeting. He had conquered fear
once, but preparing to jump again, a man knew he was but 'a mere
mortal'.[51]

★

To become an officer in the Parachute Regiment, a cadet had to pass
pre-parachute selection, P Company, and he had to complete parachute training. Officers did P Company and parachute training
separately from the other ranks, but it was one experience an officer
would share with the paratroopers who would later fall under his
command. The lives of officers and other ranks were separate. After
officers-to-be passed the Regular Commissions Board, they trained
with other officer cadets destined for all parts of the British Army at the
Royal Military Academy, Sandhurst. Going to meet his platoon of
paratroopers for the first time could be a testing time for a newly qualified lieutenant: 'Nothing in his Sandhurst training has prepared him
to meet the confidence and intelligence of the Parachute Regiment
soldier – how much he thinks and how ready he is to express his opinion within the framework of Army discipline.'[52]

The purpose of training was different for officers and soldiers.
Like recruits at Depot Para, the officer cadet attended lessons on
weapons-handling and fieldcraft, infantry tactics, military history
and international affairs. He endured daily drill and was also pushed

to his physical limits and forced by the vigilance of the sergeants into habits of cleanliness and tidiness. Mike Jackson (later General Sir) commented: 'Slightly to my surprise, I found that I had my own room, which I quickly discovered had to be kept immaculate because, like everything else, it would get inspected.'[53] Chip Chapman (later Major General) described his room as 'My space was Room 101 (George Orwell would have been proud), a tiny enclave where dust was the enemy of the righteous and bad hospital corners on blanket ends incurred the wrath of the colour sergeant . . . Duvets are a real sign of progress.'[54]

Whereas Depot Para trained recruits to be obedient, disciplined and aggressive, Sandhurst sought to make its cadets into leaders. Its motto was 'Serve to Lead'. A good officer had to have the authority to demand unquestioned compliance from his soldiers. He had to have the confidence and judgement to make good decisions under pressure, and the physical stamina to endure even more than his men could. He had to understand that he should not ask his men to do what he could not, or would not, do himself. Officers could be totally responsible for the lives of their men, and they needed to adopt a detached but genuine interest in their characters and their welfare. They might need to know those men better than their own mothers did. Sandhurst trainers reminded officer cadets that they needed to think of themselves as distinct from the ranks, and it remained the case that some officer cadets from traditional backgrounds would have had very little contact with men born into the working classes before they ended up commanding a platoon. One colonel was heard to remark, perhaps apocryphally, 'the person who is being led . . . does not believe in being led by a bigger version of himself. He wants his officers to be different.'[55] The curriculum taught officer cadets that the soldier was much like his Second World War counterpart: 'well trained, tough, resilient, good-humoured, a bit of a rogue, an eye for the girls, dependable in a tight spot, a bit sentimental'.[56]

Leadership, according to Field Marshal Montgomery, was 'the will to dominate, together with the character which inspires confidence'.[57] Field Marshal the Viscount Slim, who led the 14th Army during the Burma campaign, gave a speech on leadership in 1952 which became part of the Sandhurst curriculum. Slim isolated five qualities of leadership: courage, willpower, initiative, knowledge and integrity. Those qualities showed character, and that character was moral. The wellsprings of character were to be found in Christianity and the self-sacrifice of service. Service was a privilege: 'Your Sovereign has selected you, individually, to lead your fellow countrymen in battle, and your Queen and your country can do you no higher honour.' In return for that honour and the trust which was invested in them, men were duty-bound to follow the traditions of Britain's past, and to live up to the standards imparted by them.[58] For those of the Christian faith, religion was an enduring source of courage and the foundation of military morale. Even for agnostics or atheists, the spiritual essence of Christian thought and the character of the nation went together. Britain had consistently chosen liberty, and had never been tempted by totalitarianism.[59]

In the 1970s, Sandhurst was concerned that growing numbers of entrants from grammar school and university would alter the Army's ethos. Boys who had attended day schools lacked the 'inevitable introduction to teamwork which being thrown together with others in a boarding school brings'.[60] Sandhurst offered further educational opportunities for many young men, but officers-in-training were not expected to have a university education. The qualifications for entry for those aiming for a regular commission were five O levels (including maths, English language and a science) and two A levels; and five O levels for a short service commission.[61] Some feared that admitting more men with degrees would encourage individualist tendencies: 'Officers of the directing staff tend to see graduates as less committed, even fickle . . . They are thought to be the most interested in "looking after number one".'[62]

A group of retired officers reviewed leadership training in 1978. In the past, they felt, they had been able to take some attributes, such as discipline, self-discipline and putting the needs of others first, for granted. Now, those qualities had to be demonstrated and explained. They were prepared to teach men how to acquire the skills of leadership, and they recommended that Sandhurst introduce discussion periods into the curriculum on 'officer-like behaviour'. Those lessons would train officers to 'express themselves like officers', demonstrate courtesy at all times, dress appropriately and behave differently from other ranks.[63]

Although some signs of social variety were apparent in the intake, both in the recruit training at the Depot and at Sandhurst, the quest for men of good character meant they were likely to succeed if the selectors believed that they had the fibre to be an officer or an airborne soldier: 'It remained the prevailing view that leaders were born, not made.'[64] Men could be assessed on their gentlemanly or soldierly comportment, or commitment to the Army or the regiment's ideals, rather than just on their ability to complete the tasks demanded. Whether a man had the right character or not could still be a matter of interpretation, and thus while the tests of training were rigorous, and the Paras more diverse in background and more likely to promote on merit than the traditional regiments, character could still be subjectively observed.

★

For recruits at Depot Para, training was backed up by a robust system of discipline. Discipline often involved punishment. Sometimes punishment was formal, administered by military law through court martial, but the army was accustomed to relative autonomy and, more often than not, discipline was doled out informally. The commanding officer of a regiment could deal with many offences himself and had the authority to send men to military prison for up to sixty days and fine them up to a month's salary.[65] Company sergeant majors would often find themselves administering punishment, and corporals also had authority to deliver short, summary punishment. In fact they often preferred to do so themselves rather than bring offences to the attention of their superiors. Discipline could also be self-regulating.[66] It worked best when each man at each rank understood what was expected and used their own initiatives to come up to scratch.

The NCOs in a recruit platoon enforced discipline to ensure their underlings could meet the required standards. Punishments varied in intensity. Men could be sent into the kitchens in disgrace, and obliged to clean grease-smeared pots.[67] Another regular punishment was a 'showclean'. Anyone whose kit was found wanting was forced to go to the guardroom for a special parade in front of the duty NCO. If the uniform was still not up to standard, the 'showclean' could be repeated, and repeated. Other punishments were more physical, such as repeated press-ups, or holding themselves in stress positions against the wall.

NCOs could also subject the men to provocation. During kit inspections, for example, the platoon sergeant inspecting the room could suddenly throw 'a carefully pressed shirt out of the window and into the pouring rain, bellowing, "Next time, turn the f——ing iron on!", only to run another kit inspection a few minutes later'.[68] Michael Asher described one recruit failing to control his anger after he was goaded and attacking the corporal in charge: 'So unthinkable was it that a recruit should attack an instructor that none of us moved . . . "That's you finished in this regiment . . . You've cracked!".'[69] In some ways, too, the NCOs' riling of recruits was part of the test. Men needed psychological reserves to absorb the repeated refrain that they were not good enough: 'It was rough, it was hard, but it had to be, because of the job we had to do being paratroopers.'[70]

Some punishments were doled out collectively. If one man's locker was dirty, the whole room could be punished. That encouraged recruits to work together and to look out for each other; to find ways to assist men who could not keep up, to devise ways of circumventing the system to ensure they could finish their tasks. Sometimes, their disciplining of each other was done spontaneously and could help men to bond. A section was only as good as its weakest member, and if one man got everyone punished, then, 'when you got back to the barrack, you'd make sure that he knew – in one way or another – that he was in the wrong. That's a bit of self-discipline within the team, and it brings you closer together.'[71]

At other times, the prospect of collective discipline could encourage surveillance of each other, which could verge on intimidation. Lee Smith described giving a 'regimental bath' to one of his group. They tipped him into a bath of detergent and scoured him with brushes, for the reason that 'he was dirty' and, for the sake of the group, he needed to be cleaned.[72] This kind of self-regulating discipline could also turn into violence. Men could be 'beasted' either by their superiors or by other men in the same rank. For example, to keep a section's toilets clean, men would agree to use only one cubicle, and if there was a queue, to use another section's toilets.[73] If men were caught in the wrong toilets, the trespasser would usually face a 'beasting' in the form of violence or humiliation – a beating followed by boot polish on the testicles, for instance – dished out by the men in the other section.

In early 1978, a seventeen-year-old recruit – Private R. – went to a district court martial on a charge of Actual Bodily Harm. He was charged with battering another recruit, Private Nazzroo, over the head with an iron cudgel taken from the end of a dormitory bed. The incident happened during parachute training at RAF Brize Norton and R. was suspended from service and given nine months' detention. R. explained in court that he had passed tests to progress to parachute training, but Nazzroo had failed. However, Nazzroo had been allowed through, and when he turned up at Brize Norton, R. and the other recruits were angry. On the night of the attack, R. had been drinking and consumed ten pints of lager. Nazzroo had not been out. On returning to the barracks, R. tipped him out of bed and beat him up, giving him deep scalp wounds and body bruises. Another man assisted in the assault.

The prosecuting officer, Regimental Adjutant Captain Richard Gettings, said Nazzroo was 'potential officer material' and R. had been in the running for a champion recruit award. The attack, therefore, sounded like jealousy. The officer defending R., Lieutenant David Benest, said the attack had been sparked by spite and had the unspoken support of other soldiers who were standing by. It was, he said, 'rough justice'.[74] He meant that even if R.'s attack was spontaneous, its violent nature was just part of a system of informal discipline. If self-regulation in the ranks turned to criminal brutality, it was an issue that needed to be addressed higher up the chain of command.

★

On one occasion, in November 1981, discipline broke down, with horrible consequences. Three recruits, Privates S., P. and N. met two girls in a pub in Aldershot. One of the girls was fifteen. She had moved with her family to Aldershot ten weeks previously, and was out for the evening with a visiting friend. The girls got in a taxi with the soldiers. The fifteen-year-old later said she thought they were going on to a disco. Only when they drew up at the barracks did she discover they were not. S. persuaded her to come into the barracks and she went to his room, where several other soldiers were asleep. She lay down with him on his bed and they began to kiss.

Recruit Platoon 474 then returned from a course party. They burst into the room, surrounded the bed and began shouting 'gang bang'. Soldiers forced her legs apart, removed her shoes, trousers and knickers and tied her ankles to the bedposts with elasticated cord. Private N. went around the room waking men up and urging them to take part. One soldier was tipped from his bed several times but declined to get involved.[75] Four or five men raped the girl, she could not remember exactly how many. Before they let her go, they kicked, punched and urinated on her, and stole her knickers as a trophy. By the time the girl got home, sobbing, incoherent and with her clothes wet, her parents, afraid as to her whereabouts, had already called the police.

The case went to Winchester Crown Court in May 1983. Private N., named by the judge as the ringleader, told the jury he thought the girls were a 'couple of sluts', and she wanted to take part in a 'gang bang'.[76] He got five years in jail for rape, indecent assault and common assault. S. got six months for indecent assault; P. six months for indecent and common assault; and another soldier, C., twelve months for indecent assault. Two more men, Privates Q. and D., pleaded guilty. D. admitted rape and was sentenced to three years. Private Q. confessed to indecent assault. The judge said he 'at least had the grace to acknowledge his part in the assault', and added that Q. had been 'in a way unfortunate that there was not more adequate supervision on that evening'. The press reports said the guards on duty were seventeen.[77] One of the soldiers told the judge that women were always in the barracks: 'We are not allowed to, but it happens every night.'[78] He added, 'There are more people getting away with this than are in the dock.'[79]

The incident suggests that, even among recruits, men were routinely disobeying rules that prevented them from taking women back to the barracks. By itself, that flouting of the regulations does not suggest a total dissolution of discipline. Perhaps, in a more licentious society, those rules, and the shared living space, were becoming outdated. It was impossible for officers to control everything recruits did, and recruits were free to go into town by themselves. Most men did not behave like this.

Moreover, the rape could have little to do with the fact they were paratroopers-in-training. Those men could have been capable of such an attack anyway, and paratroopers were not the only soldiers – nor presumably the only people – in Aldershot who engaged in sexual violence. In August 1982, three gunners from the Royal Artillery indecently assaulted a nineteen-year-old who had been in a relationship with two of them. They tied her to a bed and tried to rape her, because they wanted to teach her a lesson for spreading rumours about them.[80]

Afterwards, the Army promised to tighten up its security, particularly as Paras could be targeted anywhere by IRA honey-traps. Many ordinary people were outraged. Some mothers instigated a campaign to 'clean up Aldershot'. Mrs Burt, who was married to a former paratrooper, said she grew up in Aldershot at a time when there were thousands more soldiers than there were now. Then, if you saw soldiers, you felt safe; now, their unruly behaviour had driven a wedge between civilians and soldiers. People were afraid to go out at night, and Aldershot was becoming a 'ghost town'.[81]

Other Aldershot residents blamed the girls, feeling that women who frequented certain pubs in town, or went back to the barracks with soldiers, were inviting an assault. One writer to the letters page of the *Aldershot News* asked what on earth the girl's parents were thinking, allowing her to go into pubs at night. Parents, 'instead of complaining, should endeavour to teach their children moral standards'. A twenty-four-year-old writer said, 'girls who go to such places are asking for trouble'. A sixty-two-year-old former Army wife said she had lived in married quarters for twenty-three years, some eight feet away from soldiers' sleeping quarters. Her husband had been in India for five years, and while she had offers, she was never molested. She concluded: 'Why put all the blame on the lads, when the girls egg them on?'[82]

At the time of the trial, Private N. was twenty-one, had fought with 3 Para in the Falklands, was married and expecting a child. Privates S. and P. had also been to the Falklands with 3 Para. While still a recruit, N. had encouraged them all to participate in a violent and criminal act. Perhaps N. had been out of control at the time, focusing only on his own desire at that moment to humiliate and dominate.

The circumstances of the attack do, however, hint at the importance of a group mentality. The paratroopers who took part cared not about the girl – it was so obvious she could be defiled; she was nothing – but about how they were seen in each other's eyes. If there was a dark heart of regimental violence, it was that. At that instant, N. was a drunken private, not yet through training, taking cruel relief from the tiny power he possessed among the men alongside him; he showed himself to be violent and able to command others to obey. When N. began the assault, the others did not stop him. They turned away or they joined in. Many, presumably, did not like it, or thought it was wrong, but they had to stick together and turn a blind eye to this humiliation. In an outfit like the Paras, either they were in, or they were out.

★

Training ended, and recruits found out whether they had passed or failed. Those who made it invited their families to watch them pass out. Passing-out day was a day of celebration. The new paratroopers put on their smartest uniforms, their best parade, and parachuted from a balloon cage, watched by their friends and relatives. They were rightly proud of their achievements. Passing out made them into airborne soldiers; it gave them a marker of manhood. One father thanked the sergeant in charge of 480 Platoon for 'making a man out of his son'.[83]

Together they were a collective, but at the same time – as individuals – they were different from each other. Many had ambitions to push up the ranks. A good private could look for promotion to lance corporal after two to three years, sooner if he excelled. Thereafter, perhaps after six to eight years' service, a soldier could advance to corporal, a rank that had real responsibilities as a section commander for about eight men.[84] Others wanted to develop specialisms in areas like reconnaissance or intelligence, perhaps – as I believe my uncle had planned – to build towards an application to join the SAS. They anticipated tours of Northern Ireland and exercises and postings overseas.

They were allocated to battalions, and when they arrived, they were then 'Joe Crow', at the bottom of the pile again. They could not expect to be accepted by, or even speak to, senior soldiers until they had proved their worth. Becoming a paratrooper, therefore, was always a slightly elusive goal, its standards difficult to attain, an 'endless ladder', difficult to climb.[85] How could they know whether they would match the standards of the past if they were called upon in battle?

PART TWO

4. Falkland Islands

The Falkland Islands were a loose hem of Britain's Empire. Most of the colonies gained independence after 1957, but the Falklands remained a British Crown Colony. The status of the territory was unresolved because Argentina claimed the islands, but the inhabitants wished to remain under British jurisdiction.

The islands, a remote archipelago in the South Atlantic, were taken first by the French. Then in 1766, Spain bought them for a fee. After a British ship sighted the islands, Britain and Spain came to the brink of war over them, and both empires for a time maintained separate settlements on West and East Falkland. In 1820, Argentina won independence from Spain, and inherited the title to the land. Possession of the islands' sovereignty was, for Argentina, part of its national foundation, born of the country's emergence from European colonial rule and the newly formed nation's wish for the extension and consolidation of its own borders.

In 1831, after a dispute over fishing rights, an American warship destroyed the Argentine settlement on East Falkland. Taking advantage of the flux, in 1833 a British ship, the HMS *Clio*, landed there. The captain of the *Clio* compelled the remaining dwellers – a scattering of cowboys living roughly from the sale of wool and the curing of cow and seal hides – to give way. He raised the Union flag, claimed British authority and established the conditions for an administration that was to endure.[1] Dispute over the islands' sovereignty was dormant, but Argentina continued to hold it was the rightful owner, and Britain had taken the islands from them.

In 1946, the United Nations placed the islands on a list of non-self-governing territories, and in 1965, the General Assembly of the UN noted the existence of a sovereignty dispute and invited Britain and Argentina to hasten their negotiations to resolve it. British diplomats often saw the islands as strategically unnecessary and economically worthless. The main reason Britain still owned the territory in 1982 was because the Falkland Islanders did not want to be given away. The islanders were descended from the settlers who came with the HMS *Clio*. They were accustomed to a hardy life and British habits. They drank tea and pints of bitter; they ran a post office and governed themselves in a tiny legislative assembly. They were English-speaking, white-skinned and small in population – 1,763 of them in 1982 – and they wanted their allegiance to remain in Britain's hands.

When British politicians travelled to the islands in 1968 and again in 1979 and 1980, they were taken aback by the strength of islander opinion against their transfer. Perhaps more importantly for British domestic politics, the islanders had a strong lobby in the House of Commons. Once a military dictatorship took power in Argentina in 1976, parliamentary opinion was even less likely to consent to a change in the islands' sovereign status.[2]

At the same time, the question of the Falkland Islands never demanded urgent resolution, and perhaps that was Britain's mistake. The Falkland Islands Company owned the land and baulked even at the cost of fencing to improve the pasture for the sheep. The islands were economically poor and in decline. Islanders often worked as itinerant labourers, dependent for survival on the benevolence of their absent landlords. In Britain, if diplomats and politicians thought much about it, they probably expected that lack of British investment would force the islanders gradually to leave; and in time, the balance of the islands' future would change. After 1979, under economic pressure themselves, the incoming government of Margaret Thatcher lifted the vigilant patrol Britain had maintained against possible Argentine military action around the islands. In turn, the Argentine junta saw an opportunity it believed might not recur.

By late 1981, hyper-inflation was causing distress and poverty in Argentina. The years of terrible violence against opponents of the regime slowly destroyed the legitimacy the dictatorship had earlier claimed, and protest mounted. President Galtieri, a weak and alcoholic leader of a factionalized government, craved the easy popularity that would come from this historic cause. He authorized the navy to sail to the Falklands and retake the sovereignty of Las Islas Malvinas.[3]

★

The Argentine occupation of Port Stanley on 2 April 1982 changed the politics of this dispute. In Britain in early 1982, the Conservative government was unpopular and divided. The previous summer, youths rioted in areas of some British cities, including Brixton in London and Toxteth in Liverpool. *The Sun* newspaper pictured police stooped behind riot shields, with the headline: "'To think this is England'".[4] In March 1981, 364 economists signed a letter to *The Times* denouncing the government's budget, and in July even some ministers loyal to Thatcher resisted further spending cuts.[5] The legacy of the late 1970s – the IMF loan, the union strikes, the 'winter of discontent' – hung over British politics. The Labour Party had split: in November 1980, the left-wing Michael Foot became leader and in March 1981 four prominent MPs left to form the Social Democratic Party (SDP). In January 1982, unemployment rose to over 3 million for the first time in the post-war period. Commentators asked themselves if this government, led by the novel figure of Britain's first female leader, would survive.

The Argentine occupation was a shock, and was talked of as a national humiliation. For many in Parliament, the question was how much further could Britain, this once great nation, fall? On 3 April 1982, the House of Commons met on a Saturday for the first time since the 1956 Suez crisis. Parliamentarians from left and right talked about the failure of appeasement, and restated the Falklanders' allegiance to the British Crown and Britain's duty to protect the Falkland people, who had now had their liberty removed by force. With Margaret Thatcher under pressure to act, the Commons authorized the immediate despatch of a task force. The fleet set sail from Portsmouth two days later. By the end of April, Britain had despatched approximately sixty-five ships, including twenty warships, eight amphibious landing ships and nearly forty other vessels of the Royal

Fleet Auxiliary and Merchant Navy. Fifteen thousand men had been sent, of whom about 7,000 were Marines and soldiers – the largest mobilization of British forces since Suez.[6]

The departure of the Task Force was not necessarily a declaration of war. Diplomacy could still avert it, and even many of those travelling with the fleet believed politicians would resolve things peaceably. In the United States, President Ronald Reagan saw the sovereignty dispute over the islands as a trifling, and somehow inexplicable, cause for armed violence. He referred to the islands as that 'little ice-cold bunch of land down there'.[7] US Secretary of State General Alexander Haig, a veteran of Vietnam and anxious to avoid a protracted conflict with no evident resolution, launched into a mediation mission.

Haig's diplomacy, undertaken while the heightening dispute was still at an embryonic stage, was probably the best chance for peace. The US Secretary of State flew between Washington, Buenos Aires and London with proposals that seemed sensible at first, but rapidly became confused. Initially, the British government agreed concessions. The Junta, blinkered by their own domestic politics, unable to see how international diplomacy would play out and torn by poor leadership, consistently refused to yield the gains they had made through force.

In London, the crunch came on the evening of 24 April. Lord Carrington, Britain's Foreign Secretary prior to the Argentine invasion, had resigned on 5 April, taking the blame for what he saw as his oversight. Margaret Thatcher had got on well with Lord Carrington, but, obliged to replace him, she had had little choice but to appoint Francis Pym, an old Etonian, son of a landowner, decorated in the Second World War, a Conservative 'wet' of the kind she had battled against all her career. Pym returned from Washington on the 24th with a deal he had devised with Haig. In effect, they envisaged a cessation of hostilities and a long, winding process which would probably one day result in Argentina assuming sovereignty.[8] For Thatcher, this was unacceptable. It failed to respect the wishes of the islanders, and she saw clearly that if she followed Pym's course, she would be compelled to resign.[9]

The British Cabinet could at that juncture have faced a crisis, but it never came. Pym's proposal was put to Argentina, and the Junta rejected it. Their rebuff led the Americans formally to 'tilt' towards Britain. A few days hence, on 2 May, the British government authorized what some later saw as the most controversial British action of the war and consented to attack the Argentine cruiser, the *General Belgrano*. At the time, it was a tense but not difficult decision for the government to take. The submarine HMS *Conqueror* had the *Belgrano* in its sights and the ship posed a threat to the Task Force. Those who opposed Britain's course of action argued that the cruiser was sailing away from the military Total Exclusion Zone set up around the islands and that the government covered up the ship's true position to conceal its own belligerent intentions. Some believed that Thatcher by now wanted to stifle the UN's new efforts at diplomacy.[10]

Of course, the path to military action was not so simple. Thatcher was influenced by the armed services' judgement that time was not on Britain's side. If there was to be a military response, she understood, it would have to be quick, before the South Atlantic winter prevented troops from landing on the islands. In addition, she was resolute in her belief that Argentina had broken international law. It was Britain's responsibility to restore it, as a leading Western power in a divided Cold War world.

At the same time, the prime minister felt keenly the risks of military action, and she understood the importance of international opinion. Diplomacy at the United Nations intensified after the *Belgrano* was sunk. Even after British paratroopers had fought on the islands, President Reagan called Thatcher to suggest she might settle for a ceasefire. She told him then she would not retreat: 'I didn't lose some of my finest ships and some of my finest lives to leave quietly under a ceasefire.'[11] The truth was that, once committed, Britain had to win. Failure was not an option for her and, as many believed, Britain had to maintain its reputation as a country with the fortitude to fight when circumstances demanded.

Despite international will to avoid war, throughout the conflict Britain always had allies. Thatcher could not have overseen the recapture of the islands but for the fact that the Americans offered military help, and they and the EEC and the Commonwealth gave

Britain diplomatic support. At the United Nations, the Security Council passed Resolution 502 and accepted Argentina had breached the peace (although the General Assembly had supported the principle of the Argentine sovereignty claim). This meant that British actions to repossess the islands were legitimate under the right of self-defence granted by Article 51 of the UN Charter.

Nevertheless, as the military campaign intensified in May and June 1982, even a strong-minded prime minister with international law on her side could not guarantee the outcome of events. Two days after the *Belgrano* was hit, an Argentine plane fired an Exocet missile that hit and sank the HMS *Sheffield*, with the loss of twenty lives. For the first time, popular support for the war began to waver. That night, in the privacy of her Commons room, Margaret Thatcher wept.[12] She faced the fact that British men would die, and that the conflict might not run in Britain's favour.

★

Sailing towards the South Atlantic, many soldiers were excited by the prospect of war. The 3rd Battalion, The Parachute Regiment – 3 Para – left on the cruise liner the *Canberra* on 9 April, among the first troops to sail. They were to be part of 3 Commando Brigade, under the command of Royal Marine Brigadier Julian Thompson, sailing with the Marines of 40, 42 and 45 Commando, each Commando a similar size to a parachute battalion. The Commanding Officer of 2 Para, Lieutenant Colonel Herbert 'H' Jones, immediately returned from a family skiing holiday to lobby hard for his battalion's inclusion in the fleet.[13] He did not need to. On 15 April, the Chiefs of Staff assessed that they would need more forces because of the dangers of establishing a presence on the islands. The 700 men of 2 Para sailed on the P&O ferry the *Norland* on 26 April.

The paratroopers anticipated a fight, but during the long journey south, war seemed very distant. They trained hard: weapons preparation, first aid and medical know-how, battle awareness, running around the decks and physical fitness. But the days did not have the intensity and the distractions of routine in a small barracks town and

in the Sun, he is in my platoon, unfortunately I was on the other end of the squad, I tried to make my neck stretch 6 feet when I saw the cameraman but to no avail.'[21] He had been told what might happen once they got ashore, but the prospect must have seemed in some ways like a big adventure. Dave told his father he wanted to get off the ships and have the chance to 'give the Argies a bloody nose'.[22]

It was always going to be dangerous when British forces landed on the islands. Initially, the Chiefs of Staff calculated they could lose up to 20 per cent of the landing force, up to 900 men, should Argentina oppose them.[23] Normally, a landing force would hope to have air superiority, but by the end of April the British had accepted this would be impossible. On 14 May, Brigadier Thompson apologized to his superiors for 'banging on . . . in a most boring manner', but felt he had to urge again that 'We are . . . bracing ourselves for a very unpleasant first day' if they had to land without local air control.[24] To minimize the danger of attack, the Commander of the Naval Task Force, Admiral Woodward, proposed to land at San Carlos, at the west of East Falkland, on the opposite side to Stanley. In London, the War Cabinet accepted this.

The *Canberra*, a huge ocean liner with 3 Para and the Marines aboard, could not sail right up to the islands, as it would have to bob around in Falkland Sound while the men disembarked. Instead, 3 Para had to cross to HMS *Intrepid* in the heaving sea. They had to time their jumps with the swell. 2 Para jumped from the side of the *Norland* into the landing craft. One man fell and was crushed between the craft and the ship. He was rescued but had broken his pelvis.[25] Once in, they were packed tightly together, standing in waste water, sometimes sickened by the motion. When they disembarked, some companies descended the ramps onto the beach, others into the sea. One short man said the sea was up to his neck. He had recently passed training and had been asked to carry a machine gun. He lifted it over his head to keep it dry.[26]

As they reached the shore, early in the morning of 21 May, they did not know if the landings would be opposed. Some felt that the noise of the landing craft, and the shouting, would alert any Argentines to their presence. 3 Para landed on a stony beach: 'Two hundred

Paras hobbled off the landing-crafts. The stones and the kit we carried would have made it impossible to run, even if we had needed to.'[27] 2 Para were mixed up, their direction uncertain: 'Contrary to much press speculation at the time, the first men did not "storm" ashore at all; they waded, soaked, heavily burdened like pack mules.'[28] The cost to life could surely have fulfilled Thompson's worse predictions if the Argentines had attacked them at this vulnerable moment.

Once they had landed, and established bases in the hills around San Carlos Bay, 2 Para on Sussex Mountains, and 3 Para at Port San Carlos, it was not certain what the paratroopers, or any of the troops, would do next. The commanders of the Task Force still focused on the war at sea. In the next four days, HMS *Ardent*, *Antelope*, *Coventry* and *Atlantic Conveyor* were hit and sunk; bombs also struck *Antrim* and *Argonaut* but failed to explode, and *Brilliant* and *Broadsword* were damaged. The First Sea Lord, Admiral Henry Leach, had expected up to six frigates and destroyers to be hit and believed the Task Force could endure double that.[29] In that perspective, the landings were a success. Despite British losses, they calculated they had done more damage to the Argentine air force than the Argentines had done to them. Nevertheless, it did not necessarily look like that back in Britain; and it was a shock to some in 2 Para to watch ships burning on the water and not be able to do anything to help.

The local commanders' idea was that the forces on the islands would concentrate on getting to Port Stanley, on the other side of the islands. Argentine forces were dug into hills around the islands' small capital, and it was here, the Task Force commanders judged, that the conflict would be won. The challenge, then, would be to get across the islands and then to attack uphill the Argentine positions that would be very well defended.

Most of the junior ranks in the Argentine Army were conscripts. Some of them had recently completed one year of basic training; others had finished more than a year hence and had been recalled from civilian life. Many were from hot climates and trained for tropical conditions; others in the 'Class of 1963' found themselves taken to the Malvinas before their training was complete. Once on the islands, lines of supply in the Argentine army could be chaotic. Sometimes officers failed to distribute food among the ranks and men were forced to steal food from stores in Stanley.

Some conscripts, perhaps particularly the youngest ones, were poorly treated. If they were caught stealing they could be cruelly punished. At least one was reported as being tied to tent posts on the hillside in a spread-eagled position and left to freeze.[30] One islander recalled seeing men scavenging for food in the municipal rubbish dump, and others said that Argentine soldiers came begging at their doors to wash or eat.[31] Nevertheless, the Argentine force was not exclusively conscripted. Officers and NCOs were well trained and conscripts were not all working class or poor fighters.

In contrast, the British troops were highly trained and very well motivated. Lieutenant Colonel Andrew Whitehead of 45 Commando Royal Marines said on HMS *Canberra*, 'I have never known the men so enthusiastic, motivated and with such high morale.'[32] But they were also inexperienced. Some men at the rank of major in the Paras had been in battle in Dhofar in Oman, but most troops had not. Some of them wanted it badly, but very few knew what to expect. It could be hard for some men to believe they would be going into combat. After a few days on the islands, many of the young soldiers felt as if they were on exercise. 3 Para's Post-Operational Report said: 'Some young soldiers were genuinely surprised that ENDEX [end of exercise] was not declared after the statutory period.'[33]

The men did not know what they were going to be asked to do, and waiting around could be dispiriting. The terrain was spare and rugged, like Brecon or Dartmoor only more so. On sunny, clear days – and there were some – the light was clear and acute, the sea blue, the nights dark and starry. But there were only eight hours of daylight, it was relentlessly cold, the wind roared continually and as the weather worsened it became wet and foggy and they had to sleep out in snow and sleet. 'The wind often reached speeds of 30 knots or more and this plus the rain made wind chill a problem.'[34] When the Marines got to the base of Mount Kent, a telegram noted that 'atrocious weather resulted in little more than survival being achieved'.[35] It was not physical fitness alone that determined men's ability to cope. Some of the fittest men, those who were good at running or gym, did not fare as well as men with more body fat. Rather, what was needed was resilience and robustness: 'Some [junior officers and NCOs] found the conditions so demanding that they had little or no energy left to either think or to lead others.'[36]

The physical demands on them were extraordinary, even before battle. 3 Para marched from Port San Carlos to Estancia House via Teal Inlet, 40 kilometres over nearly three days. On 8 June, Sergeant Ian McKay wrote home: 'I have never known a more bleak, wind-swept and wet place in my life. We spend our life with wet feet trying to dry out and keep warm. The wind blows constantly but it is cooling rather than drying. You cannot walk fifty paces anywhere, even on the mountainsides, without walking into a bog. To be quite honest once we have given them a hammering and put them back in their place the Argentines can have the place. It really is fit for nothing. I thought the Brecon Beacons was bad but this takes the biscuit.'[37] A corporal wrote to his father on the same day: 'As you know we are on the islands now. I don't know which is worst being in bad weather in the South Atlantic or being under shellfire from the Argies. We are just outside Stanley the capital waiting to attack it when that's over we will be on our way home hopefully. Things out here are proving difficult with the weather and soft ground but everybody's getting used to it. I'll be glad when it's all finished. But I think this has finished me in the army when I get back I think I will pack it in.'[38]

Waiting, and 3 Para's long march, did seem to exact a toll on the morale of the men. According to Lieutenant Chapman, B Company 2 Para, 'with the weather and the harshness of the conditions, we were physically degrading. We were suffering from "the actualities of war – the effects of tiredness, hunger, fear, lack of sleep, weather, inaccurate information . . .".'[39] Some men were consequently keen to give the Paras something to do, to get the Parachute Regiment into action.

5. Orders: The Battle of Darwin and Goose Green

At 2 a.m. Falklands time on 28 May 1982,* 2 Para advanced into battle for the first time in a generation. Darwin and Goose Green subsequently became a battle honour: named after these two small settlements some 4 kilometres apart, each on the narrow isthmus that connected East Falkland to its uninhabited southern part, Lafonia.

On the isthmus, the land rose gently to the top of the hill, above the six farmhouses in the hamlet of Darwin, to its eastern side. Next to the hill was a steep gully, and at its crest a thicket of gorse bushes. The gorse ran from the gully along a ridge across to the ruins of Boca House, on the west side of the isthmus. After the gorse line, a long, gentle slope descended to the fifteen houses at Goose Green. The incline between Darwin and Goose Green was flat and almost completely featureless, broken by a wooden school building, some children's swings and a tiny airstrip in front of the Goose Green settlement.

The battalion commander Lieutenant Colonel Jones's plan was for his men to move rapidly from one end of the isthmus to the other, arriving before dawn outside Goose Green. They could then capture the settlement in daylight, avoiding harm to any civilians still there. But when dawn came, elements of the battalion were pinned back around the gorse line by Argentine gunfire and could not move forward. Later, they broke through the gorse and made their way across the plain in daylight, under assault from an enemy who could see

---

* The military recorded timings in Greenwich Mean Time, or 'Zulu' time, which was four hours ahead of Falklands time. I have chosen to translate all timings into Falkland Islands time because it is easier to see what time of day it was, and therefore whether it was dark or not; and to get a sense of where the timings would fit into the men's daily rhythms.

them clearly. The commanding officer was killed at Darwin Hill, trying in his own determined way to break what seemed then to be a deadlock.

Julian Thompson, the brigadier in charge of 3 Commando Brigade, had not thought it necessary to capture the settlement at Goose Green. It was to the south, not on any direct route between Port Stanley and Sussex Mountains, where 2 Para had made camp after they had landed. One member of the Royal Marines Intelligence Corps said the battle was 'tricky and pointless'.[1]

It was certainly unorthodox. 2 Para had on call only three 105-mm light guns, stationed at Camilla Creek House, a few kilometres from the isthmus. A normal battalion allocation would be six, but it was too difficult to move more guns to help them. Those manning the three guns found it impossible to keep up with demand for artillery as the battle progressed. Positioned on the other side of the creek that separated the top of the isthmus from the island, there were in addition Machine Gun Platoon's six machine guns; and three firing posts and seventeen missiles for the MILANs, the wire-guided anti-tank missiles. These weapons could not hit the eastern side of the isthmus unless they moved forward, which they had to do at first light. Until 4.30 a.m. the powerful 4.5-inch gun on HMS *Arrow* was supposed to support them, but its gun jammed; 2 Para had only two 81-mm mortar tubes, as carrying any more was also too cumbersome and heavy for the men without any transport.

The fire support was less than would normally be expected for their mission. This lack placed even greater reliance on the physical capability of 2 Para's men. It demanded courage to fight at close quarters, and not to give up when they seemed to be outgunned. Major Dair Farrar-Hockley, the officer commanding A Company said, 'I decided that if one was brought to battle again ideally one would not go in those circumstances. There was a very high risk to the operation we were committed to and principally down to the tremendous gutter fighting capability of the soldiers, we won through.'[2] 2 Para's post-operations report said: 'The victory at Darwin and Goose Green was a remarkable tribute to the training and mentality of the British soldier . . . the ultimate success was largely due to initiative and determination, often at section commander and private soldier level, to keep moving forward.'[3]

★

Lieutenant Colonel Jones injected his own spirit into the form of 2 Para's battle. Since taking command of the battalion in April 1981, he had insisted on fitness, trying to move the men away from the strange blend of lassitude and adrenaline that Northern Ireland had some-times induced and back to the regiment's founding ethos as a highly motivated spearhead unit. Jones had never quite fitted in among the army elite. He had hated the conformity of Eton; he was shy, but also impetuous, even reckless. Before he came to command the Paras, he was rejected from his parent regiment, the Devon and Dorsets. There, a brigadier had concluded that he had relentless dynamism, but that his judgement was sometimes clouded by impatience and an unreadi-ness to accept others' counsel. In Kenya in December 1981 he had been out in the front while on a live-firing exercise – the command-ing officer, leading a company attack.

When Brigadier Thompson, a day after the landings, asked 2 Para's commanding officer to prepare a company of 2 Para to raid the settle-ments at Darwin and Goose Green, Jones was enthusiastic. He readied D Company, the company my uncle was in, and set them off to march from Sussex Mountains to Camilla Creek House, an isolated farm-house at a mid-point to their ultimate destination. It was not quite clear what D Company were expected to do once they reached the isthmus, but raiding implied arrival by stealth, firing some shots, per-haps attacking the small airstrip, creating some confusion and then retreating again. This would be a raid aimed at reminding the Argen-tines the British were there, to distract them as Thompson began to move the rest of the parachute battalions and Marines across the island to prepare to assault the high ridges around Stanley, where the main Argentine garrison was waiting.

On 24 May, D Company set off, reached Camilla Creek House, and then the next day were called back. When the *Atlantic Conveyor* was sunk, the British lost helicopters, which Thompson was planning to use to move the paratroopers across the islands towards Stanley. Without the helicopters, they would have to march. It was a long way, the weather was poor, the risks were higher, and Thompson no longer wanted the additional complication of a company stuck out in the south raiding the Argentine forces stationed at Goose Green settlement.[4] Jones did not hide his dismay. Told the raid was off, he said, 'I've waited twenty years for this, and now some fucking marine has cancelled it.'[5]

Why then, two days later, was the cancelled raid relaunched, and why did the raid end up as an operation with a more substantial objective, to capture the settlements of Darwin and Goose Green? These have always been sensitive questions. There is no written record of conversations about the orders, and therefore it is hard to be sure precisely what passed between Navy HQ in Northwood and Brigadier Thompson, and then between Thompson and Jones.[6] In London, the losses of ships affected public morale and potentially weakened Britain's diplomatic stance. In the War Cabinet on 27 May, Thatcher said 'it was important to make the earliest possible progress with the operations on land', but exactly what this meant was up to the military commanders in the field.[7] At Navy headquarters, some believed Thompson, who wanted to wait for the arrival of more troops before beginning his advance to Stanley, was too cautious.[8] Consequently, on 26 May at 10 a.m., Thompson was instructed to order the raid at Darwin and Goose Green for a second time: 'as clear and unequivocal were the orders from Northwood. The GG operation was to be remounted and more action was required all round'.[9]

What, exactly, did Admiral Fieldhouse, the Commander in Chief of the Fleet who gave Thompson his orders, intend his underling to do? It is difficult to say. London was remote from daily appreciation of the terrain, the logistics, or the timings of any operation. In his *Official History of the Falklands Campaign*, Professor Sir Lawrence Freedman said that the signal from Fieldhouse to Thompson read: 'You should do all you can to bring the Darwin/Goose Green operation to a successful conclusion with the Union Jack seen to be flying in Darwin. This will enable us to claim possession of Lafonia.'

Northwood also talked about 'eliminating the [Argentine] garrison' before withdrawing.[10] The orders from Northwood were, to an extent, ambiguous. The instructions might have intimated that London wanted Thompson to capture, and hold, the settlements on the isthmus; but on the other hand, a Union Jack could fly from Darwin without the battalion going to Goose Green, and without, presumably, anybody capturing anything bar the flagpole on Darwin Hill.

Thompson recognized the logistical and resource problems an operation on the island's southern flank could cause. After the war, he told an interviewer in the Parachute Regiment that 'he was told to order the second raid but he was not happy about the idea'.[11] He knew he could not get more than three 105-mm guns to the area because of the difficulties of moving artillery and ammunition forward. Thompson met Lieutenant Colonel Jones in the afternoon of 26 May. What passed between them is still uncertain. The written record indicates that the Brigadier told Jones to 'carry out a raid on the Goose Green isthmus and capture the settlements before withdrawing in reserve for the main thrust in the north'.[12] Possibly, there was not much distinction between a 'raid' and a 'capture'. The order suggested 2 Para should do both, and perhaps Thompson saw there was no choice but to capture the settlements, even with few resources available. Doubtlessly, Jones would have been keen to press ahead. When Jones asked for a troop of tanks to support 2 Para, Thompson refused, as he thought the vehicles could not cope with the terrain. Later, he admitted this was a mistake.[13]

Or perhaps Thompson said and Jones heard different things. Many in the Parachute Regiment believed that Jones had a role to play in the formation of the mission objective. In his *2 Para Falklands: The Battalion at War*, Major General John Frost, the former Commanding Officer of 2 Para and retired hero of Arnhem, said: '2 Para was "raring to go" and Brigadier Thompson knew that there would be no peace for him with Jones straining at the leash. For although it is always a mistake to underestimate an enemy, there was reason to believe that the Argentines' hearts were not really in the business – and if 2 Para had no doubts about the outcome, it ill behove anyone else to be too fearful.'[14]

Further evidence from the Parachute Regiment suggests, at least, that Jones was keen to take the opportunity to capture the settlements. He wanted to get on and do it, even in the knowledge he did not have the artillery support he might have wanted.[15] In October 1982, General Sir Anthony Farrar-Hockley, the Colonel Commandant of the Parachute Regiment, whose son Dair was the officer commanding A Company, began a series of interviews with officers and soldiers who had been in the conflict. 3 Para's Adjutant, Captain Kevin McGimpsey, told Farrar-Hockley that 'initially the 2 Para action was to be a raid, but the Commanding Officer of 2 Para's wishes prevailed and it became a proper attack'. He heard this developing on a radio communication between Jones and Thompson.[16] HQ Operations Officer Major Roger Miller said the second order was for a raid, but that 'The feeling in the battalion was that the brigadier had been told by Northwood to get on and go and do something, but again the orders were scanty and general in nature.'[17] Major Ryan, also with HQ Company, said: 'It was also my impression that Colonel H was not satisfied with the concept of a raid and that probably from the outset he saw it as a deliberate assault on Darwin and Goose Green, and as he himself said and this is not verbatim, what is the point of going down and hitting Darwin and Goose Green and walking 16ks back [to Camilla Creek House]. I think from the very outset he saw this as an assault to secure those two locations.'[18]

By 27 May, the attack now imminent, information from 2 Para's patrols meant Jones was aware that there was more Argentine opposition on the isthmus than perhaps he had initially supposed. He could, perhaps, have asked again for more support, but Jones did not want to run the risk that the mission would be called off. As Miller at HQ had said, he 'was worried lest the battalion be left behind and concerned to make every possible preparation for a parachute assault'. Jones was exceptionally determined, and Thompson had been ordered to mount an operation on the isthmus. It was perhaps obvious that there could be advantages, not least to distract the Argentines from the brigade's move across the islands in the north, if 2 Para did what Jones wanted and scored a notable victory at minimal cost.

★

Later that afternoon, on 27 May, Jones held his 'Orders' or 'O' group with the battalion officers. The previous night, the whole battalion had marched the 12 kilometres from Sussex Mountains to Camilla Creek House. It was an arduous walk: 'Men staggered on through the night, cold seeping up from the ground at halts chilling the sweat and sending shivers down the spine. But they were used to such moves: like an unpleasant dream, one still knows that there will be an awakening, eventually.'[19]

In the morning, men were resting in and around the farm when, at 10 a.m., they heard on the BBC World Service an announcement that a battalion of paratroopers were preparing to assault Goose Green. Jones was furious: 'The CO was livid and threatened to sue the BBC for manslaughter.'[20] It is not yet clear why the broadcast was made. Perhaps in London's eagerness for a triumph, MPs who had been told there was to be an attack were unaware it had not already taken place. Or maybe someone intended it as a deliberate deception, ignorant that 2 Para really were about to do what the broadcaster said.

Jones had called an Orders group for 11 a.m. When the time came, however, not all the company commanders turned up. In the confusion after the broadcast, some had not got the message to attend. Jones 'became incensed'.[21] One private soldier in the vicinity said he could hear a lot of 'shouting coming from the house'.[22] Jones then ordered a second meeting for 3 p.m., with only an hour and a half to go before last light. When they convened, Jones told his men that they were to conduct an attack, managed in six phases, that would result in the capture of both the settlements of Darwin and Goose Green.[23] Jones said that he did not know, in a nod to the 'raid', if the Paras would then have to withdraw, or if they would be permitted to stay at their new location.

Jones's intention was clear, but, as dusk began to fall, he wanted the Orders group over and done with, and this meant that the officers did not have time to talk about key parts of the battle plan. Jones hurried Lieutenant Thurman, attached to the regiment, who gave detailed intelligence about the terrain. He was impatient with Captain Alan Coulson, 2 Para's intelligence officer, telling him, 'for fuck's sake hurry up'.[24] Coulson said: 'I also tended to speak for a bit too long, which was upsetting Colonel Jones.'[25] Jones knew by then that there were sixteen Argentine trenches lying in the centre of the isthmus, between Darwin and Boca House. The Argentines were well dug in, and the Paras could not get past them without a fight. 2 Para patrols had identified the trenches, but in the Orders group meeting, the officers did not discuss how they would remove the threat. Nor did they instruct anyone to secure Darwin Hill, the high ground above Darwin settlement. It is hard to say why. Perhaps Jones was relying too much on what he thought he knew from an SAS patrol that had reported the Argentine forces were aimless and inefficient. Perhaps someone made a mistake with a grid reference.[26] Or maybe Jones assumed that, whatever the Argentine strength, they were no match for the Paras.

Jones ended the Orders group meeting with the statement that 'All previous evidence suggests that if the enemy is hit hard, he will crumble.'[27] Yet he had no solid grounds on which to base this assessment. It was perhaps simply his faith in the professionalism of the Parachute Regiment when matched against a conscript army. According to Major John Crosland, the officer commanding B Company, the Parachute Regiment were certain of their ability to dominate: 'Confident, not arrogant, technically proficient, physically very fit, and mentally just as tough. That combination is a very powerful combination, and correctly led, I mean can you imagine if we hadn't won Goose Green, professional Paras beaten by conscripts? I mean, give us a break.'[28]

As he brought the Orders group meeting to its conclusion, perhaps Jones realized that if he was to capture the settlements, he could not afford to delay any longer. In the dusk, as the fog began to rise, his priority was to make the most of the cover of darkness. It was 7 kilometres to the start-lines, 12 kilometres to Goose Green. The terrain was boggy and covered with unstable tussocks of grass. Even without the enemy, it would have been a tough march, just as the long trek had been the night before.

Losing the darkness at that moment, then, perhaps came to be more important than understanding fully what lay ahead. There was no time to go into detail. The officers knew there were dangers and they could not, now or later, prevent the assault nor change the way it was to proceed. Some understood it was to be a 'come as you are party', dependent on the depths of courage their men could tap into.[29] D Company Commander Major Philip Neame said he knew it was going to be 'a bloody do'.[30]

★

As night began to fall, 2 Para set off to the start-lines at the top of the isthmus. At 2 a.m. they crossed silently – ten hours of darkness had already passed. Morale was high. Private Worrall of A Company 2 Para said that on the start-line he felt 'terrific. I always wanted to do it. It's a bit like if you want to be a carpenter but you can't work the wood. I wanted to kill, I wanted to be a soldier.'[31] Corporal John Geddes, C Company 2 Para, said he felt a heightened charge when he heard B Company fixing their bayonets: 'I was thrilled and I'm not ashamed to say it. I was electrified by that sound because I'm a soldier, and the thought of the fight to come and the idea of my mates out there preparing to do battle gave me a warrior's rush.'[32] Corporal Martin Margerison, B Company 2 Para, said that he had always wanted to go to war, it was what he joined the regiment for. He was ready to die for the glory of the Paras. 'That was never a problem. And we all knew that . . . we knew we were going to die, we knew where we were going, but it was all for one and one for all, we were all going to die together, nobody was going to die on their own.'[33]

At Burntside House came their first encounter: A Company fired with 6-mm rockets, sub-machine guns and rifles. Their bigger gun, the 84-mm rocket launcher, missed. Perhaps it was fortunate. When they went to inspect, they found two dead Argentine soldiers in the barn, but inside the house were four elderly Falkland Islanders. They were hiding beneath a mattress, trying to shelter under the floor-boards. The British gunfire had knocked the teeth from their dog's mouth.

Three minutes into their advance, B Company 6 Platoon saw a figure nearby. It seemed more plausible to at least one man that they should encounter a scarecrow than an enemy soldier. Corporal

Margerison shouted to the figure to put his hands up. He replied, '*Por favor*'. The silhouette moved, and in the darkness it was not clear if he was raising his hands or readying his weapon. Corporal Geddes wrote later that 'two rifles and two gimpys [general purpose machine guns] opened up on him without a moment's hesitation'.[34] The group shot the man, taking collective responsibility for this first kill.

Margerison had a different memory of this incident later. 'I killed the first sentry, coming from our start-line up the hill, and that's a terrible thing to do. Not the fact that I killed him, but that it was up to me as to whether he should die or not.' B Company was advancing silently. Margerison knew that as soon as shots were fired, the Argentines would be alerted to B Company's position and he knew that there was an Argentine gun, a .5 Browning 'which has bullets that big, and they're going to kill every one of us, every single one of us', in a position overlooking them. When the Argentine's hands moved, 'I just fired a shot, then our machine gunners opened up. Well, you don't see tracer, which is the bit that ignites, it doesn't ignite for 110 yards. And it only goes to 1,100 yards, but all we could see was the flash of the weapons lit this guy up. And then the tracer. So you just had this imaginary line.'

Geddes, and platoon commander Lieutenant Chapman, witnessed the impressive force of their action: 'The enemy soldier literally flew through the air and the tracer ignited as it passed through him. He was hit quite a few times. [Corporal] Eiserman later searched his body and found about five rounds had penetrated a prayer book he was carrying.'[35] Later, Chapman analysed the significance of that moment for the rest of the battle: 'From that moment forth, 6 Platoon believed we were invincible and that our will to win was stronger than the enemy's. We could not lose. The attack was, for me, the seminal moment of the war.'[36]

But Margerison felt no glory, no release, no body blasted high into the air. He was aware of his responsibility, not only for the life of the Argentine, but for the safety of his men, and, after the shooting ended, there was simply an empty space. 'It wasn't like a John Wayne movie, he didn't get thrown back five or ten yards. He just collapsed like a bag of jelly. He just went on the floor. That was it. Finished.'[37]

Nothing had changed. It was what they had been waiting for, but afterwards they were in exactly the same position as before – with the absence of a figure where a man had been. Exhilarated, feeling the power of their rightful choice, they had to move forwards.

★

The darkness was worsened by fog, and D Company was lost: 'The night was so dark that we had to hold on to the kit on the back of the man in front.'[38] They found themselves ahead of the lead company. Jones became annoyed. D Company were aware of Argentine positions nearby, and although they did not know exactly where they were, Jones ordered them to attack.[39]

The battle had only just begun, and suddenly they came under fire from close range. The firepower was awesome, and it came as a shock. One officer said that his soldiers were 'completely incapable of detecting which rounds were incoming and which outgoing'. They assumed it was all outgoing. During training they had never come across artillery firing: 'Only when they were on the receiving end, did they begin to realize.'[40] The men tried to keep calm and do their jobs. Private Graham Carter, who had just come to the battalion after completing his training, said: '[I was] so absolutely petrified really. Knowing that they are trying to kill me, they are trying to kill the people that I had tried to come to terms with as new friends and new colleagues. It is very difficult to describe exactly how you feel, but petrified basically. It would be nice to say you were completely controlled and you knew that you were quite capable of getting on with the job but that is not the case.'[41]

As 10 Platoon crawled towards the direction of fire, Lance Corporal Cork was hit. Men had been trained not to waste time assisting wounded comrades, but Private Fletcher went to help him and was shot too. When later Fletcher was found, he had a dressing for a shell wound in his hand; he had been about to give first aid to his lance corporal. The deaths of Cork and Fletcher, so soon and sudden, led 10 Platoon to feel the possibility of their own mortality: 'This event had a deep impact on everyone because it was the first time most of us had come under direct fire at close range, and obviously the deaths of two in such an apparently random manner brought home the seriousness of the situation. It might sound rather naive to say so, but until then we were quite "gung-ho" and confident death would only happen to someone else.'[42]

D Company still had to deal with the enemy who were shooting at them. Major Neame, the company commander, was worried that, if they committed themselves, they might collide with B Company, but Jones urged him to keep moving. 11 Platoon fixed bayonets. Lance Corporal Bingley, keen to lead from the front, charged towards an enemy position, Private Grayling behind him. Grayling was hit in the water bottle, and the bottle exploded. As he fell, the Argentine machine-gun post stopped firing. Its final rounds hit Bingley in the head and he was killed. Corporal Harley crawled forward and grenaded the trench.[43] Some of the Argentines defending the position had already fled, but others continued to fight hard.[44] Four men appeared and a 'flare was fired revealing them to be enemy. All four vanished under a hail of shots which killed one and wounded another.' Corporals Harley and McAuley advanced to the trenches again and this time threw white phosphorus grenades into them.[45]

10 and 11 Platoons were under fire. The noise was deafening, the darkness disorienting and, for some at least, it did not feel as if they were in control. They had to force themselves to focus only on what was immediately in front of them, to prevent their minds from dwelling on what was happening, and what it meant. Corporal Harley had to keep ordering the men to separate from each other in order to spread the risk, though he understood why the men were naturally inclined to come together. They feared finding themselves alone, without comfort if they were hurt, having to take significant decisions without knowing any details, without knowing if they were doing the right thing. 'Nobody wants to die alone.'[46]

As the Argentine trenches were subdued, a bullet struck Private Parr – my uncle – and he fell to the ground.[47]

★

A Company found no Argentines at Coronation Point, where the enemy had been expected, and then the company halted. At around

5.20 a.m. on 28 May, Jones came forward to their position. He wanted to see where they were and he urged their commanding officer, Major Dair Farrar-Hockley, to move forwards as quickly as possible.[48] Dawn was beginning to break; the advantage of a night attack was receding.

The first fingers of light emerged as A Company arrived at the gorse gully on Darwin Hill.[49] They saw men on the slope of the gully, and one soldier thought they might be civilians out walking their dog. They called out, the men replied in Spanish, and the paratroopers opened fire.[50] According to Private Worrall, 'We shouted hands up, they all stood up and put their hands up. As we were advancing towards them one bent down and picked up his weapon, he actually picked it up. One of the other lads from the section wasted the four of them. Killed all four of them, sir.'[51]

Immediately, fire came heavily from the Argentine trenches. 'All hell broke loose . . . Tracer, mortar, SF [sustained fire] . . . approximately to our right, to our front. It was amazing how much. I thought I had seen company firepower but this was absolutely amazing firepower.'[52] Private Tuffen was shot in the head. It was four hours before anyone could get to him to pick him up: 'I've got no recollection of pain or anything at the time. The one thing, and again I couldn't swear to it, but the thing I think I remember was actually coming to a couple of times and looking, and I just felt so tired, and I'd look round and no one was about, so I'd fall back asleep.'[53] Corporal Melia of the Royal Engineers was killed, and Lance Corporal Shorrock was shot in the spine.

In the gully, the fire was intense. Men took individual and small-group initiatives to continue moving forward. One section attempted to flank around to the left. Worrall was hit in the stomach: 'I was crawling along the top of the bank . . . my cover was non-existent. I thought I had to make a dash for it. First couple of paces and I fell like a bag of spuds.' He lay in the open. It took nearly an hour to rescue him, to drag him to cover. During this action, Corporal Stephen Prior was shot in the head and killed: 'Did he fall over you?' 'No sir, to the side.'[54]

Farrar-Hockley wanted fire support, but there was none, and at

7.25 a.m. he called for a Harrier strike. This was impossible because of bad weather at sea. Jones's priority was speed. It was dawn, and Jones wanted A Company to advance. When they could not do so, Jones, according to his bodyguard, Sergeant Norman, said, 'I'm not having any of this', and went to join them. According to Norman, 'When he made up his mind that a thing was going to be done then it was going to be done, and off he went.' Headquarters Company struggled to keep up with his pace just behind him.[55] Jones saw battle as about determination and resolve: '2 Para's commanding officer understood, indeed was a fervent exponent of the belief, that combat is a battle of wills, that you have to be stronger willed to win.'[56]

At 8.30 a.m. Jones arrived in the gully. He initially wanted to try to get up onto the spur, where Worrall had been injured and Prior killed. But he accepted this was unwise. The C Company commander, Major Roger Jenner, offered to bring his twelve light machine guns forward onto the ridge. D Company's commander, Major Philip Neame, suggested bringing his men around in a flanking manoeuvre to help.[57] Jones rejected these suggestions, telling Neame, 'Don't tell me how to run my battle.'[58] Then he said to Farrar-Hockley, 'Dair, you've got to take that ledge [towards the top of the spur, to the right].' Farrar-Hockley was reluctant, but Jones insisted.[59] There is not one clear version of what happened next, but it seems that an uncoordinated group of about fifteen men began to scramble and crawl up the slope to make a frontal assault across the spur.[60] Captain Dent and Corporal Hardman were shot and killed.[61] Adjutant David Wood, on his hands and knees, entreated the men around him, 'That's it, lads, airborne all the way; remember Arnhem!' He was killed.[62] Private Dey said, 'You will get killed if you go any further', and another man shouted to Farrar-Hockley as they began to retreat away from the ledge, 'If you don't fucking get out now, sir, you ain't getting out.'[63]

At the bottom of the spur, Jones began to run, pursued by Sergeant Norman, in an attempt perhaps to neutralize positions on Darwin Ridge while the Argentines were distracted by the activity on the ledge. According to one account, he shouted, 'Come on A Company, get your skirts off.'[64] When he got around the spur, he must have seen a trench up the hill to the left, but perhaps he did not see the Argentine position on the right of the rise, its overhead solidly covered.

Jones's personal bravery was extraordinary: 'I noticed the Commanding Officer standing in complete dead ground to all the enemy trenches. He then changed the magazine on his SMG [sub-machine gun], cocked it, and charged up the hill towards the enemy position.' When Jones was about three to five feet from the trench, he was shot in the back from the opposite side, fell and rolled over. He lay there, mortally wounded, and the men could not reach him until the Argentines had stopped firing.[65] When Norman found him, 'I turned him over because he was lying on his back. I got his webbing off, at this point he was still conscious although slipping into unconsciousness, so I stayed there trying to keep him warm with extra windproofs and his own quilted jacket and unfortunately some time later he died.'[66]

While Jones lay wounded, men of A Company managed to get into positions where they could bring down fire into the Argentine trenches. The Company Sergeant Major fired a 66-mm rocket, which missed. Corporal Abols fired another, and made a direct hit on what turned out to be the command trench. The Argentines began to surrender. Lieutenant Mark Coe said, 'That, I think, was the straw that broke the camel's back. At that point they [the Argentines] started to come out. They had lost probably six trenches by this stage . . . we were up on the top [of the spur] . . . and then all of a sudden the whole thing just collapsed. I mean all of a sudden people were putting their hands up and coming out of their holes.'[67] A Company had been around Darwin Hill for three hours. News went over the battle-group net that the Commanding Officer had been hit – 'Sunray is down' – at approximately 9.30 a.m.[68] About an hour later, the Argentines began to fold.[69]

★

2 Para were now in the open. From Darwin Ridge and Boca House the terrain was flat, grading downwards to the handful of houses at Goose Green. The Argentines that A Company had been engaging had surrendered, but B Company were still fighting and 2 Para had still to

cover about 4 kilometres to achieve their objective. It was so flat, the Argentines could see the British troops coming and had time and space to fire on them. The plan had been to attack under cover of darkness. Now, there was nowhere to hide, the Commanding Officer was dead, and although Major Chris Keeble took over, he could not come forward immediately, so the company commanders had to take the initiative.

B Company was still trying to secure the position at Boca House. They broke through the gorse line at the top of the rise and out into open ground. Suddenly, they came under accurate fire from some distance away: '5 Platoon had nowhere to go on the featureless hill – we were fish in a bowl.' Three men were wounded, and in the chaos, as artillery rounds landed around them, Private Illingsworth was shot and killed.[70] Further down the bank, 6 Platoon were also pinned back. Smoke from their own grenades came in to cover them, and in the retreat Corporal Margerison – the man who had shot the first Argentine, the scarecrow – was shot in the back of his shoulder and jaw and lay badly injured: 'Blooming heck, the sun comes up, and we're caught . . . I got shot from 300 yards away. And we didn't have enough firepower to even give cover and fire for people to move round, because it was that open.'[71]

B Company called for firepower to help them. Crosland asked for the MILAN missiles to be brought forward and Neame amassed machine-gun support from D Company. Poor coordination between the companies could than have proved fatal. The Argentines began to fly white flags from some of their bunkers. Neame decided to take the surrender: 'a "risk calculation" of a "most stomach-churning nature".' Machine Gun Platoon, who had also come forward, were then ordered to fire on the trenches that were waving white flags, and after a brief dispute, they did. The Argentines did not retaliate, fortunately for D Company's 12 Platoon, who were now exposed. Neame got on the radio, 'For fuck's sake stop firing!'[72] The machine guns, and the use of MILAN missiles, finally secured the victory at Boca House.

Major Keeble now had to get men forward, although he must have been aware of the potential peril 2 Para were in.[73] He ordered elements of C, Support and HQ Companies to advance from Darwin Hill.

They did not have much choice but to show themselves to the Argentines. They could see the Argentines begin to run for their guns, and soon shells and mortar fire began to land all around them. 'You could feel the guns zeroing in on you,' said Major Roger Jenner.[74] According to Lieutenant Kennedy, 'The weight of fire was incredible . . . A soldier is always concerned with the question, "How will I react under fire?" As I lay on the ground I realized that the choice was not too difficult, it was either move forward and do something or die.'[75] Major Jenner called urgently for artillery, but it was not available. Within half an hour or so, the advancing men had taken twelve casualties, one of them fatal. Jenner, C Company Commander, was 'blown over and wounded' in a burst from an anti-aircraft gun, and his signaller, Private Holman-Smith, was killed.[76]

The companies were now stretched out and mixed up together. Neame moved D Company quickly towards Goose Green. Lieutenant Jim Barry, the commander of 12 Platoon, could see a white cloth waving near a flagpole and he wanted to take the surrender. He went forward with Corporal Sullivan and four other men. Barry thought the Argentines wanted to surrender, but an Argentine account shows the Argentines believed Barry was about to surrender to them.[77] When the Argentines realized that was not his intention, they gave him two minutes to get back to safety. At that moment, shots were fired, probably by the machine gunners, who were now on Darwin Hill.[78] The Argentines immediately opened fire, killing at close range Barry, Sullivan and Lance Corporal Smith.

The machine gunners could see movement, and did not know what was going on. They were firing 'thousands and thousands of rounds – you wouldn't want to be on the receiving end of that' – but they had not been given proper targets to fire on. Corporal John Gartshore said later: 'He'd [Barry had] gone forward to take the surrender, this was spoke about after the battle actually [they did not know what had happened until afterwards], because when they'd gone forward, okay they were putting their weapons down, nobody would teach you to do that, you wouldn't put your weapon down, but we was engaged with their enemy at the time, we didn't see what was happening with this white flag situation, we were engaged with the enemy . . . It made us feel guilty, because three blokes lost their lives . . . I've always thought about this, even today I'd hate to have been the cause of it.'[79]

At around the same time, men of D Company assaulted the schoolhouse. They thought they knew how to attack a building because they had seen it in films, According to Private Carter, '10 and 11 Platoons were attacking the school house, and it seemed quite funny at the time. It looked as though they were playing cowboys and Indians, running around the house throwing grenades and shooting anything that came out.'[80] 2 Para's in-house history records that, 'The way it is always done in films appealed to Chris [Lieutenant Chris Waddington, commander of 11 Platoon]. He threw a white phosphorus grenade. It landed harmlessly inside the building. Removing the pin always helps!'[81]

Corporal Jim Creaney also commented that the attack felt almost unreal: 'There were a couple of us who fired 66s [66-mm hand-held rocket launchers], and I was one of the guys who fired a 66 into the house, and missed. But the other thing in our mind when we fired afterwards, later on in the campaign, [was] always remember the old film *Rambo*, he fires the 66 into the cave, and there's a big explosion. Well, none of that ever happened. We eventually got one into the house [and] there was no big explosion. We were expecting this big "woohoo!" and there was no magic moment, as such.'[82]

In reality, the fight was confused, 'a free for all'.[83] Men threw white phosphorus and fragmentation grenades at the school, and shot at it with their rifles. They came under mortar fire, but continued the assault as well as they could. Parts of the school were alight. As dusk fell, different sections of 2 Para opted to retreat, as there was little point continuing. Two Argentine planes flew over and one crashed. Two more flew in, and one dropped napalm near to D Company. It was a terrifying moment: 'The heat was so intense that breathing was difficult as the napalm sucked the oxygen from the air.'[84]

Major Neame remembered he had brought his platoons close together to avoid fire from both sides. When a plane flew over, he was suddenly vulnerable: 'It was the only time in the battle that I was really scared. I was sure I had really fucked things up, and I imagined massive casualties among my blokes.'[85] At 4.25 p.m. British Harriers flew over. They dropped cluster bombs near the point of the isthmus on the Argentine positions there. While they may not have eliminated the Argentine firing posts, they did perhaps offer 2 Para's men some reassurance that they were not totally alone.

★

The long second night, after the battle had quietened down and they did not really know what to expect, was for many the worst period. Major Crosland of B Company told his men: 'We've done bloody well today. Okay, we've lost some lads; we've lost the CO. Now we've really got to show our mettle. It's not over yet, and we haven't got the place. We're about 1,000 metres from D Company; we're on our own and an enemy has landed to our south and there's a considerable force at Goose Green, so we could be in a fairly sticky position.'[86]

The sight of more Argentine troops arriving by helicopter had a further dampening effect on 2 Para's spirit. Lieutenant Chapman, B Company, recalled: 'The arrival of the enemy helicopters . . . was a very frightening moment as I thought it might alter the course of the battle. I remember being with John Crosland at the time and saying to him, "What the fuck do we do now?" His reply was, "It looks like Arnhem – day three". I was scared because I thought there was likely to be a big Argentinian counter-attack on our position.' Chapman also believed that 2 Para's casualties were higher than they were. He had been told that seven officers had been killed, and he thought that B Company might be the only operational company left.[87]

B Company went to the high ground slightly south of the Goose Green settlement and dug in as best they could. Private Curtis recorded: 'The whole company lay in the cold mud . . . with Crosland in the middle . . . I had about 200 rounds left on the gun – fuck all – and I began thinking, shit, this is it; they're going to come up here at any moment and we've got nowhere to go.'[88] D Company remained near the airfield. Creaney said they dug in using hands and bayonets, as obviously they had no shovels. C Company pulled back to the gorse line on Darwin Hill, where A Company had stayed all day. Some of the gorse was burning still. It was freezing, snowing, and 2 Para had been engaged unceasingly since the very early morning, but it was so cold, sleep was impossible. 2 Para's medic, Captain Steven Hughes, had a space blanket he had concealed down the back of his smock: 'Although I was exhausted I wondered whether I would sleep after the horrors of the day, and as I lay in a twilight state every rustle of my foil blanket was a machine gun and every crackle of gorse was an artillery shell.'[89]

All the men, in their various positions, drew towards each other for warmth. Corporal John Gartshore, Machine Gun Platoon, Support Company, told me: 'It was so cold, the sleet and the rain came down. It was about 100m from the gorse line, which was burning. You wanted to go back up there to keep warm, it was so cold and wet. You got all the men huddled together, and you still had to be on stag, watching for anyone moving in. You couldn't light a brew up in case they could see us. We was in a dip, anyone could have dropped anything on us really.' He continued: 'We had no ammunition left. I think between the whole platoon we had maybe only 5 or 6 rounds. It was going to be a bayonet job, do or die. It didn't matter. You'd gone this far, you might as well go the whole way. That was how it was going to be. I remember, when first light broke, Hugo [Lieutenant Hugo Lister] said we may as well have our last cup of coffee.'[90]

Private Dave Brown, C Company, remembered: 'We got to that gorse line and we were sat there thinking we're ******, we're just wiped out . . . they are either going to blow us off this gorse line the next day with artillery, they are going to send troops up under cover of darkness and over-run us, or – and the worst scenario – we will go back down the hill again tomorrow in broad daylight. We weren't going to give in, we were Airborne, we'd have rather died. Honestly.'[91] All they had left was themselves, and they were preparing now to die as the mission was not finished yet. According to Private Dean Ferguson, D Company: 'I think that was the scariest part, just the waiting, we didn't know what to expect. We were expecting attack, it came down on the grapevine . . . As far as we were concerned it was going to be a bayonet charge.'[92]

Until morning came, nobody could know that this battle was

over. Major Chris Keeble, who had assumed command after Jones's death, prepared an offer to the Argentines to spare the settlement and themselves. He convinced them they were surrounded by a superior army, told them the lives of the civilians would be on their consciences and urged them not to waste more life. The BBC journalist Robert Fox proposed that the Argentines should have a parade, thus demonstrating they had not been humiliated. In these circumstances, the Argentine commander in the field, Lieutenant Colonel Ítalo Piaggi, and the Air Force Commander Vice Commodore Wilson Pedroza agreed that the Argentine force would surrender.

6. Momentum: The Battle of Mount Longdon

On 11 June at 8.15 p.m. 3 Para began their assault on Mount Longdon. This battle was one part of 3 Commando Brigade's coordinated night attack on the hills that circled Port Stanley. As 3 Para advanced on Longdon, the Marines of 45 Commando took Two Sisters and 42 Commando Mount Harriet. In early June 1982, fresh British troops, mainly the Scots and Welsh Guards under the command of 5 Infantry Brigade, had arrived in the Falklands. They faced immediate disaster. On 8 June, the ships RFA *Sir Tristram* and *Sir Galahad*, carrying the Welsh Guards, were bombed at Fitzroy.[1] Forty-nine men were killed and 125 wounded in the single biggest loss of British life during the campaign. That bombing, and the subsequent reorganization, delayed the attack on Stanley by around two days.[2]

Mount Longdon is steep, scattered with jagged knots of light grey rock and topped with two spines, a low dip between them. It was defended by a company of Argentines, 287 soldiers, from the 7th Mechanized Infantry Regiment.[3] They had been waiting, and were well protected in bunkers formed from natural shelters.

The flow and ebb of the battle is perhaps best conceived in four parts. First, B Company ascended the mountain and took heavy casualties; second, from around midnight, there was a period of confusion as a bombardment of naval artillery was called in and as B Company continued to try to advance; third, at 2 a.m. A Company took over from B Company and pushed on to the top of the mount, forcing the Argentines to surrender; fourth, over the subsequent day and a half, 3 Para remained on the hill and were shelled by Argentine guns, firing, particularly, from Mount Tumbledown nearby.[4]

★

Like 2 Para at Goose Green, 3 Para advanced silently to contact under cover of darkness. They knew from experience the importance of firepower, and yet 3 Para's Commanding Officer Lieutenant Colonel Hew Pike opted to approach the enemy without artillery cover until the close-quarters firing started. 3 Para's Sergeant John Weeks, B Company's Sergeant Major, said, 'I was surprised because the lesson we'd learnt from Goose Green was that no way should we ever do a silent attack. I thought we should stomp everything, but we didn't have artillery on call.'[5] Sergeant Des Fuller, at battalion head-quarters, said that in retrospect: 'If I had had a good night sight, I would have called for as much artillery, mortar fire, the lot, and then attempted to take out the positions, far too many sangars [fortified enemy positions] there, if you can't see the enemy.'[6]

Captain William McCracken, 29 Commando Regiment Royal Artillery and in charge of directing artillery and naval gunfire, commented: 'I'm firmly of the view that the Argentinians were expecting us, anyway; in fact like most of us they were probably wondering what the hell was keeping us. Therefore I believe that in this situation it is much easier to put in a hefty bombardment and then go in and pick up the pieces, instead of trying to take everything with just the rifle and bayonet. Bombardment may not be quite so subtle but by God it's effective. But a fact of life was that Colonel Hew was a colonel and I was a captain so that night we would go silently.'[7]

The reasons for a silent advance rather than a bombardment seemed pragmatic. Hew Pike was worried that bombardment would alert the Argentines that 3 Para were approaching. If they knew the British were coming, the paratroopers would be very vulnerable to fire from above. Brigadier Thompson, in charge of 3 Commando Brigade, wanted to ration the artillery in case he needed to concentrate it later if anyone got bogged down.[8] At the same time, Thompson's decisions as to where to focus his artillery might also have been influenced by his perceptions of the Parachute Regiment's mentality. The ease with which 3 Para had conducted patrols perhaps led Thompson, or Pike, to believe that the enemy lacked vigilance and determination, and therefore that 3 Para would be able to take the feature more rapidly, and more easily, than they did.

Lieutenant Colonel Pike also believed in the ethos of the Parachute Regiment. When he gave his orders to company commanders, he called upon the regiment's reputation: 'If a parachute battalion couldn't do it, then nobody could.'[9] He later wrote that Mount Longdon was a battle of the sort that had not been 'undertaken by the battalion for a generation'.[10] Lieutenant Andrew Bickerdike remembered B Company Commander Major Mike Argue galvanizing the men: 'We're a band of brothers but we might not all be here tomorrow. But whatever happens, as a regiment, as a team, 3 Para are making history and we will always be remembered.'[11]

★

At the start-line, men who were not going to advance with the lead rifle company wept: 'One lad from patrol company . . . kissed me on the cheek. "Mind how you go," he said. He was crying.'[12] Others accepted that if they were to die, they wanted to die as paratroopers. Private Dominic Gray changed into his Para combat trousers so he would look like a Para in death.[13] Some had a sense of foreboding. According to John Weeks, 'My lads were getting gun happy. They thought it would be easy . . . I knew it wasn't going to be a picnic, they [the Argentines] weren't going to run away . . . After the OC's talk, I told them [B Company] a few home truths about what was going to happen. I told them some of us aren't coming back, I told them they were outnumbered . . . I told them . . . it could be any of us.'[14]

Others felt a dragging sense of sadness – not for the fact they might die themselves, but because they were in a position where it was thought right they should have to. Private Tony Gregory had grown up in various children's homes. 'I was one of the more mature toms [paratrooper in the ranks] because of the way I had had to live my earlier life. I matured quicker. I had to. I know, too, that it has been what they call human nature over hundreds of years to fight and to kill, but I couldn't help thinking there was something sad about it all.'[15] His fate was to be there because nothing had intervened to stop him; nothing or no one had loved him enough to prevent him from being there, about to step into the uncharted. He, as all of them, had no alternative but to take their chances with the lives they had. As Private Mark Eyles-Thomas said, there was no going back.[16]

At the foot of Mount Longdon, 4 Platoon B Company 3 Para advanced silently in the dark. Then Corporal Brian Milne trod on an anti-personnel mine. There was a tremendous explosion and scream-ing. 4 Platoon dived to the floor. The Argentines woke up and began to fire from their positions on the mountain. 4 Platoon were in a minefield on the open ground at the base of the hill. Lance Corporal Hedges, interviewed by a Parachute Regiment senior officer in 1982, said drily: 'Everyone hit the deck, he [Milne] started screaming, and shit poured down on top of us, all lying down.' When asked, 'What did that feel like?' Hedges responded: 'Bloody hell like, we were sort of shook out in extended lines, we split up then and we started mov-ing, eventually we got to the rocks.' 'How long did it take you?' 'Not very long at all, we ran the last part. It was a couple of hundred yards or so.'[17]

A Company, advancing steadily in an extended line, came under fire. There was something absurd about the way they were approach-ing. Private Kevin Connery later said: 'I can't tell you how fucking shocked and surprised I was when we were at the base of Longdon waiting for the order to advance and they told us to get into an extended line. I couldn't help thinking some bastard was on drugs and that they had turned back the clock and we should be lined out in red tunics.'[18]

Private Trevor Bradshaw, also with A Company, had joined the battalion in January and anticipated that battle would be controlled, like a training exercise. Someone must be in charge. He said: 'I was waiting for someone to say "We are now taking effective enemy fire, take cover!" and that didn't seem to be happening.' There was nowhere to shelter anyway until they got closer to the mount. If they had lain down, they would still have had to get to the bottom of the hill somehow.

Bradshaw forced himself to behave as the soldiers around him behaved. There was, after all, no alternative. 'We were just walking towards this incoming fire; it was coming down all around us. As I was advancing I felt incredibly vulnerable, there were rounds fizzing by me and others striking the ground and it felt like only a matter of time before one would hit me.' His body instinctively began to curl: 'I was trying to continue forward whilst at the same time making myself as small a target as possible. My chin was touching my chest as I tried to crouch lower and walk at the same time.'[19]

C Company, in reserve, reached their position, about 100 metres behind A Company, and they too came under increasingly effective small-arms fire and shellfire. Men felt urged to cover themselves, but could not: 'Geordie Nicholson and I both began to dig shell scrapes; we were lying flat to the ground as there was no cover. We had one digging tool between the two of us . . . but you couldn't raise yourself up to swing [it] because of the incoming fire.' The exposed men were desperate to protect themselves, to disappear, if they could, under the turf: 'We were hugging the ground and clawing at the sodden peat, trying to dig a hole with our hands.'[20] Nobody had explained to them that they would find themselves so quickly yearning to survive.

★

6 Platoon B Company began to work their way up from the base towards the ridge of the mount. At first, their advance went well: 'We just laced the place – laid it down thick and heavy, hard and fast, and started moving into whatever cover we could get.'[21] At the top, however, it was suddenly clear they had missed positions. Fire came down from all directions. A sniper struck and pinned down some men. Private Nick Rose was in cover behind rocks: 'There's incoming everywhere, loads of stuff going down the range, and then "bang" my pal Fester [Tony Greenwood] gets it just above his left eye, only a yard away from me. That was a terrible thing.'[22]

The sniper then hit Lance Corporal Murdoch multiple times, and over a spluttering radio set the men heard him dying. Lieutenant Jonathan Shaw, B Company 6 Platoon Commander, said, 'They forgot fieldcraft. They went to help. It's tactically wrong but no private soldier abandoned his mate. That's the problem as I saw it.'[23] Corporal Morham said Murdoch's distress was unbearable. He and Private Stewart Laing, sheltering by some rocks, agreed to rush forward to try to help him. Morham paused to take off his webbing, but Laing set off. 'Shots rang out, together with a sharp intake of breath – Stew [Laing] had been hit three times in the chest.'[24] In a short space of time, five men – Lance Corporals Murdoch and Scott, and Privates Laing, Greenwood and Dodsworth – had been killed, and eight others wounded. Almost half the platoon was out of action, and they had to stop and reorganize.[25]

B Company 4 and 5 Platoons also moved forwards, working against Argentine positions in the rocks. Operating in small teams, two men put down suppressive fire while two or three others moved towards the position they had identified. As men closed in, they fired into the Argentine bunker, or threw grenades. It was hard to maintain co-ordination and their actions became chaotic. As the young soldiers in 6 Platoon had also found: 'There was nobody to tell me what to do. I just had to do it, off my own back.'[26] When they too got closer to the rim of the mount, strong opposition halted their momentum.

They could not move forward and were taking casualties. Lieutenant Bickerdike, commanding 4 Platoon, moved into open ground to try to assess the machine-gun post that was holding them back. A bullet hit him in the thigh. He shouted, 'The bastard got me' and his men laughed.[27] His signaller Private Cullen was hit in the mouth and lost some teeth, but continued to radio although he was dribbling blood and could barely speak. It was becoming difficult for B Company to continue. They were, in the words of one writer, 'dangerously close to defeat'.[28]

Bickerdike shouted to Sergeant Ian McKay: 'It's your platoon. Crack on.'[29] McKay now assumed charge. Perhaps he felt that now he had no choice but to lead from the front, to play out the heroism passed down to him from times past. He knew he was a respected soldier, and he had a reputation for taking care of his men. He understood also that 4 and 5 Platoons' positions were critical. Perhaps he believed that inaction, retreat or delay could lead more men to their deaths.

McKay gathered three men – Corporal Ian Bailey, Lance Corporal Roger James, Private Tony McLarnon – and they advanced up a sheep track towards a machine-gun post. Bailey said, 'We had only gone a short distance when we came under fire from multiple positions. We had no choice but to attack them. We grenaded the first position and went past it without stopping, just firing into it. I had lost sight of Roger James and Tony McLarnon. I thought they had been wounded or were dead; that's when I got shot from another position, which was about three metres away . . . Sgt McKay was still charging on to the next position but there was no one else with him. I then heard a grenade explosion. I noticed that the firing had stopped as suddenly as it started, and it was now very quiet.'[30] James, McLarnon and Bailey survived the assault on the machine-gun post.[31] McKay reached the Argentine trench. His body was found next to it, shot multiple times.

Sergeant Des Fuller then assumed charge of what was left of 4 and 5 Platoons, and with members of 4 Platoon he began again to advance. They walked uphill and then were hit by heavy fire. Private Burt, aged seventeen, was shot and killed, and Corporal 'Ned' Kelly injured. Private Grose, who had turned eighteen that day, was shot through the chest. Later – in some accounts when he was taking Grose to the first-aid post – Private Scrivens, also aged seventeen, was shot in the head and killed. Grose died at the aid post.

Fuller went back to the company headquarters. Corporal Stewart McLaughlin was still fighting on, 'working among the rocks', and Fuller effectively put him in charge of the remainder of 4 Platoon.[32] Lance Corporal Hedges later recalled: 'Then we were moving forward, slowly . . . we were more or less at the top, then we were pinned down by the .5, small arms fire. We didn't know that Sergeant McKay had got it by that stage. We lay down in sort of an extended line. We put about eight grenades over the top. It sounded like moaning, but there was no way we could get over. We launched a few more grenades. We were there for quite some time.'[33]

The battle was now into its second, confused phase. At around midnight, the platoons were withdrawn so that a large naval bombardment could take place, and after that there was uncertainty about how to proceed. Major Mike Argue did not want to concede B

Company's role in the battle just yet. He suggested a second attempt on a position to the northern side of Longdon, where men had been attacked before. They advanced that way. One man, Private Crow, was killed, and at least one more, Lance Corporal Carver, wounded.[34]

Lieutenant Cox, commander of 5 Platoon, and Private Connery continued to work against the Argentines blocking them there. Connery said: 'I found myself lying next to Lieutenant Mark Cox. He was the son of a Parachute Regiment officer. Just across the bowl from us was an enemy position which looked quite strong . . . We looked at each other and agreed to take it out . . . I blasted the position with [a 66-mm anti-tank rocket], then Lieutenant Cox and I threw some grenades into it. As soon as the explosions went off we leapt in and thrust our bayonets into the enemy, firing quick double-tap rounds into them. All were dead. It had taken only seconds. We had done it quickly.'[35] Cox then tried to push further on, but three more men were injured and they had to retreat. In 1986, in a School of Infantry video recording, Cox reported: 'It proved to be a costly operation. We took the position, but had to withdraw to the area where the company had consolidated before the artillery and A Company took over the battle.'[36]

The fact they were forced to retreat seemed to affect Cox. 'When I arrived back [after the failed attempt to advance], Company Sergeant Major Johnny Weeks and Major Argue were there, and I have to admit that at this point, I was physically and mentally exhausted. I was a bit overwhelmed by events and perhaps feeling somewhat ashamed for not managing to push the platoon further.'[37] He gave an order, although he did not remember what it was. Corporal McLaughlin challenged him, and another corporal, Corporal X, took him aside and told him to pull himself together.[38]

Hew Pike then decided that B Company should be rested, and A Company should be brought up from the bottom of the hill to take their place. He wanted A Company to advance to the hilt of Mount Longdon, after a further intense artillery bombardment. Pike and Major David Collett, the officer commanding A Company, disagreed about how to advance. Collett did not want to rush directly up the side of the ridge, and he did not want his men to linger in the chaos

of the battle's wake – 'There were bodies lying everywhere . . .
I could hear captured Argentines crying and praying. It was awful.'
He told Pike he could not bring his men straight up as he would have
to walk through a minefield. Rather, he would move them up slowly,
working up through the positions B Company had already cleared.[39]

In other words, at this critical third phase of the battle, Collett
favoured stealth. The Paras were given fire support, and Collett
ordered his men to advance on their stomachs: 'Cover was very limited and all movement was on the belly. Furthermore, B Company's
experience had shown the importance of clearing enemy positions
systematically, to minimize the lethal danger of sniping from behind
the attacking platoon.'[40] A Company fixed bayonets and gradually
began to gain the upper hand: 'We could see them starting to break,
which spurred us on. But all the bunkers still had to be cleared. We
were not about to take any chances, we continued moving forward
and even those who appeared dead were shot or bayoneted unless
very obviously dead. The effects of artillery were absolutely devastating. Bodies were torn apart. It was a sight I shall never forget.'[41]

It took an artillery bombardment, and men moving slowly and
using bayonets, to gain the upper hand on Longdon. Just before daybreak, the Argentine withdrawal began.[42] A Company took no
fatalities in their trench clearance, and their action proved to be decisive. By the early morning of 12 June the Argentines on the mountain
had been defeated.

★

Brigadier Thompson's original intention was for 3 Para to take Longdon and push on to Wireless Ridge, in the direction of Stanley. But
the battle had taken longer than anticipated, and Mount Tumbledown, the largest hill, had not yet been captured. That job fell to the
Scots Guards, who wanted more time to survey the terrain. They
went into attack on the night of 13–14 June. 2 Para were called to take
Wireless Ridge that same night, while 3 Para lay in reserve.[43] Pike
did not want to withdraw 3 Para from Longdon in case they were
suddenly required to move forward.

This final phase of the Mount Longdon battle was, for many men, in some ways the hardest. They were exhausted and it was freezing cold: 'I found it too cold to sleep; Lance Corporal Phil Jones and I cuddled together for bodily warmth in between two large slabs of rock.' They often used blankets taken from the Argentine dead: 'They smelled absolutely disgusting, but we didn't care, we were just grateful . . . We all cuddled up together.'[44] They also came under frequent, sometimes nearly constant, shellfire from Argentine guns, and this could be troubling. Lieutenant Jonathan Shaw said, 'The psychological effect of artillery should not be underestimated . . . It has a constant psychological "wearing down" effect.'[45] Private Jez Dillon remembered 'sitting in a bunker and putting my arm around a member of A Company during one particularly bad period of shelling. He said, "I fucking hate this" and began to cry. I just said, "Don't worry about it, we'll be alright." But it was now getting a bit too much for all of us. I'm not religious but I remember praying to my dead father, praying that the next one didn't have our names on it. It just never seemed to stop, and for me this was the hardest part of the battle . . . it was absolutely nerve-racking . . . It's hard trying to explain actually how nerve-racking it really was.'[46]

Their lives were not in their hands. It was terrifying, sometimes exhilarating, as Sergeant Graham Colbeck explained: 'With each approaching scream I convinced myself that the coming explosion would tear off a part of my body – sometimes an arm or leg, sometimes my head – and each time the impact left me unharmed I felt reborn . . . It took great effort at times to remain calm under a rain of such terrible power.'[47] That sense that there was nothing they could do to alter the passage of their history could be life-affirming, but at the same time the sensation could drain them of the knowledge they had carried with them – there was so little between a man and his death. The next night on Tumbledown, Gurkha officer Nigel Price said: 'It was as if I saw through – in one instant – the whole sham of civilization with its artificial rank structures and carefully maintained levels of society . . . Since then it has been difficult to be awed by authority. You realize we are all muddling along together, pretending. Hiding behind our ranks and status, all of it a mirage.'[48]

★

An objective view of the way lives were lost at Goose Green and Longdon reveals something about the course of the battles. At Goose Green, British soldiers were fighting a battalion of Argentines – thus a similar number to themselves.[49] Seventeen British soldiers died at Goose Green, fifteen from the Parachute Regiment, and two from attached arms, and forty-five were injured. Three men were killed in the night, by machine-gun fire when D Company walked into a trench position they did not know was there (Lance Corporal Cork, Private Fletcher, Lance Corporal Bingley). Of the fifty Argentines who died and the 145 who were wounded, most were probably killed at night, and during A Company's fight in the gorse gully; and some when D Company attacked the schoolhouse in the afternoon.

During the day, three men were killed at very close range in a bungled attempt to take a surrender (Lieutenant Barry, Corporal Sullivan, Lance Corporal Smith). The advance over open ground in daylight – in other words, the distance between Darwin and Goose Green – claimed fourteen British lives. Two were killed by stray bullets or shrapnel (Private Mechan as dawn broke, by shellfire; Private Dixon as D Company moved towards the schoolhouse). One man was killed from gunfire at a distance when C Company and HQ Company advanced forward from Darwin Hill (Private Holman-Smith); and another was killed during B Company's engagement at Boca House (Private Illingsworth).

A Company's engagement at Darwin Hill – the assault that had not been planned – was the most deadly for the British: seven men were killed. One man was killed from a more proximate gunner at the start of the engagement (Corporal Melia, a Royal Electrical and Mechanical Engineers (REME) mine-disposal expert), one man was killed by a mortar fragment as he tried to retrieve a wounded friend as he came into the gorse gully (Corporal Prior). Three men were killed crawling up Darwin Hill (Captain Dent, Corporal Hardman, Captain Wood), and one was killed running towards a machine-gun position (Lieutenant Colonel Jones). Another man, Lieutenant Richard Nunn of 3 Commando Brigade Air squadron, Royal Marines, was killed when his helicopter was shot down as he attempted to evacuate 2 Para's Commanding Officer. The death toll was not high by historical standards, but the numbers show intense fighting. All the men died in a period of around twelve to thirteen hours, between crossing the start-line and the attempt to take the surrender in the mid-afternoon.

On Longdon, between twenty-nine and fifty Argentines died, and it is not possible to say whether they were killed by paratroopers at close quarters, or by bombardment from distant guns.[50] Of the British soldiers, eleven of the twenty-three who died were killed by Argentine artillery, four of those after the Argentines on the mountain had been defeated at daybreak on 12 June. Corporal McLaughlin, Lance Corporal Higgs, Lance Corporal Lovett and Corporal Wilson (9 Parachute Squadron Royal Engineers) were killed by shellfire during the fighting. Corporal McCarthy and Privates Hedicker and West were killed by a direct hit just before dawn on 12 June; and Privates Absolon, Bull, Jones and Craftsman Shaw (REME) all died on 13 June.[51]

Of the twelve men shot by Argentine gunfire, Private Jenkins was killed and Corporal Hope sustained fatal injuries early into A Company's advance. Lance Corporal Murdoch, Lance Corporal Scott, Private Laing, Private Greenwood and Private Dodsworth were killed by Argentine fire at close quarters after B Company 6 Platoon was pinned back, having missed the Argentine positions as they climbed the mountain. Privates Burt, Grose and Scrivens were shot during the advances of 4 and 5 Platoons and Private Crow was shot as 5 Platoon tried again to unblock the deadlock. Sergeant McKay was killed running towards a machine-gun post. Artillery fired from a distance and guns fired from close range were thus fatal in almost equal measure, and B Company, who had the task of the silent night advance, took the brunt of the casualties. Only three men across both battalions – Jones, McKay and Bingley – were killed attempting a frontal charge on a trench.

7.   Comrades

At Goose Green that first night – 28 May – early into D Company's engagement, a bullet hit Private Dave Parr in his stomach and he fell, in pain. His section commander, Corporal Walter McAuley, told me he checked him, carried him a short distance away and gave him morphine.[1] 2 Para's medics came forward, under fire, to tend to him and the other casualties. The fighting was only a hundred or so metres away. Dave was the first casualty treated by Lance Corporal Bill Bentley. Bentley cut away Dave's clothes and found no wound.

Bentley 'asked him again, "Where does it hurt?" "In my belly," he moaned painfully. I [Bentley] told the P.T. Sergeant, who was helping me, to shine his torch so that I could see what I was doing.' He was taking a risk by shining a light, but Bentley needed to see what injury this young soldier had. The sergeant shielded the torch with his body. What Bentley found was surprising. 'There, nesting in . . . [Parr's] belly button was a 7.62mm spent head!' The round had hit Dave's webbing, exploded his water bottle, gone through a pouch and followed the curve of the inside of his belt. Around his navel was a burnt ring, but 'unbelievably, [the bullet had] come to rest without breaking his skin exactly in his belly button'.[2]

In reality, the moment must have been very highly charged. Dave was afraid he had been mortally wounded, and that fear was causing the pain. Captain Steven Hughes, 2 Para's doctor, said: 'Bill was rummaging around in his webbing and found this round in his umbilicus, and then made some very caustic comments, you haven't been shot . . . you're a lazy . . .'[3] The medics had to move on to people whose lives might depend on them. They took or ordered Dave back to dead ground at the bottom of a small hill, a spot that became a collecting point for the wounded. Bentley gave Dave his sleeping bag and told him to rest. Private Parr's battle was over. Perhaps a physically bigger man – he was slender and wiry – would have better withstood the impact of the bullet. Maybe a more experienced soldier might have more easily put aside the terror of being hit and gone forward to rejoin the company right away.

Later, Private Parr was evacuated by helicopter with other casualties to the field hospital set up in a former meat-packing factory in Ajax Bay. On 30 or 31 May, he returned to the battalion and stayed with them in Goose Green until they transferred to Fitzroy. Major Neame, the Commanding Officer of D Company, and Lieutenant Colonel David Chaundler, who was flown from London to replace Jones as Commanding Officer of 2 Para, said that Dave wanted to come back. It was not normal practice for men to return to battle from the field hospital – he would have had to display some aptitude at getting himself into a helicopter to make the journey to rejoin the battalion. He returned because he still wanted to be a part of it. His fellow private Tony Banks said, 'nobody ordered him to do that'.[4]

★

Comradeship was a kind of love – a love that created the bonds between the men – but it was also the responsibility and obedience of rank, their loyalty to the Parachute Regiment and the readiness of the individual to play his part in the regimental whole. The volunteer soldier, the man who could have chosen otherwise but wanted to be there, was thus an essential element in the dedicated professional regiment. These men were not conscripts. They had passed out of one of the hardest training and selection regimes in the world, and they accepted their roles. The men leaving the UK for the Falklands felt that they could not have missed the experience: it was everything they had prepared for. Their volition, their will to be part of the battle, helped to explain the way that it progressed. It helped, too, to ease some of the anxiety about dying in battle. The regiment as a collective was larger than the sum of the individuals in it: they had chosen to be part of its mission.

After battle and the shock of being hit, the knowledge that men had died, wanting to do it looked different. Dave was in the field hospital among the wounded. Private Tony Coxall had been shot in

the leg and was also there in the makeshift ward. Coxall said that
Dave was concerned that he had used up his luck: 'He was worried
about having to go back out there.'[5] Dave wrote to his mother and
told her what had happened: 'Today I am sitting in a field hospital
waiting to return to my unit. I managed to catch a bullet in the belly
but fortunately it hit my zip first and only grazed me. I am fine now,
and have taken up a temporary new job as a tea boy while they try to
find my kit.' His letter was light-hearted, but there was a suggestion
he was thinking, not of war and his comrades, but of home: 'Please
keep writing to me as I miss you all a lot and haven't had a letter for
three weeks now, but I don't suppose it's through you not writing,
more likely to be the supply lines. Hope you are all OK (+ Gyp) and
give my love to everyone, see you soon, love, Dave.'[6]

Perhaps Dave was ordered to go back. 2 Para had taken casualties
at Goose Green and some men were out of action with trench foot.
The battalion needed to make up their numbers. It is not likely there
was a direct order, but rather that Dave knew his life in the battalion
would be over if he did not return. He had not been badly wounded.
Although men who appreciated his presence among their ranks
would understand on one level if he went home early, he would never
restore their faith and respect in him. He would always be known as
the man who had taken fright, whose bruised stomach gave him an
excuse to leave them to face the danger, while he remained safe. He
would be known as a coward. Some of the men in the regiment would
not have tolerated his departure and – most likely – he would have
been forced to leave when he got home.

One soldier, senior to Dave, told me: 'I said to him, get yourself in
that [get stuck in] . . . I've always said, I've always blamed myself, if I
hadn't have said, you be with your mates, he would still be alive. And
I've always regretted that. But he wanted to be with his mates, you
know? There was nothing I could do. He showed me his wound, he
went, look. I said, let me see your wound. He says, as far as I'm concerned, from Captain Hughes – who's the medical officer – if you
want, you're fit for battle. Anybody asks you, you're fit for battle.
And he was happy as Larry. He wanted to be with his friends. And I
don't think, I think if he had have gone back to the boat [the hospital

ship, *Uganda*], he would have hung himself anyway. He wanted to be with his friends. Simple.'[7]

Possibly, he had been told that he did not have to go back to a front-line position, or else he might have thought that 2 Para was unlikely to be in action again. In his letter home, he consoled his mother – and comforted himself – by saying that he would only be going back to routine duties: 'I should be returning to what we call a rear echelon position (stores etc.) so nothing too hectic this time. Anyway I think they will give 2 Para a rest now as we've all had our fair share, and the CO is dead. I think we will be coming home soon so please don't worry about me.'[8]

In hospital, he was concerned he had used up his portion of luck, but once he was back with the battalion he became more optimistic. At Goose Green, he slept in a house belonging to islanders Keith and Ginnie Baillie. They later told Mike Seear: 'He reckoned that luck was on his side.'[9] It was not so much that he had exhausted his ration of good fortune, but that he would always have chance with him.

8. Dave at Fitzroy, between the battles of Goose Green and Wireless Ridge, after coming back to the battalion from the field hospital.

9. 10 June 1982, waiting to move by helicopter from Fitzroy. With Private Terry Stears and Lance Corporal Neil Turner. Dave is on the left, holding his rifle.

The soldiers around him forced him, or gave him a way, to see himself as a good omen. He had dodged death once and could do it again. He wanted to be a paratrooper, and so he had no option and he found ways to feel better about it. With his comrades, he knew the things he had to say and do. That way, he gave himself hope.

★

Soldiers' first experiences of the deaths of their friends – of men they knew well, of men they looked up to and admired, of men they commanded and looked after – disrupted their perceptions of what battle was like, especially when they had time to dwell on it afterwards. They did not expect death to come to them, and in the moment their minds found ways to blot out the impact of the death of their fellow soldiers. Private Bill Metcalfe, D Company 3 Para, remembered: 'Suddenly, as we were moving through the darkness, I saw a black shape on the floor in front of me, and to be honest I thought it may have been a dead sheep. As I got nearer I realized it was a body.'[10] Sergeant Mac French, Headquarters Company, 3 Para, said: 'I saw what I thought was a tailor's dummy; for some reason I was convinced that's what it was, thinking that these crafty Argentines had been playing tricks. I went over and touched it. My fingers sunk into real flesh, completely pale and unreal looking, dead for about three days.'[11] Sometimes they just carried on. 3 Para's Corporal Morham wrote: 'the medic . . . was bending over the body of Lance Corporal Scott. He said Scott was dead and that his magazines and grenades were being removed for the use of other soldiers.'[12]

For many men, witnessing the death of comrades was shocking. It was hard to believe that a man who moments ago had been laughing, joking, asking for a cigarette, blowing on his hands to warm himself up, had been terminated. It was difficult to countenance that, before death, men were just like the men who survived. There was nothing special, or unusual, or marked about men who were about to die. As Private Dean Coady expressed it: 'Tim [Jenkins] . . . died. Only the day before we had been celebrating Tim's 19th birthday and mine the week before and I thought, "What the fuck am I doing here? Tim's dead, I'm 8,000 miles away from home, I'm being shot at and my mate is lying dead next to me". I felt numb. I lay by Tim's body for some time after he had died, and then someone gave me a mug of tea.'[13]

It was terrible to see the deadness of the dead, hard to accept that their living had just ceased. Lance Corporal Bill Bentley remembered carrying Gary Bingley's body on a poncho. Bingley had been a battalion character, so physically courageous, now incapable of preventing the involuntary movements of his head: 'I helped the Padre carry Gaz [Lance Corporal Bingley] back to the regimental aid post in a poncho. I will never forget that short walk, his head kept banging against my knee.'[14] Many men reported disbelief on learning of those who had died: ' "Are you sure he [Tim Jenkins] is dead?" And Louie said, "Yes, I'm sure." It sounds daft now, but it suddenly dawned on me, that this was the real thing, and I thought, "Fucking hell, this is happening".'[15] Under fire, the instants that turned life into death were unpredictable, and mundane. According to Private Eyles-Thomas, 'I sat there not believing what had happened. One minute I was talking to Scrivs [Ian Scrivens] with my hand on his shoulder and the next he was gone.'[16]

At other times, the men witnessed deaths that were vile and distressing. They had not previously known the effects shellfire could have on the human body: 'In front of me, there was this guy on his face, shaking and convulsing on the ground, lying on his stomach, I dropped the load that I had with some rations, and I went over and turned him over, the sight that I seen from there was absolutely horrendous. The artillery shell had landed right close to him . . . the blast had gone up and an artillery shell at that range, I found out to my horror, it takes off everything that was showing, he had no hands, and his face was completely missing, and it was horrible, absolutely horrible, and that is etched in my mind. I was so horrified, I was just stuck, looking at him, it was horrible.'[17]

The deaths of men higher in the ranks could leave the men under their command feeling vulnerable. Lance corporals, corporals – these were the men who looked after them, trained them, whom they looked up to and strove to emulate. Corporal Scott Wilson of 9 Parachute Squadron Royal Engineers was widely admired among the men who served under him. Sapper Martin Glover recalled, on learning of Wilson's death: 'I found this hard to take in as Scotty was my second-in-command during my last tour in Northern Ireland and when I first joined 9 Squadron, he was a sort of older "mentor" to me. I found it really hard to understand that he could actually be dead.'[18] Men who were highly respected, experienced, reliable soldiers were not, as they had appeared in the minds of new recruits, invincible. And if they were not invincible, then nobody was.

The strict hierarchies between ranks could be questioned if men died, or if they needed help. Private Mark Eyles-Thomas, who was seventeen, was told to look after Corporal Ned Kelly, a highly respected soldier, after Kelly sustained a bad stomach wound: 'Corporal Kelly was renowned for having a short temper . . . I feared I might fuck up and end up being shot by him . . . He winced, not wishing to show any discomfort. He was a hard man and I admired his courage. I felt useless and alien . . . Corporal Kelly stared at me and I could not look away. Without saying my name he directed me to look at his wound. In a split second, thousands of thoughts rushed through my head. What if half his stomach is hanging out. What do I tell him? What if I can't help him? What if? I braced myself . . .' Eyles-Thomas lifted Kelly's smock. Parts of his intestine were hanging out of his wound. The private knew he was supposed to push them back in: 'I asked whether he wanted me to do it. Corporal Kelly . . . looked at me menacingly . . . Finally he nodded his head . . . Removing my blood-stained gloves I pushed the protruding stomach back inside, devoid of any emotion . . . He stared at me. "Don't let me fall asleep," he said.'[19]

Lance Corporal Graham Tolson recalled being comforted by a young private soldier after he developed battle shock. He was ordered by his sergeant to collect the British dead: 'For a moment I stared at him almost in disbelief, I squatted down and began to cry, I didn't want to do it, I felt sick, I collapsed on the floor sobbing. Pete Maddocks stooped down and put his arms around me and whispered, "Okay mate, it's okay." He helped me to my feet and ushered me away to the small bunker that we had found. For a minute or two we looked at each other in total silence. I was embarrassed by my behaviour because I was the NCO and he was a private soldier. Thankfully, Geordie broke the silence and said, "Do you want a brew?" . . . It was only after I had recovered my composure that I realized I had a condition called battle shock . . . it was short term and it passed within a couple of hours.'[20]

The death of a senior soldier was, in its small way, like the death of an idol. Company Sergeant Major Peter Richens said on learning of the death of Colonel Jones: 'I was horrified. My reaction was, Commanding Officers don't get killed.'[21] Private Mike Curtis thought, 'I don't believe this; the two most powerful men in the regiment [the commanding officer and the Adjutant] had been killed. The news hit me like a stomach punch and for the first time I considered the possibility that we might lose.'[22] Private Dean Ferguson said that after Goose Green, when they learnt that the commanding officer was dead, and how many others had been killed, his joy at their victory was tainted: 'When we heard he was killed . . . it was like something being ripped out of yer . . . you were like drunk on happiness, and then it was ripped out.'[23]

Men of senior rank inspired and sustained the confidence of their juniors. Major Crosland, the officer commanding B Company 2 Para, had a ferocious reputation, partly because he had fought with the SAS in Dhofar. He always wore a black woollen hat rather than a helmet. He never got riled and he had a dry and wicked sense of humour. Surveying shell holes with his company, he suggested that they had been made by 'bloody big moles'. Lieutenant Chapman said it would have been disastrous if Crosland had been killed: 'On the company level there was a profound faith in John Crosland. As long as he was OK we believed that we, as a collective unit, were also invincible.'[24]

2 Para's doctor, Captain Steven Hughes, said that Jones was a boss 'he adored, because he was dynamic, motivated and . . . actually quite shy'.[25] Jones was a role model for Hughes. His death, like the deaths of others in positions of command, ruptured a certainty, unfixed a miniature world. Jones was killed alongside two other admired soldiers, Captains Chris Dent and David Wood. Hughes said: 'My world just sort of was falling to pieces, and I knew that if I allowed myself to break down then I would cease to function, the regimental aid post would cease to function, and I could see my medics looking at me to see what I was going to do. Because if I went down, they would go down as well, because they'd all lost friends. And I . . . it's like I just put a great big shutter over those emotions and put them to the back of my mind . . .'[26]

For older men, the deaths of young soldiers could also be hard to take. Sergeant John Weeks cried at Longdon, away from the men, to vent what he was feeling.[27] Major Roger Patton, the second in command of 3 Para, recalled: 'I stopped for a moment and sat on a rock. I got this strange feeling, it was as if I had left my body and I was up above the RAP [regimental aid post], looking down on that terrible scene. It was probably due to lack of sleep, and stress. I hadn't got much sleep over the time we were on Longdon; all I managed was the occasional cat nap.'[28] Sergeant Des Fuller said that, looking at the body-bags, and how 'bloody good' the Toms (men in the ranks) had been, 'I could feel the tears welling up in my eyes'.[29]

Thirty-four-year-old Colour Sergeant Brian Faulkner, HQ

Company 3 Para, had joined the regiment in 1964. He was in charge of the aid post on Longdon and spent three days treating and organizing the casualties. Interviewed by a senior officer after the war, he said: 'Well, yes, it was an experience, sir. The way that the men ran into the hail of fire and assaulted it, it was fantastic to watch, especially those young soldiers, I will never forget it.'[30] Faulkner knew his role was to send the men back up the mountain after they had brought wounded comrades to the aid post: 'I kept looking up and there was all this tracer and gunfire coming down and bodies being blown up by shells and I was having to say to these lads, "Up you go – get them out", and up they went without hesitation.'[31] Faulkner was not safe from death where he was, but he was also aware of the responsibility of his rank, sending younger men into the intense fire.

The death of friends – real friends – was perhaps the hardest thing of all. These were men they knew not just as soldiers, but also as men who they might have socialized with at home, and they knew details about their lives. They would miss them as people, not just as comrades. Private David Barclay, on hearing of Private Ged Bull's death, said: 'I couldn't believe it; I had only spoken to him earlier. I went back down towards the Second Bowl [one of the geographical features on Longdon] where I saw a poncho covering a body. I pulled back part of it, I am not sure why, it may have been just for absolute confirmation, but there he was. I was gutted, I knew Ged well, and I had gone out with his sister and knew his mum and dad. I felt numb and made my way back and tried to compose myself.'[32]

The young soldiers often relied on each other; and sometimes they could rely most totally on the men they had known in the Depot. They depended on each other to get by. The reliance they had on each other, and the responsibility they took for each other, could linger after death. Private Les Davis was affected by the death of a man in the battalion he had had a fist fight with one night, a man who had subsequently become his friend: 'Down in the Falklands, the day of the battle, as we're getting ready, he actually came up to me, and told me that he wasn't going to make it through the battle. No matter what I said to him, it wasn't going to go [pause]. He said, "I want you to do me a favour." I said, "Well, I'm not going to bring you off the mountain because I can't." He said he understood that. He says, "I want you to make sure I'm all there. I've got two arms, two legs, a body and a head." I said, "I can do that, but . . ." [pause]. He did die that night, he was shot in the head. From what I can remember, the way he fell, it was as if he'd just fallen asleep from exhaustion.'[33]

Private Mark Eyles-Thomas was overwhelmed by the deaths of Privates Jason Burt, Neil Grose and Ian Scrivens, the three young recruits he had trained with. He described his agony and disbelief as each one was killed. Private Mick Southall, also seventeen years old, said: 'The young man [Grose] was in an awful lot of pain. We got him on a poncho but unfortunately for him he wouldn't lie still because he was so badly injured. We did as best we could. We got him to the regimental aid post. There was one person at his head and I was at his feet. The medic . . . was trying everything he could. Neil was in an awful amount of distress. Then all of a sudden it went quiet. And [pause] that's when he went [pause] . . . Yes [the image of Neil is still with me] . . . Very much.'[34]

Southall was devastated at the death of his friend, but also angry, partly because Grose had died and there was nothing anyone could do, and partly he was angry at Grose for not being saved: 'We had risked a lot to save him [and at the cost, in some accounts, of Scrivens' death] and now it seemed it was all in vain. I felt cheated and angry . . . I just stood there for God knows how long just looking down at my friend who was now lying there, covered over with a poncho.'[35]

Private Tony Banks remembered that at Goose Green Private Steve Dixon was shot. As he died, 'he sighed his last word: "Mum". Then a single tear rolled down his face.'[36] But it was not just the obvious sadness of the scene that upset Banks and the other men who witnessed it. Rather, the men became aware of a truth that they all knew but could usually ignore. At the moment of his death, Dixon did not want his mates, his paratrooper identity. He wanted his mother. His longing for his mother exposed the fragility underneath what they all had to do. The consolations of a death for the regiment might not be quite as they had appeared, now, as life was extinguished.

Banks felt guilty. All the men around Dixon, all the men in the platoon, the regiment, but perhaps particularly his mates, had been a part of the reasons that Dixon was there in the first place. Like Faulkner sending men back up the mountain, their own roles in the regiment, in the battle, the jokes they had all made at the expense of civilians, their families, their mothers, were part of the process that had brought men to the start-line and that led some men to die. There was no reason why Dixon should have been shot and not the next man. It was, to a great extent, dependent on the nature of the incoming fire, completely random. It was down to chance, but that could be hard to accept.

The men saw themselves, in the scope of the battalion's purpose, as interchangeable with each other. It should not matter who lived and who died, because that was what war was about, but the simple fact was that it mattered more than anything else, because death was an end. If they had survived, perhaps they had not been trying hard enough. The dead had given their all, and perhaps the men who survived had not. If their mates died, perhaps they had not been good enough soldiers to prevent it.

★

Time to think was necessary, but dwelling on such things also made life harder. The period after the battle could be the most unbearable time of all. The Company Sergeant Major of B Company 2 Para, Peter Richens, said in interview: 'In the height of battle, when the adrenaline is running, when you see people shot, gory sights, people dying, a lot of men screaming, you hear a lot of noise, a lot of crying, you just roll on and do your job. But when things settle down, and you go back and look for the bodies and it is very cold, a lot of the bodies were frozen and they were not dead like many people think, lying prone hands across the chest kind of thing, it was people were shot and as they fell that's the positions they had to be picked up in.'[37]

Initially, some commanders did order men to collect the bodies of their own troops, but later, it seems, they did not insist.[38] According to Company Sergeant Major John Weeks, 'That was the hardest thing, the hardest thing I have ever done. I knew all of the people;

obviously some time had lapsed since they had died, rigor mortis had set in, I had to pick them up, take the grid reference, put them in a body bag, take them to a central location and document them one by one. You can't order a man to do it. As Sergeant Major I can order anyone to do lots of things, but you can't order a person to help you document the bodies. Especially I had Clarkson-Kearsley with me, tremendous young lad, he was in tears same as I was in tears, when you have to go forward and pick up the bodies.'[39]

The task of sorting the dead was difficult in part because it was personal. Weeks recalled: 'We weren't supposed to carry things with us, photos and that, but without exception those bodies had a photo of their mum, dad, wife, children, and it's heartbreaking, absolutely heartbreaking.'[40] It was also grim. Men had not died peacefully, but lay contorted, their bodies brutalized. Private Dean Edwards, Support Company 2 Para, said: 'I remember walking across the ground, all these bodies littering the place, I remember one kid, I remember thinking at the time, he was laid flat on his back like that, it was almost like he was beseeching, it looked to me like that.'[41] Private Ken Lukowiak from the same company said: 'The dead man's elbow was pointed skywards and his hand still gripped the clothing around his wound. Because of the protruding elbow, they could not fit the corpse into its bag. An officer . . . tried to straighten the corpse's elbow . . . He . . . got to his feet and began to kick the elbow down.'[42]

Lance Corporal Jon Cook, C Company 3 Para, recalled: 'We found out afterwards it [the shell] hit one of them direct, completely gone. Trying to find him the next day, and found an ear on the rock, and mince meat, if you know what I'm saying. That's where the explosion . . . but like, [Soldier Z], all you could see from him was a little trickle of blood out of his nose and ear, but he had his internal organs, imploded with the shockwaves of the explosion. Also, with [Soldier Y], he lived I think for 45 minutes, and we were firing on that gunline trying to treat him, I think it was for 45 minutes, but he was a big bloke . . . and apparently from his legs down was still intact, but they weren't, they'd all been imploded. He's one of the ones we had to . . . it took 4 or 5 of us the next day to put him in a body bag. His legs were like pulp. The skin was still . . . but there was nothing there. That's one little experience.'[43]

Some men reported sorrow, or feelings of physical sickness, when they saw the Argentine dead too. Private Paul Hutchinson, B Company 3 Para, said: 'The searching of the [Argentine] bodies was a very emotional job indeed, as most of the bodies were terribly damaged by shrapnel and small-arms fire. As I looked at their family photographs, personal possessions and rosary beads, etc. it really brought home to you, as one soldier to another, the madness of it all.'[44] Lance Corporal Tolson said: 'There was a guy hit in the midriff by an anti-tank rocket, his upper torso still stuck to the rock, he was spread-eagled on this rock, and he was still wearing a quilted jacket, and with his blood and that, that stuck to the rock, it sort of resembled a tarring and a feathering really, and his legs were totally separate from his body, lying on the ground below this vision, this horrible vision of this guy. I was sick, immediately sick, it made me sick, physically sick.'[45]

Other men took photographs of Argentine corpses. Lukowiak said that 'one soldier picked up a dead Argentine, supported the corpse's weight under his arm, put a cigarette in the dead man's mouth and then one in his own. He held a lighter under the corpse's cigarette and his friend took a photograph. They both laughed. I also laughed.'[46] On Wireless Ridge, men found two corpses, one with no head, the other with no legs, and photographed them.[47] Tolson said of the devastated body that had made him sick: 'Other people were filing past to where this sight, this bloke, was, and we could hear them laughing, taking the mickey, looking back it was not a normal reaction but it was the only reaction to that situation, it helped them to cope, if you had broke down at that stage you wouldn't want to go on, it was horrible.'[48]

Sorting their own dead, they could not so easily joke or deflect the horror with black humour; and nor could they treat the British bodies as objects of grotesque fascination. Rather, they tried to take care with their own dead: 'Private Harley shouted to us from the top of the ridge. He had found a severed arm which belonged to one of our bodies and he would take it to the Padre. In retrospect the action seems pointless, even macabre, but at the time it had meaning. A similar reverence for our dead seems to have prevented any photography of them, whereas the vanquished enemy were regarded as a much lower form of death.'[49] They did not want to remember their mates, their comrades, as distorted, shot-up bodies, but as the men they had been before they died. The Argentine dead were the spoils of war. The British dead were their comrades, and were a tribute to the regiment. It was not always possible, then, confronted with the evidence of British dead, to deflect emotion in the same way as when they dealt with the enemy dead, or in the same way as they did during the battle.

Men expected some level of shock or sadness at what had happened. The battalion acknowledged that men would feel sad at the loss of their comrades. At the time, the post-operations medical report said: 'Recent conflicts have not prepared the infantryman for dealing with his dead on the scale produced by this intense war. There is no doubt that some units were shocked by the relative lack of ceremony with which some funerals took place and the manner, group graves and bodybags in which the dead were buried.'[50]

Private Mark Eyles-Thomas recalled: 'I arrived at the spot where I'd left Grose's body and knelt by his side. The poncho still covered him, his army boots sticking out of the end. I stared at the poncho, removed from the situation, unable to relate to my friend. Needing to see him for a final time I lifted the poncho from his head. Nothing had changed – Grose was gone.'[51] Lance Corporal Vincent Bramley 'stood and looked down at Westy [Private Philip West]. His small, five-feet-three frame lay as if he was asleep on his back. I couldn't see any marks to show how he died. Lying on his chest, just out of reach of his fingers, was a small greyish teddy bear with a little ribbon round its neck. Westy's face was turned to one side . . . Had Westy pulled the mascot from his smock before the fatal shell, or after?'[52]

They could feel shocked and sad, but the men were not encouraged to grieve. They had to lock their feelings away. 'My mind quickly closed the door to emotion in preparation for whatever grotesque tableau might be waiting around the next rock. Soldiers quickly develop the necessary immunity to the varied sights of death, and this creates an outward appearance of indifference and callousness . . . We . . . took up new positions in sangars built by the Argentines, where we began to brew tea and eat chocolate, as if breakfasting on a hill covered in unburied corpses was something we did every day.'[53]

Most suppressed what they felt and got on with what they had to do. It was not so long until the Argentines began to surrender, and then the men felt the exhilaration that comes with survival. When the Paras returned home, Major General John Frost spoke to them of the deep pride the regiment had in what they had achieved.[54] They had succeeded. Their friends had lost their lives in the greatest victory the Parachute Regiment had scored since the Second World War, in intense close-quarters fighting that might never be seen again. Their sadness, their revulsion, their sense – if they had it – of the unhinging of their worlds, should be closed and transformed instead into the regrettable cost of victory, the turning of history, the sacrifice of war. That was how to honour the dead. That was how they must remember them. They had all been comrades. They had stepped up to the responsibility afforded them. They were united by a special pride, and bonded even closer by the combat of their generation. That was how to make sense of everything they had done.

8. Fear

The men in the Parachute Regiment dreamed about battle, and saw glory in death, but nobody fantasized about being injured. As Major Chris Keeble said, 'No, I was not scared of dying. What I was scared of was being physically maimed and returning from this conflict as a vegetable. I did not want to return to my family . . . unable to fulfil that responsibility.'[1] Being injured did not achieve the glory or recognition of death in battle. It was a half-hearted sort of reckoning. It was emasculating and left men unable to assume their military and domestic responsibilities. Once it happened, the most determined among them expected nothing: 'It was part of our briefing, that if you're injured you won't get picked up. You have to win that little battle. They [the Argentines] have to die, be put into submission, before we can start looking after others . . . I knew the moment I was hit that I was staying there until these fellas were dead, and I was quite happy to do that. Strange as it is, but that's the Parachute Regiment mentality, I'm afraid, and that's how we lived our lives.'[2]

If there was a characteristic emotion of battle, then it was not hatred, nor anger, nor love – it was fear. Lord Moran, who was a doctor with troops in the First World War and later became Winston Churchill's physician, said that everybody was afraid. Even those who appeared fearless were usually bluffing. Fear, he said, was felt differently at various times, and men could be afraid of different things. The longer they had been exposed to fear, the harder, he thought, they found to endure it.[3]

Underlying all fear was a terror of dying, but even that was not absolute. For many of the paratroopers in the Falklands, the hardest thing to make sense of was the arbitrariness of the violence; and the hardest thing to bear was not so much the prospect of death – although when it came to it, nobody wanted to die – as the way that pain, or wounding, or terror, left men unarmed. For Lord Moran, courage was a question of will. Courage was a man's determination, embedded deep in his character, to overcome fear. This deep belief informed how the paratroopers thought about fear; but what they found sometimes was that even if they possessed that courage, even if their will to carry on had not been broken, they could still be left without the means of fighting back.

★

When injury came, it was unexpected, even alien. Corporal Margerison told me: 'When I got to get up I just felt this terrific smack, like I'd been hit in the face with a shovel. Just those proverbial stars, the white light and the stars. I was already on the floor, and I just felt it.'[4] When he was shot in the leg, 2 Para's Private Coxall said that he shouted out, 'I've been hit by a brick.' For that moment, it seemed more plausible that the Argentines were throwing bricks at him than firing guns. 'I'd never been shot before,' he added.[5] Lieutenant John Page, shot on Wireless Ridge, said 'it was like being hit by a sledgehammer and having an electric shock, all at once'.[6] Corporal Phil Skidmore, on Longdon, 'was blown over, and I felt like I'd been hit by a sledge hammer'. Corporal Ian Bailey: 'At first, I thought I had tripped but a round had struck me square in the right hip.' Private Grant Grinham 'changed position and within a split second Mick got shot in the leg. I heard the round hit him. It sounded like someone had hit him with a cricket bat or something. I admit it sounds daft now, but I did have a giggle to myself, thinking that could have been me! It was weird because he didn't even shout out. He said something like, "Oh, I've been shot!" '[7]

In the shock of the moment, many men maintained a robust defence against pain. Later, Grinham's own leg was blown off. Sergeant Fuller recalled: 'Grinham was just sat there, he said "The bastards, I'm only 21, I just lost a leg." He was very calm, he just sat there.' Fuller's signaller, Private Cullen, was shot in the mouth: 'I shouted my signaller to come to me, he couldn't speak, every time he spoke he got a mouth full of spittle and teeth; Cullen, he was laughing, he thought it was funny he couldn't signal.'[8]

The extent of Margerison's injury did not dawn on him straight away, as he tried to get up: 'Then I felt my arm get hit, like another bang . . . I'm trying to shout, "I'm alright, just leave me for a minute and let me get ready to get up." But I'm not shouting because this [his mouth] is just pissing blood, that's ripped right all the way around there. All these, the top of my top lip, it was hanging down. Lots of debris, and plus I'd now been hit in my right shoulder, but I fell onto this arm . . . it was broken, smashed.'[9] Two of his colleagues dragged him to safety.

Private Worrall, who was shot with A Company in the gorse gully, felt pain immediately and started to panic about the extent of his injury. He tried, and failed, to rescue himself: 'First feeling was like fire, like burning, really really burning sensation on my left-hand side, put my hand over it, felt the blood, started to flap at first, thinking oh my God. I got my field dressing and slapped it on, and then I just lay there . . . I was conscious of what I should be doing. I was trying to do too much. I tried to crawl into cover.'[10] Private O'Connell also began to fear what had happened to him: '[What] I next remember was being thrown backwards – something had glanced across my face, my helmet had come off, and my front teeth were missing and my mouth was filling up with blood. I knew something was badly wrong with my face, and straight away I put my hand to my face, and thought, "Oh fuck! . . . Oh fuck, my nose has come off!"'[11]

Lance Corporal Carver was shot at close range as 3 Para's B Company 5 Platoon attempted to advance. He continued fighting until he could not do any more: 'It was a twenty-round magazine he let fly at us. I was in mid-air diving for cover. There wasn't any cover, I was going for the edges, the side. And the bullet hit me in the side, here, and went through my left lung, hit my front rib, and bounced back out through my back. But it threw me back about six or seven foot, and I ended up rolling down, because it was a slope. I still had my weapon in my hand. I rolled down about ten or fifteen foot, into a slight depression, and even though I knew I'd been hit – because I could feel the pain – I just put the rifle up and started returning fire. Because they were up in the rocks then, there was three of them, and they were firing down. It was a proper ambush, it was a kill zone. So the rounds were all coming in, and again like *Private Ryan*, they were winging past me, and I was in this position, and a round went through my smock sleeve, hit there, went underneath me, and a couple either side, and all of a sudden my lung just burst, where it'd been hit, and all the blood come out my nose, out my mouth, and I just thought, "Well that's it, I can't do any more." I couldn't fire any more, I just laid my weapon down, put my head on it – I had a helmet on – and I just lay there like that.'[12]

★

Of course, once they were injured, men did fear they would die. It was worse perhaps – being wounded and in pain – because they knew it could be otherwise. They wanted treatment, they wanted to survive, but they knew that others would put themselves in peril retrieving them. Sometimes they did not want to insist on help for themselves when they could see that others were wounded and sometimes they could see that there was nothing more the medics, or anyone, could do to help them. As paratroopers they had learnt to block out their emotions, to cut out their weakness, leaving only their stoicism to prepare them for lying, freezing, feeling terrible pain. Private O'Connell 'was drifting in and out of consciousness. I was absolutely frozen to the core, I honestly thought, "I'm dying here". At some point I blacked out . . . I couldn't see anything because of the shell dressings covering my face. I was completely drained and too weak to move. I could hear the voices of the stretcher-bearers chatting. I think I must have moved, because one of them said, "Fucking hell, this one's alive!"'[13]

Private Worrall waited six hours before he was evacuated: 'I was saying "get the choppers". My fear of dying had set in by then.'[14] Captain Steven Hughes, 2 Para's medic, recalled that Worrall was holding folds of his small bowel in his lap: 'he was really worried'.[15] Lance Corporal Denzil Connick was hit by a shell and his legs were blown off. His story was recounted: 'Just as they stopped to chat [Connick was with Craftsman Shaw and Private Jones, who were both killed] he heard an almighty woosh and they began diving for cover . . . He landed on his stomach with all the wind knocked out of him. His helmet had been blown off and his mouth was full of dirt. For a second he began to panic. "That was close," he told himself. But he had barely uttered the thought when he felt a burning sensation surging through his entire body. He turned over and sat up to see what the problem was. His left leg was hanging off and his right was riddled with shrapnel. The shock of it made him scream.'[16] According to Private Pat Harley, 'He [Connick] was biting the grass, he was in so much pain.'[17] Lance Corporal Cliff Legg said: 'I remember Denzil was saying, "Don't let me die, lads, don't let me die, I don't give a fuck about my legs, just don't let me die."'[18]

Margerison had dreamed of dying, but now it took effort not to die. He had to will himself not to give in to sleep: 'I remember saying . . . "Take me to the RAP [regimental aid post], I'm just going to get my head down, I'm absolutely knackered." John Crosland, the officer commanding B Company, went, "You're not going to sleep, listen to what I'm saying mate, you're dying mate, you're dying of bad shock, you need to stay awake for me." And I just said, "Yeah, alright boss, not a problem" . . . I do believe that, apart from the guys giving me rest and reassurance, and the boss saying no, you're gonna die mate, I thought fuck, I don't want to really die here, I've got things to do. I certainly wasn't going.'[19]

If it seemed that there was no choice, then it was possible to become resigned to death, to cease to struggle against it. Carver was hit and rolled down a slope. He was still being shot at. 'Rounds were coming in at me. I remember it like yesterday. I was cool, calm, I wasn't screaming, I just lay there, and I thought, "This is it, just wait for it." I knew I was hit, because [of] the pain, I could feel all the blood coming out of my wounds, out of my mouth. I was trying to stop myself from choking, so I was spitting the blood out, but it was almost like I was resigned to the fact, I've pushed it too far, I've gone one step too far and this is it.' It was not long before two comrades ran to pull him out of the fire, but during that time, as his mouth and nose filled with blood, Carver was aware of a strongly scented blossom from trees in the garden he had played in as a child, on the driveway: 'I had that smell in my nose, and straight away my thoughts went back to walking up that driveway.' He did not believe in God, but he wondered later: 'Was I walking, in my head, was I walking up that driveway towards the light, or something?'[20]

At the point of death, many men called out to their mothers. Some men – the survivors who reported their comrades' last words – believed that this was because they were transported back to innocent times, before the killing and the cruelty of combat. The dying man was no longer on the battlefield, and could die without the noise and the fear of battle, in the midst of happier memories: 'After about five or ten minutes Doc [Lance Corporal Murdoch] stopped asking for his mother and died. I believe the moment Doc Murdoch was shot his mind was not on Longdon, he was somewhere else, in his childhood maybe. I truly believe Doc passed away in his own world peacefully; it was absolutely heartbreaking.'[21]

Other men knew that their mates would forget them, no matter how hard they tried; because they knew that they would feel the same way if they survived: 'We were paratroopers – we loved no one. We had not been taught to love. If one of us died, then no it was not a happy event, but . . . not one of us had been forced to join the Army. We were professional soldiers. We fought for the living not the dead – the dead were dead.'[22]

Their mothers were the only people who would mourn for them. Perhaps they wanted to feel they had counted for something; that their death would matter to a human being outside of the regimental annals. Perhaps they felt guilty for dying; they did not want their mothers to grieve, and in their last moments they thought about the pain their death would cause. Private Lukowiak recalled: 'Bill was sad . . . [he said] that he was thinking of how much his mother would suffer if he was to lose his life.' On finding a photograph of a dead Argentine's mother, 'We became sad for her and as we passed the photograph between us it made us once again think of our own mothers, back home in England.'[23]

Other men perhaps instinctively craved their first cradling, the comfort – on the brink of death – of the first arms that had held them. Men realized, at least later, that touch and speaking gently could soothe the distress of their friends and kindle their will to fight against death. Private Eyles-Thomas said in his memoir that he held

Neil Grose in his arms 'like a brother' before Grose died; staying with Grose, supporting and reassuring him, and comforting himself, and Grose's family, he felt that he had done what he could to alleviate his comrade's suffering.[24]

*

Pain, and fear of death, also mixed with the men's sense of who they were, and of their responsibilities to the other men around them. For Private Stephen Tuffen, 'That was my biggest concern after being injured, that I hadn't let the guys down. That bothered me for a long time, because I'd been shot I didn't know what had gone on, and my biggest [pause] I suppose this goes to show, camaraderie is probably the wrong word, but the respect you have for each other, and the fact I was more concerned about not letting them down than I was about my own injury. That might sound [like] it's only being said [for the sake of it], but that is gospel honest truth.' His anxiety that he had let down his mates was blended with his sense of his own capability, of who he wanted to be: 'I thought I was good at soldiering, but I couldn't have been that good, because I got shot.'[25] It was difficult to recall the sensations of pain as they had been felt at the time, but what lingered afterwards was fear that they had not been as good as they had hoped to be.

Mixed with that fear could be a sense of shame – shame that a man had failed at his art, shame that his failure had made things worse for his colleagues, the men on whose approval his own status and reputation depended. Corporal Margerison, a highly respected soldier, said: 'I couldn't move, and I'm absolutely disgusted first of all that I've been caught out. I should have never have got . . . I should never have stopped at the top of that hill and waited, but the daylight just came so quick.' He blamed himself for getting injured; he blamed himself for failing mentally to readjust to the fact of the light. He believed he could have avoided the shot if he had, at that moment, acted at the top of his game.

What caused his fear, perhaps, was the loss of control, his feeling that he had failed and left the men under his command in peril. He had been shot in the back from 300 yards away. He was lying, defence-less, his trousers pulled down to insert an intravenous drip through his anus. When it was inserted, without a cannula, his bowels opened involuntarily: 'It was like having an enema then. It was everywhere. But that probably helped save my life.' He feared he had let his men down, and if he had let his men down, how could he be the fine soldier he was, the embodiment of the regiment he loved? 'I'm not being rude. You haven't got a fucking clue what's in my heart, in my head, what I've lived . . . You've got to feel a buzz. You've got to feel it. It's a way of life. It's there . . . lying, bleeding, blood-sucking shit through my arse, my men are going to die. It feels terrible.'[26]

Supine, near death, his will unbroken but his body unable to fight, Margerison knew his life would change. It was not the story he wanted to return to England with; he found it hard to imagine explaining to people outside the regiment what had happened to him: 'This, then, is the beginning of the rest of your life, trying to justify, how do I tell people at home that I got shot in the back? How do you tell that you left your men on the ground?'[27]

He did not fear pain. He did not fear death. He could fight against death; he could bear pain. He possessed extraordinary courage, and he was a good soldier. If he was afraid, it was, in a sense, an even more awesome fear, because he felt he had been cast adrift. If he was afraid, it was because he could no longer be sure he was the paratrooper he had trained so hard to be and had proved that he was. Where could he turn to think of himself as different?

★

Most men said they felt fear when they came under fire – 'If you're not scared, then there's something wrong with you, it's petrifying' – but they thought about that fear in different ways. Corporal Tom Harley said that 'honesty' made a good soldier: 'To be honest with himself, to be trusted. If you're honest, you're trusted.' A soldier had to accept that he would die: 'For any soldier to do his job properly, you've got to accept death. You've got to accept the fact that you're going to die. And once you've done that you can go and do a bloody good job on the battlefield.'[28] Lieutenant Chapman recorded: 'A young soldier went up to Corporal Tom Harley, who . . . was already known as fearless in battle. He inquired of Harley: "Are you scared, Corporal?" Harley replied . . ."Of course I'm fucking scared. Now get back to your position and prepare to attack".'[29] By accepting he would die, Harley, like others around him, controlled his fear. None of them intended to invite death, but fear was part of their soldiering, and control of their fear made them able to take effective decisions. Major Neame, D Company Commander, reported the influence of Harley's openness to death. As Neame stood up to advance over open ground to take the Argentine surrender on the Boca House position, 'Corporal Harley dashed ahead saying, "You wait here, sir. We don't want to risk you on this. This is Toms' work".'[30]

Other men saw their own fear as selfishness, a limitation on their willingness or ability to fulfil their work as paratroopers. Private Ken Lukowiak, 2 Para Support Company, said: 'As I lay against the hedge I was willing my body to dissolve into the ground, I could not move, I did not want to move, I also did not wish to remain where I was . . . I knew I wanted [the Argentines firing at him] to die. The sooner the better.' Lukowiak confessed that when he thought he had been injured, his first thought was that he would get out of the battle: 'I felt a sharp pain in my back. It hurt so much that it didn't . . . My back felt very warm. I was convinced I was bleeding . . . I time flashed to the future . . . I was in a bed with white sheets. The bed was on a hospital ship. I could see a nurse. I returned to Goose Green, I said to myself, "Just get me the fuck out of here."'[31] It turned out he had been hit by a small piece of metal and was unhurt.

Others experienced a terror of dying that was debilitating. A 3 Para lance corporal recalled that he was hidden in a rocky bunker when he was ordered to go and form a work party to collect the dead: 'I was extremely terrified of venturing out of that bunker, it is the fear of knowing that if you go outside that bunker that you are going to die. You convince yourself, that if you go outside that bunker, you are going to be the next man. You are going to die. One of those shells had got your name written on it, for want of a better word. You convince yourself that you are going to die at some stage, and you don't want to go outside. Unfortunately there are things to be done on the battlefield.'[32]

Fear, then, was an integral part of battle and, if they could, men tried to deal with it through force of will by owning it, by waiting for a slightly less perilous moment so they could move. They had to do this chiefly because they did not want to appear vulnerable in front of others. Private Harrison recalled: 'Something struck my thigh really hard and I thought, "I've been hit." I dived for the rocks and checked my leg for a wound. Seventeen-year-old Private Ian Scrivens had also dived into the same bit of cover . . . I only had a slight graze where a round or something had passed through my denims. It was a bit embarrassing and despite our desperate situation I could see Ian Scrivens smirking.'[33]

The lance corporal's fear was exacerbated because he did not want other men to witness it. He was part of a group sent to evacuate Corporal Milne from the minefield. They arrived in a vehicle. A medic got out and went to assess Milne. He turned to call for his colleagues to help him carry Milne. At that moment, the medic trod on a mine: 'That explosion was bright, it was dazzling, we were peppered with bits of mud and the guy's leg.' Some of the men present dashed forward to help, but the lance corporal did not: 'I thought, hey hang on a minute and I consciously got back down, because I didn't want to be in that situation and I felt guilty because of that.'[34]

What he did was a natural reaction. On Wireless Ridge, 'an intense burst of fire brought the Company to a halt. It was a critical moment. For a short time all commanders had to pull the stops out to get the attack moving again. It was a real test of leadership, as several soldiers understandably went for cover.'[35] But the lance corporal felt guilty because he saw his own actions as cowardly. He knew he did not want to die. But he felt worse about it because he might be exposed in front of his comrades. He felt he was not the courageous paratrooper who could embrace death, but what he did not know was if, at any moment, somebody might choose to bring down that edifice of his life – if, because of his perceived cowardice, his time in the regiment was over.

Even though he was not the only one, it was a burden he could hardly bear: 'I felt, I hope nobody [saw] that, you know, because it is a pretty cowardly thing to do, I felt that way. I believe now, that there [were] others who saw the situation in the same way that I did, and it was human instinct to step down, and there were a lot of others who did exactly the same thing and so now I feel OK about it. Coming back, all the way through, it was deep in my mind, it's been a thought that, you were a coward, I hope nobody [has] seen that, I hope nobody raises that issue, and nobody finds out about that. Quite frightening.'[36]

Other men, at different times, were able to deflect fear with humour. Under shellfire at Goose Green, Lukowiak recalled someone shouting out, 'If I'd known I was going to do this much lying down I would have brought a fucking pillow.'[37] Patrols Platoon passed the time by singing John Lennon's 'Give Peace a Chance' at loud volume.[38] Corporal Robinson was nearly hit in the genitals: 'If you hit me in the balls, the wife'll kill me.'[39] When one man's leg was blown off, he cried out: 'I've lost my leg' and medic Lance Corporal Bentley responded: 'No you haven't mate, it's over there.'[40] Humour was important to the regimental culture. The Paras believed they had a black humour others would not share, and that this gave them an ability to cope when others would not. One man picked up a severed foot and rolled it up in another man's sleeping bag while that man wasn't watching. 'We all laughed, it was a very funny thing to see.'[41]

Men found different ways to deal with the randomness of violence. Some were extremely superstitious and avoided a man they believed brought bad luck. He had cut ears from corpses at Goose Green and some of the men felt he would receive a just retribution.[42] Private Carter said he felt that 'somebody' was watching over him, while Sergeant French believed in God and said his prayers. Most, if they could, had to develop a cold-hearted view towards the ruthlessness of chance. As Company Sergeant Major John Weeks carried an injured man on his shoulder, the man was shot again and killed: 'I remember Clarkson-Kearsley saying to me, "It could have been you, boss", and I said, "Yes, but if it had been me, it would have been me, and there's nothing you can do about it."'[43]

It was easier to accept such randomness if they seriously believed that the dead men had been hit by bullets destined only for them. Some felt that if their number was up, it was up. It was difficult to live as if each moment might be the last and men sometimes feared a corny epitaph. Captain Steven Hughes felt most fear on the day of his twenty-fifth birthday: 'I have this awful sensation that I won't survive tomorrow, my twenty-fifth birthday . . . I was never as frightened as I had been on 12 June.'[44] Another man thought it would be 'too much of a coincidence' not to be killed on the anniversary of his wife's death.[45]

Many stories have been told of men who were nearly shot while defecating. Company Sergeant Major Alec Munro said: 'I saw Private John (Sid Vicious) Haire venturing out in front of the position and said to him, "Where the fuck are you going?" He said, "Sir, my stomach's in bulk [churning], I'm going for a crap." He was suffering badly with dysentery. He walked about 30 metres down the slope with his shovel, dropped his denims and squatted out in the open. I then heard the crump, crump of artillery shells being fired from Stanley. You could hear them pass the culminating point as they were starting to whistle on the way down. These were going to land close and Sid must have thought the same. He judged it to the last second and then launched himself sideways into a shell hole, denims still round his ankles! . . . I thought the worst for a moment, and then his head popped up from the shell hole, like a meerkat with a grin all over his face.'[46]

They all had to relieve themselves, and there was usually nowhere completely concealed to do it. They might have shared everything, but many did not relish the prospect of having to perform this function in full view of their mates. It was an invasion of their privacy, and if they were seen to be embarrassed they would be ridiculed. They were only too aware of their fleeting vulnerability. The choice they made as to where to go mirrored the myriad other mundane choices they had to make in all their actions, choices that could turn out to be fatal. Their decision as to where to empty their bowels could determine whether they lived or died, and there was really nothing they could do about it.

There was also something absurd about the idea of being shot while in a totally unaggressive position, and something very inglorious too.

Nobody wanted to die with their pants around their ankles. The men in the regiment would not be able to stifle their laughter for time immemorial. Perhaps, too, it evoked something deep but unacknowledged about the vileness of combat. The combination of death and shit summed up the arbitrariness of who was picked off by the guns.

★

Lance Corporal Len Carver said that the worst death was to tread on a mine, because it gave you no chance. Such a death was random, but it was not just the randomness that made it unpalatable. There was nothing you could do to mitigate its effects: 'My biggest fear, and I think the majority of guys, is standing on a mine and getting blown up . . . I think it's because . . . it sounds strange, it's not as personal. If someone shoots you, that's personal, whereas a mine isn't, it's indiscriminate. It's just an object and it just takes you out . . .'[47]

Fear was a feeling that could be countermanded by aggression and by the courage that had been instilled in them in training. Kill or be killed was more than survival instinct, it was the will to triumph over the enemy, to kill them so that they could not kill you and your mates. The application of violence would neutralize fear of death. The action of the paratrooper in battle would combat the passivity of fear. The worst fear, therefore – at least, for many men who survived – was that they might be unmanned, that they would find themselves without defence; they would be killed before they had the chance to prove what they could have done; they would find themselves – as they saw it – helpless.

The Army gave men ways to try to control what was happening to them, to guard against the feeling there was nothing they could do. When 2 Para were on Sussex Mountains, the Argentine air force regularly flew over and dropped bombs on ships in the bay. Private Parr wrote home: 'On the second day, the Argies sent 24 Mirage Jets to bomb us, but between us, the Navy and the RAF we shot 20 down before they had a chance, and the other 4 were shot down on their way back. We captured one of the pilots on a later date and he said that they call our positions death row.'[48] B Company's Commanding

Officer John Crosland reported that during the battle of Goose Green, he had problems because, once daylight broke, he had to prevent his men from firing. The Argentine positions were too far away to bring effective fire onto them and they needed to conserve ammunition. When there was no action they could take, the men became tense: 'I think the frustration with the Toms, they wanted to get at the Argentinians in Boca House, they wanted to shoot at them, but they couldn't reach them, and I had to restrain them, because of the ammunition problem.'[49]

Even if they were not themselves in peril, fear could be profound, not because they were scared they might die but because there was nothing they could do to help their own men who were suffering. Private Ferguson said that when 2 Para were on Sussex Mountains (after the landings, before they went to Goose Green) they watched ships being hit: 'We watched it burning all night. We were a bit shattered. We realized, there is men in [there], men dying. We thought we were the greatest fighters, it was a bit of a fright when it actually happened.'[50] Corporal John Gartshore recalled: 'I sat on Sussex Mountains and my lads were getting their head down, I was on stag, and I watched ships burn that night. It'll never ever leave me, I can see it burning now. It's always going to be imprinted there. You can't do nothing. You can't help them. You're stuck on a mountain. That's how it is. It was with me. I don't know what else to say.'[51]

He explained that, much later, he had met one of the men who had been on the ship: 'I remember sitting in Combat Stress speaking to a Navy man, about 5 o'clock in the morning, we were talking about the Falklands, and he told me what ship he was on, and that was the one I remember burning. I felt such . . . so ashamed. He couldn't run anywhere. At least on land I could run away. I would never run away, I'd go into battle, but he was burning in a tin can.' Gartshore felt a kind of shame that there had been nothing he could have done to alleviate the man's fear; nothing he could have done against the enemy action.

Margerison said, when he was at the aid post, Argentine planes flew over: 'So we were waiting to get picked up, and there's a [unclear] flying in low level, and firing on the ground. Me and Jimmy just lying there, going fuck it, we're dead, when you've just got to get out of this, because everything's out of our hands, see?' The fact that he was dispossessed made him angry. He was angry at himself for getting shot and angry that the regiment could not call on his service. In his memoir, Vince Bramley recalled being pinned down by sniper fire: 'The voices . . . of the wounded were unlike anything else . . . their shouts were desperate . . . "For Christ's sake, I'm dying. Don't let them bury me here, please."' Bramley wanted to move forward, but the platoon commander stopped him, because so many men had already been killed. 'I slumped to the ground with a feeling of total helplessness. It was the worst feeling that anyone can imagine. As I tried not to think it was real, the cries continued. "Oh God, I'm hit in the chest, I'm all wet, please help."'[52] Some men were killed trying to combat that helplessness, trying to bring their wounded to safety. They were moved to act through love and compassion perhaps, but also to guard against their own fear. They would rather die than have no means to counter the enemy.

Carver, who had come near death, also said that helplessness – having to rely on other people for his defence – was the worst feeling he experienced. At the aid post, the Argentines were shelling: 'I was just laying there, and I felt helpless, I couldn't do anything. I couldn't move, I had blankets . . . they'd requisitioned a load of Argentinian ponchos and blankets, and we were using those to keep us warm.' Then a group of men came running down the mountain, and the soldiers at the aid post believed it was an Argentine counter-attack, although it turned out to be a group of prisoners being brought in: 'Where I was laying, they were coming from my head end. I was just . . . as the medic was kneeling next to me with his head resting on the sheet, I said, "Get me a rifle, at least I can lie here and if they get in here I can . . ." Other lads laying there as well, which weren't unconscious or in too much pain, were saying the same thing. It was the feeling of helplessness . . . But I felt if I've got a weapon in my hand I'd have felt happy. It was just that feeling of you can't do anything, you're helpless and relying on other people all the time . . . Though you're probably not physically able to, your mind is still thinking self-preservation, you want to defend yourself, you want to protect yourself. That is the worst feeling I've ever had.'[53]

The thing they feared most, then, was not being able to act on the impulse to survive, and not being able to be part of the regiment that brought the Argentines into submission. To be injured and helpless was thought to be worse than death; it meant the loss of a sense of who they were, the men they wanted to be, of how they had imag-ined battle. It was a more awesome fear than the dread of lying under shellfire, a dread that could be alleviated once the shells stopped, that could be overcome by force of will, by courage. The fear was that underneath the killing and the dying, there was nothing. The whole way they had seen the war, and the world – and the way they thought about themselves – had come unhinged, leaving just a void. Nothing could explain what had happened, nothing could explain what they had felt and done. To fear was not just to die – at least for the men who survived – to fear was to surrender, to become an ordinary man with human frailty, the power of the regiment undone.

9. Killing

How did men kill?

Many men in the ranks thought it was a 'stupid question' to ask whether soldiers had killed. It was a stupid question because they were trained paratroopers and it was their job to kill – if they were called upon to do it. Some of them had, and some of them had not, and it should not matter if an individual man had killed or not. They had all been doing their jobs. After the war, civilians who wanted to know if they had killed a person were just looking for a vicarious thrill. Private Northfield, B Company 2 Para, said: 'People would ask . . . did you shoot anybody? I'd ask them if they knew what it was like to kill someone, then tell them not to fucking ask me until they did.'[1]

Killing was therefore both a professional duty and a deep taboo. Killing crossed a line, because it was forbidden in civilian society. Private Mike Curtis, with B Company 2 Para, recalled that 'pulling that trigger was the hardest thing I'd ever done. Forget parachuting. Forget P Company. Forget anything else. That moment there, that decision, that was the hardest.'[2] Killing was often also seen as the most profound experience of war, and thus at the pinnacle of the experience that proved they were men. Killing and manhood could be linked because becoming a paratrooper was the making of a man and because the sanctioned responsibility to take life, and to bear it, was the apex of the duty of armed service. Not killing could mean men missed out, though often men did not know where their shots had ended up. Lance Corporal Graham Tolson, a machine gunner with 3 Para said: 'I can't even put my hand on my heart and say that I killed anybody.'[3]

Killing close up was viewed differently to killing at a distance. Killing an invisible enemy from far away was assumed to be easy, unproblematic. Sergeant John Pettinger, D Company 3 Para, described how his patrol had practised what they would do if they stumbled across an Argentine while on reconnaissance. To make sure the enemy did not shout out they would slit him through the windpipe, a method that is used to slaughter a sheep. It was, Pettinger said, no problem to kill a man with a gun. That 'didn't matter'. It was quite another thing to stab him to death like a farmyard animal.[4] If they were up close, they could not just pull a trigger and pretend it was an exercise. According to Company Sergeant Major John Weeks, 'There are things you don't relish, firing a 66 weapon into a known position, hearing the moans and groans coming out of that position, it's not nice.'[5] It meant more because a man knew that he had killed someone. He could not, over time, hide behind the responsibility of the collective.

Testimony about killing can be both exaggerated and suppressed: some things were talked about, others were not. It was hard to relay the experience in an exact form. Corporal Martin Margerison commented: 'You make excuses, or you get the story in your head. You make an analogy of the story, or whether it sounds right.' It could be hard to look back later at an act that seemed normal at the time, but that – at home – assumed new significance. Over the years, a moment, a split second, could be forgotten, but it could also expand, and it could come to look different.

★

What kinds of killing did take place during the Parachute Regiment's battles? The greatest number of Argentines – up to one hundred – were killed at Wireless Ridge, the battle at which the Paras had the most artillery on call. The deadliest weapons were not bayonets, grenades or rifles, but the two batteries of 105-mm guns fired by 29 Commando Regiment Royal Artillery; the 4.5-inch offshore gun on HMS *Ambuscade*; the light tanks of the Blues and Royals; and 2 and 3 Para's mortars and machine guns.[6]

This kind of distant killing has attracted a lot less attention and is usually recounted in dry language of eliminating the enemy and achieving British gains. Captain William McCracken, in command of an Artillery and Naval Gunfire Forward Observation Party, tasked with bringing down artillery fire on Longdon, described his job in terms of the technical precision it required and the effective results it produced: 'The .50 gun positions at the eastern end of the feature were engaged by NGS [Naval Gunfire Support]. This was very accurate and allowed us to start manoeuvring again. I kept moving the NGS along the ridge; this was doing the trick and neutralizing the guns. It must have been pretty uncomfortable for the enemy.'[7]

The way the battles were organized meant there were episodes of close-quarters killing at Goose Green and Mount Longdon, and also at Wireless Ridge. Most of this was done by small teams of men with grenades, rifles and hand-held 66-mm rocket launchers. At Goose Green, B and D Companies cleared trenches at night, and A Company cleared trenches in the dawn's early light on Darwin Hill. There is no official source that confirms B and D Company used bayonets, but some interview and memoir testimony suggests that they did. They certainly fixed bayonets; sometimes, as Lieutenant Geoff Weighall, 5 Platoon B Company, said, to give them something to do, a signal they were about to attack.[8] One private soldier in D Company said the order to fix bayonets was necessary, because they did not have enough ammunition: '[It] is a very personal and gruesome experience to be so close to a man you can smell his breath when he dies. That may seem a little coarse but in this case these people were trying to kill me and my comrades.'[9]

On Longdon, men of B and A Companies 3 Para used bayonets during periods of close-quarters trench clearance and this was reported in 3 Para's War Diary. 3 Para's close-quarters engagement lasted for a more sustained period than 2 Para's, but probably involved fewer men overall, because it was chiefly done by two companies (B and A) rather than the three thus embroiled (A, B and D) at Goose Green. Trench clearance was usually conducted by small teams of three, four or five men working together. Generally, two or three men put down machine-gun fire so that their two or three other comrades could move forward. As men closed on a trench, they would fire into it, sometimes using a 66-mm rocket launcher, but perhaps more frequently using white phosphorus or fragmentation grenades. Two or three men would concentrate on the trench to which they were closest, while two or three more aimed fire at the subsequent trench.[10]

They often used white phosphorus grenades, although these were supposed to be used for smokescreens rather than as anti-personnel weapons. Paratroopers found them more effective than fragmentation grenades, because white phosphorus grenades were 'prettier – you get lots of lights and things . . . sparks', but, more importantly, phosphorus grenades tended to kill the occupants of a trench, whereas the fragmentation grenades did not.[11] Their use must have been terrifying for the Argentines, as white phosphorus burns through flesh and produces poison gas that would force men out of their hiding places. Once the grenades had exploded, soldiers then got closer to the trenches and killed any enemy not yet dead with bayonets or by firing into the trench with rifles.

Sometimes, enemy who were already dead, or who were beyond saving, were shot or bayoneted, because the advancing troops could take no chances on leaving anyone behind them who could subsequently re-attack.[12] This kind of group action, and the fact that many Argentines were probably killed more than once (for want of a better way of putting it), was probably one reason why there were so many accounts of personal killing.

The great majority of personal accounts of close-quarters killing in memoirs and interviews have been given by 'other ranks', that is men from the rank of sergeant and below. Officers were with their men in battle, but they had to give orders, and, in the Parachute Regiment particularly, combat usually depended on the 'gutter fighting capabilities' of men in the ranks. Philip Neame, for example, the officer commanding D Company 2 Para, said he fired very few rounds, as his soldiers were the ones 'knocking off' the enemy.[13]

The focus on other ranks and killing also suggests something uncomfortable about violence and class. Men from the ranks were more likely to carry out up-close violence and were more likely to talk about it afterwards. They had to do the dirtiest tasks; and it was they whose passions were stoked and whose feelings were of interest to others. Officers were there to take decisions, and to lead, but were not, in this period, usually called upon later to recount their actions.

Perhaps this sheds some light on an age-old concern. What would happen to men in the ranks capable of violence and blooded by combat when they returned home?

★

Falklands paratroopers thought of themselves as professional soldiers, and they talked about killing in terms of their disciplined, military identities. The essential part of that professional mindset was that, in combat, men had to 'kill or be killed'. They had to kill to survive; they had to kill to win. A soldier had to kill, or the enemy might kill him, or his mates. Private Curtis hesitated before pulling the trigger and then rounds zipped past him towards his comrade: 'I thought, fucking hell, I've killed Bob – my delay has cost a mate his life.'[14] They had to show stoicism of nerve and steadiness of emotion: 'There was very little hatred in this war. You just did the job.'[15] For many men, killing to save themselves and their mates was a distasteful necessity, no more than fulfilling the calling they had willingly agreed to undertake.

Corporal Creaney, D Company 2 Para, said that when they were on Wireless Ridge: 'As we're advancing forward, I think it was off to my left, I'd heard, "There's one off to the left there, still alive, fucking sort him out" . . . I don't know why, but at that same time, I thought it's a trap. We're going to go forward here, and because there's all rocks and that, as we get forward, someone's going to throw a grenade and we're going to get caught out here. So, initially I said to [X], we'll stand back here, shoot in the general direction, and if we hear fucking screaming, we've got him. And literally we were both shooting in the general direction, and a light went up in the distance, and this guy was probably about twenty feet in front of me, just off, and both of us happened to be changing magazines at the same time, which is not a good thing, and I just happened to be a bit quicker, and I end up shooting this guy.'[16]

Creaney said that when the battle ended, 'We then went round, and we came to the rock face where I'd shot the guy. And it was a bit strange looking at what you'd done to someone, a human being. But what was interesting was if you imagine someone lying against that rock face, all the rounds around him, and only one round actually fucking hit him out of all of that. So of course the platoon commander took the piss. Of all those rounds and you missed the guy.'[17] Creaney dwelt not on the fatal injury he had inflicted, but on his lack of expert targeting. He had killed an enemy, but his accurate shot was almost inadvertent. He had done his duty, and there was no need to linger over it too much.

Lance Corporal Carver, B Company 3 Para, regarded one-on-one killing as, in a sense, honourable, when compared to the depersonalized killing with distant guns or mines. He saw close-quarters killing as more chivalric than other forms of killing. It was honourable because each man had a chance, and because, therefore, Carver could see that his opponent was a human being – even if he could not allow himself to think of him as a human at the moment of killing. Close-quarters killing was competitive, it was a sport. Highly developed technology was indiscriminate. If it caught you, the possibility of survival was eradicated. Face-to-face, a man had options, even if they were few.

Advancing up Longdon, Carver – as with other men – had to kill what was in front of him in the best way he could, because there was no time to do otherwise: 'As I've come round the corner the Argentinian is there, with his rifle, I haven't got room to bring it round to fire on him, so all I did was brought the weapon up and hit him with it straight in the head. Luckily he didn't have a helmet on and it knocked him down.' Subsequently, Carver and his team assaulted a machine-gun position: 'I got three lads, one with me, two of the others, and we went either side of the position, put a load of fire into it, you're talking there was four Argentinians in there, and we were literally six or seven feet away from them, it was low fire, we dropped grenades in there and back out, to clear . . .'

At another point in the ascent, he came face to face with an Argentine: 'I'd come round the corner of a big rock, there was an Argentinian there, and he just come straight at me, bringing his weapon up, he didn't have a bayonet fitted, he obviously had his safety catch off ready to fire a round, and I just bayoneted him straight

in, and took him, hit him with it, flicked him on the floor, you have
to twist to get it back out again, twist and turn and pulled it out,
picked his weapon up, threw that away, and then just moved on.'

It was, Carver said, 'animalistic'. He did not mean that he was in a
frenzy or a rage. He meant that he was channelling all the self-belief
in his aggression he had built up in training, and that all his rational
thought, his civilized mind, was subsumed into the instinct to survive. If he did not kill, he would die: 'He was bringing his weapon
up, and I know that, the way his weapon was coming up I had a split
second and that weapon was pointing at me, and all his finger had to
do was close on the trigger, and if he had it on automatic I was going
to get five or six rounds into me, if he had it on single shot it'd still
be . . . and at that range it's going to hit me in the gut area anyway. So
it's a case of, no, you don't even think about it.'[18]

*

For Creaney and for Carver, the Argentine enemies were their
opponents, soldiers who had to be killed because that was what British soldiers were there to do. They must be killed so that they, and
their mates, did not die in their stead, and so that British paratroopers
would win the battle and hence the war. At other times, men relayed
a harder attitude towards the enemy, an attitude that suggested they
saw killing in a more emotive way, but it was often a negative emotion. That attitude could be there in them anyway, or it could emerge
as a reaction to the nastiness of battle, to the effort it took to shut out
empathy, and the fear that if they felt compassion, they could not do
their jobs well. They had to block everyday human feelings in order
to kill.

On occasion, perhaps that harder attitude was expressed as a casual
racism. On the *Canberra*, some Paras had put together a weekly newsletter. In one of the pamphlets they drew a cartoon of an Argentine
being anally penetrated by a tin of corned beef with the caption
'Bloody wops'.[19] The newsletter had been created primarily because
the troops on the ships were bored. But it also indicated the ready
way in which the paratroopers could see Argentines as stereotypically

Latino – as dagoes, wops or spiks. Latinos were characterized by poor cleanliness, effeminacy and homosexuality. More commonly, British paratroopers did not talk about the Argentines in racialized terms, but as 'Argies'. As 'Argies', perhaps it was simpler to see them in contrast to the professionalism of the British troops, as fearful, inefficient and lacking strong will.

That comparison probably points to the main element in the paratroopers' attitude towards their enemy. The paratroopers had had instilled in them a profound faith in the superiority of their training and the regiment of which they were part, whoever their enemy might be. These opponents were a conscript army, and could never be their match. The sense of the poor quality of the enemy could, for some men, blend with feelings of contempt and disgust. Corporal John Geddes, C Company 2 Para, wrote in his memoir of the Argentines' lax discipline. C Company was sent forward to observe at Goose Green. Although the Argentines had been dug in for some while, they had not taken the time to organize proper latrines. British patrols found themselves crawling through, and lying in, human excrement. Geddes said: 'I'd stuck my elbow into a piece of enemy excrement, a lump of Argy shit, as I'd crawled up to their position. The dirty bastards had not been digging latrines, they'd just been walking out of their slit trenches and shitting in front of their own positions.'

The Argentines had left a machine gun readied while they all slept. It made Geddes angry that the Argentine soldiers were so lazy and had such shoddy hygiene: 'They were sleeping like babes . . . What the fuck did they think they were doing? . . . [F]or some reason the soldier in me objected to their sloppy unmilitary routine . . . They were a fucking disgrace.'[20] It was not just that their ill-discipline meant that British soldiers would prevail as victors, it was that the Argentines were such poor soldiers, so unable to prevent their detection and so impotent to avert the Paras' onslaught, they were almost asking to die.

Particularly as the battles developed, the men's will to subdue their enemy could turn into kinds of hatred: if not a deep and lasting antipathy, then perhaps a temporary coarsening of their attitudes.

That was in part a sense of asserting their professional dominance –
they were required to think of the Argentines as obstacles that had to
be killed, not as human beings. At the same time, they had to keep
themselves going, to shut out the things that might make them seek
mercy or try to make everything stop. They could have no time for
pity. As Lance Corporal Vincent Bramley said: 'A wounded Argentinian lay to my right . . . He had been hit in the chest and screamed
as he held the wound. A lad from B Company ran across the clearing
at him and ran his bayonet through him. The screaming Argentinian
tried to grab the bayonet from him before it took his life. Our lad
screamed, "Shut up, shut up, you cunt!"'[21] Sergeant French observed:
'You cannot possibly imagine the depths to which you descend in
war. I shot a man at close quarters on Longdon. In all this, there was
absolutely no question at all about the morals of anything, of taking
this bloke out . . . he had crawled out of a cave and was no more than
three or four feet away . . . I had a 9-mm pistol as well as a rifle. I
decided to use the pistol. The Argentine wasn't even a human being,
he was an enemy. It was only afterwards that I thought of him as
human.'[22]

Sometimes they wanted to exact a kind of revenge for what the
Argentines were doing to them and to their comrades: 'He got a bit
of a kicking, the pilot who dropped the napalm, if it's the same one
that [X] platoon got hold of. He got a kicking for dropping this
napalm on the boys.'[23] Corporal Geddes 'felt an ice-cold anger sweep
over me . . . It was a cold clinical anger because there at Goose Green
I could see exactly where the enemy were and knew exactly what I
could do about it. Those shits . . . were going to get some.'[24] 2 Para B
Company's Private Northfield reported: 'When we heard about the
young officer being taken out by some surrendering Argentines, that
pissed us all off. We thought sod it, we're not going to take any prisoners . . .'[25] D Company's Private Tony Banks, on Wireless Ridge,
also suggested the paratroopers would not show mercy: 'These bastards had been shooting at us and now this fucker wanted to
surrender.'[26] Perhaps recounting the same incident, 2 Para's history
said that on Wireless Ridge, '10 Platoon [D Company] came across
one lone machine gunner who lay wounded in both legs with his

machine gun lying abandoned beside him. He was shot in the chest and hand unnecessarily and died instantly.'[27]

★

Men also killed because those were their orders. Corporal Abols, A Company 2 Para, said: 'I was in the army, I was ordered to attack. I was a young man, that's what I was ordered to do. That's how young men should think.'[28] Most of them were going into battle for the first time. Preparing to attack trenches in the dark, perhaps officers wanted to stiffen their men's nerves, to eliminate, in so far as they could, any possibility of hesitation. Major John Crosland, the officer commanding B Company 2 Para, said he instructed his men, as they prepared for the Goose Green attack, not to take prisoners, as somebody else could do that. B Company had to move forward, and Headquarters Company could come later to take care of the prisoners his men had disarmed: 'I said, I'm not interested in taking prisoners, that's someone else's job, we just keep the momentum of the attack going, moving forward, from trench to trench, from position to position, just overrunning these people. That was the message.'[29]

Private Northfield remembered that his section commander had instructed them: 'Regardless of what happened, we were to walk from point A to point B and kill everything in between.'[30] Company Sergeant Major Peter Richens emphasized that the plans for battle impelled men to sustain their momentum and did not allow for subtlety: 'It is very difficult when you are fighting at night to take prisoners. You are in the heat of battle, there is a lot of firing going on, you are taking trench by trench, nobody is speaking Spanish, or very little Spanish, other than somebody jumping up and throwing their weapon away. But with the heat of battle, and also it being pitch black, it was a very difficult situation and Colonel Jones was very keen to get us moving.'[31]

When the Goose Green battle started, they did not know what they were about to find. B and D companies came upon trenches, and they discovered the Argentines quite unprepared. In some of the trenches, as the '2 Para History' makes clear, the Argentines were not fighting: 'The apparent unwillingness or inability of the enemy to defend themselves was a pathetic sight . . . Many of the enemy did nothing but hide under their blankets. Some had rifles propped against the side of their trenches.'[32] Lieutenant Chapman said: 'Just about every trench encountered was grenaded . . . There was a continuous momentum throughout the attack and it was very swiftly executed. The Argentinian resistance was pretty weak. A lot of them were, I believe, trying to hide in the bottom of their trenches and ignore the fight . . . They were a scared bunch, and a lot of them were non-participants.'[33] Major Neame, the officer commanding D Company, said: 'What surprised me was the number of Argentinian soldiers who were just not fighting. Some of them were just lying supine in the bottom of their trench with their sleeping bag pulled over their heads; others pretending they were asleep . . . large numbers of them . . . certainly half.'[34]

According to Major Crosland, 'A lot of individual actions were fought at very close quarters, from trench to trench, with a grenade going in, a machine gunner raking it, then moving on. And I think consequently the number of Argentinian casualties reflected this very aggressive tactic; and I think unfortunately a lot of Argentinian soldiers were either killed or wounded in this manner purely because you can't determine at night whether a bloke is surrendering, or is going to fight, or if he's under a poncho, or whatever; and there were undoubtedly a lot of people hurt who may well have been prepared to give up.'[35]

2 Para needed to win, to do so quickly, and they needed not to be killed themselves. They did not know until they got to the trenches what they would find and they could not afford, so early into the attack, to take chances with their own lives or to lose their momentum. The nature of the engagement – dark, uncertain, dependent on speed and the belief that if the Argentines were hit hard, they would crumble – meant that they were ordered to kill what they found. At the start of the attack, 2 Para killed to dominate, to prove to the Argentines – and to each other – that they could show the enemy who was in command, and that they would win in battle.

★

In Vietnam, and in the course of the world wars, plenty of testimony points to the thrill, excitement and visceral – even sexual – pleasure of killing.[36] Nobody talked in this way about combat in the Falklands. Rather, they felt awe at the power of their weaponry; and hence they felt a kind of joy at the destruction they brought to bear, because it showed their own potency and capability, and their capacity to survive. It was that – the ability to win in combat – that marked them as men apart. Major Crosland said he told his men: 'You've got nothing further to prove. You've been into the furnace and come out the other side.'[37]

They often talked about killing in language that reiterated its power. Private Worrall said: 'We wasted the four of them. Killed all four of them, sir.'[38] Private Ferguson came upon some Argentines towards the end of the battle for Wireless Ridge. 'What did you do with the Argentinians? We blew them to bits with a 79, a grenade launcher, there was nothing left of them at all.' Ferguson called for machine-gun support and 'if anyone else tried to run away, we blasted them to pieces'.[39] Lance Corporal Graham Tolson recalled: 'From our position, we could hear the crack of rifle fire and aggressive shouting both in English and Spanish, it was tremendous, we seemed to have the upper hand, and hopefully it would soon be all over.'[40]

Corporal Gartshore, in 2 Para's Machine Gun Platoon, commented: 'You know what you're aiming at, from 50m to 100m to 1800m to 2000m . . . When you see the firepower that goes down . . . it's heartwarming.' He described shooting at Argentine planes while the battalion were at Fitzroy: 'We watched them come in. We knew when to open the guns up. We could see them, not only us but the rest of the battalion, we could see them flying into our range, that pilot, he's got to have shit himself, I don't give a damn who you are. You could see him looking at us when he went by, he didn't drop any more bombs because he was getting battered with everything we'd got, what a sight to behold, it was beautiful.'[41]

Men also described the exhilaration of survival. According to Private Dean Ferguson, 'Then it came over the radio – white flags in Stanley – I had tears coming down my face at that point, I was that happy with it just being over with.'[42] Lance Corporal Hedges felt that the 'blokes were pleased they performed alright'.[43] Sergeant Des Fuller said: 'To be honest with you, I can't remember how I felt [at the end of the battle of Longdon]. I must have been really chuffed how I managed to get through this. All the guys who got wounded or killed, I was the only one in that small group of 8 of us who hadn't been hit.'[44] Corporal Abols said afterwards he was 'very proud. Very proud to come back as well.'[45]

Men had died, and it was hard to admit subsequently that those who had survived felt elation that they themselves were not dead too. Private Lukowiak recalled: 'A toast was made. At the time I may have believed that we were toasting victory. Today, I know we were toasting life.'[46] Private Edwards said: 'I've always felt very thankful that I'm still here. Not thankful that they're not, but I'm just glad I survived it, you know? I've always very much appreciated that.'[47] To be among so much death underlined to the men what it meant to be alive; and to have cheated death, when so many had not, was to prove how good they had been as soldiers, even if they knew, rationally, that they had just been lucky. They had experienced everything that war had to offer, and they had survived. Nothing could match it.

★

Killing, particularly close up, was also indelibly tied to experiences thought of as traumatic. A direct link was hard to prove, but anecdotally, 'Memories of killing in battle haunt most soldiers – but they rarely talk about it.'[48] If they did speak of it, they tended not to do so in terms of guilt. If they confessed to feelings of guilt, that meant they wished it had not happened, and none of the emotions they felt could be explained so easily. The killing they had done had helped to keep them and their comrades alive; it had helped to win the battle and give the battalions their place in regimental history.

Rather, some men came to feel a loneliness in the face of the reality they had had to confront. Corporal Margerison, who shot the sentry, B Company's first kill at the start of the Goose Green battle, said that it was he who had to protect his men, it was he who had decided whether the sentry should live or die. He could never know what would have happened if he had made another choice; and that split-second judgement yielded consequences because he had taken a life and, probably, saved the lives of his men. He could never go back to that instant.

If he felt bad later, it was not because he was guilty, but because the responsibility that had been vested in him only made sense when he was a soldier, and at that exact point in time: 'I killed that first sentry, coming from our start-line up the hill, and that's a terrible thing to do. Not the fact that I killed him, but that it was up to me whether he should die or not.'[49] After he left the regiment, the fact that he had been in that position of responsibility did not matter to people. Outside the regiment, no man could validate his sense of himself by understanding how right he had been. Outside the regiment, the meaning of the action changed and became, in some ways, harder to control.

Killing therefore could remain in men's minds. Some developed a sense of regret – not that they had killed, because they believed what they had done was right, but that they had been in the position to have to do it in the first place. Sergeant French said: 'At the time I was quite happy with what I did. But it's funny how as the years go on, when I have a quiet moment, I always think of him . . . I've said a lot of prayers to his family . . . I'm not proud of what happened, but I'd do it again if I had to, for a just cause.'[50]

As men grew older themselves, and spent more time out of the harsh environment of the regiment, and as their feelings about other things changed – perhaps their feelings towards their wives, their parents or their children – it was hard for killing not to assume a more human dimension. Over time, they recognized the fuller meaning of taking a man's life, the extent of what the dead had been denied, and the depth of the love that others might have felt for the dead. Lance Corporal Carver bayoneted an Argentine, an action which, he said, was 'for many years just a shape in my dreams, and I could live with that, there was no problem. Then for some reason, one night, it was the face of my son. I'm in this dream, bayoneting my son. I couldn't wake up.'[51]

Men could also come to feel horrified, even ashamed, that they had been part of something so vile. Corporal Tom Howard, a medical orderly attached to the Paras, said: 'It began to hurt me that people could do these things each other – for a fucking piece of dirt in the middle of the ocean.'[52] Private Lukowiak said that after the final surrender, as they walked over Wireless Ridge, he approached a trench. His gun was cocked because he had already taken one Argentine prisoner, then: 'Crouched in the trench was a figure in grey. I saw him. He saw me. He held a rifle. I moved the first finger on my right hand. Bullets left the end of my machine gun. They hit the figure in grey. They impacted into his chest and threw him back against the side of the trench. Grey turned to red. He slid to the ground.'[53]

Lukowiak found it hard to explain the fact that he had not been angry when he shot the man. He had been calm, and that had seemed normal. Later, he felt no remorse that he had killed. What saddened him was not that he felt guilty about killing another man, but that he did not. Soldiers had to be prepared to kill, and so even when he stumbled upon an armed enemy soldier at the end of the war, killing him was not a problem. But after the war, out of the regiment, they were no longer surrounded by people who understood how straightforward it had been. Civilians might expect them to feel guilt about killing. Feeling guilt made battle palatable, because guilt would show that they felt hesitant about taking life, that somehow they felt that what they had done was wrong. But that was not necessarily how they felt.

Instead Lukowiak and perhaps others felt that killing had seemed right, and if it seemed right, then it must be the world that was wrong – the world that could place men on a battlefield and ask them to kill each other. The cruelty of mankind (because, as they saw it, it was always men) could lead men to take part in this degradation, to feel they had been so worthless that they were put on earth to do the filthiest things, while others watched for their entertainment, or passed judgement on their actions. Once they were out of the regiment and in civilian society, if they were remorseless, then surely it was they who were cruel. And if they were cruel, how could they possibly fit into civilian society; and if they did not fit into civilian society, then what could they do, how could they see themselves as good men?

*

Some men present also reported evidence of war crimes. One soldier from 2 Para was found to have ears, cut from Argentine corpses, in his kit bag. Another was 'less than fair to one of the wounded Argentines – in effect torturing him'.[54] Another cut the fingers from an Argentine soldier's body, in order to steal his rings.[55] And another was found with dental pliers, planning to extract gold or silver tooth fillings.[56]

There has been more controversy about two events alleged to have taken place on Mount Longdon. In 1991, Vincent Bramley's memoir, *Excursion to Hell,* mentioned these occurrences. Journalists began publicizing the stories, and the Metropolitan Police conducted an inquiry which had widespread media coverage, but did not find enough evidence to mount a prosecution.[57] Afterwards, the freelance journalists Christian Jennings, a foreign correspondent, and Adrian Weale, also a former British Army officer, interviewed many veterans of 3 Para and wrote *Green-Eyed Boys*, published in 1996. Their book details the allegations.

The main claims made are first, that one soldier, Corporal Stewart McLaughlin, cut ears from Argentine corpses, and perhaps even from a live Argentine prisoner; and secondly, that another corporal, Corporal X, killed a prisoner.[58] The first allegation has recently been strongly denied. McLaughlin was killed on Longdon, and it was said that Lieutenant Cox and Company Sergeant Major Weeks had found ears in his webbing when they searched his body after his death and passed this information on to the padre. Many veterans say there is no evidence ears were ever found, and in fact officers, soldiers and members of McLaughlin's family are campaigning for him to receive a posthumous award for his leadership on Longdon that night. They say that Lieutenant Colonel Pike wrote a citation for him, which was subsequently lost, and that Major Mike Argue, the officer commanding B Company, told McLaughlin's father that the citation was for the 'highest award for gallantry'.[59]

The second incident recorded by Jennings and Weale had at least one eyewitness, who said that Corporal X shot a prisoner, not in a split-second judgement – him or me – but after the battle, as he was gathering the wounded. 'X dragged the Argentine to a rocky outcrop and produced the . . . pistol . . . The terrified prisoner realized what was about to happen. Shouting with fright, he produced a crucifix that he was wearing on a chain round his neck and held it out as if to show X that he too was Christian.' The shouting brought Captain Mason, Major Dennison and Company Sergeant Major Caithness running. Mason said: 'I heard some shouting, then I heard a shot . . . and I saw a guy get shot in the head, obviously, over an open grave . . . I ran down there and . . . X was shaking visibly . . . right on the edge . . . and I thought he was going to shoot me.'[60] X said 'he [the Argentine] was a sniper' – X may have been taking what he saw as a just revenge – and Mason thought he had 'flipped'.[61]

Perhaps the important question is why any soldier might commit crimes of this nature? One explanation is that the bounty hunters were 'bad apples'. Major Collett, the officer commanding the company X was in said X was a 'loony' and Captain Tony Mason called him a 'pariah'.[62] The 2 Para man who was found after his death to have taken trophies from corpses was called a 'psychopath'.[63] These 'bad apples' might be fascinated with violence, lacking in empathy, strong in character, driven towards extremes, or more lacking in conscience than other men in the battalion.

The blend of those characteristics with the heightened stress of battle could, therefore, lead to extreme violence; or perhaps the stress of battle was itself enough sometimes to tip men over the edge into a moral void. Perhaps some men became gripped by an overwhelming urge for the fleeting satisfaction of revenge. At the same time, they could hate the enemy, and hatred of the enemy could be blended with fear: not necessarily fear of dying, but fear of the softer emotions that they had had to suppress in order to kill. They could not afford to show sympathy, lest it began to weaken the mechanisms that got them through the battle in the first place. Lukowiak said that after retrieving a wounded Argentine man, he kicked him hard in his wound: 'I have often wondered why I kicked the boy. Which is strange because I always knew – others were watching. I may have helped save him, but I wasn't soft, I was still hard. See, I just kicked him. I was still a man.'[64]

In the test of battle, their own fear of not matching up to the expectations they set for themselves, or that others set for them, could impel them towards cruelty, as could the fear that if they stopped, they might not be able to continue. Captain Adrian Logan recalled: 'There were dead and dying Argentines laying about moaning and groaning and asking for "Mama". There were a few who were completely broken gibbering wrecks, crying, and some were praying. It was awful. However, at this moment in time, we had no sympathy for them, some of the Toms told them to "fucking shut up".'[65] It was possible, too, to fear the end of the battle, because the end of the battle would invite reflection; and it would mean the end of the sensations that were awful, but also exhilarating beyond all else. Killing, and not dying, could make men feel vividly alive, and when it was nearly over, some did not want it to stop.

Looting from Argentine bodies, or desecrating corpses, was also a way to dominate the enemy. Sergeant French commented: 'In the aftermath of victory, it's something you do to assert your authority as the victor.'[66] The corpses belonged to the men who had killed them. Defiling them, by taking photographs, rearranging them, taking boots, food and personal effects, helped the paratroopers see the dead enemy not as men – men with families – but as trophies of war. The enemy dead were evidence of how successful the paratroopers had been, and the taking of ears could be seen as a violent extension of this. McLaughlin's father said he thought his son had discussed taking ears as trophies with other men as 'psychological dominance that the Argentines, a largely Latin nation, would understand: just as bullfighters cut the ears from their victims, so would the Paras'.[67]

The culture in a battalion, and the relationships between the men, both in and across ranks, might also help to explain criminal behaviour, or allegations of it. McLaughlin was respected and feared by the soldiers who served under him. During the battle, one man recalled: 'Corporal McLaughlin stood up with a pistol in his hand and screamed at the top of his voice, "Right you fuckers, get up – get up – everyone get up now!" He was waving his pistol in the air . . . I was more scared of him than I was of the Argies shooting at me.'[68] His actions in battle inspired others. At another perilous moment, McLaughlin rose and shouted, 'Come on, lads, I'm fucking bullet-proof, follow me!'[69] Had he not been killed, the subsequent claims about the contents of his webbing could not have been made, and he might have been decorated for his leadership; at the same time, he knew how to make his presence felt, and this helped his men in battle, made them afraid of him and created loyalty towards him.

The relationship between leadership and the necessity for violence makes criminality on the battlefield a difficult subject to talk about. Historically, soldiers have been reluctant to discuss it, partly because of loyalty to their colours, and partly because of feelings of complicity, whether or not those feelings were justified. In the ranks of the Paras, it would be frowned upon to report a comrade who had gone too far. Vincent Bramley, whose memoir sparked off the debate as to whether war crimes had taken place, was effectively excommunicated after he published it.[70]

In the spirit of the regiment, men wanted to believe they were interchangeable with their comrades, and some said that they did not know whether, in some circumstances, they might not have done the same thing. 2 Para's Private Lukowiak said he saw a sergeant shoot a wounded man in the back. But he told other soldiers, and his sister, that it had been him who had done the shooting.[71] According to Private Northfield, also in 2 Para, 'Some people act over the top, even in the context of war, with unnecessary waste of life – like putting a 9mm pistol to the head of a 16-year-old boy and pulling the trigger. This extreme sort of thing didn't happen very much . . . I was 18 years old, straight from training, very Parachute Regiment, filled with aggression – and at the time it didn't bother me.'[72] At the time, he said, that was how it was.

Many officers, and perhaps many men, however, believed that if soldiers misbehaved, then this was a failure not just of the man himself but of the hierarchy – a failure of rank. Criminality among the men reflected badly on the officers in command. As one retired colonel, who had been a Commanding Officer of 2 Para, said: 'It cannot be emphasized enough that where leadership has been sound, the likelihood of misbehaviour by security forces appears to have been much diminished.'[73] One platoon sergeant with 3 Para, Sergeant McCullum, appeared to agree: 'Argentine soldiers also popped up out of nowhere, and on the spur of the moment some were blown away. Things like this happen in war. You get individuals who are maniacs in their own little paradise, blowing prisoners away and enjoying it. I made sure it never happened in my platoon, but I'm not saying it didn't happen elsewhere.'[74]

If isolated criminal acts were regarded as a breach of discipline, then it raised the prospect that officers could or should have done more to prevent them. Officers were not omnipotent. They might have been unable to stop a specific act if it happened quickly and they did not have time to react, or if it was out of their purview. But more generally, during the battle, section commanders had had to take the initiative to sustain momentum. McLaughlin had challenged his platoon commander, Lieutenant Cox, and X had told Cox to get a grip. X then led A Company's advance, and his Company Commander Major Collett gave him an Argentine officer's pistol, looted from one of the surrendered bunkers.[75] McLaughlin had a pistol too, if the soldier above who saw him brandishing it remembers correctly, although we do not know what kind of pistol it was, nor where he got it. Only officers carried pistols, and so if McLaughlin had one it was a symbol of his temporarily elevated status. Collett had challenged Lieutenant Colonel Pike's tactics earlier that night, insisting he should take his time to bring his men up the side of the mountain. Whatever Collett intended in giving X a stolen pistol, it might have had the effect of granting him licence to use it, perhaps thereby, however inadvertently, encouraging a perception that the men had to do what they thought necessary, or even that some degree of lawlessness was acceptable.

One further question the issue raises is the extent to which the climate of battle made criminality inevitable. Hugh Bicheno, a former British intelligence officer who hated the Foreign Office for failing to understand the pathology of violence that was the Argentine 'dirty war', viewed the courage of young men like McLaughlin and X as in a different league from that of their superiors. Bicheno blamed Lieutenant Cox and the battalion padre for not discreetly dealing with the ears in McLaughlin's webbing. Rather, the padre made it 'the focus of his hand-wringing horror at the reeking [*sic*] havoc all around him'. X's responsibility for the shooting was diminished: 'The real question is what diminished it, and the answer to that question is all-embracing.'[76]

It is obvious that the close-up and fraught nature of the battles made criminality possible, but if the 'heat of battle' was exclusively to blame, then we could ask why more men did not succumb. Only a tiny number were said to have violated moral boundaries in these ways. On Longdon, the Paras took fifty prisoners during the night, and five of the 120 wounded Argentines were treated at 3 Para's regimental aid post.[77] The 'heat of battle' is also, in this example, a misleading phrase. It suggests that men metamorphosed into 'berserkers' in uncontrolled rage. This had happened in Vietnam and 'forward panic' – a spontaneous eruption of violence – was a recognized phenomenon.

However, in the relatively confined environment of Mount Longdon, it does not sound as if the second incident, in which X was said to have shot the prisoner, comes under that heading. It occurred after the harsh fighting on the mountain was over. Even if X had lost his mind, in that moment the 'heat of battle' was not so much hot but cold, even vindictive. Shooting a prisoner over an open grave looked less like a crime of passion than a crime of violence much in the same way that rape need not be motivated by sexual desire. Killing was a part of the way a man saw himself and criminal killing could similarly be part of how a man saw himself too. As Joanna Bourke has argued, 'At the root of such grotesque behaviour was the desire to assert one's essential "self" in the act of killing.'[78]

The comparison with other eras and battles might also be instructive in other respects. If criminal violence is placed alongside the killing done by other men, then the unifying factor was how the men thought of themselves as soldiers. Usually, regimental discipline worked well. They saw themselves as professional, acting to defend themselves and their mates, to defeat the enemy and conclude the mission. Usually, they abided by the limits of battlefield killing and they saw what they had to do within the confines of their task. But sometimes they saw themselves as invincible, hardened and cruel – and very occasionally perhaps they saw themselves as sadistic. Perhaps, therefore, those men needed, now or never, to discover the extremes they could push themselves to. Maybe, if it happened, they committed atrocity not despite its criminality – slipping over some thin line into an abyss – but precisely because they knew it was wrong, to see how far they could go.

★

The high command of 3 Para preferred not to discuss the crimes that took place on Longdon. Even if such things had occurred, the incidence must have been extremely rare. They did not point to a regiment out of control, and therefore disciplinary action could be unnecessary. For many in the Paras, what had happened in the Falklands was their business only. When the Paras came home, it was clear to everyone that discussion of atrocities that might have taken place would detract from the triumph of victory. The worst thing would be to have civilians – armchair generals, prurient journalists, worthy academics or uppity nieces, none of whom had ever had to run into a hail of machine-gun fire – asking ill-informed questions about how they had fought.

The Commanding Officer of 3 Para, Lieutenant Colonel Pike, told the Metropolitan Police inquiry he had given X the equivalent of a court martial, although Major Collett did not believe that this had taken place.[79] X, apparently, was sent home separately from the rest of the regiment. He was transferred to 1 Para and remained in the Army until 1994.

Others in the regiment believed that distinguishing between legitimate and illegitimate violence was essential. Failing to punish the taking of trophies from the dead and the execution of a prisoner was the beginning of a slippery slope into the acceptance of savagery; and if not quelled, that impulse would continue. A culture of impunity and one in which even a small amount of deviant excess was tolerated made future crimes more likely. For some men, a clear line between right and wrong, testable in courts of law, gave British violence a certain logic, and the regiment its discipline and therefore its purpose. The regiment should ask questions of itself, and society should demand answers. But those things should not detract from, and should not be clouded by, regimental loyalty and pride.

10.   Death

At 8.45 p.m. on 13 June, D Company 2 Para began their assault on
Wireless Ridge. The battalion was now commanded by Lieutenant
Colonel David Chaundler, who had been sent from London after
Jones's death, via Ascension Island and a parachute drop into the sea.
Chaundler was determined to organize the battle differently to those at
Goose Green and Longdon: 'One lesson learned by 2 Para was that
battle was much easier with plentiful firepower, and that lesson was
applied at Wireless Ridge.'[1] 2 Para were supported by two batteries of
guns on ships offshore and fire from tanks, machine guns and MILANs.
It was exemplary, a textbook battle. Despite Argentine resistance and
some fierce close-quarters fighting, 2 Para's casualties were light, with
the loss of only three men.

Wireless Ridge was long and narrow. It rose slowly, on an axis
with Longdon, from the Murrell River. Like all the hills around
Stanley, it was scattered with pale grey rock that gathered in jagged
clusters, sewn and pulled tight as if by a giant needle, before dropping
steeply down towards the capital's homesteads. That night, it was
freezing. The plan was for A and B Companies to move towards the
ridge but to stay on the lower ground, while D Company would
advance across the tundra and then press along, and take this final
feature.

This time, men did not silently sweep towards the Argentine
enemy. Rather, British artillery shelled the Argentine positions and
paratroopers came under heavy shellfire themselves. In A Company,
Colour Sergeant Gordon Findlay was hit and killed.[2] D Company
reached the first rocky outcrops, before they got to the ridge itself, and
found the Argentines dead, or fleeing. In the blackness, the spiked
grass and heather underfoot did not distinguish itself from the sucking
Falkland bogs and two men fell into a concealed pond.[3] They had to

tread water until their platoon sergeant dragged them out. They needed dry clothes, or they could have died of cold.

D Company advanced again, quickly and more confidently now. The bombardment had done its job ahead of them. They moved to the western end, to the foot of the ridge. Then they heard the sound of incoming shells. It is not clear exactly where they were when the shells hit them. One account says they were still on low ground, not yet on the ridge. Another says they had begun to advance and were in nameless ground, in a dip between two outcrops. A third says they were on higher ground, approaching the crest of the feature.[4]

The roar of the shells was different from before. Corporal Creaney recalled: 'And then, all hell fucking broke loose, [there] were all these explosions around us, and it was like, oh my God this is it, fucking time's up, this is the fucking end, we're out of here.'[5] The shells landed on their position. They did not have time to feel persistent dread, as men had on Longdon. This salvo was not sustained. The shells had come from British guns, and the men screamed immediately for fire to cease.

The men had become experienced in judging the shells from their sound: 'You know when the shells are in the air, roughly where they're going to land. And we heard this whistling, and "Take cover!" because we knew the rounds were going to land in our area. And everyone just tried to find a shell hole, a piece, anything, and just hold.'[6] They threw themselves to the ground to try to escape the barrage. When the shells stopped, the men came together and did a roll call. Private Parr did not respond.

Corporal Harley broke out from the group and went to see what he could find. Another man was missing too. He was injured, and perhaps he called out for help. Near the injured man, Harley found a body and inspected it: 'We went looking for signs of life; there were no signs of life. Whether he was dead or not I don't know.'[7] It must have been Parr, Harley realized either then or later, because everyone else had answered the roll call. Harley did not want to dwell on how the life had gone from the body he'd found. There was no time to stop. Even if this soldier was not yet quite dead, it would take too long to get him to the aid post to save him.

For the men left alive, the most important thing was to regroup.

Suffering shellfire from their own side was a blow, and they had to recover. Things had been going well until the shells landed right on top of them. They could all have been wiped out. They had been fortunate. Some men felt angry: 'Our young officer was going mental at the artillery guys, saying he would string them all up.'[8] Major Neame 'lividly attempted to get the gunners to sort themselves out'.[9] Now they had no choice but to get on with the attack. They could not risk this setback slowing them down. They could not afford to lose momentum.

★

One death remained unexplained. Dave Parr had for some reason not taken cover, as the rest of them had. When the shells came in, perhaps his reactions to the sound of the artillery were less attuned than those of the men who had been there for the whole of the Goose Green battle. Perhaps he had wanted to show that he was not afraid. Or maybe he did try to dive for the ground and was simply caught out.

Or, perhaps, it was just as it seemed – there was no reason. There was just the infinite collection of insignificant decisions, the sum of everyday movements that brought his body to collide with the trajectory of the shell. It was just chance: but for him it was the cruellest twist of fate. People make weapons to kill, and they cannot think of the individual lives they terminate, on purpose or by accident. All the training of the finest regiment on earth could not fortify the softness of his flesh and make him more than human. He was crumpled and disposed as easily as dust.

For the men in the regiment, after the fighting was over, it could be hard. They knew the men who had died, and they had to deal with their families. Back in Stanley, Major Neame, the officer commanding D Company, wrote to my grandmother. Neame had had to write ten such letters during the campaign, not falsely sentimental, but consoling to families he surely knew would be distraught. He did not delay, and he wrote, of course, by hand. He said Dave had 'died in the final stages of the battle for Stanley, as the Company were engaged in capturing Wireless Ridge, the final feature overlooking Stanley itself, the loss of which finally persuaded the Argentinians to surrender'. The company, Neame said, 'were under very heavy artillery fire for this attack and it was this that killed him'.

When he was killed, Dave was 'in the forefront of his platoon's assault on an enemy machine gun position'. He had been wounded at Goose Green and had come back to the battalion. His return showed 'a particular brand of dedication', and 'as you can see, he was always in the thick of it'. Neame wanted to soften the blow for Dave's mother in so far as he could. Her son was a respected soldier: 'Knowing the details is probably little consolation, but I hope if nothing else it helps to show how we also miss him, and how proud you can be of him.'[10] Neame thought it would be worse to tell her Dave had been killed by artillery from British guns.

In July, Lieutenant Waddington, Dave's platoon commander, visited my grieving family. He too knew he could not tell the truth about the origins of the fire that killed Dave, but perhaps he struggled with the truth in another way too. He had to say something. He could not say there had been no particular reason why it had been Parr, and not another man, who had been hit by the shell. An explanation like that would be difficult for a family to take, and it could look callous. He said that Dave had been 'at point' in the platoon, effectively leading the formation into attack, perhaps then the man most likely to take the blast. Waddington said, 'they thought a large rock had hidden the noise of the shell from Dave and the men with him'.[11] Another man was also wounded by the incoming fire and blown from his feet. That man had said he did not hear the noise of the shell.

One year later, in November 1983, Major General John Frost published his book *2 Para Falklands*, based on the in-house history written by Captain David Benest. Frost did not know my family were unaware that Dave had been killed by British artillery, and his book made this fact plain. Before the book came out, Major Neame had to visit my family again, to break the news about how he had died. It must have been a painful meeting. It cannot have been an easy thing for him to do. There was no way out but to say it as it was and, he recalled, one of Dave's brothers had been angry.

For my father and uncle, and my grandparents, the news was a shock. That shock added to the devastation already caused by his death, but I do not think that it made them more aggrieved. When a tabloid newspaper phoned, my uncle Chris put the receiver down without a word, but the paper printed that the family felt 'bitter'.[12] Maybe the news added further hollows to the sadness of his absence, to the remorseless question of why it had been him. Perhaps, if they seemed angry, it was their fury at the unkindness of the universe that had chosen him to die and them to live this diminished life, and then at the rewriting of the news of his death just as they were beginning to comprehend what had happened. Over time, it did not change much. People die in war.

Perhaps Dave died slowly, alone on that cold hill. He died never having come face to face with an Argentine in combat. He died having been active and under fire at Goose Green for no longer than twenty minutes, and at Wireless Ridge, he came under attack from an Argentine bombardment, and then only from the shells that killed him. He might have died on Wireless Ridge itself; but he could have been killed before they started their advance along it, before the fighting on the ridge began in earnest. Perhaps he never even had a chance to pull the trigger of his gun, except at the planes flying over Sussex Mountains. He did not die in action, attacking a machine-gun post. He died in an accident, killed by shells that fell where they were not intended.

★

At Dave's funeral on 2 December 1982, six months after the end of the war, the men were on edge. They had buried their comrades in the Falklands already; they had not expected that bodies would later come home. They had to go and meet the families, put on the disciplined display of sombre respect. The standard of the spectacle had to be high, and they had to submit to those civilian relatives – lives they preferred not to see. They travelled from funeral to funeral and did not have time to relax in between, did not have time really to talk with the families. It forced them to think about things they would rather forget or would want to deal with in their own Para way, through humour and drink, and sometimes through denial.

The soldiers came to my grandmother's bungalow after his burial. They knew that Dave's family had not yet been told he had been killed by friendly fire. They had been ordered not to speak about it. Anyone could see that the funeral would be the worst place to find out that British guns had killed him.

My family were grieving, trapped in that raw space between knowing it had happened and accepting that this was to be their lives from that point on. The extent of their grief had not yet been tempered with the recognition that they were not the only ones to have felt like this. They needed to hear what had happened; they were desperate to speak about him. Talking about him could, if only they tried hard enough, conjure him there; and if they could not bring him back, then they could try to be in his place. His middle brother, my uncle Chris, recalled that he spoke to Dave's platoon sergeant, Sergeant Light, in the corridor behind the front door. The corridor separated my grandmother's bedroom from the now formal front room. They were standing on the carpet, dark red and brown. Sergeant Light told him that there had been a lot of blood.[13]

When, in 2012, I spoke to paratroopers who had been with Dave at the time, one man said: 'I saw him go for his throat. And sure enough he was there, and that's what happened. All I saw was red . . . I thought, what happened, it was red.'[14] Another, Harley, was the first to his body: 'When I was doing the check, I couldn't see any, I didn't feel any blood . . . it could have been a big chunk of something hit him, I don't know. But I didn't actually feel any blood.'[15] If there was no blood, then perhaps Dave had died of shock, leaving his body intact. Perhaps when he died he still resembled himself as a teenage man alive: blond-haired, blue-eyed, clear-skinned, good-looking.

His repatriation report said a piece of shrapnel killed him, striking his chest on the left-hand side.[16] He was wounded, and if shrapnel had hit him in the heart – a fighting man's death – then Sergeant Light was right, there would have been a lot of blood. His childhood friend, Blue Cole, in 1982 a paratrooper in 1 Para, told me Dave's death had not been as clean as that. The shrapnel severed his head from his body, from his right shoulder to his left chest. He died, torn apart, decapitated. If he was hit thus, Blue said, he would not have known anything about it.

Blue and Dave had been to school together, and had been good friends, spending their leave together in Lowestoft and Oulton Broad. Blue was given leave from the Army to attend Dave's funeral, but he was not allowed to carry the pall. He knew how Dave had died. He had heard about it, and the friendly fire, on military traffic soon after it had happened while he was in Northern Ireland. He found out later the extent of his injuries. A soldier's burden, guarding the scars of war. He wept at Dave's graveside, standing stiff-legged and saluting over that open hole.

The last thing Dave heard, I imagine, was the noise of the incoming; or the silence of the air around the shells, a sound and a silence that might have blocked out the constant howl of the wind. The last thing he would have known maybe was the shrapnel's impact, as his hands instinctively reached up to combat the force of the blow. He could have felt the hot, sharp sear of the shell fragment; if he was fortunate, there might not have been time to feel pain. That was it. He was just hit. He was just killed. He was just unlucky. He was just one man. His body, I think, was devastated from the chest up. He carried his forces railcard and three photographs in his webbing – and with them his souvenirs, a handful of small denomination Falkland coins.[17]

★

Hours later, the Argentines began to surrender. Dave's body lay where he had fallen. The cold brought rigor mortis and his corpse stiffened quickly.[18] Some men of 3 Para, walking, racing from Longdon into Stanley, came past his body. He was wearing NBC rubber overboots to keep his feet dry.[19] The Paras might have been issued with them, but probably he had procured them from elsewhere.[20] The Welsh Guards had had some and some Paras had taken boots from them, after the ship they were on was bombed at Fitzroy. Or he might have removed them from an Argentine body. If he had, neither of them needed those boots now. One Para, hurrying past, said there was a waterproof jacket placed over his face. The jacket had come loose and was flapping in the wind.[21] The man stopped to reposition it, and then carried on. The Paras wanted to be first into Stanley.

PART THREE

11.   Our Boys

14 June 1982 – the day the Argentines surrendered, the day my uncle died – was, for Britain, a turning point of sorts. It was not 1940, the pivotal year upon which Britain's future turned, but it marked, in its own way, the ending of the era cast by the Second World War. Victory in the Falklands flavoured the 1980s. It was associated with the divided politics of the early Thatcher period. Nobody could deny her this triumph, and it augmented her authority, first in her party and then in the country. It also refreshed discussion of the place of the military in Britain's national life. Some people felt jubilation at Britain's success. It was a tremendous victory. National pride returned, Britain's post-1945 decline was ended. Others viewed it as a war for politics, or as a sign of increasing military authority in public life, a foreshadowing of the intensifying Cold War order. For some, Britain seemed a non-military country no longer.

The victory gave the armed services a new visibility, at least for a time. They came home national heroes, the men Margaret Thatcher called 'Our Boys'. She saw them as heirs to the nation's tradition: 'It was their generation who had done it. Today's heroes. Britain still breeds them . . . It was a miracle wrought by ordinary men and women with extraordinary qualities. Forever bold, forever brave, forever remembered.'[1] But the Falklands War was an old war in a new time. The changes to the traditions of commemoration and remembrance begun in 1982 had an unanticipated and enduring impact. Britain's relationship with its armed forces was altered, and the aftermath of war came home.

★

The systems the Parachute Regiment had in place to inform relatives of the death or injury of a man in service were relatively rudimentary.

The Paras had more experience than the Welsh or the Scots Guards because of the 1979 Warrenpoint ambush on the Irish border. In the rush to inform families, some information given out had been wrong, and the regiment was therefore anxious to avoid this kind of ghastly mix-up.

The Parachute Regiment's emphasis was on the accurate delivery of information to the right next of kin. It was a time-consuming task, even at its most basically administrative level. Tracking people down could be difficult. One officer, looking for the mother of a man who had been killed, found her away from home. Her neighbours told him she was staying with her family in Northern Ireland. He called on the local police to attempt to locate her. Another young wife was travelling with her father. A Parachute Regiment officer intercepted her car heading for the Dover to Zeebrugge ferry to inform her that her husband had been injured.[2]

Often it was not straightforward just to give information to the intended family members. One father, divorced from the mother of his son, felt moved to ask the Paras to inform his ex-wife in person because he was sure she would be very distressed.[3] A young woman had to give the regiment details to find her husband's parents, as they were not listed as next of kin.[4] Her father-in-law rang her on the morning she learnt her husband had died. 'He phoned, and . . . we were just talking away, and he said, and how are you? Are you alright? What have you been doing today? And I suddenly clicked. He didn't know . . . I couldn't tell him . . . somebody took the phone off me, and had to tell him. I felt terrible.'[5]

For the people doing the informing, it could be a harrowing task. Their brief was not extensive. The Army seemed to assume that all the people to whom they would be delivering news would be female – 'Try to be fully briefed on her circumstances . . . BEAR IN MIND. The considerable distress of the NOK [next of kin] . . . You may receive abuse, collapse, hysteria.' The officers doing the informing were all male of course, and the regiment instructed them to be empathetic: 'BE TACTFUL . . . give your message firmly but with compassion.' The regiment's final piece of advice was to take someone with you, perhaps someone who could offer practical help – for example, to mind small children – or perhaps someone to whom emotional communication might come more easily: 'Try to be accompanied by another person, preferably a woman.'[6]

By all accounts, the visiting officers did their jobs admirably, and probably did not need to be reminded to use tact. Major Bob Leitch had been a nurse and had informed relatives of death before. But this task was harder: 'For a military man, actually telling somebody that another soldier has died or has been wounded, telling relatives, it's a bit like telling family. I felt as if they were part of the family because of the closeness of the military bond. That's the first thing. And secondly I felt huge guilt, because I wasn't there, and they were, and I hadn't died, and they had.'[7]

Informing relatives about death and injury brought the purpose of the Army abruptly into civilian life. There could be none of the usual bravado or dark humour men might use to cope in the field of battle. Leitch went to tell a family their son, a Welsh Guard, was dead. They lived in Yorkshire. It was 7.30 a.m. 'So I knocked on the door, and it was opened by this little girl who just looked at me and I said, is your mummy and daddy in, and she just beckoned me through. And I walked into the kitchen and mother was there, and she looked me in the eye and she ran the whole gamut of emotions in a second. First there was total disbelief, and there was sort of real anger directed at me, you know, why are you here, why are you telling me, where is my son, and then she just broke down and just sobbed. And I felt terrible. And I sort of walked across and gave her a cuddle and had a cry with her. Which I suppose in retrospect was the most incongruent sight. A young officer in his uniform and this mum in her dressing gown sobbing at half past 7 in the morning.'

Major Leitch found it even harder to break the news to her husband. The father of the Welsh Guard was a train driver, driving the Durham to York early morning train. Leitch knew he was coming into York station and he went to meet the train. The rail strike meant rail workers were being vilified in some sections of the tabloid press. 'And so there was this incredible irony of having to go and tell a man who was being accused of lack of patriotism that his son had died.' The men did not know what to say to each other. They did not know what to do: 'I will never forget the pain in his eyes, because he knew when he saw me what had happened. And it was an incredible depth of just sheer ache and impotence and so I said what I had to say and just went to work.'[8]

★

Army wives were accustomed to absence. Men were often away for months at a time, and usually there was no contact except by letter. The expectation of silence was usually seen as easier than the constant anticipation of conversation. No news was good news; and the male sphere of the army and the female sphere of home were kept separate. The wives had many responsibilities – particularly the wives of officers – to uphold the name of the regiment and the reputations of their husbands. The chief way they did so was through their loyalty, but it was also in exhibiting an expected kind of propriety, of their control of themselves, their children and their home.

Such expectations harked back to the Second World War at least. The psychoanalyst John Bowlby, as well as writing about men in war, also wrote about female behaviour on the home front. He insisted that it was better for young children to stay with their mother, even with the risk of air raids, so long as the mother could sensibly manage her children's anxieties by her own measured display of emotion. In bombing attacks, for example, the mother should show a common-sense, practical attitude towards the threat they faced. He wrote that maternal panic would only compound the fear of the child, and that mothers could allay their children's natural fears by talking calmly and treating the bombs as something that would pass.[9] His views were influential, and helped to create the sense of an explicitly female kind of courage. However bad things were, women must tap their temperate reserves to keep the home fires burning, and female courage was an essential prop to the bravery of their men.[10]

These attitudes were widespread. One woman, whose husband was an officer with 2 Para, said that once she understood there had been casualties at Goose Green, she spent an anxious twenty-four hours before she knew for sure that her husband was safe. She constantly looked out of the window, waiting for a car that – mercifully for her – never arrived. Her children overheard that men had died, and they asked her, ' "Is Daddy alright?" And I remember saying to them, "I don't know but we've got to be terribly brave." ' She did not want to let her own feelings show for their sake; she knew that if she let her front slip, then she 'might not be able to gather the reins again'.[11]

Sara Jones was forty when her husband was killed at Goose Green. It was half-term, she had just collected her children from their schools, her mother was with her, and a friend was staying too. When she saw the regimental colonel coming to her house, she initially thought he was coming to tell her news of other men. As the wife of the commanding officer, she might be expected to go with him to inform other families: 'Poor man, he had the not enviable task, it's not an easy thing to do I suppose. All you can do is say it as it is.'

She did not remember much about what subsequently happened, but she had to go and tell her children: 'Yes. I think I just went and told them. You just have to tell them. I think they were out in the garden playing croquet or something. Poor lads.' She recalled that there was not much choice about what she should do, and how she should grapple with her emotion: 'You either take to your bed like a Victorian lady, or you get on with it.' She wanted her children to be resilient, not to feel that this was something that should dominate them, not to feel they had to look after her, not to be immersed into something so unhappy. When half-term ended, they went back to their schools. With their friends, she felt, they would be better able to do the things boys like to do – playing cricket, passing time – free from the constant reminder of what they had lost.[12]

News could only spread in person, or by telephone. Bryan and Carole Dodsworth remembered when a lieutenant from Lichfield came to tell them their son was dead. It was a hot day, and they had been working in the garden. They were watching *CHiPs* on TV and Carole had fallen asleep. Bryan already knew, he said, that Mark had died. He had woken at 5.10 in the morning from a deep sleep, said, 'Are you alright son?' and fallen back to sleep. It was his way of understanding that he had been there for his child, as he lay dying – not quickly, but bleeding to death, they later discovered, in the first dip on the hilt of Mount Longdon.

Twelve hours later, the man arrived. Bryan's parents were at a wedding, and Carole did not know whether to try to contact them, or to let them enjoy themselves and risk that they would be angry she had not told them straight away. She needed to contact her two other teenage sons. The youngest was out with a friend, so she phoned the friend's mother, who was annoyed to be disturbed. She asked why Carole wanted to know where her son was. 'And we went through this conversation, and I said, "I'm awfully sorry, but I wouldn't be phoning you if it wasn't an emergency, we've lost his brother in the Falklands, so I need to get in touch with [son's name] to tell him." That changed the whole thing. She went and found him, brought him home.'[13]

Gareth Jones was seventeen, and was alone in the family house, revising for his A levels. His nineteen-year-old brother was a private with 3 Para. It was 14 June. His mother and father were both out celebrating the end of the war, his father with work colleagues, his mother with friends in a local pub. He was taking a break from his books downstairs: 'I saw a black Vauxhall Chevette pull out-side, with a military number plate. I looked and I thought, that's a military car. For a second you think, what's that doing there? Then I thought . . . no. No, no, no.'

The doorbell rang. Gareth opened the door and a tall man stood there. Gareth explained that his parents were both out and would not be back until late. The man was uncertain: 'He wasn't briefed for this. I could see him thinking, what am I going to do?' Gareth invited him in, but the man said he would wait in his car. Gareth told him to pull round the corner so that his father would not first see the car when he arrived back at the house. There was nothing Gareth could do. 'I went and sat in the chair and looked at the telly – I wasn't watching the telly but was looking at it, thinking what am I going to do.'

When his father, Richard, came home two or three hours later, he was in a good mood: 'He walked in, and I said, "Oh Dad, a man's called" . . . and at that point the doorbell rang. Dad said, "What is it?" I said, "I think you'd better get that." Dad went to the door and let this bloke in, and Dad knew what it was, straight away. The guy stood there and went through a very brief spiel of Mr Jones, I'm very sorry to have to inform you, your son's been killed. Dad threw his car keys at him. The guy made his quick exit.'

Richard then had to inform his wife. He phoned the manager of the pub she was at. He could not tell the manager what had happened, but he asked him to find a pretext to take his wife Pam upstairs. Richard went to the pub to tell her. She was in a separate room, watching the 10 o'clock news. The manager cleared the pub. According to Gareth, 'People who were in the pub who were walking home up the road heard her screaming.'[14]

Theresa Burt's son Jason was seventeen when he was killed on Longdon. A man in an army jeep came to the family's house. Theresa and her husband Sid were out at work on their market stall on Petticoat Lane. A neighbour, Jean, stopped the man and guessed what had happened. Jean took him to the market stall. He was hesitant, but Jean forced him to wait. She wanted him to tell Jason's father, Sid, first, and then for Sid to tell Theresa.

Sid had left his stall to go to the toilet. When he came out the man was waiting for him. The man told him and he broke down.[15] Theresa recalled that she realized Sid had been missing for half an hour or so and she did not know where he was. 'And I saw a crowd, in like the middle of the market, and I thought that's where he is, there's a fight or something going on. But then he got nearer to me, and he said . . . I said, "Where have you been?" . . . And then I could see him crying. And he said two army fellas, two army men were waiting at the top of the stairs when he came out the toilet and told him. Twenty-three that died. I can't even remember getting up. I remember screaming Jason's name, for so long.'[16]

★

The news was always a shock, and the next few days passed, in all the accounts, 'in a blur'. The informants usually did not know, or give, details about how the men had died. Some people wanted desperately to know, and others preferred not to think about it. The official view was that it was of no help to pass on such details, not only because they were often so terrible, but also because there were many uncertainties, even contradictions, about the circumstances in which men had died. Carole and Bryan Dodsworth said it was hard only to get bits and pieces of information. At the memorial service at St Paul's Cathedral in July 1982, they were kept away from the soldiers, and they did not know why. It took them many years to piece together the details of Mark's death from information they got, mainly from the men who served alongside him.

Ann Townsend, whose son Neil Grose was killed on Longdon too, said: 'The first thing you want is detail. Well, where, when, how? How was he injured? How did he die? Did he suffer? But he [the informant] obviously knew absolutely nothing more than he'd been detailed to come and tell us that Neil had been killed.' She found out very gradually that Neil had died, not instantaneously, but in pain from a chest wound. He had been shot twice. She accepted that there could have been no alternative for Neil in the circumstances on Mount Longdon, but she was a nurse and she knew it could have been different: 'My feeling was if someone could have put a chest drain in him, because he was shot in the chest, or knew how to treat him for chest wounds, he may well have survived to have got back to some warmth and comfort and pain relief. But obviously that didn't happen.'[17]

Jay Hyrons, whose husband Gary Bingley was killed, said that finding out how he had died, by a seemingly bland administrative oversight, made her feel worse. On the temporary death certificate she received, through the post with no explanation, it said the cause of his death was a 'gunshot wound to the head'. She knew, of course, that any death in war would be violent, but 'I didn't need to see that on a piece of paper'.[18] Freda McKay said she wished she had not been told that Ian's body had been badly damaged. She did not want to have to think about the brutal details of the end of her son's life. Rita Hedicker said that she never wanted to know how, or exactly where, her son had been killed. She knew what he had been doing and that was enough: 'I'm not that morbid.'[19]

Some men came home to their relatives in their imaginations. According to Jay, 'There's something very different about not seeing someone dead. Gary would turn up in my dreams and say, "I told you I was coming home." You don't want to believe it. You can hold yourself subconsciously in the denial phase for quite a long time.'[20] Richard and Pam Jones said how often they imagined Craig coming home. 'I know, when they were coming back, you're scouring the faces, had they made a mistake, could I see Craig in the crowd?' Pam added: 'And of course you could. Every other one was him.'[21]

Alastair Wood, whose brother David was killed in the gorse gully at Goose Green, said: 'I kept seeing my brother. That summer I went to Glastonbury with some friends. I kept seeing him in the crowd. I dreamed about where he is. I kept trying to make things OK again. Even now, I see people, I think oh, he's like my brother.'[22] Catherine Dent, whose husband Chris was killed near David Wood, recalled: 'You'd hear things like a noise outside and you'd think, ooh, Chris is early. Then you think, oh, it can't be Chris. All the classic stages of grief, for quite a bit I kept thinking they're going to ring me up in a minute and tell me they'd made a mistake, that for some reason he'd swapped dog tags with somebody the same height, and kit, and appearance.'[23]

Gareth Jones said that for many years, if he heard a helicopter flying over, he would be startled and think his brother was coming back. Perhaps Craig was not dead, perhaps he had been conducting a mission that nobody had been able to tell them about: 'I'd look and wonder if Craig was going to jump out. And . . . it was always like, is he really dead, or is it . . . I'd stop and look up and watch it. Is that them coming to bring Craig? It'd fly off and, Gareth, don't be a fool. You idiot. Walk on.'[24]

★

The modern traditions of war commemoration began after the Great War, a cataclysm that claimed the lives in military service of between 722,785 and 772,000 Britons.[25] Once the war ended, the government had to respond to the anguish of parents, widows, siblings and relatives of those who had been killed. It did not do so financially. During the war, the government did extend the number of people eligible for war widows' and dependants' pensions, but the amount guaranteed only a minimum subsistence. After the war, facing unprecedented levels of public expenditure, as well as the question of what to do with returning disabled and potentially unemployed servicemen, and in a climate when expectations of government provision were not embedded, it was hardly likely to increase its provision for families of the dead.[26]

Nevertheless, Lloyd George's government did have to address the very pressing issue of how to recognize and to commemorate the Great War. There was no precedent for this. Some of the practices adopted had been used previously, but the industrialized slaughter of the Great War was unlike anything that had gone before.

The war assembled an idea of a British nation united against Prussian militarism, but Britain's democracy was ever developing, and the risk of social division was considerable. Nobody could look eastwards across the Continent and believe that Britons were totally immune to the attraction of communism, socialism or industrial unrest. Some 35 million working days were spent in strikes in 1919. Men had mobilized willingly to fight for their country, but the authorities feared that violence could radicalize them if there was no work and if there could be no settled home. Women had contributed to the war effort in ways that stretched the acceptable boundaries of their sex – 800,000 had worked in munitions factories – but the 1918 Representation of the People Act extended the franchise to men over twenty-one without property, but only to women over the age of thirty. The reach of Britain's Empire extended in the Middle East, but the experience of army life and the idea of national self-determination meant Britain's formal relationship with its white dominions, and the acceptance of British rule within the colonies, was changing. The boundaries of the national community were not fixed. The Great War delayed Home Rule for Ireland and a violent uprising in Dublin in 1916 escalated into a war for independence and civil war.

On top of the divisions of class, race, sex and nationality, the government faced the sharp divisions of bereavement. People had been bereaved on an extraordinary scale. More than one in seven of the adult male population under the age of twenty-five had been killed, and about one in nine households lost a man in the war.[27] But bereavement was very far from universal and the majority of men did come home. Mass bereavement was concentrated in horrible bursts, and disproportionately affected some groups, such as the Highland Scots, attendees of some public schools, and those from urban areas where men had joined up together in the 'Pals' battalions. The government's response, inspired in part by influential men like Rudyard Kipling, who had themselves been bereaved, was to universalize the sense of grief. Britain was a nation in mourning. Its lost sons were the sons of all its people.

Commemoration after the Great War flowered from the traditions of silence, respect and sacrifice that were familiar to anyone who had grown up with habits of religious teaching, even if they did not regularly attend church.[28] The government did not have a considered strategy as to how to memorialize. Even a month before 11 November 1919, it did not appear as if there had been a decision to mark the anniversary of Armistice Day.[29] Nevertheless, the rituals of memorialization that evolved in the two years after the Great War were still enormously popular and showed no signs of abating a century later. Of course, not everyone who had been bereaved felt consoled by such national commemoration.[30] But the effect of the commemorative practices they adopted was to honour sacrifice through recognition, and at the same time to allow private and individual reflection.

At the centre of national memorialization was the Cenotaph – the 'empty tomb'. Its design was simple. Originally made from wood and plaster, it proved so popular that the government commissioned Sir Edwin Lutyens to cast it in stone. The Cenotaph was imposing – symbolizing the magnitude of what had been lost – but not dominating. It was plain, but also graceful, in white, the sides almost imperceptibly curving inwards.[31] Above all, it was unchanging. The Cenotaph was the sign of an undefeated nation – a nation that had fought a greater evil and so must always look back with sorrow, but gratitude, upon the blood that had been spilt.

The ritual of the two-minute silence bound the monument with the bereaved, and it meant that people everywhere, all over the country, were connected in mourning, whether they had lost a relative or not. On 11 November 1919, at eleven minutes past 11, activity ceased: trains stopped, machinery shut down, men took off their caps and the nation stood still. Beyond the instruction to quell all noise, which the government could not possibly have enforced without the popular will to carry it out – in 1936 four men observed the silence in a diving bell in the depths of the River Tyne – there was no intrusion, no instruction as to what to think.[32] Local communities created thousands of memorials, often drawing on the design of the Cenotaph, but adding figures of soldiers and etching the names of the fallen men.[33] Each individual soldier was given his place. Relatives came to the memorials to reach out to the men who were never coming home.[34]

The question of what to do with the bodies of the dead threatened to undermine acceptance of public commemoration. Early in the war, the government decided not to bring bodies back to Britain. Partly, their decision was practical. The numbers of dead were high, the difficulties of finding, identifying and returning bodies considerable. It could be bad for morale if there were a daily procession of funerals through British streets. But relatives, including some influential people such as Foreign Secretary Arthur Balfour and Parliamentary Under-Secretary of State for Foreign Affairs Robert Cecil, continued to call for bodies to return home. The decision was never overturned.

It was costly to repatriate, but for Fabian Ware, who initiated the Imperial War Graves Commission in 1917, the principle of burying men together, where they had fallen, was more important than any consideration of cost.[35] Repatriation would expose a brutal unfairness if the families of wealthy servicemen could bring their men home and pay for opulent or even just respectable burials, while the families of the poor could not. Bringing home the bodies could allow some other horrible divisions to surface too. It could show rather bluntly which men had been too badly injured to be identified, and those who had died a painful death. Some families would have a body to mourn, and others, nothing.[36]

The decision to leave men where they had fallen, together with the men with whom they had served, consolidated British military traditions. In some ways, the British cemetery overseas became the enduring symbol of Britain's Empire, centred on an idea of a pastoral, Christian, timeless England. In 1914, Rupert Brooke – escaping from his own complicated love life into romantic morality – wrote 'If I should die, think only this of me: / That there's some corner of a foreign field, / That is for ever England.' At the same time, the reburying of Britain's war dead into neatly ordered cemeteries, each grave marked with an identical headstone, was a remarkable democratization of death in service. Each British man – and, of course, from 1916 men had been conscripted – was recognized as equal in his sacrifice.

For the bereaved, the absence of bodies could compound their pain. In reaction to this, on Armistice Day in 1920, the authorities held a funeral for the Unknown Warrior. Whose body was in the casket genuinely was unknown. With impressive attention to detail, on 9 November 1920, six bodies were exhumed from six different battle sites in Northern France. The bodies were taken to Ypres and a blindfolded officer selected one of the coffins.[37] The coffin was taken past the Cenotaph and interred in Westminster Abbey. A million and a quarter British people visited the tomb within a week, many in hope that the body might be that of their own son, husband or brother. During the silence, many could not stifle the noise of their weeping.[38]

The Great War became, as H. G. Wells put it in 1914, 'the war that will end war'. Wells intended this as justification of a good war against Germany, and during the war years the pervasive mood was that this was a necessary, if unwelcome, fight.[39] From the end of the 1920s, the publication of memoirs and poetry – by Robert Graves, Vera Brittain, Siegfried Sassoon, Wilfred Owen – suggested an altered sensibility. Even if Britain had had little choice but to fight, the First World War had taken the flower of the country's youth.[40] The 'war that will end war' became a catastrophe that had been so appalling that it had to be the last time – the only time – that people should endure such suffering.

When war came again, however, it could hardly be seen as other than a just fight against the tyranny of Nazism. The Second World War had two consequences for the remembrance of war in Britain. First, it confirmed in the public mind that the First World War had been futile. The BBC's enormously popular documentary series *The Great War*, shown in 1964, used archive film, sometimes inaccurately, that hardened an impression of thousands sent to die pointlessly in the sludge of the trenches.[41] Secondly, the civilian experience of being under attack, and the very real threat to Britain's national survival, meant that from 1940 the Second World War was remembered as 'the people's war'. Until the summer of 1942, the Germans had killed more civilians in Britain than they had British military personnel. By 1945, Britain had lost around 61,000 civilians and 270,139 servicemen.[42] The war paved the way for a majority Labour government. The welfare state and the establishment of British social democracy moved away from the old order. The people had paid for the follies of their leaders, and now it really should never be allowed to happen again.

The Second World War, at least in the short term, reasserted traditional ideas about Britain and its place in the world. Britain was an Empire, a Great Power, uninvaded and undefeated. Compared with Britain's nearest neighbours in Western Europe, and particularly with the Soviet Union, British losses had not been devastating. When the government discussed how to remember the Second World War, they could not come up with a better alternative than to absorb its losses into the existing rituals.[43] Local authorities carved names onto existing memorials, and added commemorative spaces in areas of public use: parks, gardens and community centres.[44] Commemoration of both wars would thereafter take place on 'Remembrance Sunday'.

British wars after 1945 continued to be remembered within these traditions. The often complex and sometimes protracted wars of decolonization and the Cold War that Britain fought post-1945 did not lend themselves to demonstrative acts of commemoration. Military communities took charge of memorials for specific campaigns, and Remembrance Day parades absorbed the losses of Palestine, Korea, Malaya, Kenya, Cyprus and Suez. After the end of National Service in 1963, campaign remembrance became even more of an in-house matter. The complicated conflict in Northern Ireland, as well as the threat of terrorism on the mainland, meant there was not much noise about commemoration.

★

The Falklands War brought commemoration back to the forefront of national debate. On 26 July 1982, the government held a memorial service for families of servicemen who had lost their lives at St Paul's Cathedral. The service and its planning exposed disagreements both about the use of British military force and how it should be remembered.

The Archbishop of Canterbury, Robert Runcie, had been a contemporary of Margaret Thatcher's at Oxford, and had won the Military Cross as a lieutenant with the Scots Guards in Normandy in the Second World War. The experience of war fortified his faith. He had 'touched evil' at the liberation of Belsen concentration camp, and he had killed enemy soldiers: 'When I'd been very successful in knocking out a German tank, I went up to it and saw four young men dead. I felt a bit sick. Well, I was sick, actually.'[45] He believed governments should emphasize that war was always regrettable, and should seek reconciliation after conflict.

Consequently, the Church and the government clashed about what should be included in the service. The Archbishop proposed the service should be interdenominational and thus involve the Reverend Dr Kenneth Greet and Cardinal Basil Hume. Greet was the Moderator of the Free Church Federal Council and had recently published adverse comments on the Falklands campaign in *The Guardian*. Hume supported Pope John Paul II's pleas for reconciliation with Argentina and he wanted to read from the Pope's recent address in Coventry. The Pope had prayed for those who suffered 'in that sad conflict'. The Dean of St Paul's, the Very Reverend Dr Alan Webster, was also thought by the government to have pacifist leanings. He proposed to read the Lord's Prayer in Spanish.

These sentiments displeased the government. Defence Secretary John Nott said 'this was a service for the veterans of the war and in particular the families of the British dead'.[46] He did not think they would want to hear a Spanish version of the Lord's Prayer. At the suggestion of including a Spanish translation in the written Order of Service, Mrs Thatcher queried 'Why'?[47] She said she would go public if an attempt was made to bar members of the Task Force from reading lessons, and Nott began to suggest that perhaps the service should be abandoned, 'and instead have a service under military auspices on Horse Guards Parade'.[48] The Bishop of London felt moved to meet the Prime Minister to warn her that the Dean of St Paul's could not be trusted to execute the service according to the government's wishes. He felt it 'essential that the Prime Minister should invoke the help of the Archbishop (or even the Queen) in ensuring that, once the Order of Service was agreed, it was not modified in any way'.[49]

Perhaps the threat of not holding a service at all pushed the Church authorities to compromise. In accordance with the Church's wishes, the service was called simply the 'Falkland Islands Service', and the theme was thanksgiving, remembrance, peace and reconciliation. The chaplain of 2 Para and two junior members of the Task Force were among those who read lessons, and there was no hint of a Spanish version of the Lord's Prayer. However, nobody had vetted Archbishop Runcie's sermon, and it was this that diverged most significantly from the government's mood.

Dr Runcie's speech reflected his attitude that military violence carried out by nation states had a terrible destructive power. He began by praising the courage and restraint, in the face of horror, of the British Task Force. But, he said, since 1945 the world had lived with the capacity to destroy humankind. War was a sign of human failure and the path of history should be away from war. Nobody should claim God's will for a group or a nation. Men's love and loyalty should be for God, and war might come if they transferred that love to 'some God substitute, one of the most dangerous being nationalism'. Runcie prayed for the dead of this war, and for the Argentine dead, and hoped that in sorrow there could be the seeds of reconciliation.[50]

In reaction, the government proposed a more celebratory form of commemoration. 'The boss is livid,' Denis Thatcher told the press. 'I think the pacifist, liberal, wet establishment were shocked at our going to war and even more shocked at our winning victory,' said Conservative MP Julian Amery.[51] Plans began for an event in the City of London. Paid for and organized by the City Corporation, with co-operation from the Ministry of Defence, the military march past involved over a thousand members of the Task Force and, according to police estimates, was attended by 300,000 people, many of whom burst into spontaneous rendition of 'Rule, Britannia'.[52] Afterwards, Mrs Thatcher spoke at a reception at the Guildhall to a standing ovation. Her biographer Charles Moore called it not just the best moment in her career, but quite possibly 'the happiest moment of her life'.[53]

The march past in the City caused its own controversy. Part of that was diplomatic. The twelfth of October was 'Columbus Day', the commemoration of the day that Christopher Columbus sighted American land and celebrated as a national holiday in much of that continent. The Foreign Office commented that the Argentines could hardly believe their luck that Britain had chosen to celebrate its victory on this day. Few in Latin America were likely to regard it as a coincidence.[54] At home, planning for the parade caused concern because injured veterans were not initially included.[55] The Lord Mayor of London said this was because men who were badly injured, even disabled, might be uncomfortable having to stand for long periods or to walk. In reality, the City Corporation had failed to think about it.[56]

Particularly after the service at St Paul's, Mrs Thatcher was extremely reluctant to detract from the sense that the Falklands War was a tremendous achievement. Her instinct was to foreclose on any potential criticism of the way the war had been fought, or of the fact of the war itself. She probably did not give the specific issue of the wounded too much thought, and perhaps she assumed that the injured had no place in the celebration of war.

The public often shared these attitudes. One man, who had served in the Second World War, said that he had canvassed the views of the eight middle-aged men who worked alongside him, 'at the depot'. None were surprised at the exclusion of the disabled: 'One likened it to having a display of road accident victims at the motor show, not a bad comparison I thought.'[57] Nevertheless, times were beginning to change. In reaction to complaints, the government quickly relented. They invited six men in wheelchairs to take part.

★

Margaret Thatcher's attitude towards the Falklands victory pointed to shifts in Britain's relations with its armed services. She saw Britain's performance in war as a sign that the country's post-war decline was over. On 3 July, she addressed a Conservative rally at Cheltenham racecourse. She told them 'we have ceased to be a nation in retreat'.[58] Military success, a great and emphatic triumph, pointed a way out of two decades of uncertainty about Britain's role on the international stage. That triumph also distracted attention away from the country's economic ills. Look what could be achieved, she said, when people pulled together and got on with the job. It was a brisk remedy that seemed to stand not just for her vision of Britain rediscovering its national character, but also for the forward momentum of her economic programme.

Mrs Thatcher held the armed services in frank admiration. She first used the phrase 'our boys' in 1978, in response to the threat of Irish terrorism.[59] She was comfortable with men in the ranks and she defended difficult decisions, such as the sinking of the Argentine ship the *General Belgrano* on 2 May, saying it was necessary to protect the lives of 'our boys'. Her ease with those troops was explained in part by the fact that, compared to other politicians of her era, she was distant from armed service. In the 1970s and early 1980s, as a woman and a senior Conservative, she stood out because she did not have military experience. Until the 1960s, military service was the second most common occupation of parliamentarians, behind the law.[60] In 1982, of the twenty-one male members of Thatcher's twenty-three-strong Cabinet, seven had been the age to fight in the Second World War. Peter Carrington, Francis Pym and William Whitelaw had all won the Military Cross, and Keith Joseph had been mentioned in despatches. Eleven more of the Cabinet had gained military experience when they had been conscripted during National Service.

Mrs Thatcher was aware of her own lack of military expertise. It was one reason she sought such keen counsel from military advisers. Her distance from the military meant that she could stand alongside the troops and not face unanswered questions about how she herself would have performed in combat, nor worry if, in other circumstances, she would have been giving them direct orders. Her distance from the military probably deepened her concern towards the loss of young lives. They faced a kind of peril she would never know, and her awareness of it heightened her sense of responsibility for sending them into conflict.

She was also most interested in the human stuff of military commitment. She did not share the preoccupation of many men in the government and armed services with equipment and technology. Discussing the problems of finding enough vessels to transport troops to the islands, she feigned boredom: 'The world', she said, 'is full of ships.'[61] It was endeavour that moved her. The nation seemed for a time obsessed with the activity known by the Marines as 'yomping' and by the paratroopers as 'tabbing' – that is, 'tactical advance to battle', or, in this context, the long march across boggy terrain bearing heavy kit. In the 1988 TV drama set during the Falklands War, *Tumbledown*, Scots Guards officer Robert Lawrence commented to his nurse in hospital that 'all anyone wants to know about is bloody yomping'.[62] Mrs Thatcher was also, to an extent, galvanized by the idea of 'special forces'. The SAS captured the public imagination in 1980, after special forces ended the hostage crisis in the Iranian Embassy in London, and Falklands' soldiers would come to be seen in much the same register.

Mrs Thatcher's interest in soldiers also pointed to a shift in thinking about Britain's overseas power. The Suez crisis in 1956 had been associated with the Navy – the last time a British fleet had sailed from British shores. The Falklands victory put to rest the Suez humiliation, and obviously the outcome of the war depended on the efforts of all the services. But in contrast to the Paras, who relished the chance of combat, many in the Navy were not at all gung-ho. Lieutenant David Tinker, a naval officer on board HMS *Glamorgan*, wrote to his parents before he was killed: 'I utterly oppose all this killing that is going on over a flag.'[63] Radio operator Glenn Canham, on board the frigate HMS *Arrow*, wrote to his sister and her husband: 'Honestly there are quite a few people here who are pretty fed up with the stupidity of it all.'[64] Britain sailed to the Falklands in a great spectacle of naval splendour, but returned in some ways as an army, its power associated less with its hardware – the ships assembled in the dockyards of an imperial seafaring nation – than with the rigours of its military training, the character of its will to overcome and the force of its heritage. Those qualities were best embodied by its personnel, and perhaps particularly by its young marines and soldiers.

Thatcher's blend of distance from and unambiguous admiration for the armed services was a fine line to tread. Many commentators thought she had gone too far. According to diplomat David (later Sir David) Goodall, after the Falklands Mrs Thatcher 'spoke like Queen Elizabeth I . . . She *looked* like Queen Elizabeth I.'[65] Some military leaders seemed to think that Thatcher had overstepped a boundary. Julian Thompson, the brigadier in charge of 3 Commando Brigade, said, 'Although you don't mind, if you like, dying for your Queen and your country, you certainly don't contemplate dying for politicians.'[66] Occasionally those same commentators also betrayed something of their own presuppositions about war leadership and what it should entail. As a woman, and as a woman from a lower middle-class background, nobody had expected that Thatcher might prove herself through Britain's military success.[67]

Perhaps that suggests exactly why Mrs Thatcher's change of tone about the armed services was so resonant. Some in the Conservative Cabinet had been snooty about her social background, and had talked about this in military terms. Francis Pym was reputed to have said: 'We have a corporal at the top, and not a cavalry officer.'[68] Thatcher's stress on 'our boys' was, in some ways, classless. She wanted to celebrate the achievements of the men in the ranks as much as those of their officers. She contrasted those who 'got on with the job' with the vested interests of what she saw as the liberal establishment: the BBC, the universities, the Church, the Foreign and Commonwealth Office. She favoured a new form of tradition. There was no such thing as society, only individuals and families, and the regimental family was an exemplar of the ties of loyalty and pride she admired.[69]

Her belief that she should strive to break down some embedded forms of privilege was demonstrated in her attitude to military decorations. She wanted to treat all ranks the same way, although this was not the military custom. The MP William Waldegrave proposed the abolition of divisions between ranks in the award of medals. As it stood, the Victoria Cross was the only medal that could be won by men in any rank; otherwise, officers and soldiers were eligible for different awards. Thatcher's formal reply was that the medals had reputations that went back to the Crimea, and among servicemen they were held in equal esteem. But she wrote by hand at the end of the letter that she agreed with Waldegrave, although she could do little about it until there was appetite for change in the services: 'Bravery is the same quality wherever it occurs and I dislike the distinctions.'[70]

★

What was it like, for the paratroopers who had fought in the Falklands, when they came home? The Paras did not come home by ship, but by plane from Ascension Island. They landed at Brize Norton in Oxfordshire. There was no ceremony. The Paras did not have the slow and steady sail into a triumphal welcome at Portsmouth granted to the Royal Marines. They did not see the cheering crowds, the waving flags. Many men were simply relieved to be home. They had lived to see their wives, parents and children again.

Public attention was often directed towards their valour. Almost as soon as the war had ended, *The Sun* newspaper ran a story declaring that H Jones, the Commanding Officer of 2 Para, would be awarded a posthumous Victoria Cross.[71] The Ministry of Defence's Honours and Awards Committee agreed Victoria Crosses for Jones and McKay, and a Distinguished Conduct Medal for Private Illingsworth. The Committee were unsure that Jones's courage had undermined the enemy's will to fight, as the citation suggested, but they agreed nevertheless that his 'single-minded determination to get on, to close with and destroy the enemy so inspired his battalion that they went on to achieve a feat of arms which, in the event, defied all accepted military theory'.[72]

Most men, however, were uncomfortable with public perceptions that they were heroes. They felt something far stranger. Stepping from the plane onto the tarmac, it was summer. England was warm and people were happy. Families at home had lived through uncertainty, but they had not seen the realities of combat. Private Mark Eyles-Thomas said, as he hugged his young girlfriend, 'She felt soft and warm to touch. Her fragrance was sweet and flowery. It all seemed so foreign and unreal after the hardness and violence . . . [she] hadn't changed. I, on the other hand, had, and didn't want my life overtaken or controlled by the soft touch or sweet smell of a woman, especially one that I felt no longer knew the man who was in her arms.'[73]

Corporal John Gartshore said: 'I'll be honest, it was like something out of a story where you're in a parallel world. You think, I've been here before, but why has everyone changed?' He did not want the fuss and excitement of 'Welcome Home' parties. He did not want people to refer to him as a hero or buy him drinks in the pub when they had not done so before. He needed the company of other men who had done the same as him. 'I was on a massive high, I couldn't settle, sleep, I said to [my wife] I've got to go away for a couple of days. I'd got my Bergen in my car, I said I'll be away for 3 or 4 days, I'm going up the moors. I went up the Yorkshire moors, and there was loads of blokes up there . . . and we all used to go to this pub, nobody bothered us, sit there and have a few beers, then go back up and get our heads down and think about things, cooking out of mess tins again, and that's what it was like. I spent about 5 days up there.'[74]

Lance Corporal Len Carver, whose back and shoulder were badly wounded by gunshot, said he could not bear the sympathy of his family. He had changed, and it was impossible for them and him to understand: 'I think part of my make-up is that I'm a bit like an animal, when I'm in pain or injured I tend to keep myself to myself . . . I was laying out on the sofa. My mum had come up and sat down alongside me, she said a couple of things, consoling things, and I couldn't take it and I had to get up, I ended up running . . . I shouldn't have been running because of my injuries still being open. I ended up going off across the fields, and was gone for twelve, fourteen hours. I didn't do anything, I just went and sat. I needed my space.'[75]

For men like Carver, who had been badly injured, coming home could be a relief, but it also revealed in no uncertain terms how much their lives had been changed. Private Stephen Tuffen was eighteen and had been shot in the head: 'My head injuries were very severe, they took my helmet off and brains flopped down the back of my neck.

Well, I survived, and other guys that were perceived to have lesser injuries, or less visual injuries, died. And there doesn't seem any logic to it. That can add to this guilt feeling of why? Why have I survived? Life seems so unfair to the guys with families who didn't come home, and there was me as an eighteen-year-old, and did. It's quite a strange feeling at the time.' Tuffen lost his memory too. 'When I was first injured I had virtually no memory at all . . . and as I recovered, bits would come back. Some have come back in dreams and you're never sure if it's true or not.' Their injuries obviously affected their relations with their families. For Tuffen, until his operation he had very little vision: 'It was like you were crying all the time, so it was all blurred and not a lot of it.' When his parents came to see him, he knew them, but he did not initially recognize his siblings, who were younger than him. They were upset. He was in hospital until September 1983.[76] Corporal Martin Margerison had been shot in the shoulder and jaw. He said his eldest daughter, just two years old, was frightened of him: 'My daughter, my eldest daughter, was quite shocked when she seen me, because I had nothing, just an absolute mess. And that hurt me.'[77]

That sense that everything would be different now was far removed from the press interest in the glory of war. Len Carver said that coming home made them feel shame. On the military plane, flying into Brize Norton, they were told to close the blinds. When they came off the plane, they were pushed through a covered walkway all the way to the stairs. They got on to buses, converted to put stretchers in, and all the windows were blacked out. The men realized the authorities were trying to hide them away. 'We thought, they're embarrassed.' The families had been told to go to the RAF hospital at Wroughton, just down the road from Brize Norton and, 'even they were saying, "Why were your windows blacked out?"' He wondered if returning troops were going to be spat at, as he knew American troops had been after Vietnam.[78]

Corporal Tom Harley said that the boundaries of their lives had shifted. There was nothing now that could stand above him; he was beholden to nobody. The world had wanted him to die. He had accepted it, and now he was not dead: 'But when you've accepted death and you come back and you haven't died, you've still accepted it . . . something inside of you is not quite right, because – I've accepted death but I'm not dead, what's wrong?'[79]

★

After the Falklands, soldiers' bodies were repatriated for the first time in Britain's military history. It was not a difficult decision for Mrs Thatcher to take, although the weight of tradition was against her. Bodies had been brought home after the 1956 Suez crisis, but this was because of fears for the security of the cemetery in Nasser's Egypt rather than any decisive break with military practice. When they sailed for the Falklands, the armed services assumed that bodies would be buried together, in the theatre where they had fallen. Most men in senior ranks in the army preferred to keep their men together, to honour soldiers as fallen comrades – together in death as they had been in life.

As soon as the war ended, a small number of families wrote to the government to request that bodies should be brought home. My own family was one. Dave, my father wrote to Mrs Thatcher, 'had a deep love of his native Suffolk in which he spent seventeen of his nineteen years'. His parents' lives 'had been shattered' by Dave's death, and 'they should not be denied this last, small consolation'.[80] Shocked with grief, and feeling responsible for his parents, my father, I think, thought the war should not have happened. It was Thatcher's war, and she should look squarely at the heartbreak she had caused. Other families had different reasons for requesting that the bodies be brought home. Some felt simply that the Falkland Islands were a long way away and it would be impossible to pay their regular respects.[81] Another family feared that if the Falklands returned to Argentina, their son's body would be in foreign soil. They implored Mrs Thatcher and the Queen – they were mothers too. Everyone had seen the anguish on the Queen's face as she thought of Prince Andrew, who had piloted a helicopter during the conflict; everyone had seen tears in Mrs Thatcher's eyes the previous year as her son Mark had been lost in a car rally in the Sahara desert.

But it was not just family pressure that prompted Thatcher to overturn this tradition. Only ten families – a small number – asked the government to bring the bodies home.[82] It was probably more pressing that the tabloid press supported repatriation. Their regular reporting of other hardships families faced perhaps amplified pressure for the government to act.[83] In addition, about 200 members of the public wrote in to the government to argue that bodies should come back to Britain. One of the most common reasons people gave was that they had seen TV footage of the burial of the paratroopers killed at Goose Green, broadcast after the end of the conflict. The families of the dead did not know the burial had happened, nor that it was about to be shown on TV. Catherine Dent said: 'My mother-in-law screamed and fled, and my father-in-law and I kind of flew to each other and watched it, both crying.'[84]

The footage of the burial seemed to lead to a widespread view that British soldiers had not been given a proper send-off on the islands. After the Goose Green battle, the Parachute Regiment had dug a trench at the hospital station at Ajax Bay and laid their men to rest. They had known, obviously, that this resting place would only be temporary, as nobody would want to leave Britain's dead in a small corner this far flung. The battalion, suffering its biggest loss in a battle in the post-war period, had marked the burials. Each body, wrapped in a Union flag, was carried and laid into the trench. Reverend David Cooper read a lesson, although he had not known before he went to the burial that he would be asked to do so.[85] A cameraman filmed it, and later the film was screened in Britain. The collective grave and the relative lack of ceremony shocked some viewers. They thought this was the Paras' final send-off, and they wrote afterwards to say that the men who had died deserved something better.

The practicalities also did not stand in the way of a decision to repatriate. Of the 255 British dead, 174 had been at sea, and their bodies could not be recovered. It would cost about as much to pay for all 255 families to visit the islands as it would to repatriate the bodies fallen on land, and so cost was never a factor in the government's discussions. The civil service did ask themselves whether the recovery of the bodies could cause resentment from those whose relatives had died at sea, and so could not have a body to mourn. But the truth was that families already knew whether they could bring a body home or not. Even for those whose bodies had been very badly damaged, their comrades knew where they had been when they were killed, and knew, broadly speaking, what had happened to them. Nobody was in that horrible no man's land of 'missing, presumed dead'. Repatriation would not open new divides between the bereaved families. The government also agreed to pay for families who chose for the bodies to remain in the Falkland Islands, and for all those lost at sea, to travel to the islands to visit the sites where their relatives lay.

On 8 July 1982, Mrs Thatcher announced that bodies would be repatriated for those families requesting it. Many families were then not sure what to do. They wanted, perhaps, to know what others would choose. Sara Jones opted to leave her husband's body in the Falklands: 'One had got mentally attuned to his being buried in the Falklands, so I didn't change my mind.'[86] Catherine Dent said that she did not feel it mattered deeply to her to have a body to mourn. She had seen bodies in Northern Ireland and she knew how damaged her husband's body could be. They would be bringing back remains in a lead-lined coffin, not an intact body. She left her husband in the Falklands: 'A body is an envelope, it's a nothing. It just seemed, I don't know, it still feels right.'[87] Ann Townsend said they expected the bodies to stay in the Falklands, but when they were told some were coming home, they did not want Neil to be left out there on his own.[88] Jay Hyrons said that her husband Gary Bingley had to come home, because he had wanted to be cremated and there were no facilities for cremation in the Falklands.[89]

Repatriation, then, did not happen because most military families wished it. It came about because some members of the public thought it a good idea if families wanted it, perhaps based in part on a misconception that soldiers had been buried in the Falkland Islands without due ceremony. The call for repatriation was given additional attention because the tabloid press liked stories with emotional content and generally favoured better support for families of Task Force members. Mrs Thatcher supported it because she did not want the war to leave a bitter taste for those families. She instinctively felt that families should be treated favourably. Some families, for example, were distressed when their sons' South Atlantic Medals were sent to them in cardboard cases, or in Jiffy bags. The Ministry of Defence had despatched them as per existing regulations, but Mrs Thatcher felt these habits were outdated, and following review it was agreed that all medals would from now on be case-mounted and, ideally, presented to the families in person if they wished.[90] The result of the changes to commemorative practices, however, was more far reaching than perhaps anyone had assumed.

Repatriation was an enormous change in the iconography of British military death. Sixty-four bodies were brought back to the UK. Two families chose for the bodies to remain where they fell, one was repatriated a year later, and fourteen were reburied in a new military cemetery in the Falkland Islands. Of the thirty-nine paratrooper bodies, four were reinterred in the Falklands, eighteen were reburied (including one cremation) in individual graves in a Falklands plot at Aldershot military cemetery, and seventeen were taken home to local cemeteries. Nearly all families chose to have a funeral with full military honours, and the one who did not had military representation at a private ceremony.[91] The reburials in the UK were not at all ostentatious, but it meant that military rituals were taken out into civilian settings.

Of course, the business of repatriation was unpleasant. A small team of the Pioneer Corps under Major John Robb had to dig up the remains of the dead from their temporary graves: forty-four at Ajax Bay, twenty-nine at Teal Inlet, four at Estancia House and one at San Carlos settlement. The team arrived in the islands in late September. The bodies had been buried already for over three months. Most had been buried in plastic body-bags, but some were wrapped only in blankets or sleeping bags. The bodies had to be exhumed. As the Corps team undid the body-bags, the smell was unbearable – 'one had to make the slit with the scalpel and then step quickly away' – and the bags contained not only bodies but fluids from decomposition, dismembered limbs, a severed head and unidentifiable clumps of flesh.[92]

Subsequently, the bodies were identified and a specialist team of undertakers embalmed them. The bodies were placed in coffins and put aboard the Royal Fleet Auxiliary *Sir Bedivere*. On 25 October, servicemen and locals in the Falkland Islands held a service of remembrance for the men reburied at the new cemetery at San Carlos Bay. The Commonwealth War Graves Commission felt that the rectangular design of the military cemeteries in northern Europe would not work in the Falklands – partly for practical reasons to do with the soil, but also because they wanted something that would fit more with the locality. They opted for a circular design, representing the shape of the islands; and because – with the small number of graves – a circular cemetery would look less empty.[93] The walls of the cemetery were made from Falklands stone and blended in to their surroundings. At the end of the ceremony, the *Sir Bedivere*, bearing the coffins, sailed out of San Carlos water and headed for home.[94]

On 16 November 1982, the *Sir Bedivere* arrived at Marchwood military fort, Southampton. A lone piper played a lament as it docked. The Adjutant General Sir George Cooper and two chaplains oversaw the disembarkation of the coffins.[95] Largely because of the ongoing threat of Irish terrorism, the bodies returned home with no major ceremony and very little press attention. The families were not told the date of their arrival. An unrelated legal ruling about violent deaths meant that all the returning bodies had to have inquests. The government had been slightly nervous about this – 'Prime Minister, this is unfortunate,' as John Nott said.[96] It could, one civil servant remarked, lead some relatives – however remote the prospect – to 'seek to claim that the death of the deceased was due to ineptitude of some kind, for example on the part of a platoon commander', and in turn could lead them to question government policy. The coroner's handling of the inquests would therefore be crucial.[97]

Families were invited to attend the inquests, and if they wished to attend, the MoD would pay their transport costs.[98] I do not know if anyone from my family went to Dave's inquest. If my grandmother did go – and it seems unlikely – she must have failed to absorb the information she would have learnt. Dave's section commander testified at the inquest that Dave had been killed by shrapnel from British artillery – a fact my family still did not know officially and one that strained and divided the soldiers at his funeral.[99]

After the inquests, coffins were transported in hearses to local undertakers, or to a gymnasium in Aldershot that served as a chapel of rest.[100] On the morning of the Aldershot joint funeral – 26 November 1982 – the coffins were laid out in the gymnasium for families to visit. Some relatives recalled the shock of walking into the room to see so many boxes, laid on trestle tables, draped in Union flags. Others said they did not have to be directed to their son's or husband's body. Theresa Burt said they had been designated an officer to take care of them: 'And he said, "I'll show you where to go to Jason", and Sid said, "No, if I know Terry, she knows." And I did, I went straight to where Jason was.'[101] Bette Sullivan said it felt 'surreal'. She had wanted Paul's wedding ring back, but she knew she would not be able to see his actual body. As she went into the gym, she was struck because on the coffins, 'they all had brand new berets sitting on the top . . . maroon berets . . . I thought . . . they're brand new, they don't belong to them really'.[102]

For some people, the return of the bodies only reaffirmed how much they had lost. I recall being taken to the undertakers with my parents, my grandparents and my uncle. My father and my uncle seemed agitated. The coffin was closed, with strict instructions not to open it. How could they know, I remember my father saying, what was really inside? Alastair Wood buried his brother in Kennoway Cemetery, Fife. He recalled at the undertakers his father howling, 'It's just a box.'[103]

Most people did find comfort in the return of the bodies, even perhaps if that comfort was mainly felt in retrospect. They had to accept, to a greater extent than they had previously, that their sons and husbands were not coming home, and the presence of a coffin meant they could pass through the expected rituals of bereavement. As Richard Jones said, 'It's a terrible thing. I think that's one of the reasons closure came better when the bodies were brought back home. Because you had something tangible, you had a body, and you laid him to rest . . . it just seemed . . . you could come to terms with it then.'[104]

Bette Sullivan said that she 'kind of thought to myself that I didn't need his body brought back, because I didn't quite feel like I needed a grave. But I think when the actual funeral happened, I thought that's it then. Because before that there was a story about a bloke who'd been found wandering [who had been reported dead, but then turned up], so I suppose subconsciously somewhere that must have been in my mind, that maybe he'd been wandering . . . so I suppose it was a good thing for me that he was brought back.'[105]

The families were taken by coach from the gymnasium to Aldershot garrison church. The Reverend David Cooper read a service, and the regiment's colonel commandant and the Reverend Derek Heaver each gave an address. The 800 mourners were taken to the cemetery in Aldershot. The cemetery was large, set on a hill. Guards from 2 and 3 Para lined the route from the cemetery gates to the freshly dug Falklands graves. The burial parties carried the coffins, draped in union flags, dressed with a beret, belt and medals. The mourners and other servicemen gathered together in the higher ground overlooking the plot. Each coffin was lowered separately, and in turn, into its grave.[106]

As the families came into the cemetery, it was pouring with rain. Theresa Burt recalled, 'That day it rained like it had never rained before.'[107] Gareth Jones said: 'I remember walking through the cemetery, and all the soldiers were lined up with their rifles inverted, with the muzzles resting on their boots, and it was raining, the rain was dripping off their noses, off their peaks.'[108] They stayed precisely in position, very still.

Bette Sullivan said: 'I know it started raining. Paul was the first one to go in. I just fell to bits again, and I think my sister thought I was going to climb in with him. So that was that. I don't remember what happened after.'[109] Bob Prior, whose brother Stephen was killed, had lost his nineteen-year-old daughter in a motorbike accident a few days before the ceremony. He did not know how he was going to get through the day.[110]

For many, nothing felt real. Ann Townsend remembered, 'I bought a grey coat. It was cold. It was an overcast day, there were thousands of people there. I just felt, it was as though, like living a dream. I felt absolutely numb. As though you weren't really there, you were out-side it all.'[111]

At my uncle's funeral in Oulton Broad a few days later, cars were stopped and were not allowed to park along the route. It felt like this small town stood still. All the adults around me were sad and dis-tracted. At my grandmother's house we got into the funeral car for the short ride to the church. We drove behind the army wagon, sol-diers straight-backed inside it. It pulled my uncle's coffin, draped in a Union flag, on a gun carriage. My grandmother and grandfather were in the first row of seats behind the driver, both in grey, their arms touching.

I did not speak and out of the window I could see people standing still and watching, all along the route. One elderly man took off his cap and held it to his chest. At the church the photographs show people lining the route by the houses there. The soldiers took the cof-fin from the carriage and positioned it, sombre and uncomfortable, on their shoulders, their bare hands touching the wood beneath the cloth.

We walked along the path into the churchyard and towards the church. I remember I was holding my uncle Chris's hand as we went into the cemetery. I felt a tear land on me and I thought – but I am not crying. The photographs show me entering the church alongside my grandmother. I must have moved places in the line. The service was packed and I watched a woman making notes at the front of the church. Back outside, we assembled around the sides of the freshly dug grave. The soldiers stood in two rows and fired a volley of shots into the air. Birds flew from the trees around us and I heard more cry-ing as they lowered on ropes my uncle's coffin into the ground.

★

The bodies came home, and the nation could see that the men were not just military men, but men with families who loved them. Every-thing was organized by the military and by the government, and the ceremonies were not lavishly conducted and did not put emotion deliberately on display. Even so, it was the first time that families had

10. and 11. Gun carriage arriving at St Michael's Church, Oulton Broad, 2 December 1982.

12. and 13. Mourners at Dave Parr's funeral, 2 December 1982. *Front row*: my father Harmer, sister Marian and grandfather Con. *Second row*: my mother Vivien, me, and grandmother Joy. *Third row*: my uncle Chris.

been granted such explicit recognition, not just as members of a nation in triumph or in mourning, but as people who had lost what was most precious to them. The men in the ranks of the Army – just as much as the officers – were seen by the public to be individual men.

Women were granted greater prominence in the remembrance of war. Perhaps nobody fully saw it at the time, but the repatriation of the bodies of the dead was a tremendous shift. Britain's world role had contracted. The era in many ways defined by Brooke – 'a corner of a foreign field that is for ever England' – had gone. The aftermath of war became increasingly a domestic – even a civilian – matter.

12. Grief

Grief, when it came, was raw. When people learnt of the death of a son, a husband or a brother, it was the moment when everything changed. Grief could not be stopped. Rita Hedicker, whose son Peter was killed, got her hair cut and went back to work in the nursery at the Aldershot barracks. One of the little boys said to her, 'Auntie Rita, have you got a new head?'[1] Underneath, grief could feel uncontainable. Freda McKay, the mother of Ian McKay, said it was like entering a 'long, dark tunnel'. The whole of life looked different. She felt submerged into its depths.[2] Grief narrowed vision, and nothing else mattered. Theresa Burt, whose son Jason was killed on Longdon, said, 'The only way I got through for months was blocking everyone out of my mind.'[3]

Grief was so overwhelming, it could be embarrassing. The world had been transformed, and everyone should know about it. How could other life continue when so much had been lost? Freda said that she 'found it embarrassing to walk down the street in Rotherham and see people cross the road rather than . . . I knew it was because they didn't know what to say, but I would much rather they'd come up, put their arm around me, touch me or something, they didn't have to say anything.'[4]

On the other hand, feelings of grief were usually private and experienced primarily within the family. Public rituals of bereavement, such as the wearing of mourning clothes, were no longer widely practised. In the early 1980s, the idea that grief caused personal anguish, and that the experience of grief passed through a series of stages, was widespread.[5] People could mourn as they thought fit and were increasingly expected to express individual feelings.[6] At the same time, grief also brought into view some of the inequalities of 1980s Britain, and the uneven pace of social and emotional change.

The consequences of a death did not simply go away. There was no way to speed up the pain. The Lord Chancellor Lord Hailsham said, after his wife had been killed in a riding accident in 1978, that there had been no cure for his grief. Religious belief could not anaesthetize it, it just helped the world make sense again.[7] This was a process that was played out in different ways. The bereaved did not generally say that they 'came to terms' with death. Rather, unless their lives took a turn for the worse, they learned to live with it. For most, as their private distress became more bearable, the past came with them, made tolerable in memory, in family, in faith, in dreams – and in the sense that, compared to others, they were still fortunate.

★

News of a death forced the bereaved to move uncertainly into a future they had not wanted. It led people to question who they thought they were. The death of a child blunted parents' acceptance of their past. How could they not have foreseen that it would come to this? How could they have failed to prevent it?

In one sense that was harder for parents who had not seen the Parachute Regiment as the natural or correct path for their son. Freda McKay said her husband had never wanted Ian to join the army, but she had felt he could not be constrained. Ann Townsend, whose husband and older son were also in the army, said that her younger son Neil Grose had joined up when his other ambitions – he wanted to be a gamekeeper – were thwarted. He had been told that 'gamekeepers are born, not made'. Theresa Burt, who had signed her son's papers because he threatened to leave home if she did not, said there would be no Christmas ever again; now that Jason was dead, there could be no joy. In the days after he died, his bedroom became ice-cold and even the cat refused to go in it.

Parents for whom military service was a family tradition had to deal with the fact that it was their son who had paid the price, not them. Len Carver's father had always wanted him to join the army. Len recounted that his parents were both at home when the captain came to tell them Len had been injured: 'There was a front door, which was a big oak door, massive double door, and nobody ever came to that, they always came round to the back. Anyway they said there was a bang on the oak door, and she [his mother] said, "Your father looked at me and just said, 'We've got a visit.'" Anyway, he answered the door, and it was a Para Reg captain who'd come down from Brecon, and he said . . . Dad collapsed, he fainted there and then.'[8] Bryan Dodsworth's son Mark had joined the Paras because Bryan had been a paratrooper too. He left the regiment after the Suez crisis to marry Mark's mother, Carole. Bryan expressed nothing but pride in his son's life, and Carole said that Bryan's understanding of military life had made the pain easier to bear.[9]

The death of a son could blight the future. Richard Jones, whose son Craig was killed, said: 'It was a traumatic few days, then. Of course, you don't just lose a son. You lose your future in-laws, your future daughter-in-law, new grandson, granddaughters, almost half your generation, you lose one son, half your grandchildren you don't get, your daughter-in-law, your daughter-in-law's parents you don't get. You lose the family tree, cut down the middle. The whole of life is changed. You miss that part of growing up, part of it is the bigger family and you don't get that.' Pam Jones added: 'I'm sure he would have been married with children, he just loved children. And they loved him. He just had such patience with kids.'[10]

In their absence, everyday life lacked meaning. Small things could be unbearable reminders of what the dead could no longer do, and those small things could destabilize parents' sense of who they were without their son. Richard went on: 'It was difficult to watch rugby and things after, he was mad on rugby, and every time I watch a match I think oh God, I wish he was here. That's the aftermath, it goes on and on, even today. Occasionally you'll sit there and think he'd have loved to have seen that.' For Pam it was the 'silly things that prod thoughts. He used to say to me, I'm coming home for the week-end, Mum, make lots of gravy – because he loved my gravy, he'd say, pour it into a cup, I'll drink it. And roast parsnips. And I couldn't cook them for years after. I do now of course. It was years before I could. It always reminded me of him.' 'It affects your life more than people realize. Little things that keep cropping up, it never goes away,' Richard concluded.

For young widows, the dislocation in their lives was material too. Catherine Dent, whose husband Chris was an officer killed in the gorse gully at Goose Green, had to reorder the plans she was making for the future. Chris wanted to move to Australia after he had completed sixteen years. He nearly had, and Catherine was in Adelaide with relatives when she learnt that Chris was dead. Their son was six months old. Immediately, she knew that she had to go home to the UK. Her mother expected her to move back to Scotland, back with her parents, but she wanted to stay in the south of England, where she had previously decided to live with Chris, and where she had friends and could more easily find work. Two years later she moved to a new house nearby. Had she stayed longer, she said, she might never have found the impetus to move; the memories in her old house might have weighed her down: 'It was a wrench to leave the old house . . . like having a grave to sit at and haunt. If I'd stayed too long I might never have left.'[11]

Catherine described a gradual and painful process of accepting her husband was dead. When she travelled to the Falklands in 1983 she kept expecting to see him, but also had to visit the place he had been killed – 'I had to accept what I knew was true.' Her acceptance that he was dead kept coming and going. For six or seven years, she said, she coped by doing. She was a GP and she worked hard. She looked after other people, professionally and personally, her parents, her in-laws and her son. Sometimes she felt angry: 'Then I was angry with Maggie Thatcher and Galtieri. Alongside the anger was self-pity, because I was angry that they – the bad people – had taken away the person who was my everything', and sometimes she was angry with her husband for dying and leaving her alone: 'I still get angry with Chris. Not at him, I get angry with him. How dare you be dead!'

As soon as they knew their husbands had been killed, young women married to men in the ranks lost their status as an army wife. They were often now single mothers, and they knew that they would have to leave their army accommodation within weeks or months: 'Once that paper pops through your letter box you're no longer entitled to an army quarter. It's red tape, it's what they have to do.'[12] In the first few months, there was quite a lot to organize that could distract them and hold grief at bay. Jay Hyrons, whose husband Gary Bingley was killed at Goose Green, said that she occupied herself with organizing Gary's cremation, her house move, and her daughter; and then, months later, she was at work and everything hit her. She went to stay with a relative: 'And that morning, I understood why some people die from a broken heart because I had such a pain in my chest I thought I was having a heart attack.' She lay in bed and wondered how long it would take her to die.[13]

Bette Sullivan said that when she heard the news that her husband Paul was dead: 'I don't know, I think my immediate thought was I didn't want to be there, I wanted to be with him. My second thought was I can't, because I've got a small child.' She did not want to cry in front of the people who had brought the news, and so she just sobbed quietly. She began chain-smoking, and the stress of it made her repeatedly sick. She did not remember feeling angry: 'I think I might have got a bit angry at Paul leaving me, but it wasn't a long nasty thing, it was just . . . a thought really.' Her family took her away from her quarters straight away, to live with her sister in London: 'I had to sleep in their front room, and they just had one of those . . . it's just like a cube and it folds down . . . it was my mum's, it was a foam thing. It's the most uncomfortable thing I've ever slept on. I slept on it for three months.'[14]

Attention to grief, in a way, could be a luxury, and some people did not have much choice other than to get on with the lives they had.

★

The widows and children of servicemen were comparatively better compensated than they had been after the Second World War. They also received more from the state than widows whose husbands had not been in the military.

A widow received her husband's salary for three months, or six months if she had dependent children, and for the same six months she received the standard social security payment paid to any widow. After six months, she received the war widow's pension, and also the Armed Forces Service Pension. The war widow's pension (paid by the Department of Health and Social Security (DHSS)) was £46.55 per week (equivalent spending value in 2016 was around £128), £10.75 more than a pension received by a widow whose husband was not in the services but had been paying into National Insurance (referred to in the papers as an 'NI widow'); and their children received £11.05, which was £3.40 more than an NI widow.[15]

Widows might also be eligible for rent allowance and education allowance; and there was a short-term allowance for women widowed while also claiming unemployment benefit. Widows without children, whose husbands were below the rank of major, aged under forty and capable of maintaining themselves received considerably less, at £10.74 (equivalent value around £29) per week, which would increase to the standard rate at age forty. Successive governments had taken the view that the government could not provide 'indefinitely for those widowed at an early age without children': 'A young, fit widow can be expected to enter the employment field and support herself.'[16]

In addition to the war widow's pension, since 1973, and in part because of Northern Ireland, there was also an occupational pension scheme, payable by the MoD. The service pension was 90 per cent of the amount that the man would have received had he served his full term of service, with an adjustment to take account of the DHSS pension paid when a man's death is attributable to his service.[17] That meant of course that the amount was linked to income. The widow of a colonel, for example, would receive a lump sum at a maximum of £30,522 (£84,036.34 in today's money) and an annual forces pension of £8,702 (£23,959.25) and £2,077 (£5,718.61) per child; the widow of a private soldier, a maximum lump sum of £8,922 (£24,564.98), and a maximum annual forces pension of £2,295 (£6,318.83) and £595 (£1,638.22) per child.[18]

In addition to the pensions paid by the DHSS and the MoD, most soldiers had paid into the Single Soldiers' Dependants' Fund (Soldiers' Widows' Fund, if they were married) and the Army Dependants' (Assurance) Trust. These paid out a lump sum of around £1,000 (£2,753) to the soldier's nominee on death, and then a monthly amount depending on how much the deceased had paid in. For a private soldier who had paid in the minimum amount, the payout amounted to about £81.25–£95 (around £240 in today's values) per month until the soldier would have reached the age of fifty-five.[19]

For some families, the painful question was the disparity of pension to the widows as compared to the parents of the men who had died. This was because the pensions were calculated depending on loss of income, not on the principle of loss of life. It was possible for a parent to claim a parent's pension if there was no other next of kin and if it could be demonstrated that the son had been contributing financially to the parent and the parent was incapacitated and unable to work themselves over the longer term. But even then, the amounts were extremely small. A full parent's pension seems to have been £1 (£2.75) per week.[20]

It was hard to argue against the logic that the state provided for widows but not parents, but the issue became more politically difficult when it came to charity. The public had begun spontaneously donating money as soon as there was loss of life, and the South Atlantic Fund was established to distribute it. By 1986, £15 million had been donated.

Mrs Thatcher wanted the fund to make rapid payouts.[21] She also wanted to challenge the military's view that money could only be paid out in accordance with predetermined assessments of need as linked to income. News had leaked out that one of the widows of a highly ranked serviceman had inherited £187,000 (£514,867 in today's money), 'and at first sight it appeared unlikely that she could be shown that she was in need'. The prime minister's Principal Private Secretary, Clive Whitmore, wrote to say that Mrs Thatcher found this 'disappointing. She believed that the Fund was established to compensate dependants for the loss of their fathers and husbands and that they should all therefore be treated the same way.'[22]

The trustees of the Fund, all highly ranked military personnel, consequently agreed to pay £10,000 to each widow (£27,500), £1,000 (£2,753) to each dependent child and £2,500 (£6,883) to the next of kin of single soldiers. This meant they had by mid-1983 disbursed £2 million out of the £10.5 million that had at that point been donated.[23] They kept some of the remaining money, and handed the rest to the benevolent funds of the three services in equal amounts, even though only one man from the RAF had been killed during the Falklands.[24]

Following the initial flat-rate payments, the South Atlantic Fund then allocated further money to all widows, although the way in which they calculated the amounts was abstruse. It does not seem as if there was formal means-testing, but instead assessments were made by the amounts that had been paid out by the occupational pensions. The payments to widows were diverse, between £30,000 and £70,000, and sometimes there seemed no particular reason why some received far more than others. The amounts were guided by the man's rank, but did not always fall exactly along those divisions.[25]

In 1983, Freda McKay complained to Margaret Thatcher that the amounts were uneven and inexplicable. Her criticism was that it would have been more straightforward, and more easily comprehensible, to have paid people equally, because the sacrifice of the men had been equal: 'You can't put a price on a life.' Freda disliked the privilege of birth, the hierarchy of the military that separated soldiers and officers, and the opacity of military bureaucracy.[26] She disliked the sense that anybody, including Thatcher, had profited from the war. Her protests were not about equality as a political principle – she was no socialist. Rather, she was concerned with the equality of sacrifice and the equality of feeling among the families of the bereaved. Even if they supported the war, some families felt that the Falklands had been a special case.

The senior military who ran the Fund regarded the needs of Falklands' families in a broader context.[27] Compared to the widows of men killed in the Second World War, whose needs the benevolent funds still had to meet, or compared to the hundreds of men killed each year at sea whose families did not have the benefit of enormous public sympathy, the Falklands families were well off.[28] The Fund and the service charities also had tight definitions of emotional need, and did not want to fund anything that could not be directly attributed to material hardship caused by loss of income.

Mrs Thatcher wanted to meet the demands of the families of the dead. She seemed instinctively to share Freda McKay's view of the equality of sacrifice. But, much as she had been unable to dislodge the military's preference to allow the same medals to be granted across the ranks, she also could not persuade them to change their perspective on post-conflict suffering. Although there were intermittent public outbursts about the Fund's handling of the money, both it and the service charities remained largely immune to political or to public pressure.

★

Grief took its shape within families, and it was family life that most affected how grief was experienced. Although life was changed, people wanted to hold on to family life as it had been before bereavement, difficult as that was to do.

Some parents struggled to stay together after the death of a son: the blow was too hard and felt too individually; and sometimes it destroyed the focus of parents' lives together. Ann Townsend went straight back to work: 'I suppose I felt if I could get back to work things would begin to take on normality again.' She and her husband found it hard to comfort each other.[29] Divorce had become much more common since changes to the law took effect in the early 1970s, although the rate of its increase levelled off in the late 1980s.[30] Even if it was easier to get divorced, many people felt it was an admission of failure. Freda McKay said she could not talk to her husband about her son Ian's death. He was too absorbed in his own grief: 'That was just . . . he was the only one who was suffering, he'd lost the only thing he'd loved in his life.'[31] They divorced a few years later.

Sara Jones, at forty, was the oldest wife bereaved in the Falklands War, and of course as the widow of 2 Para's Commanding Officer she had to deal with significant press interest. She did not remember a great deal about the period after her husband's death, but she felt she had to carry on and focused on the practicalities of getting through. She felt proud of what her husband had achieved, of Britain's victory, and of the fact that the islanders were grateful for what Britain had done.

Nevertheless, she was in the public eye and that cannot have been easy: 'There was so much rejoicing, lots of flag-waving, ships coming home. That was quite trying. I do remember some journalist coming to my door and saying, how do you feel about it? I think I slammed it in his face and said how the hell do you think I feel?' Sara played her role with loyalty for the sake of her husband's memory, her children, the Army and the country. I asked her if she would consider marrying again. She laughed, and said, 'Show me the man.'[32]

Catherine Dent's husband was also an officer, a captain, killed in the same part of the Goose Green battle as Jones. She was a GP, and accustomed to talking about the stages through which grief progressed. She recalled that it had been hard to find herself suddenly a widow. Widows were supposed to be old – she was thirty-one. She did not want to be a widow at all, still less to conform to the rituals of mourning, but she had to attend the memorial services: 'I remember thinking, I will not wear black, I refuse to wear black. I wore this particular dress – I hated it so much I couldn't bear . . . I think part of that was youth and part of it was denial and part was just I will not wear black.'

Catherine had always had been determined. She came from a middle-class family. Her father was a civil engineer who had done National Service, and she had a Church of Scotland background. She had battled to break down barriers to the progression of her career, and hence her life was in some striking ways unconventional. She joined the Army, went through Sandhurst, became a doctor, and when she met Chris had a higher rank than him and earned more than he did. Once, she parachuted into the sea to meet up with him during a brief leave and she stayed in the Army until she was seven months' pregnant. Now he was dead, how could she be the person she wanted to be, without him? His death initially dislocated her sense of who she thought she had become. She looked at other families and felt uncertain why it had to be her who had lost the love of her life. Her loss made everybody else's life appear perfect; and sometimes she felt as if people were judgemental, assuming her to be an unmarried or divorced mother.

Growing up in the time she did – she was born in the early 1950s – she always thought that she would not marry. It would be the price she would have to pay for her career. When she did decide to marry, it brought responsibilities, and those responsibilities changed her life. She opted then not to train as a surgeon as she had intended, but to go into general practice. She wanted to fulfil her roles as wife and mother: 'I realized in fact it was important for me to be Chris's wife, and the mother of our child.' Consequently, after he died, she did not want to find another husband. She loved her husband and longed to have him back. She missed – horribly so – the closeness and the intimate relations they shared. He had been right for her – they had accepted each other just as they were – and she had made her vows to him alone.

It did not mean in the longer term she would rule out marrying again – she had never expected to meet Chris, after all – but it was simply that she had not met anyone she felt matched her as he had. She was loyal and very close to her in-laws, particularly her mother-in-law, and she did not want actively to seek another man. She preferred to live with what she had. Her work was important to her; she had a son she loved, who could be nurtured too by trusted family friends; she had her in-laws and close friends, and the memory of the time she had had with Chris. Just because her husband was dead, it did not mean that she could live as if she had never chosen to marry him, and never had his child.[33]

Other widows often did want to find another man. They were young, perhaps in their late teens or early twenties, but not so young that they wanted to become dependent again on their own families. They may not have had such good relations with their in-laws, or they simply expected, and wanted, a life that involved a relationship with a man. In 1981, 52 per cent of women who left their parental home did so to marry or live as married. Particularly for women from the working classes, it was more common to find a partner than to live singly or with friends.[34] Following the payouts from the South Atlantic Fund, these younger women were often financially better off than they had ever been, but emotionally they could be vulnerable, and socially – as widows – their status could be weak. They could be pushed to move on before they were ready. One woman whose son was killed retained good relations with her son's wife.

When her daughter-in-law met a new boyfriend, she said he was jealous of the dead man's memory and would not allow his possessions in their new house.

Bette Sullivan got involved with a man who was 'very possessive'. He persuaded her to sign over her money to him so that he could buy his father's business and they could go into business together. Her husband's family were upset by this. Bette's daughter was staying with her in-laws and when she tried to take her home her in-laws threatened to prevent her. Her boyfriend's business went bankrupt and she lost all her money. She struggled to get rid of him for nearly three years: 'He held a pair of scissors to my throat . . . That wasn't very nice. When I moved down to my mum's . . . [he said] if I didn't tell him where I lived he would come and burn my mum and dad's house down. I didn't know whether to believe him or not. It was a horrible few years.'[35]

Janet Findlay, whose husband Gordon was killed, said she desperately craved affection after her husband died: 'I just wanted a cuddle. I wanted somebody to love me.' She did find another partner, a relationship that lasted, but her need for comfort and the reassurance men provided her caused friction with her daughter, Pauline, who was eleven and away at boarding school. Pauline wanted to come home to live with her mum: 'I did want to look after my mum, but I didn't understand what looking after my mum was. When my mum found solace in other people other than me it made me very jealous . . . a young mind doesn't understand. I was just angry and wretched. I wanted my mum all to myself.'[36]

Siblings sometimes felt displaced, a mixture of unhappiness at their brother's death and also uncertainty about their own position within the remaining family. It could give them the feeling that their brother had been the one their parents loved most. Theresa Burt said she blocked out everything, including her younger son, who was about fourteen: 'And I can remember he [her younger son] used to kneel in front [of me] and say, Mum, tell me what I've done to you. Why do you push me away?'[37] Freda McKay said she could remember one of Ian's younger brothers standing in the garden shouting at Ian's father: 'Ian's dead, Dad, but I'm still alive.'[38]

Others were pushed towards behaviour that was quite extreme. Janet Findlay had a heart attack when she was thirty-six, a reaction to the stress she had been under and the upheavals in her life. Pauline, her daughter, recalled that she 'became quite reckless as well, because I was pursuing things that were quite dangerous. Things like mountaineering, parachuting, and that sort of stuff. Because I didn't actually care whether I would survive it.'[39] In my own family in the 1980s my father used to compete regularly in marathons and triathlons, and in 1984 he ran up and down Snowdon, Scafell Pike and Ben Nevis in twenty-four hours. In the late 1980s, my uncle Chris developed an aggressive strain of malaria on a remote island off the coast of East Africa. He was travelling alone and he was aware of the dangers of going to the island. Feverish and sick, he had to find his way back to the mainland by boat, bus and hitchhiking. When he arrived, he collapsed. Some locals picked him from the dusty floor and carried him into hospital, which probably saved his life.

Through exercise and travel, my father and uncle Chris may have tried to suppress their own feelings by running – literally – away. Physical pain justified their own living, and helped them to find their brother by pushing as close to death as they dared. Chris said he had dreams that were so vivid it felt like he was a balloon coming out of his body and bouncing around his room until he could see the window and get out. He said he would have given his life for Dave's: 'In this dream, the same thing in a different way, over and over again; it came to an absolute choice – OK, you want to die, now's your chance – it manifested in someone was pointing a gun at me – the choice is, do you want to die or not, and I chickened out, or common sense took over.'[40]

Gareth Jones, whose brother Craig was killed, said that at first he got on with his life. He was young; he continued at school, did his A levels and went to university. He was incredibly driven. At university, he joined the Territorial Army SAS. He then went to Sandhurst and joined the Army as an officer, with the intention of doing SAS selection, but an injury forced him to leave. In 1992, when he was married, and his parents had recovered a little, his brother's death hit him.

He became, he said, 'overwhelmed with grief'. In a sense, he had been trying to overcome the gulf in his parents' lives by becoming his brother as well as himself, and perhaps – like my father and uncle – he had wanted to be as good as he perceived his brother had been, to earn the love the parents had spent on the son who had died. They felt guilty at being alive when their brother was dead, and they felt responsible for the unhappiness they could see in their parents. Siblings could absorb the fracturing of their parents' lives, and take it upon themselves to try to reform a family shattered by this change.

★

Poverty, and the legacy of Christian thought, even among people who did not practise religion, also influenced people's experiences of grief.

Paratroopers had often grown up in relative economic deprivation, or in uncomfortable family circumstances. The 'family' was assumed by the military to be nuclear, but more complicated set-ups were very common. One paratrooper left all his possessions to another soldier's wife.[41] Another paratrooper's sister wrote to complain that her brother had been buried at a location against the wishes of her mother. The Parachute Regiment replied that the soldier had named the father as next of kin and that therefore the decision as to where to bury his son had been his.[42] Another mother had to confront her ex-husband about the £2,500 he had received from the South Atlantic Fund. She had had no knowledge of the payment, but now she knew about it he was compelled to give her half.[43] Three men who were killed left behind offspring not automatically covered by the South Atlantic Fund's assistance. Two of the three had girlfriends to whom they were not married. One man's best friend testified that he was planning to marry his pregnant girlfriend when he got back from the Falklands. Another could not have married yet, because his girlfriend, whose child was already nearly one, was fifteen.[44]

For some families, the 1980s brought further unwelcome change, as some of those reliant on work in heavy industry lost their jobs and had to readjust. One mother wrote to the Parachute Regiment in distress. She was separated from her husband and lived with a new partner. They had planned to marry, but could no longer afford to do so. She had worked in the canteen for the National Coal Board, but had given up her job because of her grief. Her house had come with her job, and she had been planning to buy it and her son had been helping her put money towards it. Her new partner had been a miner. He had lost his job and there was little prospect of his finding re-employment. She wished she had not given up her job, but she had, and she too felt she had no prospects. They both smoked heavily and their income support was barely enough to live on.[45]

Another family suffered partly because of the legacy of illness caused by industrial work. One father, in his mid-sixties, said his 'beloved wife' had died two years before the Falklands. He did not always get along with his sons – the son who was in the Paras had named his brother as his next of kin, but had written to him during the war and he believed that when he came home, he would come back and live with him in his northern industrial town. The father lost his job as an industrial sewer labourer because of chronic ill-health, caused by prolonged exposure to sewer-cleaning chemicals. He was partially sighted. He lived on disability benefits and had no hope of finding work again.[46]

The economic and technological changes of the 1980s undoubtedly also affected my grandfather's life, but perhaps largely because it became normal practice that older men should retire and because, as a consequence, it became harder for him to find ways of passing the time. He had been a mechanic, a second-hand car salesman, and then he fixed fruit machines for a living. The fruit-machine company was bought by a multinational, and he was made redundant in March 1982. He was sixty-one. After Dave died, he saw no prospect he would work again. Cars had become more complicated, regulations governing what could be bought and sold stricter, and so he could not practise car salesmanship in the way he had formerly understood. He had left Joy, his wife, and lived with another woman, but she grew tired of his solipsistic despair. He became 'effectively a rent-paying lodger in her house' and he bought his meals out. He lived on unemployment benefit. He had had £10,000 in savings, but in December 1983 he only had £2,300 left.[47]

My grandfather had had no formal education after the age of fourteen. His life was work and the men he passed the time of day with in the pub. He needed – and expected – a woman to keep house for him, to provide food for him and to order his days. He had nothing to keep him looking outwards. After his new woman kicked him out, he lived alone in a bedsit. He was a proud man, but his flat was damp. His suits grew mildew and he could not afford to replace them. My father remembers his stove-top was thick with unwashed and burnt remnants of dinners he had tried to cook. Dad saw him once pour the dregs of his beer can onto the carpet. He had no care for himself, and he had cast aside the women who might have cared for him. In his final illness, he was sometimes found outside, sleeping in the street, too drunk or too pained and confused to make his way home. He was taken to hospital in March 1990. My grandmother tried to care for him, and visited him there: 'He's nothing but skin and bone – Belsen in fact.' When he died, she wrote: 'Poor old lad. A happy release.'[48]

I do not exactly know how my grandmother felt in the years immediately after Dave's death. I have a photograph from Christmas at my parents' house in 1982, when I was eight years old. My sister must have got a camera for Christmas, and probably the two of us forced my assembled family to pose together, and she took the shot. I am grinning, apparently oblivious, leaning on my grandmother's shoulder. She looks gaunt, even haunted, staring into the distance, as if not really there. My uncle Chris could not bring himself even to look up. He is standing, gazing at the floor. My mother's parents, who must have come along to help her, looked as they normally looked: smartly dressed, together, slightly formal but smiling firmly. My parents look uncomfortable – my mother strained, my father grimacing slightly, perhaps feeling that it was wrong to smile because the family felt so miserable.

They held it together. I do not remember often seeing my grandmother weep. I only recall knowing that I had to be careful, that there was this thing that was more important than anything else. She could not watch the news, or anything angry or violent on TV. In

1985 Paul Hardcastle's song '19', about soldiers in Vietnam, was number one for what seemed like weeks. When it came on the TV or the radio we had to leap to turn it off and hope she would not notice. Sometimes when my father called her she thought he was Dave and that made everybody sad.

I probably remember more from when I was older, and the grief was not so raw. In 1987 my family moved from Suffolk to the northeast so that my father could take up a job in Sunderland. Distant from my grandmother geographically – it was a seven-hour car journey, and she could not drive that far by herself – I think the issue of her grief was, for me, refracted through my parents' concerns that it was harder to look after her now they lived so far away. Elderly single women, along with young single mothers, were the most economically deprived groups in the UK in the 1980s.[49] But hers was not so much an economic problem. She won on the football pools in 1992, and after that she had spare money. She used it to decorate her home, buying new furniture for the back room where, after she retired, she spent a lot of her time, reading – Catherine Cookson, historical romances, the *Daily Express* – and watching videos on her new VHS machine.

She liked to go out walking, which she did until arthritis prevented it, she liked to garden and to arrange flowers for Dave's grave. She was humorous, not at all severe or sanctimonious, and she made few demands. She used to paint, but I am not sure that she did much of that after she retired. What was the point? Grief made her lazy, even slovenly at times. I remember, in what must have been the mid to late 1990s, showering in her house and realizing that what she used as shampoo was in fact washing-up liquid. By that time, she was in the early stages of dementia. Night and day blurred together and towards the end of her life she spent her time in her comfortable armchair, sleeping when she felt like it and subsisting mainly on tea, whisky and cigarettes, Craven A. She died in 2000, aged seventy-five, from a ruptured stomach ulcer.

Right up until the end, she loved Lady Diana Spencer. Diana's beauty and demure suffering appealed to her. Brought up in the country and schooled on Christian thinking, she saw suffering as part

of life. In some ways, she was ashamed of what had happened to
her and she seemed to believe that Dave's death was punishment for
her sins: the sins of her own parentage, the unmarried conception of
her eldest son, the separation from her husband, and her failings at
the womanly craft of housekeeping. Her lot was her fate, and she did
not complain about it.

Christianity informed others' perceptions of grief too. Like many
people – while 85 per cent of people in the 1980s gave a religious
affiliation if asked, only 13 per cent regularly went to church[50] – Freda
McKay said she could go through the Creed and she often found herself singing hymns, but she found it hard to believe in God: 'I couldn't
understand why God would put me through all that.' Her son Ian's
death was not the only terrible event in her life. She had separated
from her husband and found happiness with another man, Jeff. A few
years later, in 1994, Jeff died very suddenly from cancer. Both her
younger sons died too. They had been born with disabilities and had
been expected to die in childhood, but they survived and died in 1989
and 1995. It was at that point that Freda had a breakdown: 'I had
nobody to look after anymore.' During the Falklands War, she
thought she did not believe in God but she used to go to church. At
one stage, she began to see red everywhere: 'Everything was red. I'd
convinced myself that was blood. Everything seemed red around
me.' After Jeff died, the vicar giving the sermon at his funeral did not
say anything about Jeff's life, which Freda had wanted him to do.
After that, she abandoned the idea of faith.[51]

For Rita Hedicker, born in the 1930s and brought up in an orphanage, her Christian faith was a constant guiding force. She would not
submit to self-pity or to self-analysis, and she insisted on looking outwards and on not just seeing the positives in her life, but communicating
those positives to others. She gave talks in the local area about her life
and had derived great comfort from doing so. She had been abandoned as a baby and, she said, this had made her feel unloved, that
there was something wrong with her, and perhaps she felt a little
ashamed of the fact. But her mother had not left her to freeze to death
on a doorstep, but warm and comfortable. Her mother had wanted
her to live. Her son had died, but he had died quickly, he would not

have known anything about it. She thought it was better that he had died fighting for a cause he believed in – whatever she thought, because as a Christian and an internationalist she did not believe in war – rather than that he had died carelessly, pointlessly, in an accident on the motorbike he cherished. Her husband died in 1992. It was, she said, a hard time, but her husband and her son were all around her and she felt glad that they had been in her life. She spoke to her husband every day. She felt the three of them would be together again later.[52]

People re-made themselves, and the ways in which they came to understand their lives were sometimes as a result of talking about grief, expressing their feelings and thinking about themselves and the stages of recovery they might go through, but more often the result of forbearance and the expectation that life was hard – to be endured. The things that made life bearable were often everyday realities: the support of friends, families, workmates; the kindness of strangers; the ability to talk about their loss to people who would listen; work to lose themselves in; and the stability in other areas of their lives, the fact that they had homes and money to live on. It was easier if they could share their loss, if they did not feel alone. For those, like my grandfather, who had squandered what little else they had, grief could be overwhelming and grind them down. Often, as grief passed into memory, the bereaved reinforced their sense of who they were before their loss: mothers, fathers, siblings, wives. The dead came with them, as life went on.

★

Remembering the dead, for most of the people I spoke to, was an important part of living. The casting of remembrance came with distance, as layers settled over the rawness of grief and life came again to make some kind of sense. Remembrance was a feature too of longevity. In a long life, the vivid recollection of a man alive might fade from instant recall, but the importance, and the significance, of remembering might increase.

Bob Prior's brother Stephen was killed at Goose Green. Stephen's death was part of his family's history. So many of Bob's family had been killed in war, including, most recently, his nephew Daniel Prior in Afghanistan, but he did not think they were unlucky. They were a big family, and so they took more chances. Military service was a privilege, because it was fun. It was their way of life. They were part of the military and regimental family, and so their lives were not just theirs but belonged to a greater whole. They lived alongside their memories, with gratitude for the memories that were now less painful, and the knowledge that fresher memories would become less acute. They did not tend to dwell on the 'alternative histories' that had never been lived.[53]

Catherine Dent said that over time she too came to view her life with her husband with gratitude. She had been granted so much that other people had been denied, because for that too short period they had loved each other deeply and had been happy. Her memories of the five years she had had with her husband were unchanging: etched deep into her mind. She did not idolize him, she knew that he had been human and flawed, but she was grateful for the joy she had been granted, however fleeting that had proved to be. Chris lived on with her as more than a memory, because she felt his essence still with her. Not everything that had happened since Chris had died had been terrible. Her son had grown and turned out well – there was plenty to be grateful for.[54]

For my uncle Chris, Dave's death was awful: 'I'd left home and become wild and free, my world had opened up, then it went straight down the plughole. Ghastly.' He spent a year living at home with his mum because he wanted to look after her: 'The world could have disappeared for all I cared.' People avoided him in the streets, and then one day a friend's father told him that he too had lost a brother, shot down over France in the Second World War. They never knew what happened to him. Chris realized that he was not the only one, that there was a whole generation living with that loss. That, and the repeated dream that showed him he did not have the courage or the will to die, made him see that he had to live. He went and found himself some work, and two years later he was able to go travelling again. His memories remained with him, and his sense of Dave made him more determined. He said: 'Even now, running up the beach, I can hear him, "Get a move on, you fat prick."'[55]

Often, like Catherine Dent, people saw themselves as comparatively fortunate. They had known their child, their husband, for the time they had. Bette Sullivan had no illusions about her marriage. She said people often asked her if they would have stayed together, and she said she hoped and thought they would, but how could you know. Jay Hyrons remembered her husband in terms of romance. He was the paratrooper who, after they first met, had climbed up the drainpipe and through her bedroom window to woo her. She saw it as the only time she had had a man who truly loved her. Pauline Findlay said her father's death had shaped her life. She never did anything 'half-arsed'. She said it would have been easy to be bitter; but to be bitter would have been wrong, because the death of her father had helped, too, to make her how she was. She had had a good career in the Army, and was going to university: 'I wouldn't be in the position I'm in now if it wasn't for that part of my life. And I actually find myself to be really fortunate now.'[56]

Some parents compared themselves to the Argentine parents, who, they said, often did not have the comfort of knowing how their sons died or where they were buried. Most people, at least the ones I found to speak to, no longer felt angry about the war. David Wood, who was killed in the gorse gully at Goose Green, came from a family of socialists, even communists, originally from Fife. The Woods never reconciled themselves to Margaret Thatcher's governments. David's brother Alastair thought it terrible that governments could not organize themselves to avoid war and that they used people to fight for their objectives. He saw the Falklands War as a scrap for a pointless bit of land. When Alastair and his father visited the Falkland Islands in 2000, it accentuated their sense of loss. There was nothing there. His father asked simply: 'He died for this?'[57]

Some mothers, perhaps particularly those who did not come from military traditions, thought that, for them as mothers, the war had been wrong. Freda, who suffered many bereavements, saw Ian as the son who should have been there, looking after her in her old age. 'It was not worth it for me.'[58] Theresa Burt kept her house as a shrine to her son. When her son Jason joined the Paras aged sixteen he had asked her if, now that he was in the Army, he would still have a bedroom at home. In 1982, after his death, she froze his room in time. His room was as he had left it, Chelsea FC teddy bears, peeling Panini football stickers on the wall, an Easter egg, his paying-in book, some coins, small change he never got to take to the bank. He was a boy, not a soldier but a child, photographed and on her front-room wall — olive-skinned, naked from the waist up, soft-focus, delicate and gentle. It was as if, perhaps, the circumstances that had made her and Sid sign Jason's papers so he could join the Paras had never happened.

For Theresa, and perhaps for many others, it was worse to forget. Memory was, in that sense, a privilege. Each year Theresa and her husband went through rituals of memory, travelling to the military cemetery in Aldershot and laying flowers at Jason's grave. In later life, Theresa's husband developed dementia, and in his dementia he forgot about Jason. During his illness, they drove to the cemetery as usual, but they could not continue because Sid did not know what they were doing and he became too distressed. So Theresa and her son decided to take him for one last visit. He could not have known their intentions and he refused to get out of the car. Just before they were to leave, he suddenly got out and went to the grave: 'For about ten minutes he spoke to Jason and kissed the stone. And that was the last time Sid went to Aldershot.'[59]

After that, there was no more Jason for Sid. He knew that there had been something sad in his life, but he did not know what it was. Theresa found it hard that this thing, the thing that had been the most important and terrible thing to have happened, had gone from the person who bore it with her. If there could be no more memory, then Jason really was gone for ever; and then her pain and the way she had reassembled her own life after Jason died would pass into nothing, and nothing was the bleakest consequence of all.

13. Trauma

Paratroopers' post-war emotions were seen not as grief, but as trauma. To ask sufferers to explain what this trauma felt like was far from straightforward.

The Vietnam War revised American psychiatry's attitudes towards neuroses brought on by war. Up until that point, psychiatrists who worked with the military in America and Britain assumed that men could withstand the burdens of combat. In and after the First World War, despite the high numbers of men presenting with neuroses, shell shock was considered to be the result of predisposed weakness, of lack of moral fibre. In 1918, the prominent psychologist John Mac-Curdy wrote that one man presenting with shell shock was 'rather tender-hearted and never liked to see animals killed. Socially, he was rather self-conscious, inclined to keep to himself, and he had not been a perfectly normal, mischievous boy, but was rather more virtuous than his companions. He had always been shy with girls and had never thought of getting married.'[1] His breakdown was thus virtually inevitable. He did not have the masculine character to face up to the responsibilities of warfare.

By the time of the Second World War, military psychiatrists recognized that all men – no matter how manly – would feel fear.[2] Anyone, therefore, in sustained conditions of adversity, could be susceptible to battle neurosis. Nevertheless, the military still believed that men should not be incentivized to break down by excessive sympathy or the promise of compensation. Men should be treated for exhaustion as close to the front line as possible and sent back to their units after a period of recovery and rest.[3] If this could not happen, the stigma and the shame could be immense. Writer and comedian Spike Milligan was evacuated from Italy in 1944 when, despite a period of rest, he could not stop crying and stammering. 'I got up very early. I didn't say goodbye to anyone. I got into the truck . . . as I drove back down that muddy mountain road, with the morning mists filling the valleys, I felt as though I was being taken across the Styx. I've never got over that feeling.'[4]

In Vietnam, the policy of ensuring that men had a definite date for their return from military operations initially led American psychiatrists to believe there was a historically low incidence of trauma. All that changed in 1968, when the public began to realize America was not winning.[5] For some psychiatrists, the figure of the traumatized Vietnam veteran was an expression of the horror and the insanity of that war and led many in the military to wonder whether the readier recognition that men could be traumatized by combat was a social, rather than a psychological, phenomenon.[6] After Vietnam, American military psychiatrists accepted the existence of a condition called 'post-traumatic stress disorder' and in 1980 PTSD entered the world's key psychiatric manual, the *Diagnostic and Statistical Manual of Mental Disorders*. The diagnosis of PTSD reversed psychiatric assumptions about men and combat. No longer was combat trauma or war neurosis thought to be a character failing or a pre-existing weakness.[7] Rather, it was a reaction to combat. War was hell and stress-related symptoms were thus 'a normal, sane response to its horrors'.[8]

This recognition in America, however, had by 1982 had very little impact on British military psychiatry. The British still operated on some of the assumptions of the Second World War. Going to the Falklands, the Navy was in charge of psychiatry, and it was believed highly trained British military men would behave differently to American conscripts.[9] No army psychiatrists travelled with the fleet. This dismissive attitude revealed the British military's most deep-rooted presumption. Superior training, with its post-Second World War emphasis on the governance of fear by small-group cohesion, would inhibit the presentation of trauma.[10] The troops going to the Falklands, particularly those who sailed first – the SAS, the Royal Marines and the Parachute Regiment – were elite. In 1922, Field Marshal Lord Gort told the War Office inquiry into shell shock that the condition would practically cease to exist 'in face of strong morale and *esprit de corps*'.[11] Now the army was an all-volunteer force, they thought this was even more likely to be true.

★

Consequently, after the Falklands War, paratroopers who experienced symptoms of or related to trauma had to overcome profound taboos – in themselves, in their regiment, in the army and in society at large. Over time, many of those stigmas have been eroded, and, by the thirtieth anniversary of the war, post-combat trauma was talked about as a normal part of war's aftermath. In fact, there has been a very significant transformation in civilian attitudes towards war and trauma. A large proportion of the public now almost expects men to break down after combat.[12] For many people outside the armed services, therefore, trauma has lost its association with unmanliness. On the contrary, in popular representations, the idea of PTSD after combat has masculinized trauma, and has helped towards making mental-health conditions more accepted. The experience of war is often seen to be so hellish – in the film *Saving Private Ryan*, for example – that the incidence of trauma subsequently shows just how manly the sufferer was. Only real men have been to war.

That was a remarkable transformation, and it might, as the expert in military psychiatry Edgar Jones suggests, encourage some men to embellish both their combat experience and their trauma. For the men I have spoken to directly about their experiences, however, exaggeration of their trauma seems very unlikely to me. The Paras are a close-knit regiment in which everyone knows everyone else's business, and the war service of the men I have spoken to is documented. Other paratroopers would not tolerate 'Walter Mitty' characters spreading stories of horror and trauma for personal gain. The men I spoke to felt that they should speak out to help themselves to feel less ashamed, and to make it easier for other soldiers to come forward should they need to. The evolution of attitudes towards mental health has been much more profound in civilian society than it was in the military, where significant taboos about trauma persist. Presentation of traumatic symptoms can still be career-limiting.

Surgeon Captain John Sharpley, a defence consultant adviser in psychiatry, recently said that the military depends to a certain degree on stigma, because operations require cohesion: 'Stigma is bad for the individual, but good for the group.'[13] In elite units like the Paras, the refusal to admit the existence of trauma may be deeply embedded.

The experience of trauma after the Falklands – and I use the term broadly, because there are obviously challenges in isolating PTSD from other behaviours that might be troubling but not clinically diagnosed – had some similarities for the men I spoke to. Trauma often seemed to be about the complex emotions they had felt – and usually tried to suppress – on the field of battle, but it was also about loss: loss of their friends, but also of their young selves, the masculine authority granted to them by war, the impossibility of sustaining the standards of the regiment in a civilian society whose values were so distant from the military.

This last point has led some to suggest that the aftermath of war is now worse for combatants because the gulf between the military and society – and possibly the lack of opportunities for them outside the army – means that veterans have less hope for reintegration after they have handed back their ID cards. The writer Matthew Green said of one young Afghanistan veteran who committed suicide that he may have been 'a casualty of peace – unable to withstand the sense of futureless isolation that engulfed him when he left behind friendships forged under fire'.[14]

There does seem to be overwhelming evidence that after combat men need the support of other men – fellow veterans – who have experienced the same things as them, and who therefore understand without making a fuss. At the same time, the greater public recognition of trauma, the social willingness to hear the voices of men from other ranks, and the growing expectation that men can and should express difficult feelings – all things that would have been unthinkable in the aftermath of the Second World War – presumably help to make it easier for men to come forward.[15]

★

How many men in the Parachute Regiment came home with symptoms related to trauma? In 1982, the regiment regarded 'battle shock' as a temporary condition that could be alleviated by a cup of tea – a 'brew' – and a soothing word. During the conflict, both 2 and 3 Para reported one man with 'battle shock' and 3 Para also had simply a 'battle casualty'.[16] It seems possible that there were more, even at the time, but that the stigma associated with even a temporary breakdown meant that psychological casualties presented with other illnesses.

Trench foot, a gangrenous condition caused by unending cold and wetness, was the most common illness on the Falklands. There were thirty-nine reported cases of trench foot and twelve more general cold-related illnesses.[17] As far as the regimental hierarchy was concerned, men developed trench foot because of poor discipline, as they had been instructed how to avoid it, by changing their socks twice a day, keeping one pair dry by holding it in warm parts of their person, and sometimes thawing their feet in each other's armpits. Hence, the regiment suspected later that trench foot had been an excuse for a lack of will to fight, and therefore did not want to pay compensation for it after the war.

Many of the men who developed trench foot because of the inelegant landing in the sea and the inadequacy of their boots might well have felt aggrieved by the regiment's reaction. It is impossible to know whether trench foot was sometimes what an American doctor called an 'occult' psychiatric illness – an excuse for not wanting to fight – or a presentation of symptoms whose underlying cause was fear. Seven of the nineteen trench-foot cases in 3 Para went into battle, twelve did not.[18] One clue perhaps is in the rates of discharge after the war. Some of the trench-foot cases did leave the regiment when they returned home, either because they wanted to or because the regiment no longer sought their services. One other man who had reported sick with a sprained ankle was discharged, and another man who had had battle shock/confusion was transferred to another part of the Army.[19]

During the conflict, forty-five men in 2 Para were reported to be ill, and a further three out of action for unspecified reasons. In 3 Para, thirteen men were ill and seven more were out of action. We do not know how many of those reporting ill continued to fight – certainly, some did – and it is probably the case that some of the illnesses were serious and unavoidable – kidney stones or a hernia, for example – but that others, such as hospitalization with acute sickness and diarrhoea, were 'occult' presentations of bad nerves. The figures might suggest that a small number of men in each battalion developed conditions that were proxy illnesses for their fear, or possibly for neurosis. It is impossible to say with certainty, but the numbers would indicate between 2 and 3 per cent might come into this category. Even if that is the case, it was, by historical standards, extremely low. The American medic Captain H. H. Price showed in 1984 that of the casualties taken onto the hospital ship *Uganda*, only 2 per cent – sixteen men – were psychiatric cases. Of those, only one had actually been in the land campaign and was suffering from grief after his helicopter crashed and the pilot died in his arms under heavy fire.[20] Price put the low incidence down to the elite nature of the troops, as well as the shortness of the campaign and the largely offensive nature of the land operations.

The notion that the incidence of trauma had been unusually and especially low persisted when the troops returned home. In 1984, two psychologists tested the stress reactions of thirty-four men from 2 Para by exposing them to noise and giving them unavoidable electric shocks. The psychologists concluded that paratroopers exhibited fewer signs of fear than bomb-disposal experts in the same experiment. Paratroopers, the psychologists suggested, actually were fearless. In line with prevailing attitudes, they assessed this as a consequence of their paratrooper training, with its emphasis on exposure to extremes and danger.[21]

It was only in the later 1980s that psychologists began to report that these early assessments were unlikely to be an accurate reflection of the rate of psychological injury. This indicated one of the newly recognized phenomena of PTSD – that rather than being a temporary reaction, experienced at the time, war neuroses were likely to manifest after battle, sometimes a long time afterwards, and men were likely to experience flashbacks. The military and social disapproval that surrounded mental breakdown, and perhaps also the elite culture of the Paras, led men instead to suppress their symptoms, or to manage them by drinking heavily.

In 1987, two psychologists reported that, of three cases they had assessed, not one felt able to approach the service doctor, and one could only talk about his feelings under the influence of alcohol. In all cases, the men felt that the expression of emotion, including weeping, was taboo. Contrary to the deeply embedded idea that superior training, centred on the cohesion of the small group, inured men to trauma, these psychologists argued that training was part of the web of factors that suppressed symptoms, and that the importance of comradeship to those men might exacerbate their post-war distress if their friends had been killed.[22]

In 1991, a study of a group of soldiers who were still serving, and who had been to the Falklands, showed that 22 per cent had severe PTSD, and 28 per cent exhibited some symptoms of trauma. Half of these soldiers had some kind of traumatic reaction to the fighting they had been involved in. One of the doctors conducting the study, Steven Hughes, had been the medic with 2 Para during the Falklands, and it is therefore likely that the group of sixty-four veterans he scrutinized came from the Parachute Regiment. Hughes and his collaborator, Stephen O'Brien, a Senior Registrar at the Department of Psychotherapy at the Royal Liverpool Hospital, showed that of the fourteen soldiers with severe PTSD symptoms, all of them had helped with treating casualties, and all of them believed it was highly likely they had killed someone. Proximity to the intensity of battle and to the clearing up afterwards, therefore, seemed to indicate a greater likelihood of PTSD reactions.[23]

In 1993 psychologist Roderick Ørner investigated men who had left the services. He concurred that the culture of the armed services inhibited men from coming forward with symptoms. Those symptoms tended to be worse for men in the ranks, for men who had been physically injured and for men who had left the services. He found paratroopers to be less likely to report symptoms than those from other regiments (33 per cent of paratroopers responding had severe PTSD – a figure in line with Hughes and O'Brien's assessment), but among the Marines, Navy and the Welsh Guards, the numbers were extremely high – 64, 64 and 75 per cent respectively.[24] In 1997, at the fifteenth anniversary of the Falklands War, the Parachute Regiment spoke openly for the first time about the emotional scars of combat.

★

Men reporting traumatic symptoms sometimes said that the past lived in them. They could not escape it; in sleep, their minds took them back into the war and made deliverance from nightly horror impossible. Alcohol might dim it but nothing could make it go away.

They had often experienced a profound destabilization of their sense of personal autonomy. They had been left defenceless or helpless by what happened to them or by what they saw: 'I endured a prolonged sense of powerlessness, just like that on the last night of the war when we came under intensive enemy artillery and mortar fire behind the Tumbledown.'[25] Sometimes, the sense of destabilization produced physiological effects. David Benest, a captain with 2 Para in the Falklands and later Commanding Officer of 2 Para, said the whole battalion was exhausted during the tour of Belize in 1983. Many drank heavily, and few knew how to comprehend what they were feeling. Benest's job was to direct helicopters. 'I found myself extremely emotionally affected by what had happened. I used to sit on the helipad once I'd briefed the pilot, and just sit there.' In the mid-1980s he sometimes found it could take him an hour to walk a short distance, and he thought he might have an illness like ME.[26]

In many ways, war exposed men, stripped them naked, and their comrades there had been witnesses to it. The passage of time could make that sense of exposure unbearable: 'War for the combat soldier is likely to be a humiliating experience . . . He has to open himself up and prove himself to other men to such an extent that it can be, in retrospect, humiliating . . . His comrades see him terrified, hugely aggressive and even feeling guilty. Indeed they see him in a wider range of unpalatable emotional states than should his mother or wife. They witness his basest behaviour which, at its worst, is him having to kill another. The immediate reaction to such behaviour is normally positive and this can last for some time. But in the end, years later, feelings of shame and humiliation come to the fore as we judge our memories against the standards of the mature individual.'[27] Becoming old when always young was hard. Forgetting the moments that made them or broke them could prove impossible.

They were not dead, and often they wondered why. They could bear a heavy burden of guilt for their survival and sometimes they felt ashamed to be alive – afraid they had not done enough to save their comrades-in-arms. Sometimes, they felt shame that they had been there at all, and had had to do the things they were called upon to do. The past could be ever-present because to let it go would remove the one thing that they could still do for their dead: to fix themselves in the time of their death, and to honour them in memory.

★

Many men experienced extreme but unidentified symptoms, and recognized this as trauma only later, sometimes after an intense crisis.

Jim Peters was in the Scots Guards. In 2014, he lived daily with symptoms hard to control. He fought at Mount Tumbledown aged nineteen. He believed he had killed someone, and he was injured, mainly in the leg, when a shell landed on his party carrying a stretcher down Tumbledown's forbidding slope. He had just – seconds before – swapped positions with a man in his team. That man was killed outright.

He was diagnosed with PTSD around the thirtieth anniversary of the war. Since then, he has received intensive counselling that encouraged him to relive his experiences. This was difficult at first, but started to improve. He went back to the Falklands, which helped. He went straight to Tumbledown. The rocks were exactly, stone by stone, as they appeared nightly in his dreams: 'I was being haunted . . . I had to be there. Weird. That's what it felt like, it felt like going home. The amount of times I went home on leave, and you can't wait to see the lights of your city, from the train as it's coming across the bridge. That's what it felt like, I thought.'[28]

When Jim got back from the Falklands in 1982, he did not understand why he was still alive. He had been a good soldier, but now the
injury in his knee meant he could not always keep up. He felt 'surplus
to requirements'. 'Most people that came back injured couldn't do
what they were able to do before, just felt nothing, that they were
nothing . . . You just felt like you were the guy . . . the guy who . . .
in training, who was picked on, you became him, you were rubbish,
you were nothing.'

Army life depended on discipline, but now it was hard for Jim to
accept that discipline. This was a noted phenomenon in the development of post-combat traumatic symptoms: 'a continual negative
inner questioning of external authority and its capabilities'.[29] Like
many other men, Jim felt he had been to war and knew more than his
superiors who had not. Tom Harley, a corporal in 2 Para during the
Falklands, commented: 'I think once you've actually tested yourself
in battle, it's very difficult to come back and actually put on the
bloody blank firing attachment and start going bang, bang, bang
round the parade square. It just doesn't work. When you've killed
people . . . I found it embarrassing . . . If you haven't got any ammunition, just go bang instead. Well, I can't do that. It's too embarrassing.
And they shouldn't ask you to do things like that.'[30]

Jim felt worthless – he could not do what he had previously done,
but he also felt invincible, because nobody could stop him. In Cyprus,
with his battalion after the Falklands, Jim tried to kill himself five
times. He was 'so angry' – nobody understood – and he was drinking
wildly. He jumped off a cliff but missed, hitting the water rather than
the rocks. He took an overdose of paracetamol and aspirin. He was
taken into hospital and put under guard. And still, 'I managed to cut
my wrists – I was in the bath. The guy was in the bathroom with me.'
The water turned red as the bathtub filled with blood and then the
guard realized what Jim had done.

Jim was reckless, and drove his car while drunk. Finally, he drove
his car into a shop front. He was discharged from the Army and was
sent to Pentonville prison. He felt convinced none of his military colleagues would welcome him back. He was not in touch with the
Guards until many years later when he used Facebook to get in touch

with some old friends. Around the same time – in 2012 – his symptoms became impossible to suppress and he sought help.

He was still occasionally suicidal. He had nine children and he said they prevented him from taking his own life. He mentioned a scene in the film *Saving Private Ryan*, a film he could no longer watch. What if he had died, and the person he swapped sides with on the stretcher when they were hit had lived? 'What if his life . . . if he'd had the life and I never. And you get to that scene where they're in the graveyard where he says "Tell me I've been a good man, I've lived a good life" . . . and sometimes, in a lot of ways I feel a failure, and my kids tell me different. They've got good lives ahead of them. It's been a long time.'[31] He was unable to work. For a while he'd worked as a taxi driver, and at the time he spoke to me he was sleeping on friends' sofas.

Jim was later angry with the Scots Guards for not being able to identify that he had a problem when he came back from the Falklands. This kind of denial of symptoms was widespread. Les Davis, who had been attached to 3 Para on Mount Longdon, said he went to Woolwich hospital at the end of 1982, but was told there was nothing wrong with him. He felt, 'It was as if I wasn't there. You could see various things, as if I was watching . . . Behind the glass, yeah, looking at [myself]. It'd be like that. Nearest I can describe it.'[32] Bill Bentley, a lance corporal with 2 Para and a medic, said that at the time he almost never felt fear and had been conditioned to bear pain almost with pleasure: 'Pain is only a sensation.'[33] The Para attitude, the Army attitude, was to get on, and so they did.

★

Tony Banks and Phil Francom, both privates with 2 Para, and Graham Tolson, a lance corporal with 3 Para, all threw themselves into hard work when they got back from the Falklands. Tolson had been paralysed with battle shock for a period while on Mount Longdon. 'I used to work really hard. I used to blot it out. In the garden, working on the car, doing extra shifts at work . . . I coped by working hard, very hard, for instance, during the normal course of the working day when everyone else was taking a break I would be working, sometimes working till late at night, working slowly to make sure I got it done properly, when I look back it was me trying to forget, basically.'[34]

According to Phil Francom, 'I was a different person – my drinking escalated, my punishing fitness regime became obsessive.'[35] When he left the regiment seven years later, he was enormously fit and he worked all hours, holding down three jobs. Tony Banks was also driven to long hours of work. He left the Parachute Regiment for the Royal Army Medical Corps, and then left that to set up his own successful care-home business. He said he was drinking to excess, and was 'angry and bitter, but kept everything bottled up'. His older brother committed suicide, and then his younger brother died of a brain tumour. He said he 'felt like the grim reaper – anyone near me seemed to end up dead'.[36] But he did not cry once.

Banks' experience of multiple bereavement pointed to something that Hughes and O'Brien had noticed in their 1987 study of sixty-four serving soldiers. They noted that those with PTSD-type symptoms were more likely than the matched control group to report the death of someone close to them in the years since the Falklands. It could not be that Falklands' veterans were actually like the 'grim reaper', and so Hughes and O'Brien suggested that those affected by combat had become highly sensitive to death, and mentioned it, whereas those in the control group did not. It was an important observation.

In the field of battle, men had been allowed to feel a kind of inevitable sadness, and they had been encouraged to remember – but never permitted to grieve. Some symptoms of trauma could be repressed grief for the friends they had lost: not just because they loved them as friends and comrades, but because they shared those experiences with them and felt their identities were locked together. Steven Hughes, a captain and medical doctor with 2 Para, said he was haunted by his vision of the body-bags containing Jones, Dent and Wood – three men he loved and respected. He shut off his feelings. 'To see him [Wood] with a 7.62mm entry wound in the middle of his forehead had a tremendous impact on me, but I couldn't allow that to register on my emotions at the time. I had to pretend the professional detached persona and say: "He's dead, there's nothing we can do for him."' Hughes learnt later that a friend at home, a friend he had always relied on to unburden himself to, had also died. 'I came to terms with the fact that anybody close to me could die in the next minute. I began to put everybody at a distance . . . the little boy inside me putting up barriers, because in his experience anybody who came close to him died.'[37] Later, he thought his subsequent breakdown was in part a reaction to grief he had been unable, and then too afraid, to express. To confess to deep grief could bring the whole edifice down.[38] As Tony Banks said, it was a very 'male' reaction.[39] Real men did not weep.

Phil Francom said that while he was still in the regiment, 'I suppressed the feelings I had, but I started to wet the bed. I was not alone in this and we all joked and slagged each other off about it.'[40] It was as if, at night, when they could not work or control their unconscious minds, their bodies betrayed the maturity they thought they should feel, bearing the responsibility for what they had seen and done.

★

It could be difficult to become reconciled to the absence of combat, the intense feelings and camaraderie it had brought. Sometimes, men missed the high thrill and tried to find it in other ways. Francom said he chased women: 'women were easy to come by in Aldershot and I made myself known amongst them.'[41] Len Carver, a lance corporal with 3 Para who had been shot in the back and shoulder, said, 'I went off the rails, I'm not ashamed to – well, I am ashamed to admit it – I didn't go drinking or things like that, I was just looking for, shall we say, excitement. And that was the downfall for me, for my marriage. I just wanted excitement; it led to affairs, because it was exciting. Could I get caught? No. I did eventually . . . well, in the end I came clean. I was an arsehole, I admit that.'[42]

When men left the Army, adjusting to life outside was challenging. The Parachute Regiment had enabled them to make sense of themselves – and of the war. Outside it, they just felt uprooted. Martin Margerison, a corporal with 2 Para who had been shot in the shoulder and jaw, left in the late 1990s. He found work but, like many other former soldiers, found it hard to fit into masculine civilian cultures. Outside the regiment, men were lazy. They got in their vans, drove around the corner, had a butty and a cup of tea, read the paper, then went on to work, only to do the same all over again the next day. They were untidy, overweight, they complained and just seemed to want something for nothing. They did not understand loyalty or discipline. In the regiment, if a task needed to be done, it was done; it was not deferred. If somebody messed up, they were dealt with and everyone moved on.

Many men had violent fantasies and wanted to inflict violence on others. Lee Smith said he used to soothe himself to sleep thinking about beating people up.[43] That tendency was obviously not exclusive to paratroopers post-combat. Many of them had fought with civilians, and each other, before going to the Falklands too. Nevertheless, after the Falklands, violence took on a different significance. Before, they had been playing, learning the attributes of Paras and other men. Now, it was serious. They had proved themselves in war and who could challenge them? A former corporal beat up a group of teenagers who threatened him in his local town centre. He needed to show them who was boss: 'There's always some stupid little boy outside who thinks he's the local hard man, and I remember walking through my town one night, going to the bank, about half past nine at night, and about eight or nine youths, all hanging around, one of them shouted, who do you think you are walking through my street? Wrong thing to say. I just battered him. I hurt him, and his mates. The others run away.'[44]

Sometimes violence was a way of asserting their authority and the moral superiority of the codes learned in the Parachute Regiment: stand up for your mates, do not get beaten, do not get caught. At other times, they were violent because it was easier than walking away: 'The easiest thing was attack is the best form of defence. And the bigger they were the better it was for me. Because they thought this baldy old man's not going to do anything, and then it's too late, because I was never taught to stop, never taught that when he's on the floor that you had to call it a day . . . .'[45]

Paratroopers could also find it hard to ease back into their domestic lives. The Army had always come first, but the need to be with others who had been through the same experience was more intense than ever. Martin Margerison said: 'I love my family, I love my daughters, I love my boys, and I love the regiment, and I had to get down the pub. And I think that's where it all started to go wrong, really, to be honest. More and more drink, oh, I'm just having another. And there was no mobile phones then, you shoot the shit and you can get away with it for ten minutes more. I'm turning home, my kids are in bed, before you know it's eighteen months down the line and you're stuck in it. You're being told what's wrong but you're not quite listening. Then it's gone.'[46]

At other times, the experiences they had could make them feel they were not entitled to sympathy or love. Life was harsh and that was how it had to be. Lee Smith pushed his wife, his childhood sweetheart, away from him. He loved her but he wanted her gone before she realized how horrible he had become. He said he woke up one night to find himself about to strangle her, and he left.[47] Phil Francom was trapped into feelings he thought were sham. He craved female comfort and married a girl he met in 1983. He became the landlord of a pub, and gained a reputation as a hard man. All the local men who fancied themselves as tough wanted to have a go at him, and he always saw them off, even if they came with guns and knives. He thought he was invincible. The strain of his pretence got too much for him: 'In 1991 I attempted to strangle my wife and that was the last straw. I drank a bottle of vodka, took a bottle of sleeping pills and attempted to hang myself. If it had not been for my sister-in-law cutting me down and phoning an ambulance, I would not be here today.'[48] He went to a doctor, but the Army told him there was nothing in his record to suggest he might have PTSD. It was eleven more years before he got a diagnosis.

Margerison was diagnosed with PTSD around 2000, when his second wife began to say similar things to him as his first wife had done. He felt cornered. He had left the Parachute Regiment. Domestic life was lacking in discipline and could be frivolous. Now he had to live at home all the time, he could not switch off from the ways he had learnt in the Army, but those ways were not appropriate at home. Len

Carver identified his PTSD in the early to mid 2000s. He had outbursts of uncontrollable emotion: 'I felt that, if I didn't go and get help,
I would hurt someone. It was little things. I got up one morning,
walked through the kitchen door, and there was a cupboard door open,
my wife had left one of the top cupboard doors open. I just caught it
with my head, destroyed it. Just punched the crap out of it, the cupboard and the door. I had to go out and buy a new unit. Just a simple
thing like that, and I didn't know why I was doing it, even as I'm doing
it, I didn't understand why, there was no reasoning behind it.'[49]

Graham Tolson sought help after twenty-one years. He got blind
drunk and assaulted an officer at the mess bar. He wanted to commit
suicide, and broke down and confessed how he was feeling to a friend
and then to his wife.[50] John Gartshore's recognition came later, in the
late 2000s: 'I wasn't . . . I wasn't suicidal. I was a bit crazy. I was doing
stupid things. I'd lose my rag. I'd fight, even though I was too old. I'd
lost the grip on reality. I didn't know how it was affecting me. I'm not
ashamed to say, I now understand where things was affecting me, and
other people. Other people in my family could see it, I couldn't. It
hurts them to see it. But now, because I'm open with my family about
what's happened, they understand, they prefer my honesty. So I'm
being honest with you. I'm OK.'[51]

David Benest was diagnosed in 2009. He had been Commanding
Officer of 2 Para between 1994 and 1997 and gained an MBE and
OBE for services to counter-terrorism. In 2008, he volunteered to go
to Afghanistan as a counter-insurgency adviser to the British ambassador. He said: 'I was a complete mental mess.' He was not sleeping
and was drinking too much. He told the ambassador, who, he said,
discharged him without fuss. His GP recognized he had PTSD, but
the Army treated it as if he had gone AWOL and launched an investigation which lasted seven months.[52] The course of Benest's career
demonstrated that having PTSD and achieving success were not
mutually exclusive, but it also showed that the Army often still
expected men to mask troubling symptoms if they wanted to
progress.

For many men, the story of trauma was one of suppression, crisis
and then finally recognition. The containing of their feelings was a

powerful part of their masculine and regimental identity, and, in the Paras, conquering their emotions was normal, because they had had to do it even to pass their training. After the Falklands, the ways they coped – extreme fitness, overwork, drinking, risk-taking and violence – were all part of paratrooper culture. Men could have the symptoms of trauma and yet still maintain successful careers, in and out of the Army.

For these men, their post-combat trauma was a reaction – harsher perhaps because it had been delayed – to the stress of being under shellfire, the powerlessness that could come with being hit, the shame of surviving when their friends had not, the loneliness that could come with the loss of status after leaving the army, and the sense of dispossession felt as a result of not being understood. Trauma, both clinical PTSD and symptoms or behaviours related to traumatic experiences, was therefore often bound up with men's military or regimental identities, and with the sense that men should be able to bear the responsibility of combat. They often believed they could not have trauma because they had not felt fear, they had just borne pain. They frequently believed that trauma was a sign of weakness.

And now, after combat and out of the Paras, who were they? Lance Corporal Les Standish, who won the Military Medal with B Company 2 Para, became a prison officer, but left after he began having severe flashbacks. He was a hard man, and to make money to support his family, he became a bare-knuckle fighter and collector for a local drug dealer.[53] To end up in such insalubrious occupations seemed incongruous, even humiliating, after his distinguished military record. Lance Corporal Bill Bentley, who had amputated another man's lower leg with a Swiss Army knife while under fire and who had also won the Military Medal, said he was told on departure from the regiment that a suitable job for him would be a petrol-pump attendant (unsupervised).[54] Civilian society glorified war, but did not rate highly the skills paratroopers had acquired; after the war, it could feel as if fighting for your country was worth nothing.

★

Combat often validated masculine identity, and the loss of that identity came later, when men left the Army. They could doubt they had done the right thing during the war, and worry they had not performed as they should have. Mike Seear, for example, wanted a challenging job as 'a subconscious second bite at the Falklands-Malvinas apple, which might rectify my non-optimal performance during that war'.[55]

The feeling they had not lived up to their expectations was hard. Sometimes, it was because what they had been asked, or ordered, to do was impossible, or wrong. Lieutenant Jeremy McTeague, like Seear an officer with the Gurkhas, said that as they advanced towards Tumbledown his platoon came under heavy artillery and mortar fire: 'Having decided we should remain in cover, I was still without any other options and so felt powerless to protect my men further . . . The realization that there is nothing one can do is not easy to accept, and one feels a corresponding overwhelming sense of inadequacy . . . I was worried that my men thought of me as being ineffective.'[56]

John Gartshore struggled because 2 Para's Machine Gun Platoon was not used in its proper role at Goose Green. The machine guns were not given positions to fire on, and they had to pick their targets as best they could. He feared this meant his group had been firing when Lieutenant Barry attempted to take the surrender of an Argentine trench. If this was so, then their fire had led the Argentines to believe the surrender was not sincere. Those Argentines then killed Barry and the two men he was with.

Gartshore did not know if he and the machine gunners had been responsible. Even if they had fired at the wrong moment, it was not their fault, because they were doing their best with the job they had been given and the information they had. It was a burden, to remain loyal to the Parachute Regiment's battle honour and yet to know that the machine guns had been incorrectly deployed: 'If we'd been . . . given positions to fire on instead of just picking them, we would have been doing our job properly. It's a sad thing to say that . . . Don't say I don't feel guilty. I feel remorse for the men who got killed. But I can't let it get to me at times, because you think, if I'd done this or that would it have been easier? Could we have done it a different way? . . . It was embarrassing, but the answer is, if we'd been used in our correct role, I don't know, it could have been different . . . For a machine-gun platoon to be so far forward, when we took Goose Green in the morning, it was a joke.'[57]

Dave Brown, with C Company 2 Para, felt disbelief when C Company was ordered to break through the gorse line on Darwin Hill and advance down an open slope: 'The famous last words we heard from the Company commander were, "Fix bayonets". I thought, Battle of Waterloo job here. Three kilometres over this undulating open moorland in daylight and the Argies in Goose Green had obviously got a main artillery position, they'd got the mortar defences and they also had the anti-aircraft guns in two versions, 20mm and 40mm. Because we were going down an open slope, they were firing head-high at us with these 40mms and 20mms; in the first fifteen minutes C Company took eleven casualties. A fucking nightmare, put it that way . . . Out of the four-man company HQ, I was the only man not wounded that day.'[58]

Martin Margerison developed an insidious anxiety. He was shot in the shoulder and jaw. His wounds were such that he could not be sure – totally certain – who had shot him. At times he feared he had been shot by his own men, not one of his section but somebody else: 'There was no reason for them to, I hadn't had a fall out with anybody. And then you start thinking, somebody's looking at me, for no reason, he's looking at me through his sights and going, yeah, that Scouse. And it's done. He's not going to turn round and say, "Fuck me, I've just shot Scouse." And that's how your head goes. Paranoia.'[59]

Other men felt degraded. It was not so much that they had not matched their expectations, or what they were asked to do was wrong. Rather, the whole world system had become sick. Corporal Tom Howard was a medical officer with the Parachute Regiment. He saw a man die, his legs ripped apart, screaming for his mother. He began to see war as 'a dreadful, god-awful waste, a total change from my previous attitudes'. When he got home, 'I'd started drinking heavily and smoking drugs by September 1982 – while I was still in the Army. The combination provided an escape for me, and in Aldershot drugs were easy to get – from people in the Army. We smoked hash – and even opium sometimes – in the unit club. I don't know how we got away with it. I mixed with friends in 2 Para who had the same problems. We all used drugs and drink for the same purpose.'[60]

Gus Hales was a Royal Engineer with 9 Parachute Squadron. He came from a mining family and had considered becoming a vicar when he was younger. He joined the Army seeking the kind of camaraderie his father had known down the pit. At Fitzroy, he helped the Welsh Guards, some of them terribly burned and injured, after the ship they were on was bombed. He went into battle during 3 Para's attack on Mount Longdon. As he crossed the start-line, he felt 'an inexplicable sense of euphoria, as if past and future had dissolved, and his personal fate was no longer of the slightest consequence'.

His job was to clear mines. After the battle, he went to Ajax Bay to attend the burial of men killed on Longdon and Mount Tumbledown. A friend had died. He listened to one of the battalion padres talking about God. The journalist Matthew Green explained: 'He felt he was being asked to seek forgiveness from the same religious authorities who had sanctified the killing.' He could not reconcile this to himself. Hales said: 'That was like a seminal moment – the confusion set in. I couldn't square the circle. I couldn't round it off. I couldn't understand. Here was something in me saying: "For Chrissake, we're human beings, we shouldn't be engaged in this. This is awful." '[61]

Eventually, he made sense of it by understanding that he had been put in a position that he should never have been in, not necessarily because the Falklands War should not have been fought, but because any war, any violence, was the eruption of insanity into world politics. The whole structure, the whole system that enabled violence, the visions of martial masculinity that sustained it, were grim perversions of the world, so much so that one day they would surely disappear. Hales learnt to control his thoughts – 'they are just thoughts' – and took up intense meditation and became a Buddhist. He decoupled his sense of self from 'the war'. Like many veterans of the First World War, he came to see the purpose of war as the establishment of conditions of peace, peace that should be everlasting.

★

Some men found a little consolation in meeting Argentine veterans. To see the men who had been trying to kill you, and to realize that they were just men – like the British men – doing their job, helped to dissipate some of the harder emotions they had felt. Vince Bramley went to Argentina in 1993 and met veterans who had been on Longdon: 'Jorge's polite manner to me, his former enemy, put me at ease and we both relaxed completely as the evening wore on. From time to time he would smile warmly at me across the table and as he told me his life story in his soft voice I couldn't help thinking of this man as a friend. At the same time I felt great sympathy for him because his account of the war itself reminded me of the stories of some of my own comrades.'[62]

Tony Banks came back from the Falklands with a trumpet belonging to an Argentine called Omar Tabarez. Some thirty years later, he tracked Tabarez down and flew to Argentina to return his instrument. He was nervous, driving to Tabarez's house. Tabarez welcomed him warmly: 'There is no price for this act of kindness. I always dreamed of getting my trumpet back. It is a comfort. It is like getting a brother back.' Tabarez's forgiveness and his hospitality led Banks to see the Argentines in a new light. Tabarez believed the Malvinas belonged to Argentina, but, like Banks, he had been doing his job. The Argentine soldiers had suffered as the British men had, particularly after the war. In their own way, they were all victims of a political system prone to violence.[63]

Some men, therefore, found a kind of redemption in thinking beyond the national structures that had sent them to war in the first place. It seemed more common, however, that men coped by feeling pride in the achievements of their regiment, and in Britain's wartime history. The Falklands War had been worthwhile. Gartshore carried with him a picture of two island children he had liberated from the community centre at Goose Green when 2 Para finally got to the settlement. The Argentines had been holding the 115 islanders captive for twenty-nine days. When he returned to the Falklands he met those children, now adults with children of their own. He felt proud he had played a part in giving them a future. It made the war worth it for him.

Men had to find ways to make peace with their pasts, to allow themselves to let go. Margerison said: 'I need to spend time to become a civvy. I've got to stop being an ex-paratrooper. Too old, mate.' But it took a lot to release themselves from the regiment that had given them the lives they had, and had often brought about the characteristics they valued most about themselves; and it took a lot to release themselves from the war, because to forget would be to forsake the men who had died – and sometimes died, they believed, in their place. It took a lot to let go because the war made them who they were – as Gartshore said, he left a piece of himself in the Falklands. Letting go was hard.

Phil Francom was standing next to my uncle when my uncle was hit by the shell that killed him outright. Phil was not even scratched. Dave came to Phil at night. It would be wrong to say in his dreams – it was not like that. Dave was there, in his room. At first, Phil tried to make him go away, but then he began to talk to him. He got out of bed and made them two cups of tea and they talked together. Dave was there, drinking tea, night after night.

Phil told me: 'After I left my wife, I would wake up to find Dave sat on the end of my bed plain as day asking for a brew. At first it used to bother me, then I started getting up making two brews and sitting chatting with Dave for hours, laughing loudly, so loud that at times, when my children were staying with me, they would get up and ask what I was doing. I would say I am just having a brew. Looking back now they must have thought I was mad. This continued for a long time. When my son and daughter were older, I explained to them what was going on . . .

'I have not had a visit from Dave since the second time I returned to the Falklands in 2003. It was the twenty-first anniversary of his death and I went up to Wireless Ridge on or about the time we lost him. It was freezing cold but I felt warm air around me and the smell of Brut filled the air. This gave me a feeling of elation and I felt like it was Dave forgiving me for not being injured at the same time he was killed. When I returned from the Falklands the second time, I spoke to my kids about why I had been the way I was, my experiences and all about Dave and the brews. They were surprisingly understanding. I often thought that this was the reason he came to visit me – to let me know I had to speak to my kids. Once I had spoke to them both about it, Dave never returned to drink tea and chat at all (I MISS HIS VISITS).

'I felt guilty and still do that Dave came back to the platoon so that I would survive.'[64]

★

What light can paratroopers shed on British society in the 1980s? In some ways, they illustrate two extremes: the men who never worked again, and the men who did extremely well out of the end of industrial Britain and the transformation to a liberalized, finance- and service-based economy.

It is hard to say whether the loss of employment in traditional heavy industry had much direct impact on the Paras. It might have mattered more for paratroopers who entered the regiment after 1982, when unemployment sent more men to the Depot. The generation that joined in the 1970s were often from northern cities, but they usually joined to escape industrial Britain, not because it had rejected them. In addition, the Paras were not a county regiment. Men who had taken the step of joining the regiment perhaps felt less attachment to the regions of their birth than men who stayed put, and therefore less nostalgia for the communities transformed by industrial closure.

Some men did fall into what in the 1980s was called the 'underclass'. As the nature of the traditional working class changed, and as more women entered the workforce and more people took 'middle-class' jobs, at the bottom of society was a category of people whose lives were adversely affected by the erosion of predictable communities and easy to come by, laborious work. Paratroopers had often grown up in coal-mining areas, and coal mining was one example of the change in patterns of labour and worklessness during the 1980s. In 1981, the coal industry employed 229,000 men – one in four jobs – in English and Welsh coalfield areas. By 2004, 92 per cent of those men had lost their jobs, with the greatest concentration in areas of Yorkshire, Nottinghamshire, South Wales, Durham, Derbyshire and Northumberland. Although many of those posts were replaced, particularly by work in the service sector, some men were initially reluctant to take what they saw as 'women's jobs'. Many former miners took early retirement instead.[65] The people who ended up in the 'underclass' could lack stable employment and their children could also struggle to find jobs. They had few assets and little hope that life might change.[66]

Some Falklands veterans, particularly those who became addicted to alcohol or drugs, or who had undiagnosed mental-health problems, may well have joined this group. One example was 'Tinker' – Private Derek Styles – who was in B Company 2 Para. Before the Falklands, he had represented the regiment in gymnastics competitions; but afterwards he never regained his sense of equilibrium. He had terrible nightmares, and took to drink and drugs. He had been attending a drug and alcohol dependency centre in Dumfries, run by Mark Frankland. Frankland said that Tinker was addicted to heroin and alcohol and sold copies of the *Big Issue* to earn a little money. He was haunted by his own violence at Goose Green and forever saddened by his experiences.[67]

Frankland also suggested that Tinker had done time in prison. In 2012, the charity No Offence! estimated that one in ten prisoners was a former soldier.[68] However, the Ministry of Defence and Ministry of Justice put the figure at 3.5 per cent and argued that veterans were less likely to be in prison or on probation than the general population.[69] The Howard League for Penal Reform, in a sensitive recent study, argued that while veterans were less likely than the general population to offend, they were more likely to commit sexual or violent offences; and that some veterans committed offences so long after their service that it was hard to know if service had had any impact or not.

The Howard League attempted to compare the population likely to become infantry soldiers with the general population and concluded that the profile was sometimes similar. Probable offenders were proportionately more likely to come from disadvantaged backgrounds, backgrounds in which there was violence and drug abuse, and to have had periods in care. It was possible that military service delayed criminal offending for many men.[70] At the same time, some men committed offences while still serving soldiers, and some found that the institutionalization in prison life was similar to that in the Paras.

Ken Lukowiak, a private in 2 Para, received a two and a half year sentence for smuggling marijuana from Belize, after the Parachute Regiment's tour there in 1983. One of the first prison officers he encountered was a former Royal Marine; another was an ex-Para. Prison was not nice, but 'after five years in the Parachute Regiment, it wasn't that hard'.[71] He knew how to behave himself around the prison authorities, and he had an aptitude for fighting when it was necessary. His son was born when he was inside and at times he was overcome with regret: 'I was to blame . . . it was wrong because it had caused pain to others, shame to others. And with that thought I felt so helpless.' Then another prisoner came into the room he was in and they shared a joint. 'And my true sorrow and true shame and true remorse and true promise, they all hit the ceiling with the smoke.'[72]

Steven Roberts did time in the late 1980s. He had been in junior detention before joining the Paras and, like Lukowiak, his experience in the regiment meant he could cope: 'When I walked into prison onto that wing . . . I wasn't scared, because I think [with] the military training, the discipline I'd had over the years, I knew I could hold my own. Within twenty-four hours I'd had my first fight on the wing, where someone tests you, and this is prison life now, they will test you on the wing to see your weaknesses and strengths, and if they think you're a walk-over you will spend the rest of your time in debt, paying them and doing lackey jobs for bullies.'[73]

He began to get an education, but daily life was still stifling: 'Fucking boredom. When you've had an active life and you're running around doing this and that, and suddenly twenty-three hours in the cell, you're just jumping up the walls.' The boredom nurtured paranoia, because there was nothing to distract from it: 'Everything gets blown out of proportion in your brain . . . You're sitting there, and thinking I haven't had a letter from my mum, oh, I didn't get a letter – this is an example – and then by the end of the day they've disowned me, they don't want me.' Coming out into civilian life was doubly hard: 'I come out of prison, and I tell you what, it was fucking hard, because where most people come out the army and struggle, I had not only come out of the army but out of prison as well, back-to-back.'[74]

The Falklands veterans' charity, the South Atlantic Medal

Association 1982 – SAMA82 – argued that suicide had reached epidemic levels among men who had served in the Falklands. They claimed that more men had committed suicide since the conflict than the 255 who were killed during the war. The Ministry of Defence took issue with the figures, and said in 2013 that they could establish causes of death by intentional self-harm and events of undetermined intent in only 101 cases, 7 per cent of the deaths of veterans that had occurred since 1982. The MoD said that veterans were no more likely to commit suicide than men who had never been to war.[75] Falklands' veterans countered that the MoD's figures did not take account of deaths from alcohol and drug abuse like Tinker's, which could be considered a slow form of suicide from neglect; and that the MoD had surveyed everyone in the Task Force rather than those closest to intense combat.[76] Taking these factors into account, the proportion of paratroopers committing suicide could be even higher.

It is impossible to prove, but Falklands' veterans did seem to fit an at-risk profile. In the 1970s and 1980s, men aged twenty-five to thirty-four and thirty-five to forty-five became more likely to commit suicide, and in the 1990s, the twenty-five to thirty-four age group became the highest-risk group, whereas previously they had been the lowest-risk group, and at much less risk than older men.[77] Suicide was more likely in periods of societal disruption. Some sociologists considered that the rises in marital breakdown and rates of people living alone in the 1980s were possible explanations for men ending their own lives. They also argued that the rise in male unemployment could be a contributing factor. Unemployed men might be more likely to commit suicide if they lived in areas where other men were in work, and thus were able to compare themselves on a daily basis with men who had what they wanted.[78] Work was not just an activity to pass the time and bring home money, but a marker of status, a badge of identity, and its loss could be hard for all people, including for soldiers.

The rise in consumer culture might also have affected the rate of male suicide in the 1980s and beyond. In the 1950s and 1960s, there was a rise in female suicide, attributable to the availability of a new method. Women gassed themselves, putting their heads in domestic ovens to breathe in carbon monoxide. The safety of domestic gas supplies improved, but in the 1980s rates of car ownership also increased significantly, and men subsequently were more likely than women to kill themselves with the exhaust fumes from their cars.[79]

The rate of suicide almost certainly reflected the ability to carry it out and the bravery to see it through. Former SAS soldier Nish Bruce killed himself by jumping out of a plane without a parachute. He was flying with his girlfriend, a fellow skydiver, when he opened the door and tipped himself out without warning. Stephen Hood, a medic with 2 Para during the Falklands, killed himself early in 2013. He had been suffering from flashbacks, and there had been recent news reports that the Argentines were reigniting their sovereignty claim. His widow said: 'Stephen was not anti-Argentine and neither am I. I am sure their veterans are struggling too and need help.'[80] He died in his car of carbon-monoxide poisoning.

★

On the other hand, some former Paras did well from the changing economic landscape. Tony Banks and Mark Eyles-Thomas were not afraid to embrace 'women's jobs' and both made a success in the new industry of telesales. They possessed some of the qualities lauded in post-industrial Britain: persistence, energy, entrepreneurial spirit and a willingness to work long hours. Both went on to set up their own successful businesses in the service sector, Banks running care homes, and Eyles-Thomas selling and managing security products. In 2009, Banks agreed to appear on the TV show *The Secret Millionaire*. The pause in his relentlessly busy life, and the self-consciousness provoked by being interviewed, made him acknowledge things which he had allowed himself to hide, and triggered a recognition of his trauma.

Beyond these two extremes were many men who made respectable livings doing a range of work. Sometimes what they had learnt in the Falklands was useful. Jon Cook, who realized he could tolerate grim tasks other people found distressing, worked for an undertaker. One of his jobs was to collect bodies from the scenes of motor accidents. Some became paramedics, where a phlegmatic attitude to physical pain and an ability to cope with moments of high stress were useful skills. Others, inured to hard drinking and able to handle themselves, become publicans. Yet others went into the police or joined the prison service. In the 1990s, some took advantage of the rise in the numbers of people accessing higher education and went back to college. Some took jobs in the civil service, became psychologists or lecturers in further and higher education. One man taught in a primary school, others took PhDs. Some joined the SAS and many forged successful careers in the Army. Mike Curtis and John Geddes went on to pass selection for the SAS. Chip Chapman commanded 2 Para between 1999 and 2001 and retired at the rank of major general. Two other lieutenants during the Falklands War, Major General Jonathan Shaw and Lieutenant General Jonathan Page, both went on to become Colonel Commandant of the Parachute Regiment.

Perhaps the most common post-Falklands occupation was private security, itself also a sign of the changing times. Private security could mean providing protection for celebrities. Celebrities were not new, of course, but a larger number of them became absurdly rich in the 1980s and could afford to pay ex-paratroopers to act as their personal minders. Other men gave paid protection to bankers, financiers, or overseas investors with a lot of private wealth. Robin Horsfall, ex-Para, ex-SAS, worked for Dodi al-Fayed: 'I worked a twelve-hour shift, either standing on the roof guarding the site of Al Fayed's new penthouse, then under construction, or sitting at a desk beside the front door checking in visitors and monitoring the closed circuit TV screens. The money might have been OK, but the job was mind-numbingly boring.'[81] He was little more than a well-paid minder or chauffeur, and often there to give an extra frisson – a special forces soldier as a bodyguard! – in front of al-Fayed's well-heeled guests.

Private security could also mean working overseas for corporations that dealt in any number of things: guarding foreign workers in unstable parts of the world, training special forces in the deserts of Saudi Arabia, providing security for diamond mines in Sierra Leone or oil installations in Angola, advising police forces in Nigeria or devising responses to crises and disasters in Iraq.[82] These men were – much as they had been when they were in the Army – outside the sociological classifications of class. Their employment was plentiful but dangerous and unstable. They would probably live for long periods overseas, and earn money in inconsistent patterns, even if they had families based in the UK.

It is hard to know for sure, but perhaps army service did not make a huge difference to men's career trajectories once they had left. In one sense, the gap between civilian and military life might even have been comparatively greater for middle-class men, as levels of higher education increased, and as middle-class salaries in some professions, notably in finance, rapidly increased, and as military service continued to fall out of favour as a career option.

The House of Commons reviewed army salaries each year, and compared the rate of those salaries to external conditions. In 1985, they reported that the gratuities men received towards buying a house were no longer sufficient, and in 1990 they said that men often cited the difficulties in buying a house as a negative factor in army service: 'They have seen the marked trend in civilian life towards buying property as soon as it can be afforded.'[83] Men also increasingly spoke about the problems their wives had in finding stable employment. As more women wanted to work, the disruption of being a military spouse was felt more keenly. In addition, civilian competitor occupations increasingly offered a company car.[84] By the end of the 1980s, the problems of attracting recruits in the ranks had not improved, and the problem of retaining officers remained. Army pay, along with other public sector pay, did not keep up with average pay increases during the 1980s. A private joining the Army in 1989 earned less in real terms than a private joining in 1982.[85]

In some cases, the Army gave men opportunities they would not otherwise have had; in others, the experience of combat destroyed their lives. For the most part, though, armed service probably did not much alter the opportunities provided by society. When they left the services, the Paras' employment prospects perhaps reflected not just what they had done in the Falklands, but also their education and background before they had joined up.

★

Who were the paratroopers? In the early 1990s, even the Parachute Regiment seemed unsure. The Falklands War had enhanced their reputation, and in 1983 5 Airborne Brigade was formed, essentially reconstituting the 16th Parachute Brigade that was disbanded in 1977. 5 Airborne Brigade was intended for rapid deployment and it recognized the Army might need the kind of mobile spearhead unit the Paras could offer. The Falklands War brought to attention the high standard of the Parachute Regiment's NCOs and the rest of the infantry began to adopt the training course the Paras ran at Brecon. The connections between the Paras and the SAS were made more explicit, and training literature emphasized that the Parachute Regiment was a good base from which to attempt SAS selection.[86]

As the Cold War ended and Britain's world role changed, some officers in the Parachute Regiment began to review the objectives of the Paras' cherished training regime, 'P' Company. The pass rates in P Company had not improved. Only 38 per cent got through, and the wastage was costly. Post-Cold War, the Army was more likely to be engaged in peacekeeping, or low-level counter-insurgency, rather than all-out war.

In some ways, after the Cold War ended, the Parachute Regiment also began to address the shadow cast by Bloody Sunday, as well as the attitude that had served them in the Falklands. Commanding Officer of 3 Para, Lieutenant Colonel T. W. Burls, suggested that paratroopers could be too unthinkingly aggressive: 'The instinctive reaction of our soldiers is aggressive when often it need not be.' And he questioned: 'Is the aggressive spirit we foster so unremittingly a liability when our soldiers are placed in positions requiring subtlety?'[87] Far from providing men with an essential attribute of endurance and determination, the airborne ethos could enforce a rigidity of behaviour, as men placed their reputations before their lives: 'Officers, especially junior officers, must understand that the training we give our soldiers – in basic training, pre-parachute selection and in battalion – is only a means to an end, it is not a holy grail, a sacred solution to all problems which will see us through no matter what.'[88]

In 1993, Major Twentyman reviewed the assessment processes of P Company. He suggested that while it was robust and demanding, and while the assessors were dedicated and experienced, some of the selection was done in a rather subjective way. Most of the tests were timed against the clock, but three of them – the log race, the stretcher race and 'milling' – were simply judged on the degree to which a man showed 'courage, determination and team spirit', 'physical and mental courage, aggression and the will to win'.

Those qualities could be judged with preconceptions rather than against objective criteria. Twentyman found that assessors often could not exactly explain how they had come to their verdict – what 'noteworthy events' they had witnessed, to use his words. A man could pass selection, Twentyman suggested, sometimes because he attained enough points through his physical fitness, even if he was mentally unsuitable; and sometimes simply because other airborne soldiers had the feeling that he had what it took to become a Para.[89]

To the chagrin of older colonels like the Falklands' Hew Pike, who retired as Lieutenant General Sir Hew Pike, Lieutenant Colonel Poraj-Wilczynski proposed a subtle change to the goals of Pre-Parachute Selection. Rather than just filtering who could become an airborne soldier, P Company should aim to test whether a recruit had the 'ability, self-discipline and motivation' to 'serve as a military parachutist with 5 Airborne Brigade'. It was a subtle change, but it reflected a more flexible understanding of the connection between masculinity and national, or regimental, character.

A man could attain the ability to perform as a paratrooper should, but did not have to devote his entire being to the airborne brotherhood. A man could be a Para, and he could also – when he was not at work – be a man.

14. Memory

In 2012 I went to East Falkland with my father. In some respects, the Falkland Islands had always been a land of my imagination. It might seem a strange place to dream about, being so distant, isolated, windswept and cold, but I liked the idea of wilderness, and I suppose the notion I had of my father and uncles' elemental childhoods, out on the Suffolk marshes in all weathers, appealed to me. In reality, I had little sense of what the islands would be like.

We flew from RAF Brize Norton on a civilian plane commissioned by the MoD, part of a trip organized by the Falklands veterans' organization, the South Atlantic Medal Association 1982. Since 1997, SAMA82 had arranged for veterans and relatives to go to the islands, observing that it helped to lay whatever demons they had to rest and to create links between former soldiers, families and the Falkland Islanders. I had met Falkland Islander Patrick Watts, who had been the islands' radio broadcaster in 1982, at a conference at the University of Kent, and he had kindly volunteered to meet us and to be our island guide.

In the waiting room at the airport were many soldiers in sand-coloured combat clothes on their way to Afghanistan, a small number of islanders and a man who had been one of the Royal Marines forced to surrender when the Argentines arrived. He was travelling back to the islands with his sisters. At the last minute, a battalion of paratroopers arrived to board our flight. They were flying to the military camp at Mount Pleasant, near the Falklands airport, a base that had been built after the war and was now home to a larger number of army personnel than there were Falkland Islanders. I said, 'Look, Dad, 2 Para have arrived.' Dad was dozing, and he awoke slightly startled. Even then, thirty years later, I saw his momentary hope that, going to the Falkland Islands, he would finally see his brother again.

The flight left at midnight and stopped in Ascension Island about twelve hours later. Ascension was humid: 23 degrees, but cold because of the wind. We waited five or six hours, and then flew six hours more to the Falklands. I watched *The Iron Lady* film of 2011 on the flight and thought about the things that Margaret Thatcher eventually forgot. As we neared the islands, we were joined in the air by a fighter plane to escort us to the airfield – a regular show of military strength. The airfield was small, and during the descent I could see Patrick waiting by a farm gate just outside the terminal building.

★

We drove the next day along the winding road out of Stanley up to Wireless Ridge. It was early October, incipient spring. The hills around Stanley were a connected series of ridges and rises; an expanse of cropped yellow grass, patches of dark green moss and heather. Pale grey rocks rose in stunted clusters from the tundra, and some slopes descended in scattered runs of scree. The light was brilliant and lucid; and the wind howled constantly, so loud we could hardly hear ourselves speak.

On Wireless Ridge, we found the spot where my uncle might have died. We could not, even now, be certain of the exact location. There is a chance he was killed before 2 Para got onto the ridge at all, on the low ground at the foot of the incline, but he might have advanced a short way along the feature when the shells struck them.[1] Phil Neame, his commanding officer, had sent coordinates, and that grid reference pointed us to a place towards the crest of the ridge, on higher ground, as the Paras were getting closer to Stanley. It was this place we chose. Patrick had taken his time to identify and locate the position from Neame's direction as best he could. The ridge was long – longer than I expected. If this was the place, then Dave had crossed the plain with his colleagues from the start-line, about half a kilometre, and then, arriving at the base of the ridge, had advanced 300 metres or so up the slope before he was hit by the shell. Perhaps it was better to think he had had that much, at least. The spot we selected was in the open. It was near to an Argentine position among the rocks. To the other side, there was a circular shell hole, full of water, five feet across, rough-edged with grass and mud.

The British possessed the sovereignty of the islands, and the Argentines challenged that with force. To defeat them, the paratroopers impelled them into submission and took back this land. The Argentine force had begun arriving on the islands on 2 April 1982. Their troops had time to wait for the British to come. They built their defences. On this ridge, an Argentine soldier had taken large flat slabs and lined them up around the entrance to the rocky cove where we now stood. He was protecting himself, giving himself shelter. I wondered if he had survived.

Thirty years later, in the cold light, we began to build a cairn for my uncle. We picked up the stones from the place the Argentine had left them. Some of the stones took more than one person to lift. The physical trace of that Argentine's bunker was gone, and in its place was our cairn, which looked good – grey and yellowing, part of its surroundings. Remodelling history. My uncle's short life remembered. This land was British land, reclaimed with British blood.

★

The commemoration of the Falklands War matters on the Falkland Islands for countless reasons. It was a war for sovereignty, and the islanders are always aware of that. While the Argentine claim is still live, they cannot presume their allegiance to Britain is secure. The numerous British flags, red telephone boxes and Falkland Island stickers that say 'Desire the Right', are symbols, as well as expressions, of their nationalism. They are islanders first, and British because it is necessary.

The islanders promote these informal commemorations of the war in part to show the Argentines that the islands are not their country. They also want to mark their respect for what the British did for them, and they wish to express their gratitude for their liberation from foreign occupation. British soldiers are remembered as individuals. At the hilt of Mount Longdon, there are small wooden crosses bearing the names, and sometimes pictures, of the British men who died there. On Wireless Ridge, beneath a big metal cross, someone had left a small cross with my uncle's name on it.

Many people find these kinds of commemoration immensely helpful. Richard and Pam Jones were given a piece of land in one of the Falklands' many inlets by friends they made there. They named it Craig Island, a permanent tribute to their son. Soldiers returning to the islands often go to the battlefields and see them in a new light, without violence. Sometimes, it is less the commemorative efforts than the attention islanders show to people's feelings that create the most enduring ties. When it comes to it, if an individual has personal pain, or grief, or trauma, what might make the most difference is that other people should care.

The effort made to remember the British dead on the Falkland Islands contrasts to the commemoration of the Argentines. The Malvinas war toppled General Galtieri, and within a year democracy returned to Argentina. But Argentina had lost the war, and Argentina maintains strongly that the Malvinas belong to them. It was hard to fit the defeat in war into Argentine national history, and difficult to remember its dead without opening the profound wounds caused by the military dictatorship. Partly in consequence, many of the Argentine dead were not identified when the fighting ended. On the islands, the Argentine cemetery is outside the settlement at Darwin, tucked away from the road. It has 230 graves, with white crosses. It looks like a small version of the war cemeteries built in Northern Europe after the First World War. In it, 121 of the 230 graves are anonymous, dedicated to *Soldado Argentino, Solo Conocido Por Dios*.

The Falkland Islands are sometimes portrayed in Britain as a mini-England, like England was in the 1950s or 1930s: homogeneous, self-reliant, community-minded, safe. It did not strike me like that. It was a small place. The population had doubled since 1982, but it was still only as populous as a village, and quite spread out. On one isolated farmstead we visited, a dead cow dangled rigidly on a gibbet – called in the islands a plinky. Patrick explained that the farmer had strung up the animal and stripped off the beef to eat when he wanted – it would last a few weeks like that. When we drove past, all that was left was three limbs, hanging from a great swing by metal chains and hooks.

The islands felt remote, and East Falkland resembled perhaps a fishing croft in northern Norway – low houses, some brick but mostly wooden, with corrugated metal roofs painted green or red. Many younger islanders now travelled and worked abroad, and went away to university; the islands had become more outward-looking and cosmopolitan. Most of the shops and cafés were staffed by immigrants from St Helena. But the old ways had not died out. Heavy drinking still seemed common, and Falklands girls often looked for soldiers to marry or sought out the itinerant oil workers who came to Stanley once a fortnight when the shifts on the oil rigs changed over.

The island economy was transformed after the war, as the islanders were given fishing rights in the waters around the islands, and the Falkland Islands Company sold off the land it had previously kept for itself. Some had grown relatively wealthy, and the people who lived here generally loved the place; but life was hard, as it must be when there are few amenities, when people have to earn their living from

14. Commemorative cairn to Dave Parr on the crest of Wireless Ridge, built by me, my father and Patrick Watts, October 2012.

15. Dedications to British paratroopers on the summit of Mount Longdon, October 2012.

outdoors labour, farming and fishing, and when they are dependent in no small part on the elements and the military support of the geographically distant protector of their rights.

★

War has been important in Britain's history, but Britain never thought of itself as a military country. It relied on its armed services for the reach of its Empire, the defence of its shores and its interests in Europe, but the military never dominated its political or its social life. In the nineteenth and the first part of the twentieth century, the regular armed services were composed of men from landed but lesser gentry – county families – and, at the bottom, from 'society's dregs' – men who were often seen as outcasts. The experience of total war and conscription forced the armed services to greater prominence in Britain's national life. The almost spiritual idea of death as honour and

16. *Soldado Argentino*, Argentine cemetery on the Falkland Islands, October 2012.

glory was lost in the industrialized slaughter of the trenches of the Great War, and in the Second World War conscripted men saw themselves not as trained killers, but as men compelled and willing to do their duty by their country for the duration, because the alternatives were worse.

The 1982 Falklands conflict stood at a bridging point to a new era in Britain's relationship with its armed services. In 1982 the memory of the Second World War was still close, and in the 1970s British society was similar to that which created the people's army of 1939–45. It was only beginning to adjust to immigration from the former colonies; its politics and occupations were still dominated by men; only a small proportion of its population went to university; and it was still very much divided along traditional lines of social class.

The men who made up the early 1980s Parachute Regiment reflected this. Officers were beginning to come in greater numbers from non-public schools and from university, but the officer training at Sandhurst had not yet adopted changes that might hasten a fully meritocratic army, and they still wanted men with moral fibre imprinted on their character. In the ranks, paratroopers were usually poorly educated but quick witted, and sometimes from backgrounds of extreme deprivation, already acclimatized to hardship and violence. Others joined because they did not want the drudgery of repetitive industrial or unskilled labour. In a British society that was becoming more affluent, and offering greater variety of experience to more of its youth, they sought adventure.

They were a generation for whom military service and manhood often went hand in hand. Men seeking to become officers often saw service as their calling, a duty. Others loved the physical challenge of sports and competition. They all wanted to test themselves as men, against each other, against the high standards of the past. Men joining the ranks often wanted to make themselves and their families proud by showing too that they were up to the job of soldiering. They had the discipline, the emotional reserve, the moral courage, to do what it took to be a paratrooper. Men often saw marriage and fatherhood, the responsibilities of providing for a family and becoming the head of a household, as part of their progression to manhood. At the same time, the Parachute Regiment's history of serving in a variety of extreme circumstances, and the fact they were allowed to kill in combat, could encourage men to see themselves as aggressive and self-sufficient and very occasionally hardened, rebellious or unconformist.

Since the 1980s, British national life – and the British Army – have changed significantly. The working class shrank as industrial labour all but disappeared, and in its place emerged a society that was still divided and unequal, but in which a greater proportion of the population found themselves in a 'middle' class.[2] Women joined the workforce in far greater numbers, and continued to work after marriage and childbearing. The idea that a man should take sole charge of affairs outside the home and act as a patriarchal head of his family became less widespread. Many more people stayed in school until the age of eighteen, and then, in the following decade, sought further education. The aristocracy crumbled away, and a much larger proportion of society began to own property and land.[3]

The armed services came to be regarded much more as another professional occupation. Many more officers had a university education and married women who wanted to maintain their own careers. Over time, the Army was forced to adjust. It could no longer assume that wives at any rank would simply 'follow the drum', and indeed it began to allow women to enlist into some roles.[4] Men in the ranks often still came from marginalized backgrounds – and with increasing globalization proportionately more now came from Britain's former colonies, particularly Fiji, Ghana, South Africa, Jamaica and Zimbabwe.[5] In these places a career in the British Army could significantly boost status and prospects. But the position of the Army in national life remains much as it ever was: pivotal, but not central. Perhaps in the future, if historians look back on the 1970s and early 1980s, this period will appear to be the end of the era defined by total war. The ways in which manhood was linked to the responsibility of military service – the final trial of the stiff upper lip – will seem dated, perhaps even absurd.

The connections between national character, manhood and society were already beginning to be transformed soon after 1982, more intently so after the end of the Cold War in 1991. Armed service is now regarded less as a burden of masculine duty to be accepted without complaint, and more a set of special skills that can be taught to all people, not just to men. A soldier's allegiance is regarded as less to his Queen and country than to his mates, his comrades-in-arms. The Army still reflects society, but it is now seen as more moral than a society given over completely to individualism, and thus genuinely separate from and different to it.[6] In a culture based to a much greater extent than hitherto on acquisition, personal fulfilment and consumer spending, the idea of any type of service – the priesthood, the NHS, fire-fighting – is regarded by those who are not involved in it with a mix of bafflement and admiration. The infantry soldier of the future has become a warrior – fit, highly trained, glamorous, sharp-minded, adorned with high-tech kit – prepared to do and see things that for civilians are out of reach.

As for the Parachute Regiment, it was reborn in the Falklands. In the 1970s, the events of Bloody Sunday prompted questions about the regiment's suitability for counter-insurgency operations in Northern Ireland. Renowned for their aggression, the Paras also had a tight-lipped culture. Their discipline was nobody else's business. They were class-bound, conformist, and on occasions could be brutal. But the battles they won in the Falklands brought them to a national audience in a much more unambiguously heroic light. The two Victoria Crosses awarded to Lieutenant Colonel 'H' Jones at Goose Green and Sergeant Ian McKay on Mount Longdon showed the attributes the regiment wanted to remember about the war. Jones was decorated for his personal bravery, running alone to a machine-gun post, and in recognition of the Parachute Regiment's fine victory against the odds. McKay was acknowledged for his courage in close-quarters battle and the desperate intensity of that moment, the sacrifice of his life for his comrades and for the regiment's pride.

After the Falklands, the Parachute Regiment gradually became more associated with special forces. Special forces training relied less on enforcing discipline from above than on instilling discipline within the individual. The Paras see themselves as 'switched on', with 'airborne initiative', and these qualities prepared them to enter this truly elite club. The Falklands triumph raised the esteem of the regiment in the public mind. The battles of the Falklands War were the last twentieth-century battles – men of national armies facing each other over an open field or up a defended hill – but they also pointed the way to the contemporary era.

One perhaps unexpected feature of this current era is that the Army is much more widely admired than it was during the period of conscription, or in the 1970s. The post-Falklands euphoria could be regarded as marking the beginning of this shift, but it has been more noticeable since the wars in Iraq and Afghanistan. In 2004, the Army enjoyed more public trust than any other British institution except the judiciary.[7] Soldiers are increasingly viewed not as 'avatars of a nation's sanctioned violence', nor as instruments of the state's oppression, but as highly trained and professional, and as individual people put by politicians in difficult, sometimes terrible, positions. The far greater social recognition of post-combat trauma, the acceptance that women and families have a place in the aftermath of war, and the practice of repatriating bodies from the war zone, have helped to consolidate public compassion for soldiers.

During the conflicts in Iraq and Afghanistan, the public began to gather spontaneously in the streets of Wootton Bassett to mark the passing through of repatriated bodies. It was a striking display of public sympathy and in 2011 the town was given royal patronage and renamed Royal Wootton Bassett in honour of this. But sympathy could contribute to doubt about the purpose of the fighting, and the feelings on display as funeral cortèges drove slowly along Wiltshire streets became a factor in the questioning of Britain's role in world politics following those wars, and in the belief that the loss of British lives was too great a price to pay for these overseas engagements.[8]

The growth in support for the armed services is in part a consequence of the politics that came out of the Iraq War, but it is also reflects changes in social habits. As people live longer and have more leisure time, so the hobby of researching family history has become popular. Many people spend time tracing their relatives' readily documented military backgrounds, fashioning perhaps a personal affinity with the past and more of a rapport with military experiences.[9] This interest has taken place alongside an important social shift. Far fewer people nowadays have direct experience of the military. In 1997, the Army noted that 20 per cent of those aged thirty-five to forty-five (born between 1952 and 1962) had personal links with individuals with military backgrounds, but the same was true for only 7 per cent of those aged sixteen to twenty-four (born between 1973 and 1981).[10]

Distance from the military, and the fading from national consciousness of the reality of war and the compulsion of conscription, seems to have brought a new inclination to think more sentimentally about the armed services. British people remember war often and readily acknowledge its violence and horror. At the same time, the contexts within which wars were fought, and the memories of the remorseless and unfeeling grind, the restrictions and petty humiliations that could be daily life in service or in wartime, have been forgotten. More emotional attachment to the armed services contributes to an uncertainty about Britain's future direction. Britain used to be a great power whose Empire and role in the world wars was important to its sense of itself. In 1982, it was a leading power of the second rank. Since 1982, and particularly since the end of the Cold War in 1991, Britain has become a smaller though still influential power, with a much higher regard for its armed services, but with a greater sense of misgiving about why, how and when it should use them.

★

The hours of intense combat on the Falklands were in some ways the crucible into which 1970s British life was poured and came out altered. Goose Green, Mount Longdon and Wireless Ridge – as well as the Scots' Guards fight on Tumbledown, and the Marines' battles on Mount Harriet and Two Sisters – were not just the last battles of the twentieth century, they were the first close-quarters battles the British Army had fought for a generation. Those battles had symbolic power, and sometimes had long-lasting personal consequences for the people involved in fighting them.

The Parachute Regiment sailed to the Falklands as one part of the 3,000-strong 3 Commando Brigade, but once landed on the islands, 2 Para's commanding officer took his battalion's history into his own hands. Lieutenant Colonel 'H' Jones had worked to force discipline and physical fitness back to the forefront of the battalion's ethos, and he had total faith in the professional training of his men, particularly in contrast to the Argentine conscript army. As commanding officer, he had aimed to pull the Parachute Regiment away from its experiences of counter-insurgency, and he saw on the Falklands the opportunity for them to experience battle, to have their chance to take this greatest of challenges and, more simply, he wanted to get the battalion moving for the good of the men's morale. At the same time, he did not listen to counter-arguments, and he had an excess of courage and willpower at the expense of a more measured judgement.

The way the battles of Goose Green and Longdon were organized meant there were intense periods of close-quarters combat, some of it hand to hand with bayonets, particularly on Longdon. In 2 Para's first battle, the up-close violence during the initial night advance, sometimes

against an enemy who was not prepared, the uncovered advance to the
Goose Green settlement in daylight over open ground, and the long,
freezing second night with few resources, strained men's nerves. On
Longdon, many paratroopers found the period of heavy Argentine
artillery shelling, after the battle on the mountain was over, to be the
worst part. After both battles, men had to clear the bodies of the dead.
They saw the shot-up bodies of their comrades, their sometimes devastating and abject deaths, and those of the Argentine soldiers.

Their training gave them a formidable *esprit de corps* and a determination not to give up in any circumstances. They had to demonstrate
those qualities. Training gave ordinary men an aggressive spirit and
an ability to endure. Comradeship gave them heart and made them
understand they could not be the men they wanted to be – proud
paratroopers – unless they could commit themselves. But no training
could inure them to all the consequences of violence, or stop them
from dying, being injured or feeling afraid, nor prevent them from
looking back later and seeing things differently. In some respects, the
training was too powerful. It made it difficult to hold men back. One
company commander from 3 Para said: 'You are having to rein them
in rather than push them on. The difficulty is restraining them in
operations.'[11]

After the war, the consequences of combat could be far-reaching
and unanticipated. Many men – probably a majority – put the war
behind them and went on to do other things with their lives. But for
many others it was not like that. In 1982 post-combat trauma was
barely acknowledged; but by the beginning of the 1990s the fact that
combat could cause trauma was becoming much more widely accepted
in society. By the 2000s, social attitudes towards trauma had almost
completely transformed, and many people now almost assumed servicemen would have problems after combat. For the men who did
have post-war trauma, it could be awful, made worse because of
the taboos they had to overcome to acknowledge their condition. They
often believed trauma was a sign of weakness, a confession of failure,
an indication they could not bear the masculine responsibility they
had relished. Nothing had prepared them for the possibility they
could develop symptoms of trauma, even many years after the event.

Increasingly, encouraged by the definition of PTSD, trauma was regarded not as weakness – the opposite to manliness – but as a 'normal reaction to an abnormal event'. War – the 'abnormal event' – was the most profound thing a human could experience. More people could therefore dare to come forward to speak of the problems they had had. For many veterans, the hard fact was that their comrades had died, and their loyalty to them and to the regiment meant it could be difficult to dispute the reasons and the manner in which they had fought, or to question the regiment that had joined them together.[12] Much like death, trauma became an inevitable part of the sacrifice of war.

For some men, leaving the services could be the moment at which traumatic symptoms presented themselves. It was hard to shake off their training. The disappearance of a world that had made sense of violence, and in which everyone understood the ways that people were trained to behave, could leave ex-servicemen feeling suddenly very isolated. The loss of the masculine status of being a Para, a Para who had been to war, could be deeply felt. In a civilian society in which military experiences were uncommon, military identity stood out, and ex-soldiers could find it difficult to fit in.

Ex-Paras, therefore, remembered the Falklands War as the paratroopers they had been. That regimental identity bound them together and they had to remember the men who had died. Their loyalty stayed with them; there was no way out for those who had survived. In terms of their regiment's proud history, they were representatives of the duty vested in them by their country, the orders given to them by their officers and the fact that as men in the ranks they had gone into battle together. Because of that, the Falklands could be remembered as it was. It was in itself a short episode that probably could not have been avoided; it was an honour about which they should feel proud; and it was a war without end.

*

Those hours of combat on the Falklands also became part of the remembrance of war in Britain, a long tradition stretching back into the twentieth century and forward into the twenty-first. The Second World War and the Cold War were unusual because of the prominence of an external threat to Britain's continued existence. When the Cold War ended, that threat lifted and Britain's world role changed; but elements of the memory of Britain's wartime past remained the same, or even became simplified, shorn of their vital context. At its most essential – or its most emotional – what remained in the national memory was that Britain's spirit was best when Britain stood alone.

The sense of the unchanging continuum of history – the essence of British military character – meant that important lessons of the Falklands were not really remembered at all. Some of these elements were striking. The international politics of the Falklands conflict were uniquely confined: the sovereignty dispute was of interest in itself only to Britain, Argentina and the Falkland Islanders. It was unusual because it was a conflict that could be won decisively. The war did not drag out into an uneasy peace. It was over when the Argentine forces surrendered on 14 June. Britain could not have fought it without the international support of its allies in both the EEC and the United States, and without the full backing of international law. Argentina had without doubt and at the whim of the dictatorship breached the peace, and Britain had reacted in self-defence. Mrs Thatcher was successful at least in part because she proceeded with caution and because she was thorough, and listened to the views presented to her, particularly by her military advisers.

The Falklands became associated with the end of Britain's relative economic decline. Victory in the South Atlantic tempered the early 1980s: a nation rejoicing in the tradition of its past and the *élan* of its new-found present. But the Falklands scarcely changed Britain's world role. The Americans were pleased that Britain had won, but it did not transform the 'special relationship'. The conflict delayed, rather than prevented, the controversial naval cuts proposed in the 1981 defence budget.[13] By the mid-1980s, Thatcher's support for the Single Market in the European Economic Community ensured that Britain was far more integrated into the EEC, and that membership of the EEC became the root of Britain's influence not just in Europe, but also in the USA, and internationally.

The war, however, did have some enduring effects. It helped an idea to take hold that force could be used not just because it was necessary, but also because it was right.[14] The singular, decisive victory stuck in the national memory. A hope grew that a small war could be limited, that people could be liberated by military force, and that war could have a solely benign impact on a prime minister's political fortunes. In those ways, the Falklands War provided a bridge from the Second World War to Britain's more recent military interventions.

The contexts of Iraq and Afghanistan were, of course, completely different. Among other motives, the Blair government wanted to use Britain's military force for the good, not just of the country but of other people living under tyranny. The wars in Iraq and Afghanistan, and their long and complicated aftermaths, exposed the limits on British, and perhaps Western, military power, and contributed to a crisis of confidence about Britain's place in world politics.

Britain's post-1945 history has been one of gradual adjustment to the changed realities of its global power. From Empire to Europe, military force was part of the constellation of influences that enabled Britain to 'punch above its weight', but it has never been at the centre of Britain's sense of itself. The Second World War and conscription, then the Cold War and wars at the end of Empire, extended the place of Britain's armed services in society and affected the lives of millions of people. The Falklands combat had symbolic force partly because of that history, but it had direct consequences only for a few.

Their history – a history of the lives connected with the Parachute Regiment and the Falklands War – shows the vast effort it took to fight even one short war, and that even one short war could have unfolding and sometimes unanticipated consequences. Britain in the 1980s was a changing country, but its transformations were uneven, and habits and attitudes formed in a previous time persisted: Christian teachings, forbearance, the expectation of suffering and the living out of fate. The flourishing of memory showed too the relative privilege of the British way of life, the attention to its deaths in service. Despite their anguish, many grieving relatives saw themselves as fortunate, grateful for the joy they had been granted and the advantages they had had in living out a settled life.

Their histories show that Britain was never truly alone, and military force was not, by itself, enough. What was best about Britain's military character – in the vanguard of battle – could also lead to sadness and discomfort; what was tough about Britain's infantry – the paratrooper, the man apart – could also, sometimes, prove fragile. What earned those serving the most pride could also contain an almost unbearable reality, and yield pain; what gave the most comfort was often detached from the harsh world of the regiment. Violence could cast shadows into the furthest reaches of human life and across unexpected ground; but among those shadows there was also light.

★

In this book I have tried to answer the question – who were the paratroopers? When I was younger, I saw my uncle foremost as my grandmother's son: a child, a teenage boy, whose life was taken. As I researched this book, I realized that he was also a paratrooper, an elite soldier, one tiny part of a regiment whose history and reputation were composed of all the individuals within it. For many former paratroopers and former soldiers, that fact defines the memory of war. In recent times, it matters more to tell that history because so few people understand what military life is like. To honour the dead is to recount their lives as paratroopers – as paratroopers wish it to be. Thus history can be personal and intimate, and at the same time public. It is regimental history in an age of the individual.

Dave Parr was his mother's son, his father's son, and a paratrooper killed in the Falklands. Perhaps he should be more than that too. People are complicated, their lives can rarely be reduced to one thing or another; their sense of who they are not usually rigidly fixed. Dave was a son, a brother, an uncle, a friend, a paratrooper who did what he had to do because, by that point, he had developed a loyalty to his regiment; and he did his best in the narrow confines of his choice. The dead have gone, and they should be allowed to rest in peace. We do not know how they would like to be remembered. Nevertheless, should that be all? Perhaps memory could be extended to recognize the things he was denied: the chance to grow older, to try to join the SAS, to become a man, to marry and have his own children; the opportunity to tell his own history, and perhaps, if he wanted, to put it behind him. Maybe there is a way to remember the dead, and all the while to set them free.

Appendix

Units and compositions of the British Army

Unit	Composition	Approximate numbers	Commanded by
Army	2 or more corps	100,000–150,000	Field Marshal or General
Corps	2 or more divisions	25,000–50,000	General or Lieutenant General
Division	3 or more brigades or regiments	10,000–15,000	Lieutenant General or Major General
Brigade	3 or more battalions	1,500–4,000	Major General, Brigadier or Colonel
Regiment	2 or more battalions	1,000–2,500 (2,700 in the Parachute Regiment from 1977)	Colonel
Battalion	4 or more companies	400–1,000 (approx. 700 per parachute battalion from 1977)	Lieutenant Colonel
Company	4 platoons	120	Major
Platoon	3–5 sections	24–30	Lieutenant or Second Lieutenant
Section		8–12	Corporal

Sources:

Mark Adkin, *Goose Green: A Battle is Fought to be Won* (Orion, 1992)
Julian Thompson, *No Picnic: 3 Commando Brigade in the South Atlantic* (Leo Cooper, 1992)
<http://secondworldwar.co.uk/index.php/army-sizes-a-ranks/86-army-units-a-sizes>

Rank structure in the British Army

Officers

Officer Cadet	Officer in training
Second Lieutenant	First rank held on commission
Lieutenant	Command of a platoon of up to thirty
Captain	Often second in command of a sub-unit of 120
Major	Usually after eight to ten years service. Command a company of 120
Lieutenant Colonel	Command a regiment of up to 1,000
Colonel	Typically serve as staff officer
Brigadier	Command a brigade
Major General	Command formations of division size
Lieutenant General	Command formations of corps size
General	Most senior appointments, e.g. Chief of Defence Staff

Other ranks

Private	
Lance Corporal	Typically after about three years. Supervise a small team of four soldiers
Corporal	Typically after six to eight years. In charge of a section of eight to twelve soldiers
Sergeant	Typically after twelve years. Second in command of a platoon, with responsibilities for assisting junior officers
Staff/Colour Sergeant	Senior soldier, with responsibilities for up to 120 soldiers
Warrant Officer Class 2/ Company Sergeant Major	Second in command of a company
Warrant Officer Class 1/ Regimental Sergeant Major	Typically after eighteen years of outstanding service; senior adviser to the Regimental Commanding Officer

Source:

British Army website: see <https://www.army.mod.uk/who-we-are/our-people/ranks/>

Notes

Introduction

1. The National Archives [henceforward TNA], ADM 202/880, Medical Report, November 1982, pp. 19–21.
2. Airborne Forces Museum, Imperial War Museum at Duxford [henceforward AFM], 2/34/14. The record says one man, Major Thackeray, came to deliver the news. My uncle, Chris Parr, remembers it was a man and a woman who came to break the news. It is possible Major Thackeray brought a woman with him, perhaps his wife or the wife of another army officer.
3. The last photo taken of Dave, as 2 Para were waiting at Fitzroy on 10 June to transfer forward by helicopter towards Wireless Ridge, shows him to be wearing thick gloves. He must have lost them after that.
4. Sixteen paratroopers were buried in a ceremony together on 26 November 1982. Two more individual ceremonies, for Lance Corporal Gary Bingley, cremated on 23 November, and Colour Sergeant Gordon Findlay, were held on 3 December 1982.
5. Field Marshal the Viscount Montgomery of Alamein, handwritten foreword, Hilary St George Saunders, *The Red Beret: The Story of the Parachute Regiment, 1940–1945* (Michael Joseph, 1950).
6. Jean Bethke Elshtain, *Women and War* (University of Chicago Press, 1987), p. 3.
7. John Newsinger, *Dangerous Men: The SAS and Popular Culture* (Pluto Press, 1997); Michael Asher, *Shoot to Kill: From 2 Para to the SAS* (Cassell, 2004), p. 274.
8. Ministry of Defence, 'A study of deaths among UK Armed Forces personnel deployed to the 1982 Falklands Campaign: 1982 to 2013', 1 May 2014. The figures were eighty-six Royal Navy and two laundrymen from Hong Kong; twenty-seven Royal Marines; four Royal Fleet Auxiliary and six sailors from Hong Kong; six Merchant Navy; one

RAF; 123 Army, including thirty-two Welsh Guards, thirty-nine Parachute Regiment, nineteen SAS, three Royal Signals, eight Royal Engineers, eight Scots Guards and one Gurkha. See also Gordon Ramsey (ed), *The Falklands War: Then and Now* (After the Battle, 2009) and Martin Middlebrook, *The Falklands War 1982* (Penguin, revd edn, 2001).

9. For a discussion of oral history methods, see Alistair Thomson, *Anzac Memories: Living with the Legend* (Oxford University Press, 1994).

10. Mike Seear, 'Seeking "The Other" in the Post-Conflict 1982–2006', in Diego F. García Quiroga and Mike Seear (eds), *Hors de Combat: The Falklands-Malvinas Conflict in Retrospect* (CCCP Press, 2009), p. 10.

11. Samuel Hynes, *The Soldiers' Tale: Bearing Witness to Modern War* (Pimlico, 1998).

1 Britain and the Parachute Regiment

1. The idea that Britain saw itself as unmilitary is a frequent feature of British military writing; see Correlli Barnett, *Britain and Her Army, 1509–1970: A Military, Political and Social Survey* (Allen Lane, 1970). It is most robustly challenged in David Edgerton, *Warfare State: Britain, 1920–1970* (Cambridge University Press, 2006).

2. George Orwell, 'The Lion and the Unicorn', in *The Collected Essays, Journalism and Letters of George Orwell*, Volume 2: *My Country Right or Left, 1940–1943* (Secker & Warburg, 1968), pp. 58–63.

3. Kevin Morgan, 'Militarism and Anti-Militarism: Socialists, Communists and Conscription in France and Britain, 1900–1940', *Past & Present*, 202:1, 2009, p. 211.

4. For a much more detailed discussion, see Hew Strachan, *The Politics of the British Army* (Oxford University Press, 1997), pp. 44–73.

5. C. B. Otley, 'Militarism and the Social Affiliations of the British Army Élite', in Jacques van Doorn (ed.), *Armed Forces and Society* (The Hague/Paris: Mouton, 1968), p. 103.

6. Alan Allport, *Browned Off and Bloody-Minded: The British Soldier Goes to War 1939–1945* (Yale University Press, 2015), p. 31.

7. Major General Julian Thompson, *Ready for Anything: The Parachute Regiment at War* (Weidenfeld & Nicolson, 1989), p. 3.

8. Daniel Todman, *Britain's War*, Volume I: *Into Battle, 1937–41* (Allen Lane, 2016), p. 375.

9. Winston Churchill, *The Second World War*, Volume II: *Their Finest Hour* (Cassell, 1949), p. 413.

10. Robert Kershaw, *Sky Men: The Real Story of the Paras* (Hodder & Stoughton, 2010), p. 166.

11. Kershaw, *Sky Men*, p. 168; Paradata website: <https://paradata.org.uk/events/north-africa-operation-torch>.

12. Thompson, *Ready for Anything*, p. 4.

13. Major General John Frost, *A Drop Too Many: A Paratrooper at Arnhem* (Cassell, 1980; reissued Pen and Sword, 1994), p. 26.

14. Frost, *A Drop Too Many*, pp. 22–3.

15. Thompson, *Ready for Anything*, p. 111.

16. Allport, *Browned Off*, p. xviii.

17. Jeremy A. Crang, *The British Army and the People's War, 1939–1945* (Manchester University Press, 2000), p. 2.

18. Thompson, *Ready for Anything*, pp. 48–9.

19. Susan Crosland, *Tony Crosland* (Jonathan Cape, 1982), p. 20.

20. Crosland, *Crosland*, pp. 24–5.

21. Crosland, *Crosland*, p. 35.

22. Kershaw, *Sky Men*, p. 88.

23. Thompson, *Ready for Anything*, p. 110.

24. Private Baines, cited in John Parker, *The Paras: The Inside Story of Britain's Toughest Regiment* (John Blake, 2012), pp. 94–5.

25. Brigadier General James Gavin, cited in Kershaw, *Sky Men*, p. 200.

26. Paradata website: <https://paradata.org.uk/events/normandy-operation-overlord>.

27. Cited in Thompson, *Ready for Anything*, p. 162.

28. Field Marshal the Viscount Montgomery of Alamein, *Normandy to the Baltic* (Hutchinson, 1946), pp. 123–50.

29. Thompson, *Ready for Anything*, p. 223.

30. Frost, *A Drop Too Many*, p. 231.

31. Thompson, *Ready for Anything*, p. 262.

32. Richard Vinen, *National Service: Conscription in Britain, 1945–1963* (Allen Lane, 2014), the figure of 2 million is on p. xxv.

33. Chiefs of Staff, Future Defence Policy, cited in David French, *Army, Empire and Cold War: The British Army and Military Policy, 1945–1971* (Oxford University Press, 2012), p. 41.

34. Vinen, *National Service*, pp. 410–14.

35. TNA, DEFE25/326, Anonymous Paper, D/DS14/149, June 1976.

36. Hew Strachan, 'The British Way in Warfare', in David Chandler and Ian Beckett (eds), *The Oxford History of the British Army* (Oxford University Press, 1994), p. 414.

37. Leslie Ives, *A Musket for the King: The Trials and Tribulations of a National Serviceman, 1949 to 1951* (Leslie Ives Books, Tavistock, 1999), Cited in Vinen, *National Service*, p. 234.

38. Nicholas Pronay, 'The British Post-Bellum Cinema: A Survey of the Films Relating to World War II Made in Britain between 1945 and 1960', *Historical Journal of Film, Radio and Television*, 8:1, 1988, pp. 39–54.

39. Cited in Vinen, *National Service*, p. 252.

40. Kershaw, *Sky Men*, p. 261.

41. Kershaw, *Sky Men*, p. 269.

42. Thompson, *Ready for Anything*, p. 329.

43. Private Jonathan Bennetts, 3 Para, cited in Kershaw, *Sky Men*, p. 270.

44. Lieutenant Sandy Cavenagh, cited in Kershaw, *Sky Men*, p. 275.

45. Hew Strachan, 'The Civil–Military "Gap" in Britain', *Journal of Strategic Studies*, 26:2, 2003, pp. 43–63; David French, *Military Identities: The Regimental System, the British Army and the British People, c.1870–2000* (Oxford University Press, 2005), pp. 304–5.

46. David French, 'Nasty Not Nice: British Counter-Insurgency Doctrine and Practice, 1945–1967', *Small Wars & Insurgencies*, 23:4–5, 2012, pp. 744–61; Paul Dixon, ' "Hearts and Minds"? British Counter-Insurgency from Malaya to Iraq', *Journal of Strategic Studies*, 32:3, 2009, pp. 353–81.

47. Kershaw, *Sky Men*, p. 283.

48. Parker, *The Paras*, p. 208.

49. Kershaw, *Sky Men*, p. 281.

50. French, 'Nasty Not Nice', p. 752.

51. Account given by General Sir Anthony Farrar-Hockley, Paradata: <https://paradata.org.uk/article/874/related/32936>. Farrar-Hockley ended his career as Commander-in-Chief, Allied Forces Northern

Europe. His son, Dair Farrar-Hockley, was a major in charge of A Company 2 Para during the Falklands War.

52. Parker, *The Paras*, p. 227.

53. AFM, *Pegasus Magazine*, November 1970, p. 23.

54. Thomas Hennessey, *The Evolution of the Troubles, 1970–72* (Irish Academic Press, 2007), pp. 73–4.

55. Parker, *The Paras*, p. 237.

56. Andrew Sanders, 'Principles of Minimum Force and the Parachute Regiment in Northern Ireland, 1969–1972', *Journal of Strategic Studies*, May 2016, online, p. 12.

57. Aaron Edwards, *The Northern Ireland Troubles: Operation Banner, 1969–2007* (Osprey Publishing, 2011), p. 37.

58. Niall Ó Dochartaigh, 'Bloody Sunday: Error or Design?', *Contemporary British History*, 24:1, 2010, pp. 99–100.

59. Cited in Christopher Tuck, 'Northern Ireland and the British Approach to Counter-Insurgency', *Defense & Security Analysis*, 23:2, 2007, p. 174. The Derry Young Hooligans were a group – some of whom were members of the IRA or its junior wing – that had been causing major disturbances.

60. Report of the Bloody Sunday Inquiry [henceforward Saville Report] (HMSO, 2010), Volume 1, Chapter 2, outline of events before the day; and paras 4.8–4.12 on Major General Ford.

61. See <http://webarchive.nationalarchives.gov.uk/20101103103930/http://report.bloody-sunday-inquiry.org/evidence/M/M_0003.pdf>, accessed 2 January 2017.

62. Sanders, 'Principles of Minimum Force', p. 16.

63. Huw Bennett, '"Smoke without Fire"? Allegations against the British Army in Northern Ireland, 1972–5', *Twentieth Century British History*, 24:2, 2013, pp. 284–5.

64. Tuck, 'Northern Ireland', p. 173.

65. Asher, *Shoot to Kill*, p. 65.

66. Saville Report, para. 3.86.

67. Saville Report, para. 3.19.

68. Saville Report, para. 3.89; David Benest, 'Atrocities in Britain's Counter-Insurgencies', *The RUSI Journal*, 156:3, 2011, p. 84.

69. There are usually about 24–30 soldiers in a platoon.

70. Saville Report, para. 3.101.

71. Saville Report, paras 3.101–3.104, 106.

72. Saville Report, paras 3.107–9.

73. Saville Report, paras 310–11.

74. Saville Report, paras 3.112–13.

75. Parker, *The Paras*, p. 248.

76. Saville Report, paras 3.72; 3.74; 3.76–7; 3.100.

77. Caroline Kennedy-Pipe and Colin McInnes, 'The British Army in Northern Ireland 1969–1972: From Policing to Counter-Terror', *Journal of Strategic Studies*, 20:2, 1997, p. 17.

78. Asher, *Shoot to Kill*, p. 105.

79. Hugh Noyes, 'Miss Devlin Strikes Mr. Maudling in Commons', *The Times*, 1 February 1972.

80. Dominic Sandbrook, *State of Emergency. The Way We Were: Britain, 1970–1974* (Allen Lane, 2010), pp. 248–52.

81. Report of the Tribunal appointed to report into the events of 30 January 1972 (Widgery Report), Summary of conclusions, para. 8; <http.//cain.ulst.ac.uk/hmso/widgery.htm.

82. Parker, *The Paras*, p. 257.

83. Paul Burns, *A Fighting Spirit* (HarperCollins, 2010), pp. 61, 66.

84. General Sir Mike Jackson, *Soldier: The Autobiography* (Corgi, 2008), pp. 159–60.

85. Tuck, 'Northern Ireland', p. 178. The numbers were 3,289 killed and over 40,000 injured.

86. TNA, CAB129/181, C(75)21, Statement on the Defence Estimates, Roy Mason, 25 February 1975.

87. Jim Tomlinson, 'Thrice Denied: "Declinism" as a Recurrent Theme in British History in the Long twentieth century', *Twentieth Century British History*, 20:2, 2009, pp. 227–51; the classic texts on decline are Andrew Shonfield, *British Economic Policy since the War* (Penguin, 1958) and Michael Shanks, *The Stagnant Society* (Penguin, 1961).

88. Richard Clutterbuck, *Britain in Agony: The Growth of Political Violence* (Penguin, 1980), p. 19.

89. Lawrence Black, Hugh Pemberton and Pat Thane (eds), *Reassessing 1970s Britain* (Manchester University Press, 2013).

90. See <https://www.theguardian.com/news/2001/aug/14/guardianobit-
    uaries1>, obituary by Dennis Barker, 14 August 2001.

91. In a general sense, Stuart Hall, Chas Critcher, Tony Jefferson, John
    Clarke and Brian Roberts, *Policing the Crisis: Mugging, the State and Law
    and Order* (Macmillan, 1978).

92. '(White Man) In Hammersmith Palais', 16 June 1978, CBS Records, in
    Mark Garnett, *From Anger to Apathy: The British Experience since 1975*
    (Jonathan Cape, 2007), pp. 8–9.

93. By some measures, 1976 was the best year to be alive in Britain: Andy
    Beckett, *When the Lights Went Out: Britain in the Seventies* (Faber and
    Faber, 2009), p. 4.

2 *Joining Up in the 1970s*

1. Tony Banks, *Storming the Falklands: My War and After* (Little, Brown,
   2012), p. 23.

2. TNA, DEFE70/48, Paper on Racial Characteristics, 1975; and Annex
   A to that paper, dated 30 March 1973. In a Parachute Regiment of 2,687
   men, 2,617 men were British by birth, two were 'British and alien',
   twenty-three 'British and Eirean', three Australian, two Canadian,
   two Cypriot, one Dominican, twenty-six Eirean by birth, two Indian
   and Hindu, two Malayan, one New Zealander, one American, three
   South African and one South American.

3. French, *Military Identities*, p. 298.

4. TNA, DEFE70/48, Analysis of active male adult soldiers with 'D
   factor', 31 August 1972. The Army tended not to keep records on 'race',
   preferring instead to record what they called the 'D' factor – 'non-
   European facial characteristics', which might not equate exactly to
   colour or to race, however defined.

5. Tom Harley, interview with me, 16 June 2012.

6. Douglas Stevens, interview with me, 16 June 2012 (name changed).
   UDA and UVF refer to Unionist paramilitary groups, the Ulster
   Defence Association and the Ulster Volunteer Force.

7. Lee Smith, interview with me, 18 April 2013 (name changed).

8. Antony Beevor, *Inside the British Army* (Corgi Books, 1991), p. 5. There was a practice of the recruiting sergeant visiting the boy's home to get an idea of family circumstances. This was abandoned because of the risk of an IRA trap.

9. Lee Smith, interview with me, 18 April 2013 (name changed).

10. Colin Black, interview with Emma Murray, 11 September 2013 (name changed).

11. Robin Horsfall, *Fighting Scared: Para, Mercenary, SAS, Sniper, Bodyguard* (Cassell, 2002), p. 19.

12. Mark Eyles-Thomas, *Sod That for a Game of Soldiers,* 3rd edn (Kenton Publishing, 2007), pp. 27–8.

13. Janet Findlay, interview with me, 26 July 2016.

14. AFM, all from Depot Para records.

15. TNA, DEFE70/67, The Enlistment of Civil Offenders, 1974.

16. TNA, DEFE70/67, The Enlistment of Civil Offenders, Annex B, 1974.

17. Vincent Bramley, *Two Sides of Hell* (John Blake, 2009), pp. 29–35, 60–61.

18. Jon Cook, interview with me, 25 September 2013.

19. Vincent Bramley, interview with me, 12 August 2013.

20. Banks, *Storming the Falklands*, p. 61.

21. David Chaundler, interview with me, 1 June 2012.

22. Hew Pike, *From the Front Line: Family Letters and Diaries – 1900 to the Falklands and Afghanistan* (Pen and Sword, 2008), pp. viii–ix.

23. Philip Neame, interview with me, 23 May 2012.

24. Major General Chip Chapman, *Notes from a Small Military* (John Blake, 2013, Kindle edn), chapter 1.

25. G. Salaman and K. Thompson, 'Class Culture and the Persistence of an Elite: The Case of Army Officer Selection', *Sociological Review*, 26:2, 1978, pp. 283–304; C. B. Otley, 'The Social Origins of British Army Officers', *Sociological Review*, 18:2, 1970, pp. 213–39.

26. Reggie von Zugbach de Sugg and Mohammed Ishaq, 'Officer Recruitment: The Decline in Social Eliteness in the Senior Ranks of the British Army', in Hew Strachan (ed.), *The British Army, Manpower and Society into the Twenty-First Century* (Frank Cass, 2000), pp. 75–86.

27. Chapman, *Notes from a Small Military*, location 209. By the early 1990s, the Parachute Regiment officer corps had roughly even numbers of

men from grammar schools and university as from public school. I am very grateful to Major General Chapman for sending me the paper he wrote at Staff College, on which his research is based.

28. John Crosland, interview with me, 21 June 2012.

29. Simon Raven, 'Perish by the Sword', in Hugh Thomas (ed.), *The Establishment: A Symposium* (Anthony Blond, 1959), p. 56.

30. David Chaundler, interview with me, 1 June 2012.

31. John Crosland, interview with me, 21 June 2012.

32. Jackson, *Soldier: The Autobiography*, p. 24.

33. Chapman, *Notes from a Small Military*, location 108.

34. David Benest, interview with me, 12 July 2012.

35. Steven Hughes, interview with me, 5 September 2012.

36. John Wilsey, *H Jones VC: The Life and Death of an Unusual Hero*, new edn (Arrow Books, 2003), p. 25.

37. Wilsey, *H Jones VC*, p. 41; the 60 per cent figure is on p. 31.

38. Wilsey, *H Jones VC*, pp. 82–3.

39. Wilsey, *H Jones VC*, p. 129.

40. Wilsey, *H Jones VC*, p. 146.

41. Les Davis, interview with me, 15 April 2013 (name changed).

42. Dean Edwards, interview with me, 6 July 2012 (name changed).

43. Bryan and Carole Dodsworth, interview with me, 3 July 2013.

44. Phil Francom, email correspondence, 9 September 2012.

45. Graham Dawson, *Soldier Heroes: British Adventure, Empire and the Imagining of Masculinities* (Routledge, 1994), p. 238.

46. Burns, *A Fighting Spirit*, p. 5.

47. Tony Coxall, interview with me, unrecorded, 19 April 2014.

48. Martin Margerison, interview with me, 7 December 2012.

49. Vincent Bramley, interview with me, 12 August 2013.

50. Jon Cook, interview with me, 25 September 2013.

51. Freda McKay, interview with me, 19 July 2013.

52. Theresa Burt, interview with me, 26 September 2013.

53. Rita Hedicker, interview with me, 14 September 2012.

54. My parents found out when they discovered her marriage certificate after her death.

55. Dave Parr, letter to Dad, 18 May 1982. Spelling as in original letter.

56. AFM, Pamphlet in library.

57. Peter Johnston, 'Join Up and See the World! British Military Recruitment after National Service', June 2013, National Archives: <http://media.nationalarchives.gov.uk/index.php/join-up-and-see-the-world-british-military-recruitment-after-national-service/>.

58. TNA, WO163/725, The Army Board, Soldier Manning and Recruitment, AB/G/71 14, 30 July 1971.

59. Frank Hilton, *The Paras* (BBC Books, 1983), p. 18.

60. Abstract of Army Manpower Statistics, no. 90, 1980/81, p. 16. All issues of the Abstract after 1974, no. 82, were obtained by a Freedom of Information Request and do not have a TNA file reference.

61. TNA, WO384/82, Abstract of Army Manpower Statistics 1973, pp. 23–4. All these figures remain more or less consistent throughout the 1970s. In fact, the Abstract would suggest slightly worse educational attainment levels by the end of the 1970s, with more men grouped in band level 6 'school age to 15 (no certificate)', but more or less static results in the general aptitude tests.

62. Richard Hoggart, *Speaking to Each Other: Essays*, Volume I. *About Society* (Penguin, 1973), p. 60.

63. Eyles-Thomas, *Sod That for a Game of Soldiers*, p. 6.

64. Gary Williams, interview with me, 1 November 2012.

65. Paul Willis, *Learning to Labour: How Working Class Kids Get Working Class Jobs* (Ashgate, 2003).

66. Banks, *Storming the Falklands*, p. 53.

67. Cited in Jon Cooksey, *Felklands Hero: Ian McKay, the Last VC of the 20th Century* (Pen and Sword, 2012), p. 37.

68. Billy Bragg and Chris Salewicz, *Billy Bragg: Midnights in Moscow* (Omnibus Press, 1989), pp. 11–12.

69. Mike Curtis, *C.Q.B.: Close Quarter Battle* (Bantam Press, 1997), pp. 35–6.

70. Brian Harrison, *Finding a Role? The United Kingdom, 1970–1990* (Oxford University Press, 2010), p. 182.

71. TNA, ED193/25, Department of Education and Science, Report by HMI, On Junior Para at Aldershot, March 1983.

72. The phrase 'shit work' is cited in Harrison, *Finding a Role?*, p. 181.

73. Burns, *Fighting Spirit*, p. 12.

74. Asher, *Shoot to Kill*, p. 12.

75. Chris Parr, interview with me, 2 January 2017.

76. My mother insists it was not violent in the places she used to frequent.

77. Blue Cole, interview with me, 11 July 2013.

78. John Gartshore, interview with me, 6 June 2013.

3 *Training: Making Men*

1. AFM, 22/1/17, Orders for the training and administration of recruits, Parachute Regiment, 1968.

2. TNA, DEFE70/49, Wastage Rates, Annex A, Figures to 1963; Claire Gillman, *Para: Inside the Parachute Regiment* (Bloomsbury, 1993), p. 19.

3. Hilton, *The Paras*, pp. 78–100.

4. Jon Cook, interview with me, 25 September 2013.

5. Banks, *Storming the Falklands*, p. 71.

6. Asher, *Shoot to Kill*, p. 89.

7. Eyles-Thomas, *Sod That for a Game of Soldiers*, p. 33.

8. Asher, *Shoot to Kill*, p. 3.

9. AFM, 2/34/14.

10. AFM, 2/1/17, Orders for the training and administration of recruits, Parachute Regiment, 1968.

11. Rory Bridson, *The Making of a Para* (Sidgwick & Jackson, 1989), pp. 16 and 17.

12. Letter from Dave to Mum, Chris and Gyp (the dog), 6 June 1980. Spelling and grammar of this and all subsequent letters retained as in the originals.

13. John Hockey, *Squaddies: Portrait of a Subculture* (University of Exeter, 1986), pp. 46–64.

14. Letter from Dave to Mum, 19 June 1980.

15. S. L. A. Marshall, *Men against Fire: The Problem of Battle Command* (University of Oklahoma Press, 1947); the other two influential studies were Samuel A. Stouffer, *The American Soldier: Combat and Its Aftermath* (Princeton University Press, 1949); and Edward Shils and Morris Janowitz, 'Cohesion and Disintegration in the Wehrmacht in World War II', *Public Opinion Quarterly*, 12:2, 1948, pp. 280–315.

16. Joanna Bourke, *An Intimate History of Killing: Face-to-Face Killing in Twentieth-Century Warfare* (Granta, 1999), pp. 69–102; Anthony King, *The Combat Soldier: Infantry Tactics and Cohesion in the Twentieth and Twenty-First Centuries* (OUP, 2013), pp. 345–62. The analysis King

makes that cohesion is less about friendship and more about the *esprit de corps* created in training is supported by the research here.

17. AFM, 22/1/14, Scotter speech, 1977. From 1978 Scotter was the Commander-in-Chief of the British Army on the Rhine.
18. Bridson, *The Making of a Para*, pp. 161–2.
19. Hilton, *The Paras*, pp. 76, 66, 22.
20. Hilton, *The Paras*, pp. 21, 43.
21. Eyles-Thomas, *Sod That for a Game of Soldiers*, p. 61.
22. Bridson, *The Making of a Para*, p. 28.
23. Eyles-Thomas, *Sod That for a Game of Soldiers*, p. 48.
24. Stephen Tuffen, interview with me, 9 July 2012.
25. Martin Margerison, interview with me, 7 December 2012.
26. John Gartshore, interview with me, 6 June 2013.
27. AFM, Depot Para Record Cards.
28. Gillman, *Para*, p. 9.
29. Asher, *Shoot to Kill*, p. 20.
30. Hilton, *The Paras*, p. 72.
31. Antony Beevor, 'The Army and Modern Society', in Strachan (ed.), *The British Army, Manpower and Society*, p. 69. There were known to be homosexuals in 3 Para's Mortar Platoon. Homosexuals who behaved in particular ways – they were hard and intimidating men – therefore were tolerated, even accepted, although perhaps they tended not to get promoted.
32. BBC, *The Paras*, Episode 3, *Basic Wales*, 1983.
33. TNA, WO384/81, Abstract of Army Manpower Statistics, no. 79, 1972/3, and no. 90, 1979/80.
34. Lee Smith, interview with me, 18 April 2013.
35. Jon Cook, interview with me, 25 September 2013.
36. Christopher Jessup, 'Transforming Wives into Spouses: Changing Army Attitudes', in Strachan (ed.), *The British Army, Manpower and Society*, pp. 89–99.
37. Curtis, *C.Q.B.*, p. 64.
38. Hockey, *Squaddies*, pp. 114–16.
39. Hockey, *Squaddies*, pp. 34–6; Lt Col. Dave Grossman, *On Killing: The Psychological Cost of Learning to Kill in War and Society* (Little, Brown, 1995), pp. 104–18.

40. War Office, and British Army Review, during WWI, cited in Bourke, *Intimate History*, pp. 89–93.

41. I am grateful to Anthony King for a discussion on this point.

42. Hilton, *The Paras*, p. 82.

43. Horsfall, *Fighting Scared*, p. 53; Eyles-Thomas, *Sod That for a Game of Soldiers*, p. 57.

44. Bramley, *Two Sides of Hell*, pp. 17–18.

45. Horsfall, *Fighting Scared*, p. 54.

46. Hilton, *The Paras*, p. 147.

47. Cited in Bridson, *The Making of a Para*, p. 54.

48. Hilton, *The Paras*, p. 158.

49. Eyles-Thomas, *Sod That for a Game of Soldiers*, p. 74.

50. Gideon Aran, 'Parachuting', *American Journal of Sociology*, 80:1, 1974, pp. 124–52.

51. Bridson, *The Making of a Para*, p. 99; Eyles-Thomas, *Sod That for a Game of Soldiers*, p. 78.

52. Bridson, *The Making of a Para*, p. 78.

53. Jackson, *Soldier: The Autobiography*, p. 34.

54. Chapman, *Notes from a Small Military*, location 204.

55. Cited in Beevor, *Inside the British Army*, p. 118.

56. Sandhurst Archives, Box 248a, Lecture on 'The officer–soldier relationship', 1987.

57. Field Marshal the Viscount Montgomery of Alamein, *The Path to Leadership* (HarperCollins, 1961), as cited in Royal Military Academy Sandhurst, Box 248a, Report on Leadership Training, 1978, 'Leadership and Morale'.

58. Sandhurst Archives, Box 248a, Slim speech, 14 October 1952. Slim was also Chief of the Imperial General Staff in 1949 and Governor General of Australia in 1952.

59. Sandhurst Archives, Box 248a, Field Marshal Slim, 'From Defeat into Victory', extract.

60. Sandhurst Archives, Box 248a, Sandhurst leadership training and Report by Lieutenant Colonel Crawford, March 1978.

61. AFM, Uncatalogued Pamphlet, Officer Parachute Regiment, HMSO, March 1984.

62. Beevor, *Inside the British Army*, p. 103.

63. Sandhurst Archives, Box 248a, Sandhurst leadership training and Report by Lt Col. Crawford, March 1978.

64. French, *Military Identities*, p. 321.

65. David Benest, interview with me, 14 July 2017.

66. French, *Military Identities*, pp. 181–91.

67. Asher, *Shoot to Kill*, pp. 27, 37.

68. Bridson, *The Making of a Para*, p. 25.

69. Asher, *Shoot to Kill*, pp. 51–2.

70. Jon Cook, interview with me, 25 September 2013.

71. Jon Cook, interview with me, 25 September 2013.

72. Lee Smith, interview with me, 18 April 2013.

73. Banks, *Storming the Falklands*, p. 73.

74. 'Barrack room assault by soldier', *Aldershot News*, 18 April 1978.

75. 'Schoolgirl tells of rape ordeal', *Aldershot News*, 6 May 1983; Clive Emsley, *Soldier, Sailor, Beggarman, Thief: Crime and the British Armed Services since 1914* (Oxford University Press, 2013), pp. 197–8.

76. 'Army orders security check after soldiers are jailed for rape', *The Times*, 17 May 1983.

77. 'Para rapists jailed', *Aldershot News*, 20 May 1983.

78. 'Army orders security check after soldiers are jailed for rape', *The Times*, 17 May 1983.

79. 'Para rapists jailed', *Aldershot News*, 20 May 1983.

80. 'New army sex shocker', *Aldershot News*, 3 June 1983.

81. 'Mums slam the Army', *Aldershot News*, 20 May 1983.

82. Letters page, *Aldershot News*, 27 May 1983.

83. Hilton, *The Paras*, p. 226.

84. Bridson, *The Making of a Para*, p. 64.

85. Cited in Thomas Thornborrow and Andrew D. Brown, '"Being Regimented": Aspiration, Discipline and Identity Work in the British Parachute Regiment', *Organization Studies*, 30:4, 2009, p. 362.

4 Falkland Islands

1. Sir Lawrence Freedman, *The Official History of the Falklands Campaign*, Volume I: *The Origins of the Falklands War* (Routledge, 2005), pp. 4–7.

2. Aaron Donaghy, *The British Government and the Falkland Islands, 1974–1979* (Palgrave Macmillan, 2014); Martín Abel González, *The Genesis of the Falklands (Malvinas) Conflict* (Palgrave Macmillan, 2013). On Nicholas Ridley's visit to the Falkland Islands in 1980, see Charles Moore, *Margaret Thatcher: The Authorized Biography*, Volume One: *Not for Turning* (Allen Lane, 2013), p. 659.

3. Lawrence Freedman and Virginia Gamba-Stonehouse, *Signals of War: The Falklands Conflict of 1982* (Faber and Faber, 1990), pp. 65–83.

4. *The Sun*, 6 July 1981.

5. Richard Vinen, *Thatcher's Britain: The Politics and Social Upheaval of the 1980s* (Simon and Schuster, 2009), pp. 113–15.

6. Martin Middlebrook, *The Falklands War 1982* (Penguin, 2001), p. 83.

7. Richard Aldous, *Reagan and Thatcher: The Difficult Relationship* (Hutchinson, 2012), p. 90.

8. TNA, CAB148/212, OD(SA)(82)25, Falkland Islands: Washington Discussions with Mr Haig, Memorandum by the Foreign Secretary, 24 April 1982.

9. Margaret Thatcher, *The Downing Street Years* (HarperCollins, 1993), pp. 205–9.

10. See, for example, Clive Ponting, *The Right to Know: The Inside Story of the Belgrano Affair* (Sphere Books, 1985).

11. Moore, *Margaret Thatcher*, Volume One, pp. 737–8, Margaret Thatcher Foundation, <http://www.margaretthatcher.org/document/110526>, Ian Glover-James, 'Reagan phone call to Thatcher [31 May 1982]', *Sunday Times*, 8 March 1992.

12. Moore, *Margaret Thatcher*, Volume One, p. 716.

13. Wilsey, *H Jones VC*, pp. 192–3.

14. TNA, WO305/5040/2, Commander's War Diary, pp. 34–5.

15. Imperial War Museum [henceforward IWM], Sound Collection, no. 20696, Company Sergeant Major John Weeks, 3 Para (Blakeway Associates).

16. David Benest, 'History of 2 Para in the Falklands' [henceforward '2 Para History']. This was compiled by Captain Benest soon after his return from the Falklands and was based on interviews done at the time.

17. Dave Parr, letter to Mum, 18 May 1982.

18. TNA, WO305/5040/2, Commander's War Diary, p. 45.

19. AFM, tape recording, Private Dean Ferguson.

20. AFM, tape recording, Colour Sergeant Brian Faulkner.

21. Dave Parr, letter to Mum, 18 May 1982.

22. Dave Parr, letter to Dad, 18 May 1982.

23. Sir Lawrence Freedman, *The Official History of the Falklands Campaign*, Volume II: *War and Diplomacy* (Routledge, 2005, Kindle edition), location 1919.

24. Cited in Freedman, *Official History*, Volume II, location 9775.

25. IWM, Sound Collection, no. 17143, Sergeant John Meredith, 2 Para (Barraclough Carey/Channel 4).

26. Stephen Tuffen, interview with me, 9 July 2012.

27. Vincent Bramley, *Excursion to Hell: Mount Longdon, a Universal Story of Battle* (Bloomsbury, 1991), p. 36.

28. '2 Para History'.

29. Freedman, *Official History*, Volume II, location 10340.

30. Daniel Kon, *Los Chicos de la Guerra: The Argentine Conscripts' Own Moving Accounts of Their Falklands War* (New English Library, 1983), pp. 65, 73.

31. Toby Green, *Saddled with Darwin: A Journey through South America on Horseback* (Weidenfeld & Nicolson, 1999), p. 169; Lisa Watson, *Waking Up to War: Lisa Watson Tells a Story of Life as an Eleven-year-old during the Falklands War* (Stanley Services Limited, 2010), pp. 19–20.

32. Cited in Max Hastings and Simon Jenkins, *The Battle for the Falklands* (Michael Joseph, 1983), p. 187.

33. TNA, WO305/5603, 3 Para Post Operational Report.

34. TNA, WO305/5603, 3 Para Post Operational Report, Annex E, Infantry Support Weapons.

35. TNA, WO305/5041, Sit Rep 04/01, 42 Commando RM.

36. TNA, WO305/5603, 3 Para Post Operational Report, Annex C, Training and Tactics.

37. Ian McKay, letter to his parents and brothers, 8 June 1982, cited in Cooksey, *Falklands Hero*, p. 176.

38. AFM, 2/34/17.

39. Chapman, *Notes from a Small Military*, location 781. Chapman was quoting from Lord Wavell's memoirs to show the difficult conditions the infantryman has had to put up with over time.

5 Orders: The Battle of Darwin and Goose Green

1. Nicholas van der Bijl, *Nine Battles to Stanley* (Leo Cooper, 1999), p. 141.

2. IWM, Sound Collection, no. 17141, Major Dair Farrar-Hockley, 2 Para (Barraclough Carey/Channel 4).

3. AFM, 2/34/1, 2 Para Post Operational Report.

4. Freedman, *Official History*, Vol. II, location 12418; AFM, 2/34/1, log kept by intelligence officer Alan Coulson, notes for 25 May: 'CO went to an O group at Brigade HQ where it was stated that future operations would be delayed until air superiority had been guaranteed. The intention is now for the Brigade to head straight to Port Stanley and the Darwin peninsula could only be considered a secondary objective.'

5. Hastings and Jenkins, *Battle for the Falklands*, p. 237.

6. The most thorough books about it are Mark Adkin, *Goose Green: A Battle is Fought to be Won* (Orion, 1992); Major General John Frost, *2 Para Falklands: The Battalion at War* (Buchan and Enright, 1983); Spencer Fitz-Gibbon, *Not Mentioned in Despatches: The History and Mythology of the Battle of Goose Green* (Lutterworth Press, 1995). Hugh Bicheno, *Razor's Edge: The Unofficial History of the Falklands War* (Orion, 2006) and Freedman, *Official History*.

7. TNA, CAB148/211, OD(SA)(82)45th, 27 May 1982.

8. Freedman, *Official History*, Vol. II, location 12464.

9. Julian Thompson, *No Picnic: 3 Commando Brigade in the South Atlantic: 1982* (Leo Cooper/Secker & Warburg, 1985), p. 81.

10. Freedman, *Official History*, Vol. II, location 12511.

11. AFM, 2/34/2, statement by Brigadier Thompson.

12. Freedman, *Official History*, Vol. II, location 12620

13. Thompson, *No Picnic*, p. 76.

14. Frost, *2 Para Falklands*, p. 45.

15. Bicheno, *Razor's Edge*, p. 159. Bicheno quotes part of their conversation, although does not give a source for this: '"Do you think you can do it?" Thompson asked after telling the bristling Jones he could count on no additional artillery or transport. "Yes," Jones replied.'

16. AFM, 2/34/7, 3 Para Adjutant Captain McGimpsey transcript. There is no recording for McGimpsey.

17. AFM, 2/34/22, Miller transcript.

18. AFM, 2 Para Major Ryan, tape recording.

19. '2 Para History'.

20. '2 Para History'.

21. '2 Para History'.

22. AFM, 2 Para Private Worrall, tape recording.

23. One ambiguity is the elision of these two settlements. Jones ordered 2 Para to capture both. They were and are two separate places.

24. Fitz-Gibbon, *Not Mentioned in Despatches*, p. 12.

25. AFM, 2 Para Captain Alan Coulson, tape recording.

26. John Geddes, *Spearhead Assault: Blood, Guts and Glory on the Falklands Frontline* (Arrow Books, 2008), p. 153. (Geddes later joined the SAS.) Adkin, *Goose Green*, p. 149, agrees the SAS patrol was unsatisfactory, but puts the failure to allocate anyone to remove the sixteen trenches down to a mistake with a grid reference, p. 166.

27. Van der Bijl, *Nine Battles*, p. 129.

28. John Crosland, interview with me, 21 June 2012.

29. Adkin, *Goose Green*, p. 168.

30. Adkin, *Goose Green*, p. 158.

31. AFM, 2 Para Private Worrall, tape recording.

32. Geddes, *Spearhead Asssault*, p. 179.

33. Martin Margerison, interview with me, 7 December 2012.

34. Geddes, *Spearhead Assault*, p. 185.

35. Chapman, cited in Adkin, *Goose Green*, p. 190.

36. Chapman, *Notes from a Small Military*, location 840.

37. Martin Margerison, interview with me, 7 December 2012.

38. Robert Fox, *Eyewitness Falklands: A Personal Account of the Falklands Campaign* (Methuen, 1982), p. 165.

39. Adkin, *Goose Green*, pp. 199–200.

40. Hugh McManners, *The Scars of War* (HarperCollins, 1993), p. 123.

41. IWM, Sound Collection, no. 13004, Private Graham Carter, 2 Para (Barraclough Carey/BBC).

42. Cited in Adkin, *Goose Green*, p. 201.

43. Adkin, *Goose Green*, pp. 203–4; Fitz-Gibbon, *Not Mentioned in Despatches*, P. 48.

44. Van der Bijl, *Nine Battles*, pp. 130–31.

45. Adkin, *Goose Green*, p. 204.

46. Tom Harley, interview with me, 16 June 2012.

47. Adkin, *Goose Green*, p. 204.

48. Frost, *2 Para Falklands*, p. 66.

49. Adkin, *Goose Green*, p. 216; A Company were minus 3 Platoon, who had gone around the inlet to cover the Darwin settlement from across the causeway.

50. Adkin, *Goose Green*, p. 224.

51. AFM, 2 Para Private Worrall, tape recording.

52. AFM, 2 Para Private Worrall, tape recording.

53. Stephen Tuffen, interview with me, 9 July 2012.

54. AFM, 2 Para Private Worrall, tape recording.

55. Adkin, *Goose Green*, p. 240.

56. Adkin, *Goose Green*, p. 244.

57. '2 Para History'.

58. Frost, *2 Para Falklands*, pp. 73–4.

59. Adkin, *Goose Green*, p. 244.

60. Fitz-Gibbon, *Not Mentioned in Despatches*, pp. 110–19.

61. '2 Para History' says Hardman was killed first, before Dent and Wood.

62. Adkin, *Goose Green*, pp. 245–6.

63. Frost, *2 Para Falklands*, p. 76.

64. Fitz-Gibbon, *Not Mentioned in Despatches*, p. 111, citing Lt Mark Coe.

65. AFM, 2/34/22, Norman statement.

66. Sergeant Barry Norman, interviewed on *The Falklands War: The Untold Story*, Yorkshire Television, 1987. A version also appears in Michael Bilton and Peter Kosminsky, *Speaking Out: Untold Stories from the Falklands War* (Grafton Books, 1990), pp. 192–248.

67. Fitz-Gibbon, *Not Mentioned in Despatches*, pp. 124–5. Geddes, *Spearhead Assault*, also argues it was Abols' direct hit that led to the Argentine surrender.

68. Fitz-Gibbon, *Not Mentioned in Despatches*, p. 134.

69. '2 Para History'.

70. Curtis, *C.Q.B.*, pp. 124–6. Illingsworth was awarded the Distinguished Conduct Medal for his bravery, first dragging a wounded comrade to safety, and then retrieving his ammunition. According to his citation, he went back to pick up the ammunition and was killed.

71. Martin Margerison, interview with me, 7 December 2012.

72. Fitz-Gibbon, *Not Mentioned in Despatches*, pp. 140–41.

73. Adkin, *Goose Green*, pp. 297, 305.

74. '2 Para History'.

75. Adkin, *Goose Green*, p. 300.

76. AFM, 2 Para Major Roger Jenner, tape recording.

77. Martin Middlebrook, *The Fight for the 'Malvinas': The Argentine Forces in the Falklands War* (Viking, 1989), pp. 180–81.

78. Bicheno, *Razor's Edge*, p. 187. Bicheno says that the machine gunners fired on 10 Platoon D Company, and it was probably this that prompted the Argentine to whom Barry had been talking to fire.

79. John Gartshore, interview with me, 6 June 2013.

80. Carter, cited in McManners, *Scars of War*, p. 177.

81. '2 Para History'.

82. Jim Creaney, interview with me, 29 June 2012.

83. Captain Farrar, in Adkin, *Goose Green*, p. 320.

84. '2 Para History'.

85. Adkin, *Goose Green*, pp. 334–5.

86. Adkin, *Goose Green*, p. 338.

87. Adkin, *Goose Green*, pp. 340–41.

88. Curtis, *C.Q.B.*, p. 139.

89. AFM, 2/34/22, Captain Steven Hughes, written account.

90. John Gartshore, interview with me, 6 June 2013.

91. Private Dave Brown, in Christopher Hilton, *Ordinary Heroes: Untold Stories from the Falklands Campaign* (History Press, 2011, Kindle edn), location 1916.

92. AFM, 2 Para Private Dean Ferguson, tape recording.

6 Momentum: The Battle of Mount Longdon

1. It is often reported that this took place at Bluff Cove. But this is inaccurate, the ships were at Port Pleasant by the Fitzroy settlement.

2. Freedman, *Official History*, Vol. II, location 13566.

3. Jon Cooksey, *3 Para Mount Longdon: The Bloodiest Battle* (Pen and Sword, 2004), p. 52.

4. James O'Connell, *Three Days in June: 3 Para Mount Longdon* (E-book, 2013), location 2927. O'Connell's book is an immensely detailed collection of first-hand accounts, annotated with information from 3 Para's War Diary to put the recollections into context. It is the most comprehensive account that exists of Britain's part in this operation.

5. John Weeks, cited in Max Arthur, *Above All, Courage: Personal Stories from the Falklands War* (Cassell, 2002), p. 300.

6. AFM, Sergeant Des Fuller, tape recording.

7. Cited in Arthur, *Above All, Courage*, p. 323.

8. Freedman, *Official History*, Vol. II, location 13857.

9. TNA, WO305/5612, 3 Para War Diary, p. 117.

10. Hew Pike, 'With Fixed Bayonets', *Elite Magazine*, 2:20, 1985, p. 381; cited in Jon Cooksey, *Falklands Hero: Ian McKay, the Last VC of the 20th Century* (Pen and Sword, 2012), p. 187.

11. Cited in Cooksey, *Falklands Hero*, p. 191.

12. Cited in Christian Jennings and Adrian Weale, *Green-Eyed Boys: 3 Para and the Battle for Mount Longdon* (HarperCollins, 1996), p. 127.

13. Cited in Bramley, *Two Sides of Hell*, p. 180.

14. IWM, Sound Collection, no. 20696, Company Sergeant Major John Weeks (Blakeway).

15. Cited in Bramley, *Two Sides of Hell*, p. 82.

16. Eyles-Thomas, *Sod That for a Game of Soldiers*, p. 158.

17. AFM, Lance Corporal Hedges, tape recording.

18. Cited in Bramley, *Two Sides of Hell*, p. 190.

19. O'Connell, *Three Days in June*, location 4912.

20. O'Connell (quoting himself), *Three Days in June*, location 6363.

21. Private Nick Rose, cited in Cooksey, *3 Para Mount Longdon*, p. 64.

22. Cited in Cooksey, *3 Para Mount Longdon*, p. 65.

23. 'Falklands Experiences: 6 Platoon B Company 3 Para', School of Infantry video production, 1986; see <https://www.youtube.com/watch?v=eaDRoeTrnfs>.

24. Cited in Jennings and Weale, *Green-Eyed Boys*, p. 133.

25. Cooksey, *3 Para Mount Longdon*, p. 68.

26. Lance Corporal Gannon, cited in 'Falklands Experiences: 6 Platoon B Company 3 Para', School of Infantry video production, 1986. Gannon

was a private at the time of the Falklands War; see <https://www.you tube.com/watch?v=eaDRoeTrnfs>.

27. Cited in Cooksey, *Falklands Hero.,* p. 211.

28. Van der Bijl, *Nine Battles,* p. 174.

29. Cited in Cooksey, *Falklands Hero.,* p. 210.

30. Bailey in O'Connell, *Three Days in June,* location 2221.

31. McLarnon subsequently had PTSD and died in 2009. He was one of the men who attempted to sue the MoD for negligence in 2007; see <http://www.manchestereveningnews.co.uk/news/greater-manchester-news/falklands-ruined-my-life-says-ex-para-1167436>.

32. TNA, WO305/5612, 3 Para War Diary, p. 122.

33. AFM, Hedges, tape recording.

34. TNA, WO305/5612, 3 Para War Diary, p. 122.

35. Bramley, *Two Sides of Hell,* p. 207. The fact Cox and Connery were responsible for taking out the position is also mentioned in TNA, WO305/5612, 3 Para War Diary, p. 122.

36. Lieutenant Cox in 'Falklands Experiences: Commanding Officer 3 Para', School of Infantry video production, 1986; see <https://www.youtube.com/watch?v=O-j4oX9ouA8>.

37. O'Connell, *Three Days in June,* location 2906.

38. From Cox's testimony in Jennings and Weale, *Green-Eyed Boys,* p. 151; Bicheno, *Razor's Edge,* p. 272.

39. O'Connell, *Three Days in June,* location 5190.

40. TNA, WO305/5612, 3 Para War Diary, p. 125.

41. Private Jez Dillon in O'Connell, *Three Days in June,* location 5464.

42. TNA, WO305/5612, 3 Para War Diary, p. 125.

43. Thompson, *No Picnic,* p. 146.

44. Private Len Baines and Lance Corporal Tolson, in O'Connell, *Three Days in June,* location 5996.

45. 'Falklands Experiences: 6 Platoon B Company 3 Para', School of Infantry video production, 1986; see <https://www.youtube.com/watch?v=eaDRoeTrnfs>.

46. O'Connell, *Three Days in June,* locations 5849 and 5331.

47. Graham Colbeck, *With 3 Para to the Falklands* (Greenhill Books, 2002), pp. 186–7.

48. Cited in Mike Seear, *Return to Tumbledown: The Falklands–Malvinas War Revisited* (CCCP Press, 2012), p. 436.

49. Adkin, *Goose Green*, p. 362.

50. Argentine death toll on Longdon: the post-operational report says fifty bodies were retrieved, and this is the number Freedman cites. Jennings and Weale say twenty-nine, and Vincent Bramley, *Two Sides of Hell*, gives thirty-six names. The Intelligence Corps' Nicholas van der Bijl says thirty-one died: Van der Bijl, *Nine Battles*, p. 177. Argentine death toll at Goose Green and Wireless Ridge, Freedman, *Official History*, Vol. II, location 14320.

51. Private Richard Absolon (9.34 a.m.); Private Gerald Bull; CFN Alexander Shaw REME; and Private Craig Jones (Bull: 4.15 p.m. Jones and Shaw; 4.30 p.m. on 13 June).

7 Comrades

1. Correspondence with Walter McAuley, 9 March 2018.

2. Adkin, *Goose Green*, pp. 204–5. I am grateful to Bill Bentley for supplying additional information about this incident: correspondence, 15 February 2013.

3. Steven Hughes, interview with me, 5 September 2012.

4. Banks, *Storming the Falklands*, p. 153.

5. Tony Coxall, interview with me, 19 April 2014. I did not record this interview, so the quote is based on notes made immediately afterwards.

6. Dave Parr, letter to Mum, 30 May 1982.

7. Anon., interview with me, 16 June 2012.

8. Dave Parr, letter to Mum, 30 May 1982.

9. Email correspondence with Mike Seear, 13 September 2013. The Baillies were upset when they heard he had been killed; Mike Seear, *With the Gurkhas in the Falklands: A War Journal*, (Leo Cooper, 2003), p. 291.

10. O'Connell, *Three Days in June*, location 4967.

11. Cited in McManners, *Scars of War*, p. 349.

12. Morham's written account, cited in Jennings and Weale, *Green-Eyed Boys*, pp. 130–31.

13. O'Connell, *Three Days in June*, location 5083.

14. Adkin, *Goose Green*, p. 202.

15. O'Connell, *Three Days in June*, location 5090.

16. Eyles-Thomas, *Sod That for a Game of Soldiers*, p. 270.

17. IWM, Sound Collection, no. 20697, 3 Para Lance Corporal Graham Tolson (Blakeway).

18. O'Connell, *Three Days in June*, location 3175.

19. Eyles Thomas, *Sod That for a Game of Soldiers*, pp. 178–9.

20. O'Connell, *Three Days in June*, location 5722.

21. AFM, Company Sergeant Major Peter Richens, tape recording.

22. Curtis, *C.Q.B.*, p. 131.

23. AFM, Private Dean Ferguson, tape recording. He was being interviewed by General Farrar-Hockley, and so he may have felt he had to express sorrow at the death of Jones. Even if this is so, it still shows awareness of the reaction that men were supposed to have to the death of a commanding officer.

24. Cited in Adkin, *Goose Green*, p. 191.

25. Hughes, interview with me, 5 September 2012.

26. Hughes, interview with me, 5 September 2012.

27. IWM, Sound Collection, no. 20696, Company Sergeant Major Weeks (Blakeway).

28. O'Connell, *Three Days in June*, location 8526.

29. Fuller, cited in Jennings and Weale, *Green-Eyed Boys*, p. 168.

30. AFM, Colour Sergeant Faulkner, tape recording.

31. Faulkner, in Arthur, *Above All, Courage*, pp. 294–5.

32. O'Connell, *Three Days in June*, location 5974.

33. Les Davis, interview with me, 15 April 2013 (name changed).

34. Private Mick Southall, interviewed on *The Falklands War Documentary: 3 Para Mount Longdon* (Forces TV, 2016); see <https://www.youtube.com/watch?v=05wbJbiaR38>.

35. O'Connell, *Three Days in June*, location 2566.

36. Banks, *Storming the Falklands*, p. 129.

37. IWM, Sound Collection, no. 16074, Company Sergeant Major Peter Richens (Conrad Wood).

38. IWM, Sound Collection, no. 20697, Lance Corporal Graham Tolson (Blakeway).

39. IWM, Sound Collection, no. 20696, Company Sergeant Major John Weeks (Blakeway).

40. IWM, Sound Collection, no. 20696, Company Sergeant Major John Weeks (Blakeway).

41. Dean Edwards, interview with me, 6 July 2012 (name changed).

42. Ken Lukowiak, *A Soldier's Song: True Stories from the Falklands* (Secker and Warburg, 1993), p. 100.

43. Jon Cook, interview with me, 25 September 2013.

44. O'Connell, *Three Days in June*, location 3239.

45. IWM, Sound Collection, no. 20697, Lance Corporal Graham Tolson (Blakeway).

46. Lukowiak, *A Soldier's Song*, pp. 99–100.

47. Lukowiak, *A Soldier's Song*, p. 147.

48. IWM, Sound Collection, no. 20697, Lance Corporal Graham Tolson (Blakeway).

49. Colbeck, *With 3 Para to the Falklands*, p. 189.

50. TNA, ADM202/880, Medical Report, November 1982, p. 30.

51. Eyles-Thomas, *Sod That for a Game of Soldiers*, p. 182.

52. Bramley, *Excursion to Hell*, pp. 144–5. The teddy was a mascot given to Private West by his sister.

53. Colbeck, *With 3 Para to the Falklands*, pp. 177–8.

54. Coxall, interview with me, 19 April 2014.

8 Fear

1. Keeble, interviewed by Lt Col. Peter Bates, 'An Investigation into Whether Religion has a Place on the Modern Battlefield and Whether It has Any Influences on the British Soldier', MA dissertation, Cranfield University, School of Defence Management, 1995, cited in David Charles Eyles, '"Seeking the Bubble Reputation": Continuities in Combat Motivation in Western Warfare in the Twentieth Century with Particular Emphasis on the Falklands War of 1982', (PhD thesis, University of Sussex, December 2012), p. 228.

2. Martin Margerison, interview with me, 7 December 2012.

3. Lord Moran, *The Anatomy of Courage* (Constable, 1945; revd edn, 2007); Joanna Bourke, *Fear: A Cultural History* (Virago, 2005), pp. 197–221.

4. Martin Margerison, interview with me, 7 December 2012.

5. Tony Coxall, interview with me, 19 April 2014.

6. '2 Para History'.

7. O'Connell, *Three Days in June*, locations 3066, 2222 and 2466.

8. AFM, Sergeant Fuller, tape recording.

9. Martin Margerison, interview with me, 7 December 2012.

10. AFM, Private Worrall, tape recording.

11. O'Connell, *Three Days in June*, location 6393.

12. Len Carver, interview with me, 21 September 2015.

13. O'Connell, *Three Days in June*, location 7849.

14. AFM, Private Worrall, tape recording.

15. Hughes, in McManners, *Scars of War*, p. 276.

16. Bramley, *Two Sides of Hell*, pp. 254–5.

17. O'Connell, *Three Days in June*, location 4656.

18. O'Connell, *Three Days in June*, location 8640.

19. Martin Margerison, interview with me, 7 December 2012.

20. Len Carver, interview with me, 21 September 2015.

21. Private Simon Clarke, in O'Connell, *Three Days in June*, location 588.

22. Lukowiak, *A Soldier's Song*, p. 54.

23. Lukowiak, *A Soldier's Song*, p. 41.

24. Eyles-Thomas, *Sod That for a Game of Soldiers*, p. 174.

25. Stephen Tuffen, interview with me, 9 July 2012.

26. Martin Margerison, interview with me, 7 December 2012.

27. Martin Margerison, interview with me, 7 December 2012.

28. Tom Harley, interview with me, 16 June 2012.

29. Chapman, *Notes from a Small Military*, location 958.

30. Adkin, *Goose Green*, p. 282. 'Toms' work' as in 'Tom', the slang word for a paratrooper of the ranks.

31. Lukowiak, *A Soldier's Song*, pp. 56, 64.

32. IWM, Sound Collection, no. 20697, Lance Corporal Graham Tolson (Blakeway).

33. O'Connell, *Three Days in June*, location 2358.

34. IWM, Sound Collection, no. 20697, Lance Corporal Graham Tolson (Blakeway).

35. '2 Para History'.

36. IWM, Sound Collection, no. 20697, Lance Corporal Graham Tolson (Blakeway).

37. Lukowiak, *A Soldier's Song*, p. 57.

38. Geddes, *Spearhead Assault*, p. 116.

39. Crosland, in Arthur, *Above All, Courage*, p. 205.

40. McManners, *Scars of War*, p. 284.

41. Lukowiak, *A Soldier's Song*, p. 101.

42. McManners, *Scars of War*, p. 350.

43. Jennings and Weale, *Green-Eyed Boys*, p. 148.

44. Hughes, in Arthur, *Above All, Courage*, citing from his own diary, pp. 244–6.

45. McManners, *Scars of War*, p. 325.

46. O'Connell, *Three Days in June*, location 5845.

47. Len Carver, interview with me, 21 September 2015.

48. Letter from Dave Parr to Mum and Dad, 30 May 1982.

49. AFM, Major John Crosland, tape recording.

50. AFM, Private Ferguson, tape recording.

51. John Gartshore, interview with me, 6 June 2013.

52. Bramley, *Excursion to Hell*, p. 109.

53. Len Carver, interview with me, 21 September 2015.

9 Killing

1. Cited in McManners, *Scars of War*, p. 334.

2. Curtis, *C.Q.B.*, p. 117.

3. IWM, Sound Collection, no. 20697, Lance Corporal Graham Tolson (Blakeway).

4. IWM, Sound Collection, no. 28301, Sergeant John Pettinger (Graham Bound).

5. IWM, Sound Collection, no. 20696, Company Sergeant Major John Weeks (Blakeway).

6. Frost, *2 Para Falklands*, p. 138.

7. Cited in Arthur, *Above All, Courage*, p. 325.

8. AFM, Lieutenant Geoffrey Weighall, tape recording.

9. Phil Francom, account given in email correspondence, 9 September 2012.

10. Geddes, *Spearhead Assault*, pp. 223–52.

11. IWM, Sound Collection, no. 17143, Sergeant John Meredith (Barraclough Carey/Channel 4).

12. TNA, WO305/5612. This is mentioned in the 3 Para post-operations report by Major David Collett.

13. Cited in Peter Johnston, 'Culture, Combat and Killing: A Comparative Study of the British Armed Forces at War in the Falklands' (PhD thesis, University of Kent, 2013), p. 125.

14. Curtis, *C.Q.B.*, p. 117.

15. Carter, in McManners, *Scars of War*, p. 332.

16. Jim Creaney, interview with me, 29 June 2012.

17. Jim Creaney, interview with me, 29 June 2012.

18. Len Carver, interview with me, 21 September 2015.

19. AFM, 2/34/5.

20. Geddes, *Spearhead Assault*, pp. 165–7.

21. Bramley, *Excursion to Hell*, p. 121.

22. French, cited in McManners, *Scars of War*, p. 175.

23. Anon., interview with me, June 2012.

24. Geddes, *Spearhead Assault*, p. 279.

25. Northfield, cited in McManners, *Scars of War*, p. 175.

26. Banks, *Storming the Falklands*, p. 154.

27. '2 Para History'.

28. IWM, Sound Collection, no. 17146, Corporal Dave Abols (Barraclough Carey/Channel 4).

29. John Crosland, interview with me, 21 June 2012.

30. McManners, *Scars of War*, p. 166.

31. IWM, Sound Collection, no. 16074, Company Sergeant Major Peter Richens (Conrad Wood).

32. '2 Para History'.

33. Chapman, cited in Adkin, *Goose Green*, p. 191.

34. Cited in Fitz-Gibbon, *Not Mentioned in Despatches*, p. 49.

35. Cited in Fitz-Gibbon, *Not Mentioned in Despatches*, p. 35.

36. Joanna Bourke, *An Intimate History of Killing: Face-to-Face Killing in Twentieth-Century Warfare* (Granta, 1999), pp. 12–43.

37. John Crosland, interview with me, 21 June 2012.

38. AFM, Private Worrall, tape recording.

39. AFM, Private Ferguson, tape recording.

40. Tolson, in O'Connell, *Three Days in June*, location 5416.

41. John Gartshore, interview with me, 6 June 2013.

42. AFM, Private Ferguson, tape recording.

43. AFM, Lance Corporal Hedges, tape recording.

44. AFM, Sergeant Fuller, tape recording.

45. IWM, Sound Collection, no. 17146, Corporal Dave Abols (Barraclough Carey/Channel 4).

46. Lukowiak, *A Soldier's Song*, p. 145.

47. Dean Edwards, interview with me, 6 July 2012 (name changed).

48. McManners, *Scars of War*, p. 334.

49. Martin Margerison, interview with me, 7 December 2012.

50. French, cited in McManners, *Scars of War*, p. 365.

51. Len Carver, interview with me, 21 September 2015.

52. Cited in McManners, *Scars of War*, p. 324.

53. Lukowiak, *A Soldier's Song*, pp. 150–52.

54. Hughes, in McManners, *Scars of War*, p. 350.

55. Geddes, *Spearhead Assault*, pp. 294–5. Geddes called the man a 'ghoulish bastard' and threatened to shoot him so that he would stop.

56. Lukowiak, *A Soldier's Song*, p. 39; it is possible that this is the same as the incident named above.

57. Lucy Robinson, 'Soldiers' Stories of the Falklands War: Recomposing Trauma in Memoir', *Contemporary British History*, 25:4, 2011, pp. 569–89.

58. Christian Jennings and Adrian Weale, *Green-Eyed Boys: 3 Para and the Battle for Mount Longdon* (HarperCollins, 1996). There is also a third allegation that three American mercenaries, or Argentine soldiers who spoke English with American accents, were executed on Longdon: Jennings and Weale, *Green-Eyed Boys*, p. 135; Bramley, *Excursion to Hell*, p. 190.

59. Letter delivered by McLaughlin's son and brothers to Prime Minister David Cameron, 4 July 2015; <http://www.parachuteregiment-hsf.org/Prime%20Minister.docx>; John Ingham, 'Paras march on Downing Street in campaign for Falklands War hero', *Daily Express*, 4 July 2015; John Beales, 'Putting the Record Straight: Motivation for Testimony and Counter-Narratives of a Contested History in a British Veteran's Account of the Battle of Mount Longdon, 1982' (MA assignment, University of Bristol, 2018).

60. Tony Mason, in Jennings and Weale, *Green-Eyed Boys*, p. 163. The main eyewitness was Captain Tony Mason. He was with Company Sergeant Major Thor Caithness and Major Peter Dennison, although it is not clear whether these two men also saw what happened, although they were certainly aware that it had, and they were involved in its immediate aftermath. Private Stuart Dover also gave Jennings and Weale details about the man X shot.

61. Jennings and Weale, *Green-Eyed Boys*, p. 164. The incident is also referred to in Colbeck, *With 3 Para to the Falklands*, p. 185 and Bramley, *Excursion to Hell*, p. 144.

62. Jennings and Weale, *Green-Eyed Boys*, p. 163.

63. Anon., interview with me, July 2012.

64. Lukowiak, *A Soldier's Song*, p. 49.

65. O'Connell, *Three Days in June*, location 1642.

66. French, in McManners, *Scars of War*, p. 349.

67. Jennings and Weale, *Green-Eyed Boys*, p. 189.

68. Private Martyn Clarkson-Kearsley, in O'Connell, *Three Days in June*, location 2501.

69. Grinham, in O'Connell, *Three Days in June*, location 2047.

70. Luke Jennings, 'On Mount Longdon', *The Independent*, 15 May 1993; see <http://www.independent.co.uk/arts-entertainment/on-mount-longdon-parachute-regiment-came-back-from-the-falklands-with-their-reputation-for-bravery-2323239.html>.

71. Lukowiak, *A Soldier's Song*, p. 37.

72. Private Northfield, in McManners, *Scars of War*, p. 187.

73. David Benest, 'Atrocities in Britain's Counter-Insurgencies', *The RUSI Journal*, 156:3, 2011, p. 85.

74. Cited in McManners, *Scars of War*, p. 304.

75. Jennings and Weale, *Green Eyed Boys*, p. 156.

76. Bicheno, *Razor's Edge*, pp. 228, 275.

77. Number of prisoners taken from Freedman, *Official History*, Vol. II, location 13910; number of Argentines treated at the aid post from the 3 Para post-operations report. Number of wounded from Van der Bijl, *Nine Battles*, p. 177.

78. Bourke, *An Intimate History of Killing*, p. 38.

79. Jennings and Weale, *Green-Eyed Boys*, pp. 189–90.

10 Death

1. Freedman, *Official History*, Vol. II, location 14257.
2. '2 Para History'.
3. '2 Para History'.
4. Frost, *2 Para Falklands*, pp. 139–45, based on '2 Para History', says first they cleared positions on the ridge itself (the Argentines had already fled), and then, in a dip between two parts of the ridge, the shells dropped on them; Bicheno, *Razor's Edge*, pp. 306–7, suggests that the shells fell when they were still forming up to begin their assault along the ridge. The death certificate at Dave Parr's (Parr was killed by shrapnel from these shells) inquest in the UK (AFM, 2/34/18) says he was killed at 0230, which, if we assume it refers to Greenwich Mean Time, was 10.30 p.m. Falklands time on 13 June, and therefore early into D Company's assault. Bicheno, however, gives the time of the shell drop as 0400, which, assuming he means GMT, was midnight in the Falkland Islands, and therefore, conversely, suggests that D Company might have got further into their assault before these shells dropped. Philip Neame, the officer commanding D Company, provided a grid reference for the position they were at which puts them further along the ridge, towards its higher, eastern end and nearing Stanley.
5. Jim Creaney, interview with me, 29 June 2012.
6. Tom Harley, interview with me, 16 June 2012.
7. Tom Harley, interview with me, 16 June 2012.
8. Banks, *Storming the Falklands*, p. 153.
9. '2 Para History'.
10. Major Neame, letter to Mrs Parr, 19 June 1982.
11. Notes made by my uncle, Chris Parr, on 22 July 1982, following a visit by Lieutenant Waddington to Joy Parr's home.
12. 'Why weren't we told', *Daily Mirror*, 23 November 1983; also reported in *The Sun*, John Kay, 'Storm over Para killed by our shells', and 'Why tell us this tragic lie', 23 November 1983.
13. Chris Parr, discussion with me, 31 August 2014.
14. Anon., interview with me, 16 June 2012.

15. Tom Harley, interview with me, 16 June 2012.

16. TNA, ADM202/845, Captain Hancock's medical reports. Identification and cause of death, Private David Allen Parr.

17. TNA, ADM202/845, medical report.

18. Rick Jolly, *The Red and Green Life Machine: A Diary of the Falklands Field Hospital and Aftermath of the 1982 South Atlantic Conflict with Argentina* (Century, 1983; expanded edn, Red & Green, 2007), pp. 193–4.

19. Note that the body must have been Dave's, because the other D Company soldier killed during the assault on Wireless Ridge was Private Slough, who died in the field hospital, Frost, *2 Para Falklands*, p. 146.

20. AFM, 2/34/1, Battalion Log, 17/5/82, 'NBC overboots were issued'; Or the boots may have been scrounged from the Welsh Guards: Crosland, in Arthur, *Above All, Courage*, p. 213.

21. Colbeck, *With 3 Para in the Falklands*, p. 196; also, in O'Connell, *Three Days in June*, location 4838, Private Andy Dunn says he walked past his body, which was next to a large crater. Lukowiak, *A Soldier's Song*, p. 76, also recalled walking past a body, which he says was wearing Argentine boots. Perhaps he meant the NBC overboots. Lukowiak says, as in *All Quiet on the Western Front*, looting boots will catch up with you. Someone might kill you to get your boots.

11 *Our Boys*

1. Moore, *Margaret Thatcher,* Volume One: *Not for Turning*, p. 750; on the impact of the Falklands in Britain, Lucy Noakes, *War and the British: Gender and National Identity, 1939–91* (I. B. Tauris, 1997), pp. 103–33.

2. AFM, 2/34/14.

3. AFM, 2/34/12.

4. AFM, 2/34/13. In this period, soldiers were generally permitted to list only one next of kin.

5. Bette Sullivan, interview with me, 19 September 2012.

6. AFM, 2/34/10, Operation Corporate, Brief for Visiting Officers.

7. IWM, Sound Collection, no. 13186, Major Bob Leitch (BBC).

8. IWM, Sound Collection, no. 13186, Major Bob Leitch (BBC).

9. Juliet Gardiner, *The Blitz: The British Under Attack* (Harper Press, 2010), pp. 192–9; John Bowlby, *Maternal Care and Mental Health* (World Health Organization, 1951); D. W. Winnicott, *The Ordinary Devoted Mother and Her Baby: Nine Broadcast Talks* (C. A. Brock & Co., 1949); Selina Todd, 'Family Welfare and Social Work in Post-War England, *c.*1948–*c.*1970', *English Historical Review*, 129:537, April 2014, p. 368.

10. Lucy Noakes, 'Gender, Grief and Bereavement in Second World War Britain', *Journal of War & Culture Studies*, 8:1, 2015, pp. 72–85.

11. Anon., interview with me, June 2012.

12. Sara Jones, interview with me, 15 July 2013.

13. Carole and Bryan Dodsworth, interview with me, 3 July 2013.

14. Gareth Jones, interview with me, 15 January 2014.

15. TNA, PIN 88/95. The official record states that there was one man, although Theresa remembered that there were two.

16. Theresa Burt, interview with me, 26 September 2013.

17. Ann Townsend, interview with me, 16 May 2013.

18. Jay Hyrons, interview with me, 25 June 2012.

19. Rita Hedicker, interview with me, 14 September 2012.

20. Jay Hyrons, interview with me, 25 June 2012.

21. Richard and Pam Jones, interview with me, 11 September 2012.

22. Alastair Wood, interview with me, 21 August 2012.

23. Catherine Dent, interview with me, 24 January 2014.

24. Gareth Jones, interview with me, 15 January 2014.

25. J. M. Winter, *The Great War and the British People* (Macmillan, 1986; new edn Palgrave Macmillan, 2003), pp. 66–72.

26. Adrian Gregory, *The Silence of Memory: Armistice Day 1919–1946* (Berg, 1994), p. 97.

27. Dan Todman, *The Great War: Myth and Memory* (Bloomsbury, 2007), p. 44.

28. Adrian Gregory, *The Last Great War: British Society and the First World War* (Cambridge University Press, 2008), pp. 152–8.

29. Gregory, *The Silence of Memory*, pp. 8–9.

30. Pat Jalland, *Death in War and Peace: A History of Loss and Grief in England, 1914–1970* (Oxford University Press, 2010), pp. 60–82.

31. David Reynolds, *The Long Shadow: The Great War and the Twentieth Century* (Simon & Schuster, 2013), pp. 179–80.

32. Gregory, *The Silence of Memory*, p. 169.

33. Catherine Moriarty, 'The Absent Dead and Figurative First World War Memorials', *Transactions of the Ancient Monuments Society*, 39, 1995, pp. 7–40; see <http://arts.brighton.ac.uk/__data/assets/pdf_file/0007/79576/The-Absent-Dead.pdf>.

34. Jay Winter, *Sites of Memory, Sites of Mourning: The Great War in European Cultural History* (Cambridge University Press, 1995), pp. 78–116.

35. David Crane, *Empires of the Dead: How One Man's Vision Led to the Creation of WWI's War Graves* (William Collins, 2013), pp. 77–96.

36. Winter, *Sites of Memory*, pp. 15–28.

37. Gregory, *The Silence of Memory*, p. 25.

38. Todman, *The Great War*, p. 51.

39. Catriona Pennell, *A Kingdom United: Popular Responses to the Outbreak of the First World War in Britain and Ireland* (Oxford University Press, 2012), pp. 57–91.

40. Janet S. K. Watson, *Fighting Different Wars: Experience, Memory and the First World War in Britain* (Cambridge University Press, 2004), pp. 185–218.

41. Todman, *The Great War*, pp. 31–5.

42. Allport, *Browned Off*, p. xix; Gardiner, *The Blitz*, p. 360.

43. George L. Mosse, *Fallen Soldiers: Reshaping the Memory of the World Wars* (Oxford University Press, 1990), p. 221.

44. Allport, *Browned Off*, pp. 302–3.

45. Cited in Eliza Filby, *God and Mrs Thatcher: The Battle for Britain's Soul* (Biteback, 2015), pp. 50–51.

46. Freedman, *Official History*, Vol. II, location 14745.

47. TNA, PREM 19/658, Coles to Whitmore, 2 July 1982.

48. TNA, PREM 19/658, Note by John Nott, 9 July 1982.

49. TNA, PREM 19/658, Coles to Whitmore, 14 July 1982.

50. 'Runcie praises courage in the Falklands and remembers Ulster and Argentina', *The Times*, 27 July 1982.

51. Clifford Longley, 'Little rejoicing in Falklands service', *The Times*, 27 July 1982; Filby, *God and Mrs Thatcher*, p. 159.

52. Rupert Morris, 'A victory parade, noisily enjoyed', *The Times*, 13 October 1982; Alan Hamilton, 'City gives marching orders for Falklands parade', *The Times*, 28 Sept 1982.

53. Moore, *Margaret Thatcher*, Volume One, p. 758.

54. TNA FCO7/4456, telegram, 15 September 1982. Thatcher did not want to change the date – she said it could make Britain 'appear weak' and, if there was an adverse response, they should remind Latin America of Britain's part in the liberation of many Latin American countries, 16 September 1982.

55. Klaus Dodds, *Pink Ice: Britain and the South Atlantic Empire* (I. B. Tauris, 2002), p. 178.

56. Alan Hamilton, 'Falklands wounded join the salute', *The Times*, 5 October 1982.

57. Mass Observation Archive, Falklands and Falklands postscript directive, 1982, respondent R470.

58. Margaret Thatcher, speech to Conservative Party rally at Cheltenham, 3 July 1982; <https://www.margaretthatcher.org/document/104989.

59. John Campbell, *Margaret Thatcher*, Volume Two: *The Iron Lady* (Jonathan Cape, 2003), p. 137.

60. Strachan, 'The Civil-Military "Gap" in Britain', p. 46.

61. Vinen, *Thatcher's Britain*, p. 149.

62. *Tumbledown*, BBC, 1988. Written by Charles Wood, directed by Richard Eyre.

63. Hugh Tinker (ed.), *A Message from the Falklands: The Life and Gallant Death of David Tinker, Lieut. R.N., from His Letters and Poems* (Junction Books, 1982; Penguin, 1983), pp. 186–7.

64. IWM, Doc. 2690, Canham to Mel and Kev, 12 May 1982.

65. Moore, *Thatcher*, Volume One, p. 758.

66. Bilton and Kosminsky, *Speaking Out*, p. 317.

67. Vinen, *Thatcher's Britain*, pp. 308–11.

68. Eric J. Evans, *Thatcher and Thatcherism* (Routledge, 1997), p. 48.

69. David Cannadine, *Class in Britain* (Penguin, 1998), pp. 171–80.

70. Margaret Thatcher Foundation, Thatcher to Waldegrave, 12 July 1982.

71. TNA, DEFE47/31, clipping from *The Sun*, 'H to have the VC', 21 June 1982.

72. TNA, DEFE47/31, Honours and Awards: Victoria Cross, 22 July 1982.

73. Eyles-Thomas, *Sod That for a Game of Soldiers*, pp. 208–9.

74. John Gartshore, interview with me, 6 June 2013.

75. Len Carver, interview with me, 21 September 2015.

76. Stephen Tuffen, interview with me, 9 July 2012.

77. Martin Margerison, interview with me, 7 December 2012.

78. Len Carver, interview with me, 21 September 2015.

79. Tom Harley, interview with me, 16 June 2012.

80. Mr Harmer Parr to Mrs Thatcher, 22 June 1982.

81. AFM, 2/34/17.

82. TNA, FCO7/4453, Secretary of State for Defence, Paper on Repatriation.

83. Jean Carr, *Another Story: Women and the Falklands War* (Hamish Hamilton, 1984). Carr, a journalist with the *Daily Mirror*, collated stories from relatives and the difficulties they faced.

84. Catherine Dent, interview with me, 24 January 2014.

85. McManners, *Scars of War*, p. 340.

86. Sara Jones, interview with me, 5 July 2013.

87. Catherine Dent, interview with me, 24 January 2014.

88. Ann Townsend, interview with me, 16 May 2013.

89. Jay Hyrons, interview with me, 25 June 2012.

90. TNA, DEFE47/32, Letters, 21 December 1982, 28 January 1983, 3 February 1983, 28 February 1983.

91. AFM, 2/34/18.

92. Major M. Wilson, 'After the Battle: The Grisly Task of Grave Registration', *The Pioneer*, The Newsletter of the Pioneer Corps Association, October 2009, p. 15.

93. IWM, Sound Collection, no. 13186, Major Bob Leitch (BBC).

94. AFM, 2/34/18.

95. 'The Dead Heroes of the Falklands Are Home At Last', *East Anglian Daily Times*, 17 November 1982.

96. TNA, PREM19/640, Note from Nott to Prime Minister, 22 September 1982.

97. TNA, PREM19/640, Note to John Nott, 22 September 1982.

98. AFM, 2/34/18.

99. AFM, 2/34/18.

100. 'The Dead Heroes of the Falklands Are Home At Last', *East Anglian Daily Times*, 17 November 1982.

101. Theresa Burt, interview with me, 26 September 2013.

102. Bette Sullivan, interview with me, 19 September 2012.

103. Alastair Wood, interview with me, 21 August 2012.

104. Richard and Pam Jones, interview with me, 11 September 2012.

105. Bette Sullivan, interview with me, 19 September 2012.

106. AFM, 2/34/18, Report.

107. Theresa Burt, interview with me, 26 September 2013.

108. Gareth Jones, interview with me, 15 January 2014.

109. Bette Sullivan, interview with me, 19 September 2012.

110. Bob Prior, interview with me, 7 July 2016.

111. Ann Townsend, interview with me, 16 May 2013.

12 *Grief*

1. Rita Hedicker, interview with me, 14 September 2012.

2. Freda McKay, interview with me, 19 July 2013.

3. Theresa Burt, interview with me, 26 September 2013.

4. Freda McKay, interview with me, 19 July 2013.

5. Tony Walter, *On Bereavement: The Culture of Grief* (Open University Press, 1999), pp. 149–52; Peter Marris, *Widows and Their Families* (1958; Psychology Press, 2004); for two seminal publications about grief, Geoffrey Gorer, *Death, Grief and Mourning in Contemporary Britain* (Cresset Press, 1965), and C. S. Lewis, *A Grief Observed* (Faber and Faber, 1961).

6. David Cannadine, 'War and Death, Grief and Mourning in Modern Britain', in Joachim Whaley (ed.), *Mirrors of Mortality: Studies in the Social History of Death* (Europa Publications, 1981; revd edn, Routledge, 2011), p. 238.

7. Cited in Jalland, *Death in War and Peace*, p. 244.

8. Len Carver, interview with me, 21 September 2015.

9. Bryan and Carole Dodsworth, interview with me, 3 July 2013.

10. Richard and Pam Jones, interview with me, 11 September 2012.

11. Catherine Dent, interview with me, 24 January 2014.

12. Jay Hyrons, interview with me, 25 June 2012.

13. Jay Hyrons, interview with me, 25 June 2012.

14. Bette Sullivan, interview with me, 19 September 2012.

15. TNA, PIN 59/442, typed note.

16. TNA, PIN 59/442, typed note.

17. TNA, PIN 59/442, answer to a parliamentary question. It sounds as if the DHSS pension is more favourable when a man's death is directly attributable to service. I am not sure if the figures given are that or not.

18. TNA, PIN 59/442, answer to a parliamentary question. To convert the amounts into 2016 money, I used the government's GDP deflater: <https://www.gov.uk/government/statistics/gdp-deflaters-at-market-prices-and-money-gdp-march-2018-quarterly-national-accounts>.

19. AFM, 2/34/16. Appendix to meeting of committee on After Care of Soldiers, 13 April 1983.

20. TNA, PIN 59/442.

21. TNA, PREM 19/639, Coles to Nott, 28 July 1982.

22. TNA, PREM 19/639, Whitmore to Jim Nursaw (Law Services Dept), 29 July 1982.

23. AFM, 2/34/17, note, 18 June 1983.

24. See <http://hansard.millbanksystems.com/written_answers/1988/jan/13/falklands-campaign#S6CV0125P0_19880113_CWA_370>. Responses by Mr Freeman to Jack Ashley MP.

25. Carr, *Another Story*, pp. 105–6.

26. Carr, *Another Story*, p. 109.

27. TNA, PREM 19/639, Arnold Foster to Coles, 30 July 1982.

28. Carr, *Another Story*, p. 112.

29. Ann Townsend, interview with me, 16 May 2013.

30. Office of National Statistics, Marriages in England and Wales, 11 June 2014: see <https://www.ons.gov.uk/peoplepopulationandcommunity/birthsdeathsandmarriages/marriagecohabitationandcivilpartnerships/bulletins/marriagesinenglandandwalesprovisional/2014-06-11>.

31. Freda McKay, interview with me, 19 July 2013.

32. Sara Jones, interview with me, 5 July 2013.

33. Catherine Dent, interview with me, 24 January 2014.

34. Ann Berrington and Mike Murphy, 'Changes in the Living Arrangements of Young Adults in Britain during the 1980s', *European Sociological Review*, 10:3, 1994, p. 236.

35. Bette Sullivan, interview with me, 19 September 2012.

36. Pauline and Janet Findlay, interview with me, 26 July 2016.

37. Theresa Burt, interview with me, 26 September 2013.

38. Freda McKay, interview with me, 19 July 2013.

39. Pauline and Janet Findlay, interview with me, 26 July 2016.

40. Chris Parr, interview with me, 2 January 2017.

41. AFM, 2/34/11. List of Next of Kin.

42. AFM, 2/34/18.

43. AFM, 2/34/17.

44. Information from AFM, 2/34/11; 2/34/17 and TNA, PIN59/442.

45. AFM, 2/34/17.

46. AFM, 2/34/17.

47. AFM, 2/34/18, Harmer Parr to Parachute Regiment, 5 December 1983. Con had spent the equivalent of around £21,200 in today's money in about eighteen months.

48. This quote came from contemporaneous notes my grandmother took when she was visiting Con in hospital between 15 March 1990 and 2 April, when he died. The causes of death were given as 'death by natural causes due to fluid on lung, collapsed kidney and cancer'.

49. Patricia M. Thane, 'What Difference Did the Vote Make? Women in Public and Private Life in Britain since 1918', *Historical Research*, 76:192, May 2003, pp. 268–85.

50. Emyr Williams, Leslie J. Francis and Andrew Village, 'Changing Patterns of Religious Affiliation, Church Attendance and Marriage across Five Areas of Europe since the Early 1980s: Trends and Associations', *Journal of Beliefs & Values*, 30:2, 2009, pp. 177–8.

51. Freda McKay, interview with me, 19 July 2013.

52. Rita Hedicker, interview with me, 14 September 2012.

53. Bob Prior, interview with me, 7 July 2016.

54. Catherine Dent, interview with me, 24 January 2014.

55. Chris Parr, interview with me, 2 January 2017.

56. Pauline Findlay, interview with me, 26 July 2016.

57. Alastair Wood, interview with me, 21 August 2012.

58. Freda Mckay, interview with me, 19 July 2013.

59. Theresa Burt, interview with me, 26 September 2013.

13 Trauma

1. John T. MacCurdy, *War Neuroses* (1918; Cambridge University Press, 2013), cited in Joanna Bourke, 'Effeminacy, Ethnicity and the End of Trauma: The Sufferings of "Shell-Shocked" Men in Great Britain and Ireland, 1914–39', *Journal of Contemporary History*, 35:1, 2000, p. 59.

2. Bourke, *Fear: A Cultural History*, pp. 201–221.

3. Edgar Jones and Stephen Ironside, 'Battle Exhaustion: The Dilemma of Psychiatric Casualties in Normandy, June–August 1944', *Historical Journal*, 53:1, 2010, pp. 111–13.

4. Spike Milligan, *Mussolini: His Part in My Downfall* (Michael Joseph, 1978), pp. 276–88, cited in Ben Shephard, *A War of Nerves: Soldiers and Psychiatrists, 1914–1994* (Jonathan Cape, 2000), p. 220.

5. Simon Wessely, 'Twentieth-Century Theories on Combat Motivation and Breakdown', *Journal of Contemporary History*, 41:2, 2006, p. 280.

6. Robert H. Fleming, 'Post Vietnam Syndrome: Neurosis or Sociosis?', *Psychiatry*, 48:2, 1985, pp. 122–39.

7. Edgar Jones and Hugh Milroy, 'Stolen Trauma: Why Some Veterans Elaborate Their Psychological Experience of Military Service', *Defense & Security Analysis*, 32:1, 2016, pp. 55–6.

8. McManners, *Scars of War*, p. 14.

9. Shephard, *War of Nerves*, p. 378.

10. Nora Kinzer Stewart, *Mates & Muchachos: Unit Cohesion in the Falklands/ Malvinas War* (Brassey's, 1991); Hew Strachan, 'Training, Morale and Modern War', *Journal of Contemporary History*, 41:2, 2006, pp. 211–27.

11. Cited in Jones and Ironside, 'Battle Exhaustion', p. 109.

12. Jones and Milroy, 'Stolen Trauma', pp. 58–9.

13. Matthew Green, *Aftershock: The Untold Story of Surviving Peace* (Portobello Books, 2015, Kindle edn), location 2099.

14. Green, *Aftershock*, Conclusion; Sebastian Junger, *War* (Fourth Estate, 2010).

15. Alan Allport, *Demobbed: Coming Home after the Second World War* (Yale University Press, 2009), chapter 7, shows how difficult it was for men after the Second World War who did not feel themselves to be 'normal'.

16. Lists in TNA, ADM202/880.

17. Figures from TNA, ADM202/880, 2 and 3 Battalions casualty list; also AFM, 2/34/11, 3 Para casualties, June 1982.

18. TNA, WO305/5603, 3 Para Post Operational Report, Annex L, Medical Staffing. It is not reported how many of 2 Para's trench-foot cases went into battle.

19. AFM, 2/34/12. List of casualties.

20. H. H. Price, 'The Falklands: Rate of British Psychiatric Combat Casualties Compared to Recent American Wars', *Journal of the Royal Army Medical Corps*, 130:2, 1984, pp. 109–13.

21. T. M. Mcmillan and S. J. Rachman, 'Fearlessness and Courage: A Laboratory Study of Paratrooper Veterans of the Falklands War', *British Journal of Psychology*, 78:3, August 1987, pp. 375–83.

22. Gareth H. Jones and Jonathan W. T. Lovett, 'Delayed Psychiatric Sequelae among Falklands War Veterans', *Journal of the Royal College of General Practitioners*, 37:2945 January 1987, pp. 34–5.

23. L. S. O'Brien and S. J. Hughes, 'Symptoms of Post-Traumatic Stress Disorder in Falklands Veterans Five Years after the Conflict', *British Journal of Psychiatry*, 159, July 1991, pp. 135–41.

24. Roderick J. Ørner, Timothy Lynch and Paul Seed, 'Long-Term Stress Reactions in British Falklands War Veterans', *British Journal of Clinical Psychology*, 32:4, 1993, pp. 457–9.

25. Mike Seear, 'Seeking "The Other" in the Post-Conflict 1982–2006', in García Quiroga and Seear (eds), *Hors de Combat*, p. 11.

26. David Benest, interview with me, 19 September 2017.

27. Jeremy McTeague, 'Who Cares about the Enemy?', in García Quiroga and Seear (eds), *Hors de Combat*, p. 58. McTeague was 10 Platoon Commander, D Company, 1st Battalion, 7th Duke of Edinburgh's Own Gurkha Rifles.

28. Jim Peters, interview with me, 5 February 2014.

29. Eduardo C. Gerding, 'The Anglo-Argentine Post-Conflict Common Ground: The Combat Veterans' Aftermath', in García Quiroga and Seear (eds), *Hors de Combat*, p. 66. Gerding served in the Argentine Navy, and was Chief of the Medical Department of the Batallón de Infantería de Marina de Comando y Apoyo Logístico (Marine Corps Logistics Battalion) and then 5th Marine Infantry Battalion, 1987–90.

30. Tom Harley, interview with me, 16 June 2012.

31. Jim Peters, interview with me, 5 February 2014. I spoke to Jim on 24 October 2017, and asked him, as he had requested, if he was happy for me to use these quotes. He said I could, but he was unsure if I had captured his experiences exactly, particularly concerning the scene in *Saving Private Ryan*. He said he had done a lot more therapeutic work since our interview, and while he still had strong symptoms of PTSD, he saw things a little differently from previously.

32. Les Davis, interview with me, 15 April 2013 (name changed).

33. Bill Bentley, correspondence with me, 15 February 2013.

34. IWM, Sound Collection, no. 20697, Lance Corporal Graham Tolson (Blakeway).

35. Phil Francom, email correspondence, 9 September 2012.

36. Banks, *Storming the Falklands*, pp. 168–82.

37. Hughes, cited in McManners, *Scars of War*, pp. 302–3.

38. Steven Hughes, interview with me, 5 September 2012.

39. Banks, *Storming the Falklands*, p. 183.

40. Phil Francom, email correspondence, 9 September 2012.

41. Phil Francom, email correspondence, 9 September 2012.

42. Len Carver, interview with me, 21 September 2015.

43. Lee Smith, interview with me, 18 April 2013 (name changed). The phenomenon of violent fantasies is discussed in McTeague, 'Who Cares about the Enemy?', p. 57.

44. John Gartshore, interview with me, 6 June 2013.

45. Martin Margerison, interview with me, 7 December 2012.

46. Martin Margerison, interview with me, 7 December 2012.

47. Lee Smith, interview with me, 18 April 2013 (name changed).

48. Phil Francom, email correspondence, 9 September 2012.

49. Len Carver, interview with me, 21 September 2015.

50. IWM, Sound Collection, no. 20697, Lance Corporal Graham Tolson (Blakeway).

51. John Gartshore, interview with me, 6 June 2013.

52. David Benest, interview with me, 19 September 2017.

53. Cited in Ramsey (ed.), *The Falklands War*, p. 579.

54. Bill Bentley, correspondence with me, 15 February 2013.

55. Seear, 'Seeking "The Other"', in Quiroga and Seear (eds), *Hors de Combat*, p. 10.

56. Mc Teague, 'Who Cares about the Enemy', in García Quiroga and Seear (eds), *Hors de Combat*, P. 55.

57. John Gartshore, interview with me, 6 June 2013.

58. Cited in Hilton, *Ordinary Heroes*, location 1882.

59. Martin Margerison, interview with me, 7 December 2012.

60. Cited in McManners, *Scars of War*, pp. 290, 324.

61. Cited in Green, *Aftershock*, location. 3751–3.

62. Bramley, *Two Sides of Hell*, p. 10.

63. Banks, *Storming the Falklands*, pp. 229–302.

64. Phil Francom, email correspondence, 9 September 2012.

65. Christina Beatty, Stephen Fothergill, Ryan Powell, 'Twenty Years On: Has the Economy of the UK Coalfields Recovered?', *Environment and Planning A: Economy and Space*, 39:7, 2007, pp. 1667–8; Harrison, *Finding a Role*, p. 181.

66. Harrison, *Finding a Role*, pp. 175–86.

67. Mark Frankland, 'Goodbye Tinker'; see <http://marksimonfrankland.blogspot.co.uk/2013/07/goodbye-tinker.html>.

68. See <http://www.independent.co.uk/news/uk/crime/one-in-10-prisoners-is-a-former-soldier-new-research-reveals-7944479.html>.

69. Defence Analytical Services and Advice, 'Estimating the Proportion of Offenders Supervised by Probation Trusts in England and Wales who are Ex-Armed Forces', March 2011, accessed at: <https://www.gov.uk/government/uploads/system/uploads/attachment_data/file/280539/16-march-2011.pdf>.

70. Howard League for Penal Reform, 'Report of the Inquiry into Former Armed Service Personnel in Prison', 2011, accessed at: <http://howardleague.org/wp-content/uploads/2016/05/Military-inquiry-final-report.pdf>.

71. Ken Lukowiak, *Marijuana Time* (Orion, 2000), p. 271.

72. Lukowiak, *Marijuana Time*, pp. 289–90.

73. Steven Roberts, interview with me, 6 March 2014 (name changed).

74. Steven Roberts, interview with me, 6 March 2014 (name changed).

75. 'Ministry of Defence, Defence Statistics (Health), A Study of Deaths among UK Armed Forces Personnel Deployed to the 1982 Falklands Campaign: 1982 to 2013', 1 May 2014. See <https://www.gov.uk/government/news/falklands-official-statistics-released>.

76. Green, *Aftershock*, location 1900.

77. Kyla Thomas and David Gunnell, 'Suicide in England and Wales, 1861–2007: A time-Trends Analysis', *International Journal of Epidemiology,* 39:6, 2010, pp. 1464–75.

78. M. J. Crawford and M. Prince, 'Increasing Rates of Suicide in Young Men in England during the 1980s: The Importance of Social Context', *Social Science and Medicine,* 49:10, 1999, pp. 1419–23.

79. David Gunnell, Nicos Middleton, Elise Whitley, Daniel Dorling and Stephen Frankel, 'Why are Suicide Rates Rising in Young Men but Falling in the Elderly? – A Time-Series Analysis of Trends in England and Wales 1950–1998', *Social Science and Medicine,* 57:4, 2003, pp. 595–611.

80. 'Tributes paid to "proud" Falklands War hero found dead in car', *North Wales Daily Post,* 7 January 2013; < https://www.dailypost.co.uk/news/north-wales-news/tributes-paid-proud-falklands-war-2640696>.

81. Horsfall, *Fighting Scared*, pp. 213–14.

82. Deborah D. Avant, *The Market for Force: The Consequences of Privatizing Security* (Cambridge University Press, 2005).

83. Review Body on Armed Forces Pay, 1990, Cm 936, Parliamentary Papers online.

84. Review Body on Armed Forces Pay, May 1986, Cmnd 9784, Parliamentary Papers online.

85. Review Body on Armed Forces Pay, 1981, Cmnd. 8241 Parliamentary Papers online; Review Body on Armed Forces Pay, May 1986, Cmnd. 9784; Review Body on Armed Forces Pay, 1990, Cm. 936.

86. Bridson, *The Making of a Para*, p. 69.

87. AFM, 22/1/14, Discussion paper by Lieutenant Colonel Burls.

88. AFM, 22/1/14, Discussion paper by Lieutenant Colonel Burls.

89. AFM, 22/1/14, Major Twentyman, Review of P Company assessment process, November 1993.

14 Memory

1. Bicheno, *Razor's Edge*, pp. 306–7; Frost, *2 Para Falklands*, pp. 139–45.

2. Mike Savage, *Social Class in the 21st Century* (Penguin, 2015), pp. 168–73.

3. Richard Roberts and David Kynaston, *City State: A Contemporary History of the City of London and How Money Triumphed* (Profile Books, 2001), p. 25.

4. Beevor, 'The Army and Modern Society', in Strachan (ed.), *The British Army, Manpower and Society into the Twenty-First Century*, pp. 63–74.

5. Vron Ware, *Military Migrants: Fighting for YOUR Country* (Palgrave Macmillan, 2012), p. xvii.

6. Beevor, 'The Army and Modern Society' in Strachan (ed.), *The British Army, Manpower and Society into the Twenty-First Century*, pp. 65–74.

7. Anthony Sampson, *Who Runs This Place? The Anatomy of Britain in the 21st Century* (John Murray, 2004), p. 168.

8. Susan Schulman and Hew Strachan, 'The Town that Weeps: Commemorating Life and Loss in Wootton Bassett', *The RUSI Journal*, 155:6, 2010, pp. 76–85.

9. Helen B. McCartney, 'The First World War Soldier and His Contemporary Image in Britain', *International Affairs*, 90:2, 2014, pp. 299–315.

10. Hew Strachan, 'Introduction' in Strachan (ed.), *The British Army, Manpower and Society into the Twenty-First Century*, p. xv.

11. Cited in Bridson, *The Making of a Para*, p. 82. That urge compelled men to keep going when things were tough; it meant that men went to the aid of their dying comrades at the risk of peril to themselves; it led a tiny number towards violent excess. The will to be a Para sometimes meant men could later feel a terrible shame, if they believed they had not lived up to their own expectations, and if they thought other men had seen them fall short.

12. Lucy Robinson, 'Explanations of Post-Traumatic Stress Disorder in Falklands Memoirs: The Fragmented Self and the Collective Body', *Journal of War Culture Studies*, 5:1, 2012, pp. 91–104.

13. Andrew Dorman et al. (eds), 'The Nott Review, Witness Seminar held at the Joint Services Combined Staff College, 20 June 2001' (ICBH, 2002); see <https://www.kcl.ac.uk/sspp/departments/politicalecon omy/British-Politics-and-Government/Witness-Seminars/defence/ Nott.aspx>; A. Dorman, The Nott Review: Dispelling the Myths?', *Defence Studies*, 1:3, 2001, pp. 113–21.

14. Freedman, *Official History*, Vol. II, location 16431.

Bibliography

Primary Sources

Interviews, and correspondence, conducted by the author; ranks given as they were at the time of the Falklands War

Benest, Captain David, 2 Para, 12 July 2012, 14 July 2017 and 19 September 2017
Bentley, Lance Corporal Bill, 2 Para, 15 February 2013 (email correspondence)
Bramley, Lance Corporal Vincent 3 Para, 12 August 2013
Burt, Theresa, 26 September 2013
Carver, Lance Corporal Leonard, 3 Para, 21 September 2015
Chaundler, Lieutenant Colonel David, 2 Para, 1 June 2012
Cole, Private John (Blue), 1 Para, 11 July 2013
Cook, Lance Corporal Jon, 3 Para, 25 September 2013
Coxall, Private Anthony, 2 Para, 19 April 2014
Creaney, Corporal James, 2 Para, 29 June 2012
Crosland, Major John, 2 Para, 21 June 2012
Davis, Private Les (attached to 3 Para) , and Davis, Christine, 15 April 2013 (names changed)
Dent, Catherine, 24 January 2014
Dodsworth, Bryan, and Dodsworth, Carole, 3 July 2013
Edwards, Private Dean, 2 Para, 6 July 2012 (name changed)
Findlay, Janet, and Findlay, Pauline, 26 July 2016
Francom, Private Philip, 2 Para, 9 September 2012 (email correspondence)
Gartshore, Corporal John, 2 Para, 6 June 2013
Harley, Corporal Thomas, 2 Para, 16 June 2012
Hedicker, Rita, 14 September 2012
Herring, Sergeant Thomas, 3 Para, 24 March 2013
Hughes, Captain Steven, 2 Para, 5 September 2012
Hyrons, Jay, 25 June 2012
Jones, Gareth, 15 January 2014
Jones, Richard, and Jones, Pamela, 11 September 2012
Jones, Sara, 5 July 2013
Margerison, Corporal Martin, 2 Para, 7 December 2012
McAuley, Corporal Walter, 2 Para, 9 March 2018 (email correspondence)

McKay, Freda, 19 July 2013
Neame, Major Philip, 2 Para, 23 May 2012
Parr, Christopher, 31 August 2014 and 2 January 2017
Parr, Harmer, 9 August 2011
Peters, Guardsman James, Scots Guards, 5 February 2014
Prior, Robert (Bob), 7 July 2016
Roberts, Lance Corporal Stephen, 3 Para, 6 March 2014 (name changed)
Seear, Mike, Queen's Own Gurkha Rifles, 13 September 2013 (email correspondence)
Smith, Lee (attached to 3 Para), 18 April 2013 (name changed)
Stevens, Corporal Douglas, 2 Para, 16 June 2012 (name changed)
Sullivan, Bette, 19 September 2012
Townsend, Ann, 16 May 2013
Tuffen, Private Stephen, 2 Para, 9 July 2012
Williams, Private Gary, Royal Marines, 1 November 2012
Wood, Alastair, 21 August 2012
Anonymous, Non-Commissioned Officer, 3 Para and wife, 24 April 2013
Anonymous, wife of officer, June 2012
Anonymous, Private soldier, 24 September 2013
Anonymous, Captain, 10 January 2013

Interviews conducted by Emma Murray

Black, Colin, 11 September 2013 (name changed)
Coventry, Steven Peter, Guardsman, Scots Guards, 22 August 2013
Lynch, Timothy, 4 October 2013

Papers in private possession

Letters of Private David Parr
Papers of Joy Parr

Imperial War Museum (IWM)

Sound Collection

17146, Corporal Dave Abols, 2 Para (Barraclough Carey/Channel 4)
17138, Lance Corporal Bill Bentley, 2 Para (Barraclough Carey/Channel 4)
23277, Private Dave Brown 2 Para, *Falklands Families: The Soldier's Story* (BBC)
28300, Major Pat Butler, 3 Para (Graham Bound)
13004, Private Graham Carter, 2 Para (Barraclough Carey/BBC)

13189, Sarah Constance (BBC)

13008, Captain Paul Farrar, 2 Para (Barraclough Carey/Channel 4)

17141, Major Dair Farrar-Hockley, 2 Para (Barraclough Carey/Channel 4)

13186, Major Bob Leitch (BBC)

17147, Corporal Martin Margerison, 2 Para (Barraclough Carey/Channel 4)

17143, Sergeant John Meredith, 2 Para (Barraclough Carey/Channel 4)

13030, Guardsman Jim Mitchell, Scots Guards (Barraclough Carey/Channel 4)

28299, Major Roger Patton, 3 Para (Graham Bound)

28301, Sergeant John Pettinger, 3 Para (Graham Bound)

16074, Company Sergeant Major Peter Richens, 2 Para (Conrad Wood)

20697, Lance Corporal Graham Tolson, 3 Para (Blakeway Associates)

20696, Company Sergeant Major John Weeks, 3 Para (Blakeway Associates)

17149, Captain Mal Worsley-Tonks, A Company 2 Para (Barraclough Carey/Channel 4)

Private Papers

2690 Glenn Canham (aboard HMS *Arrow*)

1182 Graham Colbeck (3 Para)

5595 Murray Duffin (aboard HMS *Arrow*)

20152 Paul Easten (aboard HMS *Antrim*)

6842 Bernard Hesketh (aboard HMS *Hermes*)

317 Ian McKay/Freda McKay (3 Para)

3921 T. J. D. Miller (Falkland Islander)

3898 Nick van der Bijl (Royal Marines Intelligence Officer)

National Army Museum collections

1990-01-20 – Papers relating to Colour Sergeant Brian Faulkner, 3 Para

1991-12-110 – Oral History interview with Major Gareth Pugh, Royal Artillery

1992-01-13 – Papers of Corporal Brian Nicholas Washington, 3 Para

Airborne Forces Museum, Imperial War Museum, Duxford (AFM)

File series

2/34/1–10: Falklands War

2/34/11–16: Falklands War, material related to casualties

2/34/17–22: Falklands War, claims and payments; burials; repatriation; honours and awards; reunions; commemorations; memorial services

22/1/17, Orders for the training and administration of recruits 1968
22/1/14, Depot – all arms P Company – orders, reports, charters and discussions
27/1/60, Parachute Regiment Files – Standing Orders
Record Cards of Depot Para, 1976–82
Pegasus: The Journal of the British Airborne Forces, 1970–83
Captain David Benest, 'History of 2 Para in the Falklands' (1982)

Recorded interviews

Chaundler, Lieutenant Colonel David, 2 Para
Collett, Major David, A Company 3 Para
Coulson, Captain Alan, Intelligence Officer, 2 Para
Crosland, Major John, B Company, 2 Para
Farrar-Hockley, Major Dair, A Company 2 Para
Faulkner, Colour Sergeant Brian, HQ Company 3 Para
Ferguson, Private Dean, 10 Platoon D Company 2 Para
Fuller, Sergeant Desmond, 3 Para
Hedges, Lance Corporal J., B Company 3 Para
Jenner, Major Roger, HQ Company 2 Para
Keeble, Major Chris, 2 Para
Miller, Major Roger, Operations Officer, HQ Company 2 Para
Neame, Major Philip, D Company 2 Para
Patton, Major Roger, 3 Para, second in command
Rice, Major Tony, Royal Artillery, 29 Field Battery
Richens, Company Sergeant Major Peter, B Company 2 Para
Ryan, Major Mike, HQ Company 2 Para
Weighall, Lieutenant Geoffrey, B Company 2 Para
Worrall, Private Graham 2 Platoon A Company 2 Para

Royal Military Academy, Sandhurst (RMAS), Archives

Box 248a, 1978–88, RMAS Student Precis and Study Guides: Leadership
Box 246, Department of Military History, Syllabi
Box 259a, Training Notes, Tactics, 1970–72

House of Commons

Parliamentary Debates, Hansard online, 1982 and various
Review Body on Armed Forces Pay, 1981, Cmnd. 8241, Parliamentary Papers
   online

Review Body on Armed Forces Pay, May 1986, Cmnd. 9784, Parliamentary Papers online

Review Body on Armed Forces Pay, 1990, Cm., 936, Parliamentary Papers online

Reports and Inquiries

Report of the Bloody Sunday Inquiry (Saville Report) (HMSO, 2010)

Report of the Tribunal appointed to report into the events of 30 January 1972 (Widgery Report) (HMSO, 1972)

Defence Analytical Services and Advice, 'Estimating the Proportion of Offenders Supervised by Probation Trusts in England and Wales Who are Ex-Armed Forces', March 2011, accessed at: <https://www.gov.uk/government/uploads/system/uploads/attachment_data/file/280539/16-march-2011.pdf>

Howard League for Penal Reform, 'Report of the Inquiry into Former Armed Service Personnel in Prison', 2011, accessed at: <http://howardleague.org/wp-content/uploads/2016/05/Military-inquiry-final-report.pdf>

Ministry of Defence, Defence Statistics (Health), 'A Study of Deaths among UK Armed Forces Personnel Deployed to the 1982 Falklands Campaign: 1982 to 2013', 1 May 2014, accessed at: <https://www.gov.uk/government/news/falklands-official-statistics-released>

Office of National Statistics, 'Marriages in England and Wales', 11 June 2014, accessed at: <https://www.ons.gov.uk/peoplepopulationandcommunity/births deathsandmarriages/marriagecohabitationandcivilpartnerships/bulletins/marriagesinenglandandwalesprovisional/2014-06-11>

National Archives, Kew, London (TNA)

War Office

WO305, War Office and Ministry of Defence: Army Unit Historical Records and Reports

WO163, Minutes and Decisions of the Army Council

WO384, War Office and Ministry of Defence: Army Statistical Organisation, later Defence Statistical Organisation: Abstracts of Army Statistics, 1950–76

Abstract of Army Manpower Statistics. From 1974 onwards obtained by Freedom of Information Request

Ministry of Defence

DEFE47, Second Permanent Under Secretaries of State: Registered Files and Branch Folders

DEFE25, Ministry of Defence: Chief of Defence Staff
DEFE13, Ministry of Defence: Private Office
DEFE70, Ministry of Defence: Army Registered Files

Admiralty and Ministry of Defence

ADM202, Royal Marines: War Diaries, Unit Diaries, Detachment Reports and Orders

Cabinet Office

CAB128, Cabinet Conclusions and CAB129, Cabinet Memoranda
CAB148, Defence and Overseas Policy Committee, OD(SA), Sub Committee on the South Atlantic and the Falkland Islands

Prime Minister's Office

PREM19, Margaret Thatcher

Foreign Office

FCO7, American and Latin American Departments

Department of Health and Social Security

PIN88, Ministry of Pensions and Successors: War Pensions Department: Registered Files
PIN59, Ministry of Pensions and Successors: War Pensions Policy: Registered Files

Department of Education

ED193, Ministry of Education, Department of Education and Science: Inspectorate: Reports on HM Forces Educational Establishments.

Newspapers

The British Library

The Aldershot News, 1976–83
The East Anglian Daily Times, various 1982–3

Cambridge University Library

The Sun, 1981–2
The Daily Mirror, 1982
The Guardian, various 1970s and 1982
The Daily Mail, 1982

Online

The Times, 1971–82
The Independent, various
The Pioneer, newsletter of the Pioneer Corps Association

Internet sources

Margaret Thatcher Foundation Website, various sources
Paradata: The living history of the Parachute Regiment and the Airborne Forces; see
   <https://paradata.org.uk/>
Mark Frankland, 'Goodbye Tinker'; see <http://marksimonfrankland.blogspot.
   co.uk/2013/07/goodbye-tinker.html>

Sussex University

Mass Observation Archive: Falklands and Falklands postscript directive, 1982

Films and documentaries

The Paras, BBC, 1982
The Battle for the Falklands, ITV, 1982
Task Force South: The Battle for the Falklands, BBC, 1982
The Price of Victory, BBC, 1983
The Falklands War: The Untold Story, Yorkshire Television, 1987
'Falklands Experiences: 6 Platoon B Company 3 Para', School of Infantry video pro-
   duction, 1986; accessed at: <https://www.youtube.com/watch?v=eaDR0eTrnfs>
'Falklands Experiences: Commanding Officer 3 Para', School of Infantry
   video production, 1986; accessed at: <https://www.youtube.com/watch?
   v=O-j4oX9ouA8>
'Falklands Experiences, as seen by OC A Company 3 Para', School of Infantry
   video production, 1986; accessed at: <https://www.youtube.com/watch?
   v=t1n84u4ZQos&t=34s>
Tumbledown, BBC, 1988; written by Charles Wood, directed by Richard Eyre
The Falklands War, Channel 4, 1992

Return to the Falklands, ITV1, 2012
Call to Arms: The Battle for Goose Green, BBC, 2012
The Falklands War Documentary: 3 Para Mount Longdon (Forces TV, 2016)
Back to the Falklands: Brothers in Arms, BBC *Panorama*, 2017

Collections of Falklands voices or memories

Arthur, Max, *Above All, Courage: Personal Stories from the Falklands War* (Cassell, 2002)

Bilton, Michael and Kosminsky, Peter, *Speaking Out: Untold Stories from the Falklands War* (Grafton Books, 1990)

Dale, Iain (ed.), *Memories of the Falklands* (Biteback, 2012)

Hilton, Christopher, *Ordinary Heroes: Untold Stories from the Falklands Campaign* (History Press, 2011)

Kon, Daniel, *Los Chicos de la Guerra: The Argentine Conscripts' Own Moving Accounts of Their Falklands War* (New English Library, 1983)

McManners, Hugh, *Forgotten Voices of the Falklands: The Real Story of the Falklands War* (Ebury Press, 2008)

O'Connell, James, *Three Days in June: 3 Para Mount Longdon* (E-book, 2013)

Parker, John, *The Paras: The Inside Story of Britain's Toughest Regiment* (John Blake, 2012)

Memoirs

Asher, Michael, *Shoot to Kill: From 2 Para to the SAS* (Cassell, 2004)

Banks, Tony, *Storming the Falklands: My War and After* (Little, Brown, 2012)

Bragg, Billy, and Salewicz, Chris, *Billy Bragg: Midnights in Moscow* (Omnibus Press, 1989)

Bramley, Vincent, *Excursion to Hell: Mount Longdon, a Universal Story of Battle* (Bloomsbury, 1991)

Bramley, Vincent, *Two Sides of Hell* (John Blake, 2009)

Burns, Paul, *A Fighting Spirit* (HarperCollins, 2010)

Chapman, Major General Chip, *Notes from a Small Military* (John Blake, 2013, Kindle edn)

Colbeck, Graham, *With 3 Para to the Falklands* (Greenhill Books, 2002)

Curtis, Mike, *C.Q.B.: Close Quarter Battle* (Bantam Press, 1997; Corgi Books, 1998)

Dempster, Chris, and Tomkins, Dave, with Michel Parry, *Fire power: Two Professional Mercenaries Reveal the Shattering Facts behind Today's Mercenary Scene* (Corgi Books, 1978)

Eyles-Thomas, Mark, *Sod That for a Game of Soldiers*, 3rd edn (Kenton Publishing, 2007)

Fox, Robert, *Eyewitness Falklands: A Personal Account of the Falklands Campaign* (Methuen, 1982; revised edition, Mandarin, 1992)

Frost, Major General John, *A Drop Too Many: A Paratrooper at Arnhem* (Cassell, 1980; reissued Pen and Sword, 1994)

Geddes, John, *Spearhead Assault: Blood, Guts and Glory on the Falklands Frontline* (Arrow Books, 2008)

Horsfall, Robin, *Fighting Scared: Para, Mercenary, SAS, Sniper, Bodyguard* (Cassell, 2002)

Jackson, General Sir Mike, *Soldier: The Autobiography* (Corgi, 2008)

Jolly, Rick, *The Red and Green Life Machine: A Diary of the Falklands Field Hospital and Aftermath of the 1982 South Atlantic Conflict with Argentina* (Century, 1983; expanded edn, Red & Green, 2007)

Lawrence, John, and Lawrence, Robert, *Tumbledown. When the Fighting is Over. A Personal Story* (22 Books, 1997; first published 1988)

Lukowiak, Ken, *A Soldier's Song: True Stories from the Falklands* (Secker & Warburg, 1993)

Lukowiak, Ken, *Marijuana Time* (Orion, 2000)

McNally, Tony, *Watching Men Burn: A Soldier's Story* (Monday Books, 2007)

Pike, Hew, *From the Front Line: Family Letters and Diaries – 1900 to the Falklands and Afghanistan* (Pen and Sword, 2008)

Seear, Mike, *Return to Tumbledown: The Falklands-Malvinas War Revisited* (CCCP Press, 2012)

Smith, John, *74 days: An Islander's Diary of the Falklands Occupation* (Century, 1991; new edn, Quetzal, 2002)

Thompson, Julian, *No Picnic: 3 Commando Brigade in the South Atlantic: 1982* (Leo Cooper/Secker & Warburg, 1985; 2nd edn, Leo Cooper, 1992)

Thatcher, Margaret, *The Downing Street Years* (HarperCollins, 1993)

Tinker, Hugh (ed.), *A Message from the Falklands: The Life and Gallant Death of David Tinker, Lieut. R.N. from His Letters and Poems* (Penguin, 1983; first published Junction Books, 1982)

Watson, Lisa, *Waking Up to War: Lisa Watson Tells a Story of Life as an Eleven-year-old during the Falklands War* (Stanley Services Limited, 2010)

Weston, Simon, *Moving On* (Judy Piatkus, 2003)

Williams, Philip (with M. S. Power) *Summer Soldier: The True Story of the Missing Falklands Guardsman* (Bloomsbury, 1990)

Secondary Sources

Addison, Paul, and Calder, Angus (eds), *Time to Kill: The Soldier's Experience of War in the West, 1939–1945* (Pimlico, 1997)

Adkin, Mark, *Goose Green: A Battle is Fought to be Won* (Orion, 1992)

Aldous, Richard, *Reagan and Thatcher: The Difficult Relationship* (Hutchinson, 2012)

Allport, Alan, *Demobbed: Coming Home after the Second World War* (Yale University Press, 2009)

Allport, Alan, *Browned Off and Bloody-Minded: The British Soldier Goes to War 1939–1945* (Yale University Press, 2015)

Aran, Gideon, 'Parachuting', *American Journal of Sociology*, 80:1, 1974, pp. 124–52

Avant, Deborah D., *The Market for Force: The Consequences of Privatizing Security* (Cambridge University Press, 2005)

Barnett, Correlli, *Britain and Her Army, 1509–1970: A Military, Political and Social Survey* (Allen Lane, 1970)

Beatty, Christina, Fothergill, Stephen, and Powell, Ryan, 'Twenty Years On: Has the Economy of the UK Coalfields Recovered?', *Environment and Planning A: Economy and Space*, 39:7, 2007, pp. 1654–75

Beckett, Andy, *When the Lights Went Out: Britain in the Seventies* (Faber and Faber, 2009)

Beevor, Antony, *Inside the British Army* (Corgi Books, 1991)

Beevor, Antony, 'The Army and Modern Society', in Strachan (ed.), *The British Army, Manpower and Society into the Twenty-First Century*, pp. 63–74

Benest, David, 'Atrocities in Britain's Counter-Insurgencies', *The RUSI Journal*, 156:3, 2011, pp. 80–87

Bennett, Huw, '"Smoke without Fire"? Allegations against the British Army in Northern Ireland, 1972–5', *Twentieth Century British History*, 24:2, 2013, pp. 275–304

Berrington, Ann, and Murphy, Mike, 'Changes in the Living Arrangements of Young Adults in Britain during the 1980s', *European Sociological Review*, 10:3, 1994, pp. 235–57

Bicheno, Hugh, *Razor's Edge: The Unofficial History of the Falklands War* (Orion, 2006)

Black, Lawrence, Pemberton, Hugh, and Thane, Pat (eds), *Reassessing 1970s Britain* (Manchester University Press, 2013)

Bourke, Joanna, *An Intimate History of Killing: Face-to-Face Killing in Twentieth-Century Warfare* (Granta, 1999)

Bourke, Joanna, *Fear: A Cultural History* (Virago, 2005)

Bourke, Joanna, 'Effeminacy, Ethnicity and the End of Trauma: The Sufferings of "Shell-Shocked" Men in Great Britain and Ireland, 1914–39', *Journal of Contemporary History*, 35:1, 2000, pp. 57–69

Bourke, Joanna, 'Bodily Pain, Combat and the Politics of Memoirs: Between the American Civil War and the War in Vietnam', *Histoire Sociale*, 46:91, 2013, pp. 43–61

Bowlby, John, *Maternal Care and Mental Health* (World Health Organization, 1951)

Boyce, D. George, *The Falklands War* (Palgrave Macmillan, 2005)

Bridson, Rory, *The Making of a Para* (Sidgwick & Jackson, 1989)

Campbell, John, *Margaret Thatcher*, Volume Two: *The Iron Lady* (Jonathan Cape, 2003)

Cannadine, David, 'War and Death, Grief and Mourning in Modern Britain', in Joachim Whaley (ed.), *Mirrors of Mortality: Studies in the Social History of Death* (Europa Publications, 1981; revd edn, Routledge, 2011), pp. 187–242

Cannadine, David, *Class in Britain* (Penguin, 1998)

Carr, Jean, *Another Story: Women and the Falklands War* (Hamish Hamilton, 1984)

Chandler, David, and Beckett, Ian (eds), *The Oxford History of the British Army* (Oxford University Press, 1994)

Churchill, Winston, *The Second World War*, Volume II: *Their Finest Hour* (Cassell, 1949)

Clutterbuck, Richard, *Britain in Agony: The Growth of Political Violence* (Penguin, 1980)

Connelly, Mark, *We Can Take It! Britain and the Memory of the Second World War* (Pearson Longman, 2004)

Cooksey, Jon, *3 Para Mount Longdon: The Bloodiest Battle* (Pen and Sword, 2004)

Cooksey, Jon, *Falklands Hero: Ian McKay, the Last VC of the 20th Century* (Pen and Sword, 2012)

Crane, David, *Empires of the Dead: How One Man's Vision Led to the Creation of WWI's War Graves* (William Collins, 2013)

Crang, Jeremy A. *The British Army and the People's War, 1939–1945* (Manchester University Press, 2000)

Crawford, M. J., and Prince, M., 'Increasing Rates of Suicide in Young Men in England during the 1980s: The Importance of Social Context', *Social Science and Medicine*, 49:10, 1999, pp. 1419–23

Crosland, Susan, *Tony Crosland* (Jonathan Cape, 1982)

Damousi, Joy, *Living with the Aftermath: Trauma, Nostalgia and Grief in Post-War Australia* (Cambridge University Press, 2001)

Dawson, Graham, *Soldier Heroes: British Adventure, Empire and the Imagining of Masculinities* (Routledge, 1994)

Delap, Lucy, and Morgan, Sue (eds), *Men, Masculinities and Religious Change in Twentieth-Century Britain* (Palgrave Macmillan, 2013)

Dixon, Paul, '"Hearts and Minds"? British Counter-Insurgency from Malaya to Iraq', *Journal of Strategic Studies*, 32:3, 2009, pp. 353–81

Dodds, Klaus, *Pink Ice: Britain and the South Atlantic Empire* (I. B. Tauris, 2002)

Donaghy, Aaron, *The British Government and the Falkland Islands, 1974–79* (Palgrave Macmillan, 2014)

Dorman, Andrew, 'The Nott Review: Dispelling the Myths?', *Defence Studies*, 1:3, 2001, pp. 113–21

Dorman, Andrew et al. (eds), 'The Nott Review, Witness Seminar held at the Joint Services Combined Staff College, 20 June 2001' (ICBH, 2002); see <https://www.kcl.ac.uk/sspp/departments/politicaleconomy/British-Politics-and- Government/Witness-Seminars/defence/Nott.aspx>

Dudink, S., Hagermann, K., and Tosh, J. (eds), *Masculinities in Politics and War: Gendering Modern History* (Manchester University Press, 2004)

Edgerton, David, *England and the Aeroplane: Militarism, Modernity and Machines* (1991; revd edn Penguin, 2013)

Edgerton, David, *Warfare State: Britain, 1920–1970* (Cambridge University Press, 2006)

Edwards, Aaron, *The Northern Ireland Troubles: Operation Banner, 1969–2007* (Osprey Publishing, 2011)

Eley, Geoff, 'Finding the People's War: Film, British Collective Memory and World War II', *American Historical Review*, 106:3, 2001, pp. 818–38

Elshtain, Jean Bethke, *Women and War* (Chicago University Press, 1987)

Emsley, Clive, *Soldier, Sailor, Beggarman, Thief: Crime and the British Armed Services since 1914* (Oxford University Press, 2013)

Evans, Eric J., *Thatcher and Thatcherism* (Routledge, 1997)

Filby, Eliza, *God and Mrs Thatcher: The Battle for Britain's Soul* (Biteback, 2015)

Fitz-Gibbon, Spencer, *Not Mentioned in Despatches: The History and Mythology of the Battle of Goose Green* (Lutterworth Press, 1995)

Fleming, Robert H., 'Post Vietnam Syndrome: Neurosis or Sociosis?', *Psychiatry*, 48:2, 1985, pp. 122–39

Francis, Martin, *The Flyer: British Culture and the Royal Air Force, 1939–1945* (Oxford University Press, 2008)

Freedman, Sir Lawrence, *The Official History of the Falklands Campaign,* Volume I: *The Origins of the Falklands War* (Routledge, 2005)

Freedman, Sir Lawrence, *The Official History of the Falklands Campaign,* Volume II: *War and Diplomacy* (Routledge, 2005)

Freedman, Lawrence, and Gamba-Stonehouse, Virginia, *Signals of War: The Falklands Conflict of 1982* (Faber and Faber, 1990)

French, David, *Military Identities: The Regimental System, the British Army and the British People, c.1870–2000* (Oxford University Press, 2005)

French, David, *Army, Empire and Cold War: The British Army and Military Policy, 1945–1971* (Oxford University Press, 2012)

French, David, 'Nasty Not Nice: British Counter-Insurgency Doctrine and Practice, 1945–1967', *Small Wars & Insurgencies*, 23:4–5, 2012, pp. 744–61

Frost, Major General John, *2 Para Falklands: The Battalion at War* (Buchan and Enright, 1983)

García Quiroga, Diego F., and Seear, Mike (eds), *Hors de Combat: The Falklands-Malvinas Conflict in Retrospect* (CCCP Press, 2009)

Gardiner, Juliet, *The Blitz: The British Under Attack* (Harper Press, 2010)

Garnett, Mark, *From Anger to Apathy: The British Experience since 1975* (Jonathan Cape, 2007)

Gerding, Eduardo C., 'The Anglo-Argentine Post-Conflict Common Ground: The Combat Veterans' Aftermath', in García Quiroga and Seear (eds), *Hors de Combat*, pp. 62–70

Gillman, Claire, *Para: Inside the Parachute Regiment* (Bloomsbury, 1993)

González, Martín Abel, *The Genesis of the Falklands (Malvinas) Conflict* (Palgrave Macmillan, 2013)

Gorer, Geoffrey, *Death, Grief and Mourning in Contemporary Britain* (Cresset Press, 1965)

Green, Matthew, *Aftershock: The Untold Story of Surviving Peace* (Portobello Books, 2015)

Green, Toby, *Saddled with Darwin: A Journey through South America on Horseback* (Weidenfeld & Nicolson, 1999)

Gregory, Adrian, *The Silence of Memory: Armistice Day 1919–1946* (Berg, 1994)

Gregory, Adrian, *The Last Great War: British Society and the First World War* (Cambridge University Press, 2008)

Griffiths, Stuart, *The Myth of the Airborne Warrior* (Photoworks, 2011)

Grossman, Lt Colonel Dave, *On Killing: The Psychological Cost of Learning to Kill in War and Society* (Little, Brown, 1995)

Gunnell, David, Middleton, Nicos, Whitley, Elise, Dorling, Daniel, and Frankel, Stephen, 'Why are Suicide Rates Rising in Young Men but Falling in the Elderly? – A Time-Series Analysis of Trends in England and Wales 1950–1998', *Social Science and Medicine*, 57:4, 2003, pp. 595–611

Hall, Stuart, Critcher, Chas, Jefferson, Tony, Clarke, John, and Roberts, Brian, *Policing the Crisis: Mugging, the State and Law and Order* (Macmillan, 1978)

Harrison, Brian, *Finding a Role? The United Kingdom, 1970–1990* (Oxford University Press, 2010)

Hastings, Max, and Jenkins, Simon, *The Battle for the Falklands* (Michael Joseph, 1983)

Hennessey, Thomas, *The Evolution of the Troubles, 1970–72* (Irish Academic Press, 2007)

Higate, Paul Richard, *Military Masculinities: Identity and the State* (Praeger, 2003)

Higate, Paul Richard, 'Theorizing Continuity: From Military to Civilian Life', *Armed Forces and Society*, 27:3, 2001, pp. 443–60

Hilton, Frank, *The Paras* (BBC Books, 1983)

Hockey, John, *Squaddies: Portrait of a Subculture* (University of Exeter, 1986)

Hoggart, Richard, *Speaking to Each Other: Essays,* Volume I: *About Society* (Penguin, 1973)

Hynes, Samuel, *The Soldiers' Tale: Bearing Witness to Modern War* (Pimlico, 1998)

Jalland, Pat, *Death in War and Peace: A History of Loss and Grief in England, 1914–1970* (Oxford University Press, 2010)

Jennings, Christian, and Weale, Adrian, *Green-Eyed Boys: 3 Para and the Battle for Mount Longdon* (HarperCollins, 1996)

Jessup, Christopher, 'Transforming Wives into Spouses: Changing Army Attitudes', in Strachan (ed.), *The British Army, Manpower and Society into the Twenty-First Century*, pp. 87–104

Johnston, Peter, 'Join Up and See the World! British Military Recruitment after National Service', June 2013, National Archives: see <http://media.national-archives.gov.uk/index.php/join-up-and-see-the-world-british-military-recruit ment-after-national-service/>

Jones, Edgar, and Ironside, Stephen, 'Battle Exhaustion: The Dilemma of Psychiatric Casualties in Normandy, June–August 1944', *Historical Journal*, 53:1, 2010, pp. 109–28

Jones, Edgar, and Milroy, Hugh, 'Stolen Trauma: Why Some Veterans Elaborate Their Psychological Experience of Military Services', *Defense & Security Analysis*, 32:1, 2016, pp. 51–63

Jones, Gareth H., and Lovett, Jonathan W.T., 'Delayed Psychiatric Sequelae among Falklands War Veterans', *Journal of the Royal College of General Practitioners*, 37:294, January 1987, pp. 34–5

Junger, Sebastian, *War* (Fourth Estate, 2010)

Kennedy-Pipe, Caroline, and McInnes, Colin, 'The British Army in Northern Ireland 1969–1972: From Policing to Counter-Terror', *Journal of Strategic Studies*, 20:2, 1997, pp. 1–24

Kershaw, Robert, *Sky Men: The Real Story of the Paras* (Hodder & Stoughton, 2010)

King, Anthony, *The Combat Soldier: Infantry Tactics and Cohesion in the Twentieth and Twenty-First Centuries* (Oxford University Press, 2013)

King, Anthony, 'The Afghan War and "Postmodern" Memory: Commemoration and the Dead of Helmand', *British Journal of Sociology*, 61:1, 2010, pp. 1–25

Leed, Eric J., *No Man's Land: Combat and Identity in World War I* (Cambridge University Press, 1979)

Lewis, C. S., *A Grief Observed* (Faber and Faber, 1961)

MacCurdy, John T., *War Neuroses* (1918; Cambridge University Press, 2013)

Marris, Peter, *Widows and Their Families* (1958; Psychology Press, 2004)

Marshall, S. L. A., *Men against Fire: The Problem of Battle Command* (University of Oklahoma Press, 1947)

McCartney, Helen B., 'The First World War Soldier and His Contemporary Image in Britain', *International Affairs*, 90:2, 2014, pp. 299–315

McGuirk, Bernard, *Falklands-Malvinas: An Unfinished Business* (Seattle: New Ventures, 2007)

McManners, Hugh, *The Scars of War* (HarperCollins, 1993)

McMillan, T. M., and Rachman, S. J., 'Fearlessness and Courage: A Laboratory Study of Paratrooper Veterans of the Falklands War', *British Journal of Psychology*, 78:3, August 1987, pp. 375–83

McTeague, Jeremy, 'Who Cares about the Enemy?', in García Quiroga and Seear (eds), *Hors de Combat*, pp. 53–61

Middlebrook, Martin, *The Falklands War 1982* (Penguin, 2001)

Middlebrook, Martin, *The Fight for the 'Malvinas': The Argentine Forces in the Falklands War* (Viking, 1989; republished Leo Cooper, 2003)

Montgomery of Alamein, Field Marshal the Viscount, *Normandy to the Baltic* (Hutchinson, 1946)

Moore, Charles, *Margaret Thatcher: The Authorized Biography*, Volume One: *Not for Turning* (Allen Lane, 2013)

Moran, Lord, *The Anatomy of Courage* (Constable, 1945; revd edn, 2007)

Morgan, Kevin, 'Militarism and Anti-Militarism: Socialists, Communists and Conscription in France and Britain, 1900–1940', *Past & Present*, 202:1, 2009, pp. 207–44

Moriarty, Catherine, 'The Absent Dead and Figurative First World War Memorials', *Transactions of the Ancient Monuments Society*, 39, 1995, pp. 7–40; see <http://arts.brighton.ac.uk/__data/assets/pdf_file/0007/79576/The-Absent-Dead.pdf>

Mosse, George L., *Fallen Soldiers: Reshaping the Memory of the World Wars* (Oxford University Press, 1997)

Newsinger, John, *Dangerous Men: The SAS and Popular Culture* (Pluto Press, 1997)

Noakes, Lucy, *War and the British: Gender and National Identity, 1939–91* (I. B. Tauris, 1997)

Noakes, Lucy, 'Gender, Grief and Bereavement in Second World War Britain', *Journal of War & Culture Studies*, 8:1, 2015, pp. 72–85

Ó Dochartaigh, Niall, 'Bloody Sunday: Error or Design?', *Contemporary British History*, 24:1, 2010, pp. 89–108

O'Brien, L. S., and Hughes, S. J., 'Symptoms of Post-Traumatic Stress Disorder in Falklands Veterans Five Years after the Conflict', *British Journal of Psychiatry*, 159, July 1991, pp. 135–41

Ørner, Roderick J., Lynch, Timothy, and Seed, Paul, 'Long-term Stress Reactions in British Falklands War Veterans', *British Journal of Clinical Psychology*, 32:4, 1993, pp. 457–9

Orwell, George, 'The Lion and the Unicorn' (1941), in *The Collected Essays, Journalism and Letters of George Orwell*, Volume 2: *My Country Right or Left, 1940–1943* (Secker & Warburg, 1968), pp. 56–109

Otley, C. B., 'Militarism and the Social Affiliations of the British Army Élite', in Jacques van Doorn (ed.), *Armed Forces and Society* (The Hague/Paris: Mouton, 1968), pp. 84–108

Otley, C. B., 'The Social Origins of British Army Officers', *Sociological Review*, 18:2, 1970, pp. 213–39

Paris, Michael, *Warrior Nation: Images of War in British Popular Culture, 1850–2000* (Reaktion Books, 2000)

Pennell, Catriona, *A Kingdom United: Popular Responses to the Outbreak of the First World War in Britain and Ireland* (Oxford University Press, 2012)

Ponting, Clive, *The Right to Know: The Inside Story of the Belgrano Affair* (Sphere Books, 1985)

Price, H. H., 'The Falklands: Rate of British Psychiatric Combat Casualties

Compared to Recent American Wars', *Journal of the Royal Army Medical Corps*, 130:2, 1984, pp. 109–13

Pronay, Nicholas, 'The British Post-Bellum Cinema: A Survey of the Films Relating to World War II Made in Britain between 1945 and 1960', *Historical Journal of Film, Radio and Television*, 8:1, 1988, pp. 39–54

Ramsey, Gordon (ed.), *The Falklands War: Then and Now* (After the Battle, 2009)

Raven, Simon, 'Perish by the Sword', in Thomas, Hugh (ed.), *The Establishment: A Symposium* (Anthony Blond, 1959)

Reynolds, David, *The Long Shadow: The Great War and the Twentieth Century* (Simon & Schuster, 2013), pp. 179–80

Roberts, Richard, and Kynaston, David, *City State: A Contemporary History of the City of London and How Money Triumphed* (Profile Books, 2001)

Robinson, Lucy, 'Soldiers' Stories of the Falklands War: Recomposing Trauma in Memoir', *Contemporary British History*, 25:4, 2011, pp. 569–89

Robinson, Lucy, 'Explanations of Post-Traumatic Stress Disorder in Falklands Memoirs: The Fragmented Self and the Collective Body', *Journal of War & Culture Studies*, 5:1, 2012, pp. 91–104

Roper, Michael, *The Secret Battle: Emotional Survival in the Great War* (Manchester University Press, 2009)

Rose, Sonya O., *Which People's War? National Identity and Citizenship in Wartime Britain, 1939–1945* (Oxford University Press, 2003)

Salaman, G., and Thompson, K., 'Class Culture and the Persistence of an Elite: The Case of Army Officer Selection', *Sociological Review*, 26:2, 1978, pp. 283–304

Sampson, Anthony, *Who Runs This Place? The Anatomy of Britain in the 21st Century* (John Murray, 2004)

Sandbrook, Dominic, *State of Emergency. The Way We Were: Britain, 1970–1974* (Allen Lane, 2010)

Sanders, Andrew, 'Principles of Minimum Force and the Parachute Regiment in Northern Ireland, 1969–1972', *Journal of Strategic Studies*, 2016, online, pp. 1–25

Saunders, Hilary St George, *The Red Beret: The Story of the Parachute Regiment, 1940–1945* (Michael Joseph, 1950)

Savage, Mike, *Social Class in the 21st Century* (Penguin, 2015)

Schulman, Susan, and Strachan, Hew, 'The Town that Weeps: Commemorating Life and Loss in Wootton Bassett', *The RUSI Journal*, 155:6, 2010, pp. 76–85

Seear, Mike, 'Seeking "The Other" in the Post-Conflict 1982–2006', in García Quiroga and Seear (eds), *Hors de Combat*, pp. 8–15

Shanks, Michael *The Stagnant Society* (Penguin, 1961)

Shay, Jonathan, *Achilles in Vietnam: Combat Trauma and the Undoing of Character* (New York: Scribner, 1994)

Shephard, Ben, *A War of Nerves: Soldiers and Psychiatrists, 1914–1994* (Jonathan Cape, 2000), p. 220

Shils, Edward, and Janowitz, Morris A., 'Cohesion and Disintegration in the Wehrmacht in World War II', *Public Opinion Quarterly*, 12:2, 1948, pp. 280–315

Shonfield, Andrew, *British Economic Policy since the War* (Penguin, 1958)

Spiers, Edward M., *The Army and Society, 1815–1914* (Longman, 1980)

Stewart, Nora Kinzer, *Mates & Muchachos: Unit Cohesion in the Falklands/Malvinas War* (Brassey's, 1991)

Stouffer, Samuel A., *The American Soldier: Combat and Its Aftermath* (Princeton University Press, 1949)

Strachan, Hew, *The Politics of the British Army* (Oxford University Press, 1997)

Strachan, Hew (ed.), *The British Army, Manpower and Society into the Twenty-First Century* (Frank Cass, 2000).

Strachan, Hew, 'The British Way in Warfare', in David Chandler and Ian Beckett (eds), *The Oxford History of the British Army* (Oxford University Press, 1994), pp. 399–415

Strachan, Hew, 'The Civil–Military "Gap" in Britain', *Journal of Strategic Studies*, 26:2, May 2003, pp. 43–63

Strachan, Hew, 'Training, Morale and Modern War', *Journal of Contemporary History*, 41:2, 2006, pp. 211–27

Strange, Julie-Marie, *Death, Grief and Poverty in Britain, 1870–1914* (Cambridge University Press, 2005)

Thane, Patricia M., 'What Difference Did the Vote Make? Women in Public and Private Life in Britain since 1918', *Historical Research*, 76:192, May 2003, pp. 268–85

Thomas, Kyla, and Gunnell, David, 'Suicide in England and Wales 1861–2007': A Time-Trends Analysis, *International Journal of Epidemiology*, 39:6, 2010, pp. 1464–75

Thompson, Major General Julian, *Ready for Anything: The Parachute Regiment at War* (Weidenfeld & Nicolson, 1989)

Thomson, Alistair, *Anzac Memories: Living with the Legend* (Oxford University Press, 1994)

Thornborrow, Thomas, and Brown, Andrew D., "Being Regimented": Aspiration, Discipline and Identity Work in the British Parachute Regiment', *Organization Studies*, 30:4, 2009, pp. 355–76

Todd, Selina, 'Family Welfare and Social Work in Post-War England, c.1948–c.1970', *English Historical Review*, 129:537, April 2014, pp. 362–87

Todman, Daniel, *The Great War: Myth and Memory* (Bloomsbury, 2007)

Todman, Daniel, *Britain's War*, Volume I: *Into Battle, 1937–1941* (Allen Lane, 2016)

Tomlinson, Jim, 'Thrice Denied: "Declinism" as a Recurrent Theme in British History in the Long Twentieth Century', *Twentieth Century British History*, 20:2, 2009, pp. 227–51

Tuck, Christopher, 'Northern Ireland and the British Approach to Counter-Insurgency', *Defense & Security Analysis*, 23:2, 2007, pp. 165–83

Van der Bijl, Nicholas, *Nine Battles to Stanley* (Leo Cooper, 1999)

Vernon, Alex (ed.), *Arms and the Self: War, the Military and Autobiographical Writing* (Kent State University Press, 2005)

Vinen, Richard, *Thatcher's Britain: The Politics and Social Upheaval of the 1980s* (Simon and Schuster, 2009)

Vinen, Richard, *National Service: Conscription in Britain, 1945–1963* (Allen Lane, 2014)

Walter, Tony, *On Bereavement: The Culture of Grief* (Open University Press, 1999)

Ware, Vron, *Military Migrants: Fighting for YOUR Country* (Palgrave Macmillan, 2012)

Watson, Janet S.K., *Fighting Different Wars: Experience, Memory and the First World War in Britain* (Cambridge University Press, 2004)

Wessely, Simon, 'Twentieth-Century Theories on Combat Motivation and Breakdown', *Journal of Contemporary History*, 41:2, 2006, pp. 269–86

Williams, A. T., *A Very British Killing: The Death of Baha Mousa* (Jonathan Cape, 2012)

Williams, Emyr, Francis, Leslie J., and Village, Andrew, 'Changing Patterns of Religious Affiliation, Church Attendance and Marriage across Five Areas of Europe since the Early 1980s: Trends and Associations', *Journal of Beliefs & Values*, 30:2, 2009, pp. 173–82

Willis, Paul, *Learning to Labour: How Working Class Kids Get Working Class Jobs* (Ashgate, 2003)

Wilsey, John, *H Jones VC: The Life and Death of an Unusual Hero*, new edn (Arrow Books, 2003)

Wilson, Major M., 'After the Battle: The Grisly Task of Grave Registration', *The Pioneer*, The Newsletter of the Pioneer Corps Association, October 2009, pp. 13–16

Winnicott, D. W., *The Ordinary Devoted Mother and Her Baby: Nine Broadcast Talks* (C. A. Brock & Co., 1949)

Winslow, Donna, *The Canadian Airborne Regiment in Somalia: A Socio-Cultural Inquiry* (Minister of Public Works and Government Services, Canada, 1997)

Winter, Jay, *Sites of Memory, Sites of Mourning: The Great War in European Cultural History* (Cambridge University Press, 1995)

Winter, J. M., *The Great War and the British People* (Macmillan, 1986; new edn, Palgrave Macmillan, 2003)

Woodward, Rachel, '"Not for Queen or Country or Any of that Shit . . .": Reflections on Citizenship and Military Participation in Contemporary British Soldier Narratives', in Deborah Cowen and Emily Gilbert (eds), *War, Citizenship, Territory* (Routledge, 2008)

von Zugbach de Sugg, Reggie, and Ishaq, Mohammed, 'Officer Recruitment: The Decline in Social Eliteness in the Senior Ranks of the British Army', in Strachan (ed.), *The British Army, Manpower and Society into the Twenty-First Century*, pp. 75–86

Unpublished PhD theses and MA and BA dissertations

Beales, John, 'Putting the Record Straight: Motivation for Testimony and Counter-Narratives of a Contested History in a British Veteran's Account of the Battle of Mount Longdon, 1982' (MA assignment, University of Bristol, 2018)

Eyles, David Charles, '"Seeking the Bubble Reputation": Continuities in Combat Motivation in Western Warfare in the Twentieth Century with Particular Emphasis on the Falklands War of 1982' (PhD thesis, University of Sussex, December 2012)

Johnston, Peter, 'Culture, Combat and Killing: A Comparative Study of the British Armed Forces at War in the Falklands' (PhD thesis, University of Kent, 2013)

Karner, Tracy X., 'Masculinity, Trauma and Identity: Life Narratives of Vietnam Veterans with Post Traumatic Stress Disorder' (PhD thesis, University of Kansas, 1994)

O'Neill, Esther Margaret, 'British World War Two Films 1945–65: Catharsis or National Regeneration?' (PhD thesis, University of Central Lancashire, 2006)

White, Jade, 'The Falklands Conflict 1982: A Study of 2 and 3 Para and the Significant Role They Played' (BA dissertation, University of Swansea, 2012)

Index

Page references in *italic* indicate illustrations.

Abols, Dave 111, 171, 174
Absolon, Richard 129
Aden 16–17
adultery 68
Afghanistan War 247, 291, 297
Aldershot
  Bruneval Barracks 60
  Depot Para *see* Depot Para
  gang rape by Para recruits 78–80
  joint funerals of repatriated Paras
    223, 224
  junior barracks 60, 78
  married quarters 68
  military cemetery xi, xii, 221,
    224, 250
Allen, Billy 45
Ambuscade, HMS 163
Amery, Julian 210
Andrew, Duke of York 218
Antelope, HMS 94
Antrim, HMS 94
Ardent, HMS 94
Argentina 85, 89
  Falklands War *see* Falklands War
  junta 86, 88, 89
  and Malvinas commemoration 285
  occupation of Port Stanley 87
Argentine air force 158
Argentine Army 94–5, 104, 111–13,
    115, 117, 118, 126, 128, 143, 145,
    168–9, 284
  Falklands War *see* Falklands War

meetings with British veterans 271
  Soldado Argentino, Falklands *288*
Argonaut, HMS 94
Argue, Mike 120, 124–5, 177
Arnhem, battle of xii, xiii, 11–12, 26,
    45, 64
Arrow, HMS 98, 213
Asher, Michael 20, 53, 59, 76
Atlantic Conveyor, SS 94, 99
atomic bombs 12
Attenborough, Richard: *A Bridge Too
    Far* 26

Bailey, Ian 124, 147
Baillie, Keith and Ginnie 133
Balfour, Arthur 206
Banks, Tony 27, 29, 35, 50–51, 54, 59,
    131, 140, 170, 261, 262, 263, 271, 277
Banks family 29
Barclay, David 139
Barry, Jim 113, 128, 268
bayonet training 69
Belgrano 89, 212
Benest, David 40, 77, 188, 258, 266
Bentley, Bill 130, 135, 156, 261, 267
Bicheno, Hugh 181–2
Bickerdike, Andrew 120, 123
Bingley, Gary 108, 128, 129, 135, 202,
    203, 220, 233
Black, Colin 32
Blacker, C. H. 17
Blair government 297

Bloody Sunday xiii, xiv, xv, 21–3, 280, 290–91
Boca House, Falklands 97, 104, 112–13, 128, 154, 159
Boot, Private 17
Borneo 16
Bourke, Joanna 182
Bowlby, John 198
Bradshaw, Trevor 121–2
Bragg, Billy 51
Bramley, Vincent 34–5, 43–4, 144, 149–50, 160, 170, 180, 271
  Excursion to Hell 177
Britain
  armed services and British society xvii, 4–5, 13–14, 26, 34–45, 49–57, 254, 273–7, 287–90, 291–3, 296–8
  British cemetery overseas as symbol of Empire 206–7
  consumer culture 276–7
  contracting world role 14, 24, 25
  Defence Review of 1975 24
  economy 25, 87, 212, 273, 277, 296
  and the European Community/EEC 24, 80, 296
  Falklands War *see* Falklands War
  hooliganism 25
  industrial strikes 25
  Labour party 87
  Ministry of Defence xv, 210, 221, 222, 234, 274, 276, 282
  national pride 63–4, 195
  Navy *see* Royal Navy
  the Parachute Regiment and inception of modern Britain 3–26
  Representation of the People Act 204
  riots of 1981 87
  in Second World War 4–12, 42, 63, 297 *see also* Second World War
  social/moral decay in 1970s 25–6

Social Democratic Party 87
unemployment 52, 87, 273, 276
war commemoration 203–11, 284–5
'winter of discontent' 87
youth counter-culture 25, 49
British Army
  5 Airborn Brigade 280, 281
  and the 1975 Defence Review 24
  advertising campaigns 49
  Airborne Division, 1st 6, 11–12, 14
  Airborne Division, 6th 10, 12
  and British society xvii, 4–5, 13–14, 26, 34–45, 49–57, 273–7, 287–90, 291–3, 296–8
  and competitiveness 38
  conscription *see* conscription, military
  Devon and Dorsets 41, 99
  education and Army ethos 74
  Essex Regiment, 10th Battalion 9
  Falklands War *see* Falklands War
  First Battalion, 7th Duke of Edinburgh's Own Gurkha Rifles xiii
  and manhood/masculinity 5, 39, 44, 59, 67, 81, 162, 254, 266, 268, 270, 281, 289, 290, 295
  and marriage 67–8
  in Northern Ireland *see* Northern Ireland
  as Old Britain 25
  Parachute Brigade *see* Parachute Brigade
  Parachute Regiment *see* Parachute Regiment
  and public school education *see* public schools
  Queen's Own Cameron Highlanders, 7th 9
  Queen's Own Highlanders 23

racism 28–9

rank structure 301–2

recruits (1970s) 27–57

Royal Artillery, 29 Commando
Regiment 163

Royal Green Jackets 20

Royal Warwickshires, 13th
Battalion 9

Royal Welch Fusiliers, 10th
Battalion 9

salaries 279

SAS *see* SAS

Scots Guards xiii, 118, 126, 209,
259, 261

in Second World War *see* Second
World War

Somerset Light Infantry, 10th
Battalion 9

units and compositions 300–301

veteran offenders 274

Welsh Guards xiv, 118, 191, 197–8,
257–8, 270

women recruits 32

Brittain, Vera 207

Brixton riots 87

Brize Norton, RAF 58, 71–2, 77,
215, 282

Brooke, Rupert 207, 228

Brown, Dave 116, 269

Browning, Frederick 7

Bruce, Nish 277

Bull, Gerald 129, 139

Burls, T. W. 280

Burns, Paul 23, 29, 43, 53

Burntside House, Falklands 105–7

Burt, Jason 44, 124, 129, 140, 201, 223,
230, 249, 250

Burt, Mrs, of Aldershot 79

Burt, Sid 201, 223, 250

Burt, Theresa 44, 201, 223, 224, 229,
230, 240, 249–50

Caithness, Thor 178

Camilla Creek House, Falklands 98,
99, 103

Canberra 90, 91, 93, 168

Canham, Glenn 213

Carrington, Peter, 6th
Baron 88, 212

Carter, Graham 107, 114, 156

Carver, Len 125, 148–9, 150–51, 158,
160–61, 167–8, 175, 216, 217,
230–31, 266

Carver family 230–31

Cecil, Robert 206

Cenotaph 205–6

Chamberlain, Neville 3

Chapman, Chip 38, 40, 73, 96, 106–7,
115, 138, 154, 172, 278

Chaundler, David 36–7, 38, 39,
131, 185

Christian faith/thinking 74, 242,
245–7, 297

Churchill, Winston 3, 6

Clarkson-Kearsley, Martyn 142, 156

Clash 26

Clio, HMS 85, 86

Clutterbuck, Richard 25

Coady, Dean 135

coal mining 273

Coe, Mark 111

Colbeck, Graham 127

Cold War 13, 24, 195, 208, 296, 297

Cole, Blue (John) 46–7, 55–6, 190–91

Collett, David 125–6, 178, 181, 183

Commonwealth War Graves
Commission 222

comprehensive schools 50

comradeship 108, 122–3, 130–45,
151–2, 294

Connery, Kevin 70, 121, 125

Connick, Denzil 149–50

Conqueror, HMS 89

conscription, military 4–5, 8–9, 12–14,
    42, 212
  see also National Service
Cook, Jon 34, 43, 44, 58, 68, 142, 277
Cooper, David 219, 224
Cooper, Sir George 222
Cork, Anthony 107, 128
Coulson, Alan 103–4
counter-culture 25, 49
Coventry, HMS 94
Cox, Mark 125, 182
Coxall, Tony 43, 131–2, 147, 177, 181
Craig Island 285
Creaney, Jim 114, 115, 166–7, 186
Crosland, Anthony (Tony) 9
Crosland, John 39, 104, 112, 115, 138,
    150, 159, 171, 172, 173
Crow, Jonathan 125, 148
Cullen, Private 123, 147
Curtis, Mike 51–2, 68, 115, 137, 162,
    166, 278
Cyprus 15, 17

Darwin 97, 100, 103
  battle of Darwin and Goose Green
    see Goose Green, battle of
Davis, Les 42, 139–40, 261
death
  Argentine deaths in Falklands *see*
    Falklands War: Argentine deaths
    and dead
  British cemetery overseas as symbol
    of Empire 206–7
  fear of 130, 146–61
  and grief *see* grief
  and guilt at survival 216–17,
    242, 273
  notifying relatives of ix–x, 187–8,
    195–202
  Para deaths in Falklands *see*
    Falklands War: Para deaths

remembering the dead 203–11,
    247–50, 284–5, *286, 287, 288*, 298–9
  and repatriation 206, 218–28, 292
  and war commemoration 203–11,
    284–5
  see also killing
Dennison, Peter 178
Dent, Catherine 203, 220, 232, 238–9,
    248, 249
Dent, Chris 110, 128, 138, 203, 220,
    232, 238, 239, 248, 262
Depot Para 27, 28, 30, 51
  records 28, 32, 35–6, 42, 52–3
  recruit training 58, 59–62, 64–6, 69,
    73, 75–8
  recruits arriving at 28–36
Derry Young Hooligans 19
Devlin, Bernadette 22
Dey, Dilip 110
Dillon, Jez 127
discipline 75–8
divorce 68, 237
Dixon, Steve 128, 140–41
Dodsworth, Bryan 43, 199–200, 202, 231
Dodsworth, Carole 43, 199–200, 202, 231
Dodsworth, Mark 43, 123, 129,
    199–200, 202, 231
Doherty, Patrick 22
Donaghey, Damien 20
Donaghey, Gerald 21–2
Dover, Victor 8
du Maurier, Daphne 7
Duddy, Jackie 21

education 50–51, 289–90
  of 1980 intake to Parachute
    Regiment 49–50
  and Army ethos 74
  of officers in Parachute Regiment 8,
    38–41, 288–9
  at Sandhurst 74 *see also* Sandhurst

schools *see* schools
streaming 50
Edwards, Dean 42–3, 142, 174
Elizabeth II 218
EOKA 15, 17
Eton 38, 40, 99
European Community/EEC 24, 80, 296
Eyles-Thomas, Mark 29, 50, 59, 66, 121,
   135–7, 140, 144, 151–2, 215–16, 277
Eyles-Thomas family 32

Falkland Islands x, 25, 85–96, 218, 282–7
   Argentine cemetery *288*
   commemorative cairn, Wireless
     Ridge *286*
   Craig Island *285*
   dedications to Paras, Mount
     Longdon *287*
   East Falkland ix, 85, 93
   economy 86, 286
   Parachute Regiment's posting and
     start of mission 90–96
   Service (of commemoration) 209–10
   Task Force *see* Task Force
   war *see* Falklands War
   West Falkland 85
Falkland Islands Company 86, 286
Falklands War xiii–xiv, xvi, 296–7
   Argentine deaths and dead 126, 143,
     144, 163–5, 177–8, 179, 210, 294
     see also killing
   Argentine prisoners ix, 126, 160,
     171, 176, 177, 178, 182, 183
   Argentine surrender ix, 191, 195, 296
   battle of Goose Green *see* Goose
     Green, battle of
   battle of Mount Harriet xiii, 118
   battle of Mount Longdon xiii, xiv,
     118–29, 164, 182, 270, 294
   battle of Mount Tumbledown xiii,
     126, 127, 259

battle of Mount William xiii
battle of Two Sisters xiii, 118
battle of Wireless Ridge xiii, xiv,
   147, 155, 163, 164, 166, 170–71,
   173, 185–91
Belgrano sinking 89, 212
and British national pride 195
British ship losses 90, 94
City of London's Columbus Day
   march 211
commemoration 209–11, 284–5
comradeship 108, 122–3, 130–45,
   151–2, 294
and creation of modern paratrooper
   xiii–xiv, 291
and criminality 177–84, 294
and the EEC 80, 296
as end of an era 195, 211–12, 288, 296
and fear of death 130, 146–61
and grief *see* grief
Para deaths ix–x, xiv, 108, 109,
   110–12, 113–14, 115, 122–3, 124, 125,
   128–9, 135–42, 143–4, 151, 156–7,
   186–91, 294 *see also* death; grief
Paras' experiences of, and attitudes
   to killing *see* killing
Paras' post-war emotions and
   trauma *see* trauma and emotional
   reactions, post-war
Paras' return home and to civilian
   society 166, 176–7, 215–18, 254,
   259–78 *see also* trauma and
   emotional reactions, post-war
and repatriation 218–28, 292
and Thatcher *see* Thatcher, Margaret
and the UN 89
and the USA 88, 89, 296
Farrar-Hockley, Sir Anthony 17, 37, 102
Farrar-Hockley, Dair 37, 38, 98, 109–10
Faulkner, Brian 91, 138–9, 140–41
fear of death 130, 146–61

Ferguson, Dean 91, 116, 137, 159, 173–4
Fieldhouse, John, Baron 100
Findlay, Gordon 185
Findlay, Janet 32, 240, 241
Findlay, Pauline 240, 241, 249
First World War commemoration 203–7
Fitzroy 118, *133–4*, 270
Fletcher, Mark William 107, 128
Foot, Michael 87
football hooliganism/violence 25, 33, 34
Ford, Sir Robert 19
Fox, Robert 117
Francom, Phil xi, 43, 261, 262, 263, 265, 272
Frankland, Mark 274
Freedman, Sir Lawrence: *Official History of the Falklands Campaign* 100
French, Mac 135, 156, 170, 175, 179
Frost, John 7, 8, 11–12, 101, 145, 188
Fuller, Des 119, 124, 138, 174
funeral, Parr, Dave xi
Fursman, Peter 24

Galtieri, Leopoldo 86–7, 232, 285
Gartshore, John 57, 66–7, 113–14, 116, 159, 173, 216, 266, 268–9, 271
Gavin, James 10
Geddes, John 105, 106, 169, 170, 278
General Belgrano 89, 212
Gettings, Richard 77
Gilmour, Hugh 21
Glover, Martin 136
Goodall, David 214
Goose Green, battle of xiii, xiv, 97–117, 128, 164, 171, 174–5, 268–9, 293–4
    TV footage of Para burials 219
Gort, John Vereker, 6th Viscount 252–3
Graves, Robert 207
Gray, Dominic 33–4, 120
Gray family 33–4

Grayling, Barry 108
Great Britain *see* Britain
Great War commemoration 203–7
Great War, The (BBC series) 207–8
Green, Matthew 254, 270
Greenwood, Tony 'Fester' 122, 123, 129
Greet, Kenneth 209
Gregory, Tony 120–21
grenades 108, 113, 114, 123, 124, 125, 135, 164
    white phosphorous 108, 165
grief 189, 203, 229–50
    and Christian thinking 242, 245–7
    and family complications 242–3
    of mothers 151, 218, 229, 231, 237, 244–7, 249–50
    and poverty 242
    and remembering the dead 247–50
    repressed 262–3
    resisted whilst in combat 144, 262
    of widows 203, 232–3, 237–41, 247, 248
Grinham, Grant 147
Grose, Neil 124, 129, 140, 144, 152, 202, 220, 230
Guardian 19, 209

Haig, Alexander 88
Hailsham, Quintin Hogg, Baron 230
Haire, John 157
Hales, Gus 270
Hardcastle, Paul: '19' 245
Hardman, David 'Chuck' 110, 128
Harley, Pat 150
Harley, Tom 30, 108–9, 143, 153–4, 186, 190, 217–18, 260
Harriet, battle of Mount xiii, 118
Harrison, Private 155
Heath, Edward 22
Heaver, Derek 224
Hedges, John 121, 124, 174
Hedicker, Peter 45, 129, 202

Hedicker, Rita 44–5, 202, 229, 246–7
Higgs, Peter 129
Highland Scots 205
Hill, Stanley James L. 10–11
Hitler, Adolf 5
Holman-Smith, Mark 113, 128
homosexuality 49, 67, 169
Hood, Stephen 277
hooliganism 25
    football violence and 25, 33, 34
Hope, Stevie 129
Horsfall, Robin 32, 54, 71, 278
Howard, Tom 176, 269–70
Howard League for Penal Reform 274
Hughes, Steven 116, 130, 132, 138, 149,
    157, 257, 262–3
Hume, Basil 209
Hutchinson, Paul 143
Hyrons, Jay 202–3, 220, 233, 249

Illingsworth, Stephen 112, 128, 215
Imperial War Graves Commission 206
Intrepid, HMS 93
Iranian Embassy, London xv
Iraq War 291, 292, 297
Irish Republican Army (IRA/PIRA)
    18–19, 20, 21–2, 23–4, 30
Ives, Leslie 14

Jack, Parr family's lodger, and
    biological father of Joy Parr 45–6
Jackson, Sir Mike 24, 39, 73
James, Roger 124
Jenkins, Tim 129, 135
Jenner, Roger 110, 113
Jennings, Christian 177–8
John Paul II 209
Johnston, John 20
Jones, Craig 129, 200–201, 203, 231, 241
Jones, Edgar 253
Jones, Gareth 200, 201, 203, 224, 241–2

Jones, Herbert 'H' xiv, 36, 38, 40–42,
    90, 97, 99, 100, 101, 107, 108, 109,
    110, 111, 128, 129, 137, 138, 171,
    215, 220, 237, 262, 291, 293–4
Jones, Pam 201, 203, 231, 285
Jones, Phil 127, 149
Jones, Richard 200–201, 203, 223–4,
    231, 285
Jones, Sara 199, 220, 237–8
Joseph, Keith 212

Keeble, Chris 38, 112, 117, 146
Kelly, Michael 21
Kelly, Ned 124, 136–7
killing 126, 162–84, 259
    after enemy surrender 64, 112, 176
    and battalion culture 179–80
    and the class–violence connection
        165–6
    close-up 126, 162–3, 164–5, 170–71,
        174–6, 178
    and criminality 177–84, 294
    and dehumanization 170
    distant 119, 163–4
    with grenades *see* grenades
    haunting memories of 174, 175
    on orders 171–2
    paratroopers' attitudes to 162–3,
        166–71, 172–3, 174–7
    and racism 168–9
    return to civilian society after 166,
        176–7, 254
    as a taboo 162
    trench/bunker clearance 108, 111,
        112, 123, 124, 126, 164–5, 171–2
Kipling, Rudyard 205

Laing, Stewart 123, 129
Leach, Henry 94
leadership training 73–5
Legg, Cliff 150

Leitch, Bob 197–8
Leonard, Graham, Bishop of
    London 210
Light, Sergeant 190
Loden, Edward C. 21
Logan, Adrian 179
Londonderry shootings, Bloody Sunday
    xiii, xiv, xv, 21–3, 280, 290–91
Longdon, battle of Mount xiii, xiv,
    118–29, 164, 182, 270, 294
Lovett, Chris 129
Lowestoft 54, 55–6, 190
Lukowiak, Ken 142, 143, 151, 154, 156,
    174, 176, 178–9, 180, 275

McAuley, Walter 108
McCarthy, Keith 129
McCracken, William 119, 163–4
McCullum, Sergeant 181
MacCurdy, John 251
McElhinney, Kevin 21
McGimpsey, Kevin 102
McGuigan, Bernard 22
McKay, Freda 44, 202, 229, 230, 236,
    237, 240, 246
McKay, Ian xiv, 44, 51, 96, 123–4, 129,
    215, 230, 246, 291
McKinney, Gerard 21
McKinney, William 22
McLarnon, Tony 124
McLaughlin, Stewart 124, 125, 129,
    177, 179–80, 181, 182
MacLellan, Patrick 19, 20–21
McTeague, Jeremy 268
Maddocks, Peter 137
Malaysia 16
Margerison, Martin 43, 66, 105–6, 112,
    147–8, 150, 152–3, 159–60, 163,
    174–5, 217, 263, 265, 269
Marley, Bob 51
marriage 67–8, 289

Mason, Tony 178
Maudling, Reginald 22
Mechan, Thomas 128
Melia, Michael 109, 128
mental health, post-war problems *see*
    trauma and emotional reactions,
    post-war
Merchant Navy xiii, 30, 43, 88
Metcalfe, Bill 134–5
MILAN missiles 98, 112, 185
Miller, Roger 102
Milligan, Spike 251–2
milling 69–71
Milne, Brian 121, 155
Montgomery, Bernard, 1st Viscount
    xii, 11–12, 73
Moore, Charles 211
Moran, Charles Wilson, 1st
    Baron 146–7
Morham, Jimmy 123, 135
mothers
  attitudes to sons' recruitment to
    Paras 44–5, 48
  dying Paras calling out for their
    mother 140, 151, 269
  grieving 151, 218, 229, 231, 237,
    244–7, 249–50
  informing mothers and relatives of
    Paras' deaths ix–x, 187–8, 195–202
  and returning sons from
    Falklands 216
  single 232–3
Motorman, Operation 22
Munro, Alec 157
Murdoch, James Hamilton 'Doc'
    122–3, 129, 151

napalm 115
Nash, Alexander 21
Nash, William 21
Nasser, Gamal Abdel 15

national pride 63–4, 195
National Service xvi, xvii, 12–13, 16, 43, 44, 56, 212
Nazism 5, 6
    see also Second World War
Nazzroo, Private 77
Neame, Philip 37, 38, 105, 108, 110, 112, 113, 114–15, 131, 154, 165, 187–8, 283
Nicholson, Geordie 122
No Offence! 274
Norland 90, 91, *92*, 93
Norman, Barry 110, 111
Normandy 10
North Africa 7
Northern Ireland
    Bloody Sunday shootings by paratroopers xiii, xiv, xv, 21–3, 280, 290–91
    Direct Rule 22, 23
    girls agreeing to sexual requests from visiting soldiers 68
    Operation Motorman 22
    Parachute Regiment in xiii, xiv, xv, 3, 17–25, 290–91
    paratrooper recruits from 30
    Troubles 17–25, 30, 208 *see also* Bloody Sunday
    Warrenpoint ambush 23, 29, 30, 196
    Widgery Report 23
Northfield, Private 162, 170, 171, 180
Northwood, Navy HQ 100–101, 102
Nott, John 209, 210, 222
Nunn, Richard 128

O'Brien, Stephen 257, 262
O'Connell, James 148, 149
Operation Motorman 22
Ørner, Roderick 257
Orwell, George 4
Oudna 7

Oulton Broad ix, 27, 56, 190, 225, *226, 227*
Owen, Wilfred 207

Page, John 147
Page, Jonathan 'Jacko' 278
Palestine 14–15, 43
Parachute Brigade
    1st 7, 12
    3rd 11
    16th 15, 24, 280
Parachute Regiment
    1st Battalion xiii, xiv, xv, 7, 21–3
    2nd Battalion xiii, 27, 36, 37, 40, 42, 90, *92*, 94, 98–117, 171–2, 185–91, 268–9, 293–4
    3rd Battalion xiii, 37, 90–91, 93–4, 95, 96, 118–29, 177, 182, 183, 191, 255–6
    10th Battalion 45
    battle of Arnhem Bridge xii, xiii, 11–12, 26, 45, 64
    becoming officers in 36–42, 72–5
    in Borneo 16
    Bruneval raid 7
    and Churchill 3, 6
    common written approaches to xii
    comradeship 108, 122–3, 130–45, 151–2, 294
    creation at Falklands of modern paratrooper xiii–xiv, 291
    creation of regiment 3, 5–7, 8–9
    in Cyprus 15, 17
    death notification to relatives ix–x, 187–8, 195–202
    deaths in Falklands *see* Falklands War: Para deaths
    dedications, Mount Longdon *287*
    demographical data on recruits 52–3, 290
    discipline xii, xvi, 8, 35, 71, 75–8, 80, 182–3, 184, 260, 291

Parachute Regiment – (cont.)
  educational background of 1980
    intake 49–50
  educational background of officers
    8, 38–41, 288–9
  Falkland battles see Goose Green,
    battle of; Longdon, battle of
    Mount; Wireless Ridge, battle of
  Falklands posting and start of
    mission 90–96
  at Falklands thirtieth anniversary xi
  fear of death 130, 146–61
  in Federation of South Arabia 16–17
  HQ of 3 Para 91
  humour 156
  and inception of modern Britain 3–26
  killing see killing
  Londonderry shootings xiii, xiv,
    xv, 21–3
  Machine Gun Platoon, 2 Para
    112–14, 116
  and marriage 67–8
  meetings with Argentine veterans 271
  members with convictions 33–4
  meritocracy 8–9
  and Montgomery xii
  mothers of Paras see mothers
  in Northern Ireland xiii, xiv, xv, 3,
    17–25, 290–91
  P Company selection week 58, 65,
    70, 281
  in Palestine 14–15, 43
  Paras' post-war emotions and
    trauma see trauma and emotional
    reactions, post-war
  Paras with military childhood 8, 34,
    36–7, 39, 42–3
  post-war counter-insurgency
    operations 14–15, 16–24, 291, 293
  post-war cuts and reorganization 14
  racism 28–9

recruit company, Aldershot see
    Depot Para
recruiting pamphlet from 1960s 49
recruits (1970s) 27–57
regimental loyalty and pride 62–3,
    64–6, 145, 169, 184, 214, 294, 295
repatriation 218–28, 292
reputation xv, 3, 7–10, 16, 20, 22,
    120, 280, 291
return home and to civilian society
    after Falklands 166, 176–7,
    215–18, 254, 259–78 see also trauma
    and emotional reactions, post-war
  and SAS 280, 291
  in Second World War xi, xii, xiii,
    5–12, 26, 45, 63–4
  and society xvii, 26, 34–45, 49–57,
    254, 273–7, 291, 296–8
  and Suez 15–16
  training see training of paratroopers
  veteran careers 277–9
  wives see wives
Parr, Billy 45–6
Parr, Chris x, 27, 28, 48, 54, 55, 56, 189,
    190, 223, 225, 227, 241, 244, 248
Parr, Con x, 27, 45, 46, 225, 227, 243–4
Parr, Dave xi–xii, 27–8, 29, 36, 45, 46–8,
    47, 48, 49, 53–4, 54–5, 218, 298–9
  commemorative cairn, Wireless
    Ridge 286
  Falklands service and death ix–x,
    91–3, 92, 108, 130–34, 133–4,
    158–9, 186, 187–8, 190–92, 222–3,
    245, 248, 272, 283
  funeral xi, 189–90, 191, 225, 227
  as Para trainee 60–62
Parr, Harmer 27, 28, 29, 46, 218, 223,
    227, 241, 244, 245, 282–3, 286
Parr, Joy ix, x, xi–xii, 27, 29, 45, 46,
    48, 187, 222–3, 225, 227, 243,
    244–6, 248

Patton, Roger 138
Pedroza, Wilson 117
Pegasus emblem 7
Pegasus magazine 18
Persian Gulf 17
Peters, Jim 259–61
Pettinger, John 162–3
Phillips, Jerry 34
Piaggi, Italo 117
Pike, Hew 37, 119–20, 125, 177, 181,
    183, 281
Pike family 37
Poraj-Wilczynski, Joseph J. P. 281
Port Stanley *see* Stanley
post-traumatic stress disorder (PTSD)
    252, 253–4, 256–7, 259–61, 262,
    265–6, 294–5
    see also trauma and emotional
    reactions, post-war
Price, H. H. 256
Price, Nigel 127
Prior, Bob 224, 247
Prior, Daniel 248
Prior, Stephen 109, 128, 224, 247
private security work 278
Provisional IRA *see* Irish Republican
    Army (IRA/PIRA)
PTSD *see* post-traumatic stress
    disorder
public schools 8, 38–40, 50, 99, 205
Pym, Francis 88, 89, 212, 214

racism 168–9
Radfan 17
Randle, John Pomeroy 41
rape 78–9
Reagan, Ronald 88, 89
Remembrance Day 208
repatriation 206, 218–28, 292
Richens, Peter 137, 141, 171
Robb, John 221

Roberts, Steven 275
Robinson, Corporal 156
Rose, Nick 122
Royal Fleet Auxiliary xiii, 87–8
Royal Gurkha Rifles, First Battalion,
    7th Duke of Edinburgh's Own
    Gurkha Rifles xiii
Royal Marines xiii, 90, 93, 95, 118, 215,
    252, 257–8
Royal Navy 7, 41, 158, 213, 252, 257–8
    HQ 102
    Marines *see* Royal Marines
Royal Ulster Constabulary 18
Royal Wootton Basset 292
Runcie, Robert 209, 210
Ryan, Mike 102

San Carlos 93–4
Sandhurst 8, 39, 40, 41, 72–5, 241,
    288–9
SAS xiv, xv, 16–17, 46, 47, 81, 104, 213,
    241, 252, 277, 278
    and Parachute Regiment 280, 291
Sassoon, Siegfried 207
Saving Private Ryan 253, 261
schools
    and Army ethos 74
    comprehensive 50
    public 8, 38–40, 50, 99, 205
Scots Guards xiii, 118, 126, 209,
    259, 261
Scott, David 123, 129, 135
Scotter, Sir William 63
Scrivens, Ian 124, 129, 136, 140, 155
Second World War 4–12, 42, 56, 63,
    288, 296, 297
    battle of Arnhem Bridge xii, xiii,
    11–12, 26, 45, 64
    comics and books 43
    commemoration 207–8
Seear, Mike xv, 133, 268

sex
  adultery 68
  and barracks talk 68–9
  cohabiting before marriage 68
  gang rape by Para recruits 78–80
  girls in Northern Ireland agreeing to
    sexual requests from visiting
    soldiers 68
  homosexuality 49, 67, 169
  and violence 69, 78–80
Shanks, Michael 25
Sharpley, John 254
Shaw, Alex 129
Shaw, Jonathan 122–3, 127, 149, 278
Sheffield, HMS 90
shell shock 251, 252–3
  see also trauma and emotional
    reactions, post-war
Shonfield, Andrew 25
Shorrock, Lance Corporal 109
Sicily 10
Sir Bedivere, RFA 222
Sir Galahad, RFA 118
Sir Tristram, RFA 118
Skidmore, Phil 147
Slim, William, 1st Viscount 73–4
Smith, Lee 31, 68, 76, 264, 265
Smith, Nigel Robert 113, 128
Smith family 31
South Atlantic Fund 235–7, 239, 242
South Atlantic Medal Association 1982
  (SAMA82) 275–6, 282
Southall, Mick 140
Soviet Union 12
special forces *see* SAS
Standish, Les 267
Stanley ix, 94, 283
  Argentine occupation 87
Stears, Terry 134
Styles, Derek 'Tinker' 274
Suez 15–16, 213

suicide 33, 254, 260, 262, 266, 276–7
Sullivan, Bette 223, 224, 233, 240, 249
Sullivan, Paul 113, 128, 223, 224, 233
Sun 87, 215
Sussex Mountains 94, 98, 99, 158–9

Tabarez, Omar 271
tabbing (tactical advance to battle) 213
Task Force xiii, xvi, 87–8, 89, 209–10,
  211, 221
  commanders 94
terrorism 23–4, 25
Thatcher, Denis 210
Thatcher, Margaret
  and Carrington 88
  and the Falklands/Task Force xvi, 87,
    88, 89–90, 100, 195, 209–10, 211–15,
    218–19, 220–21, 232, 236, 296
  and *The Iron Lady* 283
  loss of son, Mark 218
  and Pym 88
  and Reagan 89
  and the South Atlantic Fund 235, 236–7
Thatcher, Mark 219
Theirs is the Glory 14
Thompson, Julian 90, 93, 98, 99–101,
  102, 119–20, 126, 214
Thurman, John L. 103
Tinker, David 213
Tolson, Graham 137, 143, 162, 173,
  261–2, 266
Townsend, Ann 202, 220, 224–5, 230, 237
Toxteth riots 87
Tragino Aqueduct, Italy 7
training of paratroopers xvi, 6, 36,
  58–81, 280, 294
  480 Platoon 58, 64
  bayonet training 69
  Brecon Basic Wales week 58, 280
  at Depot Para 58, 59–62, 64–6, 69,
    73, 75–8

and discipline 71, 75–8, 80, 291
drill 60
infantry's adoption of Brecon
    course 280
leadership training 73–5
life in junior barracks 60–61
and manliness 66–7
milling 69–71
and national pride 63–4
officer training 72–5
P Company selection week 58, 65,
    70, 280–81
parachuting 71–2
passing-out day 59, 80
physical training 65
at RAF Brize Norton 58, 71–2, 77
and regimental loyalty and pride
    62–3, 64–6
at Sandhurst 72–5, 288–9 *see also*
    Sandhurst
and self-perception 58
timetable 69
wastage rate 58
trauma and emotional reactions,
    post-war 251–76, 295
  'battle shock' 255
  career-limiting presentation of
    traumatic symptoms 254, 266
  and doubt in correct conduct of
    war 268–9
  and feelings of degradation 269–70
  guilt at survival 216–17, 242, 273
  and gulf between military and
    society 254, 263–5, 279
  incidence in Parachute Regiment
    255–6, 257
  and loss of masculine identity
    268, 295
  PTSD diagnosis, experience and
    representation 252, 253–4, 256–7,
    259–61, 262, 265–7, 294–5

public recognition of 254
reports of traumatic symptoms 258–63
and repressed grief 262–3
shell shock 251, 252–3
and suicide 254, 260, 266, 276–7
and support 254
and suppression 254, 256–7,
    261–3, 266–7
symptom denial by authorities
    261, 265
taboos about trauma 253–4
and trench foot 255
veteran offenders and prison
    sentences 274
and violent fantasies/tendencies
    264, 265–6
trench clearance 108, 111, 112, 123, 124,
    126, 164–5, 171–2
trench foot 255
Tuffen, Stephen 109, 152, 216–17
Tumbledown (drama) 213
Tumbledown, battle of Mount xiii,
    126, 127, 259
Turner, Neil *134*
Twentyman, Major 280–81
Two Sisters, battle of xiii, 118

Uganda, SS 256
Ulster Special Constabulary 18
unemployment 52, 87, 273, 276
Unison in Action 26
United Nations 85, 89, 90
United States of America 5, 296
    and the Falklands War 88, 89, 296
    Vietnam War 16, 173, 182, 217, 251, 252

Victoria Cross xiv, 37, 64, 215, 291
Vietnam War 16, 173, 182, 217, 251, 252

Waddington, Chris 114, 188
Waldegrave, William 214–15

Walker, Sir Walter 25, 26
war commemoration 203–11, 284–5
war crimes/criminality on the
    battlefield 177–84, 294
war widows' pensions/benefits/
    payments 204, 233–7, 239
Ware, Fabian 206
Warrenpoint ambush 23, 29, 30, 196
Watts, Patrick 282, 283, 285, *286*
Weale, Adrian 177–8
Webster, Alan 209
Weeks, John 91, 119, 120, 125, 138,
    141–2, 156, 163, 177
Weighall, Geoff 164
Wellington School 8, 38–9
Wells, H. G. 207
Welsh Guards xiv, 118, 191, 197–8,
    257–8, 270
West, Phil 129, 144
white phosphorous grenades 108, 165
Whitehead, Andrew 95
Whitelaw, William 212
Whitmore, Clive 235
Widgery, John Passmore, Baron 23
widows xvii, 203
    grieving 232–3, 237–41, 247, 248
    as single mothers 232–3
    war widows' pensions, benefits and
        payments 204, 233–7, 239

Wilford, Derek 20–21
William, battle of Mount xiii
Williams, Gary 50
Wilsey, John 40
Wilson, Scott 129, 136
Wilson, Thomas 8
Wireless Ridge, battle of xiii, xiv,
    147, 155, 163, 164, 166, 170–71,
    173, 185–91
wives 68, 80, 198, 199, 201, 279, 290
    and ex-Falklands Paras with
        PTSD 265–6
    grieving 203, 232–3, 237–8, 239, 247
    informing wives and relatives of
        Paras' deaths ix–x, 187–8, 195–202
    see also widows
Wood, Alistair 203, 223, 249
Wood, David 110–11, 128, 138, 203,
    223, 249, 262
Woodward, Sir John 'Sandy' 93
Wootton Basset 292
Worrall, Graham 105, 109, 148,
    149, 173
Wray, Jim 21
Wroughton RAF hospital 217

Yemen 17
yomping 213
youth counter-culture 25, 49

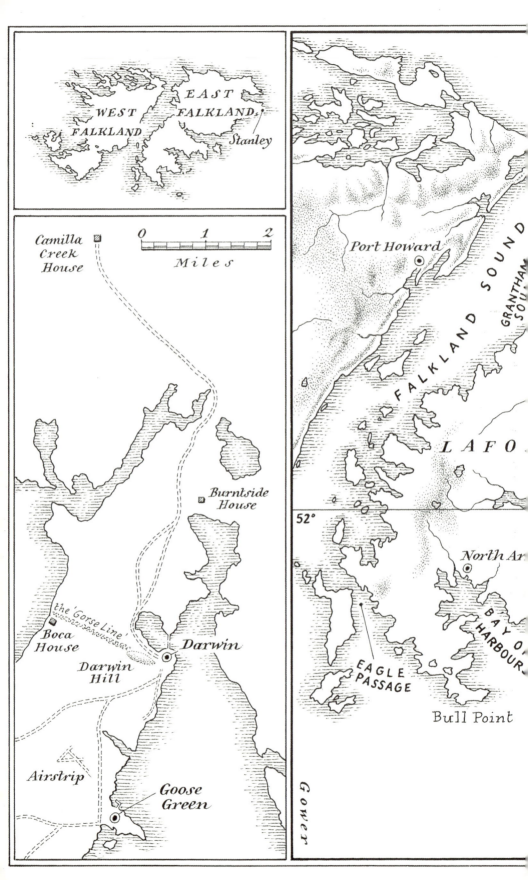

WEST FALKLAND

EAST FALKLAND

Stanley

Camilla Creek House

0   1   2
Miles

Burntside House

the 'Gorse Line'

Boca House

Darwin Hill

Darwin

Airstrip

Goose Green

Port Howard

FALKLAND SOUND

GRANTHAM SOUND

LAFO

52°

North Ar

EAGLE PASSAGE

BAY OF HARBOUR

Bull Point

Gower